Business Finance
Theory and Practice

Fourth Edition

E J McLaney

Plymouth Business School
University of Plymouth

PITMAN
PUBLISHING

London · Hong Kong · Johannesburg · Melbourne · Singapore · Washington DC

PITMAN PUBLISHING
128 Long Acre, London WC2E 9AN
Tel: +44 (0)171 447 2000
Fax: +44 (0)171 240 5771

A Division of Pearson Professional Limited

First published in Great Britain in 1986
Published as *Business Finance for Decision Makers* in 1991 and 1994
Fourth edition 1997

© E J McLaney 1986, 1991, 1994, 1997

ISBN 0 273 62694 9

British Library Cataloguing in Publication Data
A CIP catalogue record for this book can be obtained from the British Library

10 9 8 7 6 5 4 3 2 1

Typeset by Create Publishing Services
Printed and bound in Great Britain by William Clowes Ltd

The Publishers' policy is to use paper manufactured from sustainable forests.

Contents

Preface

This book attempts to deal with financing and investment decision making, with particular focus on the private sector of the UK economy. An attempt has been made to set out the theories which surround each area of financial decision making and to relate these to what appears to happen in practice. Where theory and practice diverge, the book tries to reconcile and explain the differences. It also attempts to assess the practical usefulness of some of the theories which do not seem to be applied widely in practice.

Though the focus of the book is on the UK private sector, the theories and practices examined are, for the main part, equally valid in the context of the private sector of all the world's countries which have private sectors. It is also the case that much of the content of the book is relevant to many parts of the public sector, both in the UK and overseas.

Most of the organisations to which the subject matter of this book relates will be limited companies or groups of companies, though some may be partnerships, co-operatives or other forms. For simplicity the word *firm* has been used as a general term for a business entity, referring to specific legal forms only where the issue under discussion relates specifically to a particular form.

Though the topics in the book are interrelated, the book has been divided into sections. Chapters 1 to 3 are concerned with setting the scene, Chapters 4 to 7 with investment decisions, Chapters 8 to 12 with financing decision areas, leaving Chapters 13 to 15 to deal with hybrid matters.

The book attempts to make the subject as accessible as possible to readers coming to business finance for the first time. In doing this, unnecessarily technical language has been avoided as much as possible and the issues are described in a narrative form as well as in more formal statements. Detailed proofs of theoretical propositions have generally been placed in appendices to the relevant chapters. Readers should not take this to mean that these proofs are particularly difficult to follow. The objective was to make the book as readable as possible and it was felt that sometimes formal proofs can disturb the flow if they are included in the main body of the text.

Nothing in this book requires any great mathematical ability on the part of the reader. However, some basic understanding of correlation, statistical probabilities and of basic differential calculus would be helpful. Any reader who feels that it might be necessary to brush up these topics could refer to Harper (1982 and 1991). These references and each of the others given in the chapters are listed alphabetically at the end of the book.

At the end of each chapter there are six 'review questions'. These are designed to enable readers to assess how well they can recall key points from the chapter. Suggested answers to these are contained in Appendix 3, at the end of the book. Also at the end of most chapters are up to six 'problems'. These are questions designed to test readers' understanding of the contents of the chapters and to give some practice in working through questions. The problems are graded either as 'basic', i.e. fairly straightforward questions or as 'more advanced' which may contain a few practical complications. Those problems marked with an asterisk (about half of the total) have suggested answers in Appendix 4 at the end of the book. Suggested answers to the remaining problems are contained in the *Lecturer's Guide* which is available as an accompaniment to this text.

The book is directed at those who are studying business finance as part of an undergraduate course, for example a degree or Higher National Diploma in business studies. It is also directed at postgraduate, post experience students who are either following a university course, or who are seeking a qualification like the Certified Diploma in Accounting and Finance. It should also prove useful to those studying for the professional examinations of the accounting bodies.

Edward J. McLaney
January 1997

Plan of the book

PART 1 – THE BUSINESS FINANCE ENVIRONMENT		
Chapter 1 Introduction	**Chapter 2** A framework for financial decision making	**Chapter 3** Financial accounting statements and their interpretation

PART 2 – INVESTMENT DECISIONS			
Chapter 4 Investment appraisal methods	**Chapter 5** Practical aspects of investment appraisal	**Chapter 6** Risk in investment appraisal	**Chapter 7** The pricing of securities and its relevance to real investment decisions

PART 3 – FINANCING DECISIONS				
Chapter 8 Sources of long-term finance	**Chapter 9** The secondary capital market (the Stock Exchange) and its efficiency	**Chapter 10** Cost of capital estimations and the discount rate	**Chapter 11** Gearing, the cost of capital and share-holders' wealth	**Chapter 12** The dividend decision

PART 4 – MIXED DECISIONS		
Chapter 13 Management of working capital	**Chapter 14** Corporate restructuring (including takeovers and divestments)	**Chapter 15** Small firms

REFERENCES	APPENDICES	INDEX

PART 1

The business finance environment

Business finance is concerned with making decisions about which investments the firm should make and how best to finance those investments. This part of the book attempts to explain the context in which those decisions are made. This is important in its own right, not just as an introduction to later parts of the book. Chapter 1 explains the nature of business finance. It continues with some discussion of the legal framework in which most private sector firms operate. Chapter 2 considers the decision making process, with particular emphasis on the objectives, in the pursuit of which, firms invest. It also considers the problem faced by managers where people, affected by a decision, have conflicting objectives. Chapter 3 provides an overview of the source and nature of the information provided to financial decision makers by accounting reports. As is explained in Chapter 1, business finance and accounting are distinctly different areas. Accounting statements are, however, a very important source of information upon which to base financial decisions.

CHAPTER 1

Introduction

OBJECTIVES

In this chapter we shall deal with the following:

- the role of business finance
- its relationship with other disciplines, particularly with accounting
- the importance of the consideration of risk in financial decision making
- the importance of the limited company as the legal form in which most UK businesses exist
- the nature of the limited company
- what is meant by limited liability
- the formation of limited companies
- directors and their relationships with shareholders
- the duty of directors to account for their actions
- typical means of financing companies and the rights of suppliers of corporate finance
- the requirement for firms trading as limited companies to signal the fact to the world through the company name
- liquidation of companies
- the nature of derivatives

THE ROLE OF BUSINESS FINANCE

Business firms may fairly be regarded as investment agencies or intermediaries. That is to say that their role is to raise funds from members of the public and from other investors and to invest those funds. Usually funds will be obtained from the legal owners of the firm (the shareholders) and from long-term lenders, with some short-term finance being provided by banks (perhaps in the form of overdrafts), other financial institutions, and trade creditors. Firms typically invest in 'real' assets such as land, buildings, plant and trading stocks, though they may also invest in 'financial' assets including making loans to, and buying shares in, other firms. People are employed to manage the investments, i.e. to do all those things necessary to create and sell the goods and services in the provision of which the firm is engaged. Surpluses remaining after meeting

3

the costs of operating the business – wages, raw material costs, etc. – accrue to the investors.

Central to the firm will be decisions involved with questions of the types and quantity of finance to raise, and with the choice of investments to be made. Business finance is the study of how these financing and investment decisions should be made in theory, and how they are made in practice.

A practical subject

Business finance is a relatively new subject. Until the 1950s it mostly consisted of narrative accounts of decisions that had been made and how, if identifiable, the decisions had been reached. More recently theories of business finance have emerged and been tested so that the subject now has a firmly based theoretical framework – a framework which stands up pretty well to testing with real life events. In other words, the accepted theories which attempt to explain and predict actual outcomes in business finance broadly succeed in their aim.

Business finance draws from many disciplines. Financing and investment decision making relates closely to certain aspects of economics, accounting, law, quantitative methods and the behavioural sciences. Despite the eclecticism of business finance in drawing what it finds most useful from other disciplines, it is nonetheless a subject in its own right, vital to the business firm.

Decisions on financing and investment go right to the heart of the business firm and its success or failure. This is because:

● Such decisions often involve financial amounts which are very significant to the firm concerned.
● Once made, such decisions are not easy to reverse, so the firm is typically committed in the long term to a particular type of finance or to a particular investment.

Though modern business finance practice relies heavily on sound theory, we must be very clear that business finance is an intensely practical subject which is concerned with real-world, practical, decision making.

RISK AND BUSINESS FINANCE

All decision making involves the future. We can only make decisions about the future; no matter how much we may regret it, we cannot alter the past. Financial decision making is no exception to this general rule.

There is only one thing certain about the future, which is that we cannot be sure what is going to happen. Sometimes we may be able to predict with confidence that what actually occurs will be one of a limited range of possibilities. We may even feel able to ascribe statistical probabilities to the likelihood of occurrence of each possible outcome, but we can never be completely certain of the future. Risk is therefore an important factor in all financial decision making, and one which must be considered explicitly in all cases.

In business finance, as in other aspects of life, risk and return tend to be related. Intuitively we expect returns to relate to risk in something like the way shown in Fig. 1.1. In investment, for example, investors require a minimum rate to induce them to invest at all but they require an increased rate of return, the addition of a risk premium, to compensate them for taking risk. We shall see in Chapter 7 that, when considering marketable stocks and shares, there does actually appear to be the linear relationship, which Fig. 1.1 suggests, between levels of risk perceived and the returns which investors expect to receive. Much of business finance is concerned with striking the appropriate balance between risk and return.

**Fig. 1.1
Relationship
between return
and risk**

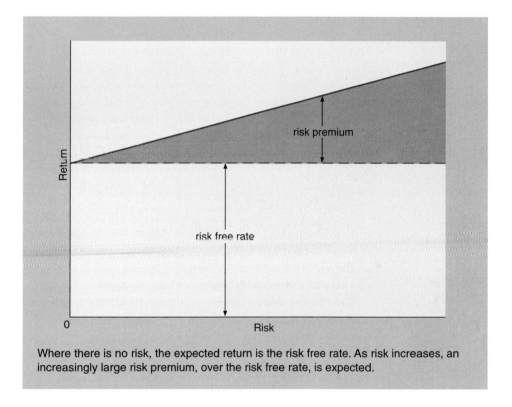

Where there is no risk, the expected return is the risk free rate. As risk increases, an increasingly large risk premium, over the risk free rate, is expected.

THE RELATIONSHIP BETWEEN BUSINESS FINANCE AND ACCOUNTING

Business finance and accounting are not the same thing. Accounting is concerned with financial record keeping, the production of periodic reports, statements and analyses, the dissemination of information to managers and, to some extent, to investors and the world outside the firm. It is also much involved with the quality, relevance and timeliness of its information output. Obviously financial decision makers will rely heavily on accounting reports and the accounting database generally. Knowledge of past events may well be a good pointer to the future, so reliable information on the past is invaluable. However, the role of the financial manager is not to provide financial information but to make decisions involving finance.

In smaller firms, with narrow portfolios of management skills, the accountant and the financial manager may well be the same person. In the large firm the roles are most likely to be discharged by different people or groups of people. Not surprisingly many financial managers are accountants by training and background but some are not. With the increasing importance of business finance in the curricula of business schools and in higher education generally, the tendency is probably towards more specialist financial managers, with their own career structure.

THE ORGANISATION OF FIRMS

This book is primarily concerned with business finance as it affects firms in the private sector of the UK economy. Most of our discussion will centre on larger firms, i.e. firms which are quoted in the secondary capital market (e.g. the International Stock Exchange of the United Kingdom and the Republic of Ireland) and where there is fairly widespread ownership of the firm amongst individual members of the public and the investing institutions (insurance companies, pension funds, unit trusts, etc.). Towards the end of the book we shall take a look at the smaller, owner-managed firms to see how the issues, discussed up to that point in the context of large firms, apply to this important sector of the economy.

Irrespective of whether we are considering large or small firms, virtually all of them will be limited companies. There are businesses in the UK, indeed many of them, which are not limited companies. Most of these, however, are very small (one or two-person enterprises) or they are highly specialised professional service firms such as solicitors and accountants.

Since the limited company predominates in the UK private sector, we shall in this book discuss business finance in this context. Many of the principles which will emerge apply equally, however, irrespective of the precise legal status of the firm concerned.

In this chapter we shall consider briefly the legal and administrative environment in which limited companies operate. The objective here is by no means to provide a detailed legal examination of the limited company, it is simply to outline its more significant features. More particularly the aim is to explain, in broad terms, those aspects which impinge on business finance. A lack of a broad understanding of these aspects may make life difficult for us in later chapters.

WHAT IS A LIMITED COMPANY?

A limited company is an artificially created legal person. It is an entity which is legally separate from all other persons including those who own and manage it. It is quite possible for a limited company to take legal action, say for breach of contract, against any other legal persons, including those who own and manage it. Actions between limited companies and their owners or managers do occur from time to time.

Obviously an artificial person can only function through the intervention of human beings. Those who ultimately control the company are the owners who each hold one or more shares in the ownership or equity of it.

Limited liability

One of the results of the peculiar position of the company having its own separate legal identity is that the financial liability of the owners (shareholders) is limited to the amount which they have paid (or have pledged to pay) for their shares. If the company becomes insolvent (financial obligations exceed value of assets) its liability is, like that of any human legal person, limited only by the amount of its assets. It can be forced to pay over all of its assets to try to meet its liabilities, but no more. Since the company and the owners are legally separate, owners cannot be compelled to introduce further finance. The position of a shareholder in this regard does not depend upon whether the shares were acquired by taking up an issue from the company or as a result of buying the shares from an existing shareholder.

Transferability

As a separate legal entity, the company does not depend on the identity of its shareholders for its existence. Transfer of shares by buying and selling or by gift is therefore possible. Thus a part, even all, of the company's ownership or equity can change hands without it necessarily having any effect on the business activity of the company.

Since the company can continue irrespective of precisely who the shareholders happen to be at any given moment, the company can theoretically have a perpetual lifespan, unlike its human counterparts.

FORMATION OF A LIMITED COMPANY

Creating a new company is a very cheap and simple operation which can be carried out with little effort on the part of the promoters, for very little cost (from about £100).

Formation basically requires the promoters to make an application to the Registrar of Companies (Department of Trade and Industry). The application must be accompanied by several documents, the most important of which is a proposed set of rules or constitution for the company defining how it will be administered. These rules are contained in two documents known as the Memorandum of Association and the Articles of Association.

All of the documentation becomes public once the company has been formally registered. A file is opened at Companies House in Cardiff on which are placed the various documents; the file is constantly available for examination by any member of the public who wishes to see it.

SHAREHOLDERS AND DIRECTORS

The shareholders (or members as they are often known) are the owners of the company; profits and gains accrue to them, losses are borne by them up to a maximum of the amount of their investment in the company. The shareholders, at any particular time, need not be the original shareholders, i.e. those who first owned the shares. Transfers by sale or gift (including legacy on death) cause shares to change hands.

For a variety of sound practical reasons the day-to-day management of the company is delegated by the shareholders to directors, who may or may not themselves own some shares in the company. Shareholders elect directors in much the same way as citizens elect Members of Parliament in a parliamentary democracy. They also fail to re-elect them if the directors' performance is judged by shareholders to be unsatisfactory. Usually one-third of the directors retire from office each year, frequently offering themselves for re-election. Typically each shareholder has one vote for each share owned. Where a company has a large number of shareholders, a particular individual holding a large number of shares, even though not a majority of them, can wield tremendous power. The board of directors is the firm's top level of management, so to control its composition is substantially to control the company.

ACCOUNTABILITY OF DIRECTORS

The law imposes a duty on directors to account annually, both to the shareholders, and, to some extent, to the world at large, on the performance of the company's trading and on its financial position.

Each year directors are required to prepare (or to have prepared on their behalf) a report for the shareholders. The minimum contents of the report are prescribed by law, though in practice this minimum is often exceeded. Principally the report consists of a profit and loss account, a balance sheet and a cash flow statement. These accounting statements are subject to audit by an independent firm of accountants whose principal role is to express an opinion on the truth and fairness of the view shown by them. The auditor's expression of opinion is attached to the annual report.

A copy of the report must be sent to each shareholder. A copy must also be sent to the Registrar of Companies for insertion on the company's file in Cardiff. This file must be available for inspection by anyone wishing to do so. In practice large companies also send copies of the report to financial analysts and journalists. They will usually comply with a request from any private individual for a copy.

The annual report is a major, but not the only, source of information for interested parties, including existing and prospective shareholders, on the progress of the company. Companies whose shares are quoted on the Stock Exchange are required by its rules to publish summarised accounting statements each half year. In practice most large companies, from time to time, issue information over and above that which is contained in the annual and half-yearly reports.

The nature of the accounting statements which appear in the annual report, and how those statements can be interpreted, are discussed in Chapter 3.

RECOGNITION OF COMPANIES

Limited companies are required to use the words *Limited (Ltd)* or *Public Limited Company (plc)* after their name in all formal documentation to warn those dealing with the company that its members' liability is limited.

Limited is used by private limited companies. These are basically the smaller, family-type companies which have certain rights on the restriction of transfer of their shares. Public companies are typically the larger companies with more widespread share ownership.

LONG-TERM FINANCING OF COMPANIES

Much of the semi-permanent finance of companies, in some cases all of it, is provided by shareholders. Many companies have different classes of shares. Most companies also borrow money on a long-term basis. (Many borrow finance on a short-term basis as well.) In later chapters we shall examine in some detail how and why companies issue more than one class of share and borrow money; here we shall confine ourselves to a brief overview of long-term corporate finance.

Ordinary shares

These are issued by the company to investors who are prepared to expose themselves to risk in order also to expose themselves to the expectation of high investment returns, which both intuition and the evidence, which we shall come across later in the book, tell us is associated with risk. It is normal for companies to pay part of their realised profits, after tax, to the shareholders in the form of a cash dividend. The amount which each shareholder receives is directly linked to the number of shares he or she owns. The amount of each year's dividend is at the discretion of the directors.

Dividends are often portrayed as being the reward of the shareholders, in much the same way as a payment of interest is the reward of the loan creditor. This is, however, a dubious interpretation of the nature of dividends. All profits, whether paid as dividends or reinvested by the directors, belong to the shareholders. If funds generated from past profits are reinvested, they should have the effect of causing an increase in the value of the shares. This increase should be capable of being realised by shareholders who sell their shares. It remains the subject of vigorous debate as to whether reinvesting profits is as beneficial to the shareholders as paying them a dividend from the funds concerned. This debate is examined in Chapter 12.

If the company were to be liquidated (wound up) each equity holder would receive an appropriate share of the funds left after all other legitimate claimants had been satisfied in full.

Where shares are traded between investors, there is no reason why shares should be priced according to their original issue price or according to their face value (nominal or par value). Perceptions of the value of a share in any particular company will change with varying economic circumstances, so that share prices will shift over time.

Historically, in the UK, increases in the market value of equities have tended to represent a larger element than have dividends in returns to shareholders, i.e. dividends have tended to be less important to shareholders than have capital gains.

It should be noted that a shareholder selling shares in a particular company for some particular price has no direct effect on that company. The company will simply pay future dividends and give future voting rights to the new shareholder.

It is the ordinary shareholders who have the voting power within the company. Thus it is the equity holders who control the company.

Each ordinary share confers equal rights on its owner in terms of dividend entitlement, repayment on liquidation and voting power. Two shares carry exactly twice as much of these rights as does one share. The law forbids the directors from discriminating between the rights of different shareholders other than on the basis of the number of shares owned (assuming that the shares owned are of the same class). Ms X owning 100 shares in Z plc should have equal rights in respect of her shareholding to those of Mr Y who owns a similar number of shares in the same company. The Stock Exchange and other non-statutory agencies also seek to promote this equality.

Preference shares

These represent part of the risk-bearing ownership of the company though they usually confer on their holders a right to receive the first slice of any dividend which is paid. There is an upper limit on the preference share dividend per share, which is usually defined as a percentage of the nominal value of the share. Preference share dividends are usually paid in full. Preference shares give more sure returns than equities, though they by no means provide certain returns. Preference shares do not usually confer voting rights nor do they usually give the same preference in repayment in a liquidation as they do in payment of dividends, though in some companies they do.

Preference shares of many companies are traded in the capital market. As with equities, prices of preference shares will vary with investors' perceptions of future prospects. Generally preference share prices are less volatile than those of equities as dividends tend to be fairly stable and usually have an upper limit.

For most companies, preference shares do not represent a major source of finance.

Loan stocks

Most companies borrow funds on a long-term, occasionally on a perpetual, basis. Lenders enter into a contractual relationship with the company with the rate of interest, its date of payment, the redemption date and amount all being terms of the contract. Many long-term lenders require rather more by way of security for their loan than the rights conferred on any lender under the law of contract. Typically they insist that the principal and sometimes the interest are secured on some specific asset of the borrowing company, frequently land. Such security might confer on lenders a right to seize the asset and sell it to satisfy their claims where repayment of principal or interest payment is overdue. Loan stocks (debentures) are, in the case of many companies, traded in the capital market. It is thus possible for someone owed £100 by company X to sell this debt to another investor who, from the date of the sale, will become entitled to receive interest, and repayment of the principal in due course. Such payment amounts and dates are contractual obligations, so there is less doubt surrounding them than applies to dividends from shares, more particularly where the loan is secured. For this reason the market values of loan stocks tend to fluctuate even less than those of preference shares.

The relationship between the fixed return elements (preference shares and loan stocks) in the long-term financial structure and the equity is usually referred to as *capital gearing* (leverage in the USA).

Broadly speaking, companies have a fair amount of power to issue and redeem ordinary shares, preference shares and loan stocks. Where redemption of shares is to be undertaken, the directors have a duty to take certain steps to safeguard the position of creditors which might be threatened by significant amounts of assets being transferred to shareholders.

LIQUIDATION

A limited company, because it has separate existence from its shareholders does not die when they do. The only way in which the company's demise can be brought about is by following the statutorily defined steps to liquidate the company. Liquidation involves appointing a liquidator to realise the company's assets, to pay the claimants and formally to lay the company to rest.

The initiative to liquidate the company usually comes either from:

● the shareholders, perhaps because the purpose for which the company was formed has been served; or
● the company's creditors (including loan creditors), where the company is failing to pay its debts. In these circumstances the objective is to stop the company from trading and to ensure that non-cash assets are realised, the proceeds being used to meet (perhaps only partially) the claims of the creditors. This type of liquidation is sometimes referred to colloquially as *bankruptcy*.

Order of paying claimants

Irrespective of which type of liquidation is involved, the liquidator, having realised all of the non-cash assets, must take great care as to the order in which the claimants are paid. Broadly speaking the order is:

(1) *Secured creditors.* Where the security is on a specified asset or group of assets, the proceeds of disposal of the asset are to be applied to meeting the specific claim. If the proceeds are insufficient, the creditor must stand with the unsecured creditors for the shortfall. If the proceeds exceed the amount of the claim, the excess goes into the fund available to unsecured creditors.

(2) *Unsecured creditors.* This would usually include most trade creditors. It would also include any unsecured loan creditors.

In fact, ranking even before the secured creditors come a set of claimants who have preferential rights. These include the Inland Revenue for the company's Corporation Tax liability (if any) and the employees for their wages or salary arrears.

Only after the creditors have been paid in full will the balance of the funds be paid out to the shareholders. If the preference shares carry no right to priority of payment, each share (ordinary and preference) will be entitled to an equal portion of the residue of funds. Where preference shares bestow the right to payment before ordinary shareholders, each ordinary share will command an equal slice of the funds remaining after the creditors and preference share-holders have had their entitlement.

The order of payment of creditors will be of little consequence except where there are insufficient funds to meet all claims. Where this is the case, each class of claim must be met in full before the next class may participate.

DERIVATIVES

A striking development of business finance, and other areas of commercial management, since around 1980, is the use of *derivatives*. Derivatives are assets or obligations whose value is dependent on some asset from which they are derived. In principle any asset could be the subject of a derivative. In practice, assets such as *commodities* (e.g. coffee, grain, copper) and *financial instruments* (e.g. shares in companies, loans, foreign currency) are the ones which we tend to encounter as the basis of a derivative.

A straightforward example of a derivative is an option to buy or sell a speci-fied asset, on a specified date or within a specified range of dates (the exercise date), for a specified price (the exercise price). For example, a manufacturer of instant coffee may buy the right to buy a specified quantity of coffee beans from a supplier in six months' time for a specified price per tonne. Note that this is a right to buy but not an obligation. Thus if the price of coffee in six months' time is below the exercise price specified in the option contract, the manufacturer will ignore the option contract and buy in the open market. Here the option will be worth nothing. On the other hand, if the market price of coffee in six month's time is above the option contract exercise price, the manufacturer will exercise the option and buy from the seller of the option contract according to the terms of that contract. In this case, at the exercise date, the option will be worth the difference between what the manufacturer will have to pay for the coffee speci-fied in the option contract and the current market price.

Why should the manufacturer want to enter into such an option contract? Who would sell the manufacturer such a contract, and why? A manufacturer of instant coffee needs a constant supply of coffee. Coffee prices, like those of everything else, particularly traded commodities, tend to fluctuate according to supply and demand. In order to be able to plan ahead, perhaps particularly to be able to plan future pricing of instant coffee, the manufacturer needs a reliable supply of coffee at a specified maximum price. Entering into the option contract eliminates risk so far as the manufacturer is concerned. In fact the risk is transferred to the other party (known as the *counterparty*) in the option contract. This is exactly the same principle as insurance. When we pay a premium to insure one of our possessions against theft, we are paying a counterparty (the insurance firm) to bear the risk. If the object is not stolen we do not claim; if coffee prices turn out to be below the option contract exercise price, the manufacturer does not exercise the option. In both cases a sum has been paid to transfer the risk.

The manufacturer is under no obligation to transfer the risk; it can bear the risk itself and save the cost of buying the option. This is a matter of commercial judgement.

The seller of the coffee option (the counterparty) might be a coffee trader, or simply a trader in options. This firm enters into the option contact because it makes the commercial judgement, taking account of possible movements in coffee price between the contract date and the exercise date, that the price it charges for the option is capable of yielding a reasonable profit. This is rather like the attitude taken by an insurance firm when setting premiums.

Many types of derivative are concerned with transferring risk, but not all. Derivatives pervade many areas of business finance and we shall consider various derivatives, in context, at various stages in this book.

SUMMARY

Business finance is the study of how investment and financing decisions should be made in theory and how they are made in practice. It is a relatively new discipline which has drawn liberally from disciplines with which it shares common borders.

Risk is a feature of all decision making and so it is one which must be considered explicitly with finance decisions.

Business finance is a separate discipline from accounting but it is obviously closely related, financial managers often having backgrounds in accountancy and leaning heavily on accounting reports to aid their decision making.

In the UK, most business firms except those of very small size are limited companies.

Limited companies are artificially created legal personalities possessing many of the rights and obligations possessed by their human counterparts. They are owned and controlled by human beings whose liability to potential claimants of the company is limited to the amount paid for the shares, i.e. they cannot be legally required to put their personal assets at the disposal of claimants. The owners of the company hold shares in the company. Shares are equally sized slices of the ownership of the company which may be transferred from one owner to the next, for value or by gift. The number of shares which a shareholder owns dictates the entitlement to dividends, voting power, and the share of any surplus if the company is liquidated. Companies are cheap and easy to create.

Companies are ultimately controlled by the shareholders but are managed on a day-to-day basis by directors elected by the shareholders. The directors are accountable for their actions to shareholders, and to some extent to the world at large. They formally account through the annual report and accounts.

Companies typically involve themselves in capital gearing, i.e. they usually raise part of their long-term finance from preference shares and part from long-term lenders, as well as some from ordinary (or equity) shares.

Long-term lenders have contractual rights as to payment of interest and repayment of capital. Shareholders, both ordinary and preference, as owners of the company have no such rights and are therefore the ultimate risk takers. Since preference shares usually entitle their owners to a dividend before ordinary shareholders become so entitled, the preference shareholders are somewhat less at risk than ordinary shareholders. Preference shareholders do not usually have the right to vote which the ordinary shareholders have.

Companies are able to issue and to redeem shares and loan stocks as they see fit and without excessive legal restriction.

Limited companies must warn those who deal with them that this is their status by use of the word Limited (Ltd) or plc after their name.

Some positive action by shareholders or creditors must be undertaken in order to bring the life of a company to a close or to liquidate the company. Where there are insufficient funds to meet all claims against the company, care must be taken by the liquidator to pay claimants in the legally prescribed order.

Derivatives are an increasingly important aspect of business finance, generally used to transfer risks.

FURTHER READING The role of business finance is discussed by Brealey and Myers (1991) and by Puxty and Dodds (1991). Numerous books deal with the provisions of UK company law. Cole, Shears and Tiley (1990) include a very readable chapter outlining the more important aspects. For more detailed coverage, see Keenan (1994).

REVIEW QUESTIONS

Suggested answers to review questions appear in Appendix 3.

1.1 What factors seem likely to explain the popularity of the limited liability company as the legal form of so many UK firms?

1.2 How does the position of a limited company compare with that of a human person regarding liability for commercial debts?

1.3 How does the position of a shareholder in a limited company differ from that of a sole trader?

1.4 'Preference shares and loan stocks are much the same.' Is this statement correct?

1.5 Why are many investment and financing decisions of particular importance to the firm?

1.6 How are risk and return related, both in theory and in practice?

CHAPTER 2

A framework for financial decision making

OBJECTIVES

In this chapter we shall deal with the following:

● the steps in financial decision making

● the various objectives which, it has been suggested, might be followed by firms

● some evidence on objectives which UK firms actually follow

● some theoretical rules for financial decision making; the separation theorem

FINANCIAL DECISION MAKING

Like any other decision-making area, financial decisions involve choices between two or more possible courses of action. If there is only one possible course of action, no decision is needed. Often continuing with a situation which has existed until the time of the decision is one option open to the decision maker. All decision making should involve the following considerations

Defining objectives

The decision maker should know what the course of action which is the subject of the decision is intended to achieve, or at least towards what goal it is intended to work. A person leaving home in the morning needs to make a decision on which way to turn into the road. In order to do this it is necessary to know what the immediate objective is. If the objective is to get to work, it might require a decision to turn to the right; if it is a visit to the local shop, the decision might be to turn left. If our decision maker does not know the desired destination, it is impossible to make a sensible decision on which way to turn. Likely objectives of the business firm will be considered later in this chapter.

Identifying possible courses of action

The available courses of action should be recognised. In doing this, consideration should be given to any restrictions on freedom of action imposed by law or other forces not within the control of the decision maker.

Good decision making requires that the horizon should constantly be surveyed for opportunities which will better enable the objectives to be achieved. In the business finance context, this includes spotting new investment opportunities and the means to finance the firm. Such opportunities will not often make themselves obvious and firms need to be searching for them constantly. A firm failing to do so will almost certainly be heading into decline, and opportunities will be lost to its more innovative competitors.

Assembling data relevant to the decision

Each possible course of action must be reviewed and the relevant data identified. Not all data on a particular course of action are necessarily relevant. Suppose that a person wishes to buy a car, the only objective being to get the one with the best trade-off between reliability and cost. Only data related to reliability and cost of the possible cars available will be of any interest to that particular person. Other information such as colour, design or country of manufacture is irrelevant. That is not to say that a car buyer's objectives should be restricted to considerations of cost and reliability, simply that if they are in a particular case, then other factors become irrelevant.

Even some data which bear directly on running cost, such as road tax, should be ignored if they are common to all cars. As decisions involve selecting from options, it is on the basis of differences that the decision can sensibly be made. If the decision were between buying or not buying a car, then road tax would become relevant as it is one of the costs of car ownership. It will not be incurred if the car is not bought.

It is important therefore to recognise what information is relevant to the decision and what is not. Gathering the information can be costly and time consuming; thus restricting it to the relevant may well lead to considerable savings in the costs of making the decision. Also, the presence of irrelevant information can cause decision makers not to be able to see the wood for the trees, leading to sub-optimal decisions.

Assessing the data and reaching a decision

This involves comparing the options by using the relevant data in such a way as to identify those courses of action which will best work towards the achievement of the objectives.

Much of this book will be concerned with the ways in which assessment of data relating to financial decisions should be carried out.

Implementing the decision

It is pointless taking time and trouble to make good decisions if no attempt is to be made to ensure that action follows the decision. This action is not restricted to what is necessary to set the selected option into motion, but includes controlling it through its life. Steps should be taken to ensure, or to try to ensure, that what was planned actually happens.

Monitoring the effects of decisions

While perhaps not strictly central to the decision-making process, good decision making requires that the effects of previous decisions are closely monitored. There are broadly two reasons for this:

(a) It is valuable to assess the reliability of forecasts on which the decision was based. If forecasts prove to be poor, then decision makers must ask themselves if reliability could be improved by using different techniques and bases. It is obviously too late to improve the decision already made and acted upon, but this practice could improve the quality of future decisions.

(b) If a decision is proving to be a bad one for any reason, including unforeseeable changes in the commercial environment, monitoring should reveal this so that some modification might be considered which could improve matters. This is not to say that the original decision can be reversed. Unfortunately we cannot alter the past, but we can often take steps to limit the bad effects of a poor decision. For example, suppose that a firm makes a decision to buy a machine to manufacture plastic ducks as wall decorations, for which it sees a profitable market for five years. One year after buying the machine and launching the product it is obvious that there is little demand for plastic ducks. At that point it is not possible to decide not to enter into the project a year earlier, but it is possible and may very well be desirable to abandon production immediately to avoid throwing good money after bad.

In practice most of the monitoring of financial decisions is through the accounting system, particularly the budgetary control routines.

OBJECTIVES OF THE FIRM

What business firms are seeking to achieve and therefore what investment and financing decisions should seek to promote is a question central to business finance and one which has attracted considerable discussion as the subject has developed. We shall now review some of the more obvious and popular suggestions and try to assess how well each of them stands up to scrutiny.

(a) Maximisation of profit

Profit here would normally be interpreted as accounting profit which is discussed at some length in Chapter 3. This suggested objective arises from the fact that the shareholders are the owners of the firm and as such both the exercisers of ultimate control and the beneficiaries of profits. It is therefore argued that the shareholders will cause managers to pursue policies which would be expected to result in the maximum possible profit. This analysis is acceptable up to a point, but maximising profit could easily be sub-optimal to the shareholders. Profit may be able to be increased by expanding the scale of operations of the firm. If the increase merely results from the raising of additional external finance it might mean that profit per share could actually decrease, leaving the shareholders worse off.

Firms which make pharmaceutical products typically spend vast amounts of money on developing and testing new products. It is in the nature of the industry that the time taken to bring a new drug to the market can easily be ten years. A particular firm which stopped spending money on research and

17

development would enhance current profit because costs would be cut, and revenues, arising from development costs in past years, would continue for the time being. Thus current profits would be buoyant but the firm would have a bleak future since there would be no new drugs to replace the old ones.

It is probably open to most firms to increase their profits without additional investment, if they are prepared to take additional risks. For example, cost cutting on the control of the quality of the firm's output could lead to increased profits, at least in the short term. In the longer term substandard products being sold could lead to the loss of future sales and profits.

Clearly, increasing profitability through greater efficiency is a desirable goal from the shareholders' point of view. However maximisation of profit is far too broad a definition of what is likely to be beneficial to shareholders.

(b) Maximisation of the return on capital employed

This is probably an improvement on profit maximisation since it relates profit to the size of the firm; however, as with profit maximisation, no account is taken of risk and long-term stability.

(c) Survival

Undoubtedly most firms would see survival as a necessary but insufficient objective to pursue. Investors would be unlikely to be attracted to become shareholders in a firm which had no other long-term ambition than merely to survive. In times of economic recession and other hardship many firms will see survival as their short-term objective, but in the longer term they would almost certainly set their sights somewhat higher.

(d) Long-term stability

This is similar to survival and is similarly unrealistic in its lack of ambition as a long-term target.

(e) Growth

Growth of profits and/or assets does seem a more realistic goal and appears to reflect attitudes articulated by managers. Growth implies that short-term profit will not be pursued at the cost of long-term stability or survival. Growth is not really a precise enough statement of an objective. This is because growth (as we have seen) can be achieved merely by raising new finance. It is doubtful if any firms would state their objective as being to issue as many new shares as possible.

(f) Satisficing

Many see objectives which relate only to the welfare of shareholders as unrealistic in the 1990s. They see the business as a coalition of suppliers of capital, suppliers of managerial skills, suppliers of labour, suppliers of goods and services, and customers. None of the participants in the coalition is viewed as having pre-eminence over any of the others. This coalition is not seen as a self-contained entity but viewed in a wider societal context. Cyert and March (1963) were among the first to articulate this view.

The objectives, it is argued, should reflect this coalition so that the firm should seek to give all participants a satisfactory return for their inputs, rather than seek to maximise the return to any one of them.

(g) Maximisation of shareholders' wealth

This is probably a more credible goal than either those concerned with return/growth or risk/stability/survival as single objectives, since wealth maximisation takes account of both return and risk simultaneously. Rational investors will value firm A more highly than firm B if the returns expected from each firm are equal but those from firm B are considered more risky (less likely that expectations will be fulfilled). Wealth maximisation also balances short- and long-term benefits in a way that profit-maximising goals cannot.

A wealth maximisation objective should cause financial managers to take decisions which balance returns and risk in such a way as to maximise the benefits, through dividends and enhancement of share price, to the shareholders.

Despite its credibility, wealth maximisation seems in conflict with the perhaps still more credible *satisficing*. Wealth maximising seems to imply the pursuit of the interests of only one member of the coalition, perhaps at the expense of the others. To the extent that this implication is justified, the shareholder wealth maximisation criterion does give a basis for financial decisions which must then be balanced against those derived from objectives more directed towards the other members of the coalition.

It could, however, be argued that satisficing and shareholder wealth maximisation are not necessarily as much in conflict as they might, at first sight, appear to be. That is to say that wealth maximisation might best be promoted by other members of the coalition receiving satisfactory returns. Consider one of the members of the coalition, say the employees. What would be the effect on share prices and dividend prospects if employees do not receive satisfactory treatment? Unsatisfactory treatment seems likely to lead to high rates of staff turnover, lack of commitment by staff, the possibility of strikes, etc. – in short, an unprofitable and uncertain future. Clearly this is not likely to be viewed with enthusiasm by the investing public. This in turn would be expected to lead to a low share price. Conversely, a satisfied workforce seems likely to be perceived favourably by investors. It seems reasonable to believe that a broadly similar conclusion will be reached if other members of the coalition are considered in the same light.

Maximisation of shareholders' wealth may not be a perfect summary of the typical firm's financial objective(s). It does however provide a reasonable working basis for financial decision making which probably leads firms following it to make decisions which promote their goals. What must be true is that firms cannot continually make decisions which reduce their shareholders' wealth since this would imply that the worth of the firm would constantly be diminishing. Each firm has only a finite amount of wealth, so sooner or later it would be forced out of business by the results of such decisions.

Evidence on objectives

A number of studies has been conducted in the UK, most of which have involved questioning senior managers of large firms by interview or postal questionnaire.

Pike and Ooi (1988) conducted a postal questionnaire at two points in time, 1980 and 1986. The 1980 questionnaire was sent to 208 large UK firms. The 1986 questionnaire was sent to the firms that had responded in 1980, provided that they had not disappeared as a result of amalgamations, takeovers, etc. In both surveys the usable response rate exceeded 70 per cent. In both surveys senior finance executives were asked, *inter alia*, to indicate on a five-point scale the importance to their firms of five financial objectives, two of which were short term and three of which were long term.

The mean rankings for the objectives were as shown in Table 2.1. Note that a ranking of 5 implies that the objective is very important and a ranking of 1 implies an unimportant objective.

Table 2.1 The importance of financial objectives (1980–6)

Objective	1980	1986
Short-term (1 to 3 years):		
Profitability (e.g. percentage rate of return on investment)	4.28	4.61
Profits or earnings (i.e. a profit target)	4.01	4.41
Long-term (over 3 years):		
Growth in sales	3.18	2.97
Growth in earnings per share	2.83	4.38
Growth in shareholders' wealth	3.07	4.06

Source: Pike and Ooi (1988)

These results indicate a number of goals, important to the firm, being simultaneously pursued. They also imply an increasing importance of four of them (sales growth being the exception) over time. It appears that shorter-term objectives were more important to the respondents than were the longer-term ones. However, by 1986, EPS (earnings per share) and growth in shareholders' wealth had become nearly as important as the shorter-term goals.

The Pike and Ooi results show some consistency with evidence from other surveys conducted both in the UK and in the USA over recent years.

It should be noted that profit or earnings are properly defined as the net increase in a firm's wealth as a result of its commercial activities. Thus goals which emphasise an importance being placed on profits or EPS are not necessarily in conflict with a shareholder wealth objective. It is only where the longer-term benefit is being jeopardised in favour of short-term profitability that there is conflict. Thus when Pike and Ooi's respondents identified short-term profitability as a goal they were presumably not identifying it at the expense of longer-term goals. In fact the importance placed on EPS and shareholders' wealth growth by the same respondents emphasises this point.

Conflicts of interests: shareholders versus managers

Whoever may control the firm in theory, in practice it is controlled on a day-to-day basis by the managers. It has been suggested that most firms pursue policies which are likely to maximise the welfare of their managers, at the same time giving the other participants in the firm sufficient rewards to stop them from becoming too dissatisfied and causing discomfort to the managers. The ways in which managers might seek to maximise their welfare include:

- paying themselves good levels of salary and 'perks', but not too much to alert shareholders to whom, by law, directors' salaries must be disclosed,
- providing themselves with larger empires, through merger and internal expansion, thus increasing their opportunities for promotion and social status,
- reducing risk through diversification which, as we shall see in Chapter 7, may not benefit the shareholders, but may well improve the managers' security.

There is no reason to believe that professional managers are all rogues, feathering their own nests at the expense of all other participants in the firm. However, human nature being as it is, only unusual people would make a decision without considering its possible effect on themselves. This, no doubt, can cause decisions to be made which are sub-optimal from the shareholders' viewpoint. Unfortunately the costs of undertaking some sort of management audit to monitor managers' decisions are likely to be considerable, making it unreasonable to attempt. There is however a strong sanction against the management which continually makes sub-optimal decisions and that is the possibility of takeover. A firm whose share price reflects under-utilisation of assets is likely to become a prime target for a takeover which might well leave the delinquent managers without jobs. Buoyant share prices make firms unattractive as takeover targets, so that managers have a vested interest in promoting buoyancy, if not maximisation, of share prices.

The existence of this sanction may not be sufficient to cause management to be completely selfless in its conduct of the firm's affairs. We shall, however, assume that any tendency towards nest-feathering by managers is not of any great significance in practice.

One area where the takeover sanction may not be effective is where managers take too short-term a view. Though the best interests of the shareholders may be served by an emphasis on long-term profitability, the best interests of managers could be served by so-called *short-termism*. Managers may see their careers as lasting only two or three years with a particular firm before they move on to other employment. Their reputations may therefore depend on what happens while they are still with the firm rather than on the ultimate effect of their actions. Perhaps more importantly, management remuneration may well be based on immediate profit flows. Both of these factors could promote a tendency to concentrate on the short term. To what extent, if any, this produces a real conflict of interests between managers and shareholders is not clear.

For the remainder of this book we shall assume that shareholder wealth maximisation is the major financial goal of the firm. However, we should continually bear in mind that, in reality, decisions reached on the basis of this objective might be in conflict with a firm's non-financial goals. If this is the case, the final decision may need to be a compromise.

FINANCING, INVESTMENT AND SEPARATION

If we accept that firms should seek to maximise the wealth of the shareholders in making their financial decisions, we can now turn our attention to how, in theory at least, managers should approach their decision making so as to promote this objective. Let us do this by consideration of an example.

EXAMPLE

Project X – to invest or to spend

Industries Ltd is a firm owned by a number of independently minded shareholders. Three of these, Eager, Patient and Steady, each owns 20 000 of the firm's total of 200 000 ordinary shares. At present Industries only has one asset, namely £100 000 in cash. The firm's management is undecided whether to pay this cash to the shareholders as a dividend, which would amount to £10 000 (one-tenth of £100 000) in the case of each of the above trio, or to invest it in Project X. This investment project requires an initial cash investment of the whole of the £100 000 payable now, and will produce a cash receipt of £120 000 in a year's time, then come to a close. If the project is undertaken the whole of the cash proceeds will be paid as a dividend next year (£12 000 each for Eager, Patient and Steady). For the time being let us assume that there is no alternative investment project available to the firm, nor are there any shareholdings in other firms available to investors, also that it is not possible to borrow or lend money.

Suspecting that there might be disagreement between shareholders on Project X, the management decided to call a shareholders' meeting to sound out opinion. During the discussion at the meeting the following three comments were made.

(a) Eager said that she thought Industries should not make the investment but should pay the dividend immediately because, whilst she does not necessarily want to spend the money now, it would be nice to have it available should some need arise. She does not consider the additional £2000 of dividend will compensate her for delaying.

(b) Patient said that he would prefer Project X to be undertaken because he would not, in any case, spend his dividend before next year and would prefer to have £12 000 than £10 000 when he does come to spend it.

(c) Steady said that she would be in favour of Project X but that, since she needs the cash in six months' time to pay for a new extension to her house, she would reluctantly have to vote for the immediate dividend.

Similarly, diverse views were expressed by the firm's other shareholders.

Clearly, management has a problem. If it is trying to maximise the wealth of the shareholders then perhaps a decision to undertake Project X would be the correct one. This would not be acceptable to at least two shareholders; Eager would rather have her money now and Steady must have it in six months at the latest. Clearly £12 000 is more wealth than £10 000, but if it is not to be available to spend when it is wanted or needed, the £10 000 may be preferred. It seems impossible to maximise the satisfaction that each shareholder gets from the firm; satisfying some dissatisfies others because timing of spending matters to people, but not to each person in the same way.

Borrowing and lending

If we introduce a bit more realism into the example by assuming that both Industries Ltd and its shareholders can borrow and lend money, management's dilemma disappears. To illustrate this, let us assume that the interest rate is 15 per cent p.a. and see how the introduction of borrowing and lending affects the position of the trio if Project X is undertaken.

(a) Eager, who wants her money now, could borrow from the bank such an amount that would, with interest, grow to £12 000 by next year. The borrowings could then be discharged using the cash from the dividend to be received in a year's time.

   The borrowed amount would be £10 435, i.e. £12 000 × 100/(100 + 15) (check £10 435 + (15 per cent × £10 435) = £12 000). Thus she could immediately have £435 more to spend than were Project X to be rejected by the firm. Of course she would still owe the bank £12 000 by the end of the year, but she would use her dividend to pay this.

(b) Patient, who prefers to wait the year, will receive and spend his £12 000 in a year's time. If Project X were to be rejected, the best that he could do would be to lend the £10 000 dividend to the bank which, with interest at 15 per cent, would grow to £11 500 over the year.

(c) Steady, who needs her money in six months' time could at that time borrow such an amount which will grow with interest to £12 000 by the end of the year. Since she does not need the money during the first six months she will only need to borrow for the second half of the year. The borrowed amount would be £11 163, i.e. £12 000 × 100/(100 + 7½). If Project X were rejected by the firm and Steady lent her £10 000 to the bank for six months, it would grow to only £10 750, i.e. £10 000 + (£10 000 × ½ × 15 per cent).

It seems clear that all three investors will have more to spend if Project X is undertaken than if it is not, irrespective of when they wish to spend. It also seems likely that this is true for each of the firm's other shareholders. The shareholders will be unanimous that Project X should go ahead.

Project Y

Now let us suppose that Project X is not available but that the choice lies between paying the dividend now or undertaking Project Y. This project also requires an immediate cash investment of £100 000, but will only produce £110 000 next year when it will cease.

Let us consider how accepting Project Y will affect Eager, who wants her money now. Again she could borrow against next year's dividend (£11 000); the amount which she could borrow will be £9565 (i.e. £11 000 × 100/(100 + 15)). On the other hand, if Project Y is rejected she would have £10 000 to spend. Clearly she would prefer rejection of the project. We could easily illustrate, using the same logic as that which we applied to Project X, that Patient and Steady would agree with her, as indeed would all of the other shareholders. Project X and Project Y suggest what is obviously true, namely that where the firm undertakes projects whose rates of return are greater than the interest rate at which shareholders can borrow or lend, their wealth will be increased. Projects which yield a lower rate than the shareholders' interest rate will have the effect of reducing the wealth of the shareholders. Project X produces a return of 20 per cent p.a. (i.e. (£120 000 – £100 000)/£100 000), Project Y makes a 10 per cent return; the interest rate is 15 per cent. It is obvious that a project yielding 15 per cent would not alter the wealth of shareholders.

Opportunity cost of finance

The borrowing/lending interest rate represents the *opportunity cost* to the shareholder of making investments in the projects. The existence of the facility to borrow or to lend means that those who have the cash but do not want to spend have the opportunity to lend at the interest rate as an alternative to investing. Any investments in projects must therefore compete with that opportunity and, to be desirable, produce returns in excess of the interest rate.

Borrowing by the firm

Suppose that Industries' management decided to undertake Project X, but for some reason or another, it also decided to pay an immediate dividend of £50 000, making up the shortfall of the cash needed for the investment by borrowing, at 15 per cent p.a., for the duration of the project. This would mean that the £50 000 borrowed with interest, a total of £57 500, will have to be repaid from the £120 000 proceeds from the investment, leaving £62 500 of the £120 000 proceeds from Project X to be paid as a dividend next year.

For Eager this would mean a dividend of £5000 now and another one of £6250 next year. What effect will this have on her present wealth? She can borrow the amount which will, with interest, grow to £6250; this will be £5435 (i.e. £6250 × 100/(100 + 15)) which together with the £5000 dividend will give her £10 435, an increase in wealth of £435. Note that this is identical to the increase in her current wealth that we found when we assessed Project X assuming that it was to be financed entirely by the shareholders. Not surprisingly it could equally well be shown that this would also be true for the other shareholders and no matter what proportion of the £100 000 the firm borrows, Project X will remain equally attractive.

Therefore, it seems not to matter where the cash comes from; if the investment will increase shareholders' wealth under one financing scheme, it will increase it by the same amount under some other scheme.

The theoretical implications of Projects X and Y

This example illustrates three important propositions of business finance.

(a) *Firms should invest in projects which have higher rates of return than the prevailing interest rate.* By doing this the wealth of the shareholders will be increased. By investing in as many such projects as are available, shareholders' wealth will be maximised.

(b) *Personal consumption/investment preferences of individual shareholders are irrelevant in making corporate investment decisions.* Irrespective of when and how much individuals wish to spend, there will be more available to them (their wealth will be maximised) provided that the investment policy outlined in (a) above is followed. This is because individual shareholders can use borrowing or lending to adjust the dividends from the firm to match their personal tastes. Put another way, the pattern of dividends does not affect the wealth of the shareholders.

(c) *The financing method does not affect the shareholders' wealth.* Provided that the investment policy outlined in (a) above is followed, it does not matter whether the investment is financed by the shareholders or by borrowing.

These may be summarised as the *separation theorem* which says that *investment decisions* and *financing decisions* should be made independently of one another. This proposition was first identified by Irving Fisher in the 1930s and was formally set out by Hirshleifer (1958).

These propositions may seem like not-too-subtle glimpses of the obvious, yet when they were first formally propounded they met with quite a lot of scepticism, not entirely because of the lack of reality of some of the assumptions which we have made.

The assumptions Our consideration of Projects X and Y, and indeed of the separation theorem generally, is based on four major assumptions:

(a) that investments only last for one year;
(b) that returns from investments are known with certainty, e.g. there is no doubt that if Project X is undertaken, £120 000 will flow in next year;
(c) all individuals prefer more wealth to less;
(d) borrowing and lending rates are equal as between one another, and as between individuals and firms.

Clearly some of these assumptions are unrealistic, particularly (a) and (b). Whether this seriously weakens the separation theorem and its implications is probably impossible to assess directly. Even if the theorem does not strictly hold true in practice, it does give some insights into the relationship between shareholders and managers in the context of real investment decisions. The theorem certainly provides a foundation for several major financial theories which we shall encounter later in this book.

The formal derivation of the separation theorem by Hirshleifer is reviewed in the Appendix to this chapter.

THEORY AND PRACTICE

We have discussed what business finance is about and what financial decisions are intended to achieve. We have also considered some theoretical propositions of how we should make financing and investment decisions. In the remainder of this book we shall explore in more detail how in theory such decisions should be made, how in practice they appear to be made and we shall try to reconcile the differences between theory and practice where they occur.

SUMMARY

Good financial decision making requires the adherence to a sequence of steps, the first one of which is to define the firm's objectives.

Many suggestions have been made in the literature as to what are and should be the objectives of firms. Maximisation of shareholder wealth is generally assumed to be the single objective which most adequately summarises firms' financial goals.

The separation theorem provides some theoretical guidelines for financial decision makers. These may be summarised as:

● firms should take on all investment projects which offer returns of a higher rate than the prevailing interest rate; and

● firms should make their investment decisions without regard to how the investment is to be financed and what preferences individual shareholders may have as regards the timing of their spending.

These guidelines are theoretical and much of the remainder of the book will be devoted to consideration of how valid they are in practice.

FURTHER READING The subject of corporate objectives has been widely dealt with in the literature. Cyert and March (1963), to which reference was made in the chapter, discuss it at length. Most finance texts devote some space to it as do most business economics texts. The article by Pike and Ooi (1988) to which reference was made in the chapter is worth reading, as is the original article by Hirshleifer (1958) referred to in the chapter and reviewed in the Appendix. Lumby (1994) clearly explains the separation theorem and its formal derivation.

REVIEW QUESTIONS

Suggested answers to review questions appear in Appendix 3.

2.1 When making a decision, an item of information needs to satisfy two criteria in order to be relevant and worthy of taking into account. What are these two criteria?

2.2 Why is profit maximisation considered incomplete as the definition of what most businesses seek to achieve?

2.3 Is exploitation of customers by a monopoly supplier, who charges very high prices, consistent with the objective of maximising shareholders' wealth?

2.4 A firm has £1 million at its disposal. The firm's financial managers feel that this could either be invested in new production facilities or paid to shareholders as a dividend. What does the separation theorem suggest that the firm should do? Can the firm both pay the dividend and make the investment?

2.5 Explain why, according to the separation theorem, the financing method (equity or loan) does not affect shareholders' wealth.

2.6 Why, in practice, would borrowing by the firm to raise cash to pay a dividend not be economically equivalent to borrowing by the individual shareholders to provide themselves with cash?*

(* Note that the answer to this question is not really provided in the chapter. A combination of background knowledge and common sense should enable you to come up with some relevant points, however.)

APPENDIX – FORMAL DERIVATION OF THE SEPARATION THEOREM

The nature of investment

Investment is essentially outlaying cash in order to give rise to future cash receipts. Usually most or all of the outlay occurs before the inflows. Thus investment has a time dimension.

Let us now consider the position of an investor who has an amount of wealth, which may either be spent (consumed) or invested in productive assets (plant, machinery, trading stocks, etc). At this stage let us restrict ourselves to considering only investment horizons of one period (say a year). Thus the individual may invest part or all of the current wealth for one year and consume the proceeds of the investment next year, or consume it all immediately.

In Fig. 2.1, $0W_0$ represents the total amount of wealth available for present consumption and/or investment by an individual. The curved line W_0W_1 represents the investments available to our investor. All of the present wealth ($0W_0$) may be invested, thus yielding $0W_1$ after a year, or all of the present wealth ($0W_0$) could be consumed, leaving no wealth at the end of the year. A third (and perhaps more likely) possibility is that the investor would choose to consume part of the present wealth and invest part – after all there is a need to eat, both now and next year. If our investor decided to invest C_0W_0 of the present wealth (and consume $0C_0$), this investment would result in $0C_1$ at the year end.

Note incidentally that the investment opportunities become less and less attractive as the amount invested by the individual increases, i.e. the line W_0W_1, becomes less steep as it rises – meaning that increasing amounts of present wealth will need to be invested to yield an extra £1 of wealth after a year. An investment XW_0 will yield wealth of $0Y$ after a year, but a similar-size investment C_0X will only increase next year's wealth by YC_1.

Line W_0W_1 does not represent a single investment opportunity but a large number of them – in fact all of the opportunities available to the investor at the time. The shaded space between the two sets of unbroken parallel lines in Fig. 2.1 represents just one of that large number of hypothetical investments available. This particular one involves an investment now (reduction in current consumption) of amount £a,

Fig. 2.1
The productive investment opportunities available to an individual whose wealth totals W_0

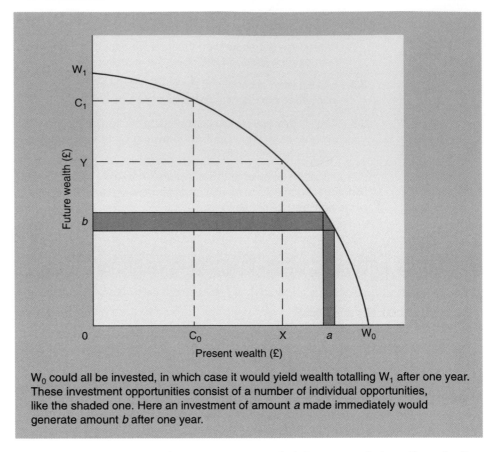

W_0 could all be invested, in which case it would yield wealth totalling W_1 after one year. These investment opportunities consist of a number of individual opportunities, like the shaded one. Here an investment of amount a made immediately would generate amount b after one year.

which will yield (increase future consumption by) £b in a year's time. Since the line W_0W_1 flattens towards the horizontal as it goes from right to left, the better investment prospects (greater return per £1 invested) lie to the right, the less good ones to the left. The investment opportunity lying closest to W_0 is the best one and opportunities decrease in desirability as the curve moves from right to left. This reflects reality in that investors, particularly those who invest in real assets, find that as they take on more and more investments the yield from each subsequent one becomes less. This is because they will tend to undertake the most advantageous investments first, leaving the less desirable ones.

Investment and utility

The investor whose wealth and investment opportunities are shown in Fig. 2.1 will want to know how much to invest, but will probably not want to invest all of the present wealth because this leaves nothing with which to buy food, shelter or indeed any luxuries which may be desired. On the other hand it would be an unusual person who decided to spend all of the money now and face starvation next year. How much would be invested and how much would be spent, which is clearly a question of personal taste, could be represented by the utility curves shown in Fig. 2.2. These curves depict this individual's attitude to the trade-off between consumption now and consumption after one year.

Each point on any particular curve represents some combination of present and future consumption which will render this individual similar amounts of satisfaction or utility. The higher the curve, the greater the satisfaction. (Readers who are unfamiliar with the notion of utility and utility curves should refer to p. 141.)

The curves in Fig. 2.2 indicate that the investor is very reluctant to forgo consumption completely, either now or next year. The fact that the curves are moving towards the vertical at the top left and towards the horizontal at the bottom right shows this. For example, at the lower levels of present consumption (i.e. reduction in present wealth, where the curves are steepest) any further lowering of consumption will only be undertaken if large increases in future consumption will follow. This tendency increases as the level of present consumption is reduced until we should reach a point where no amount of future consumption would justify further reductions in present consumption. The converse applies at low levels of future consumption. The curves depicted in Fig. 2.2 do, of course, represent the present/future consumption preferences of an individual. Other individuals might well have different attitudes. It is not likely, though, that their attitudes would be fundamentally different since they too would need to eat, both now and next year. The consumption/investment utility curves of all rational individuals would therefore be broadly similar to those shown in Fig. 2.2.

Fig. 2.2
Utility of present/ future consumption for some individual

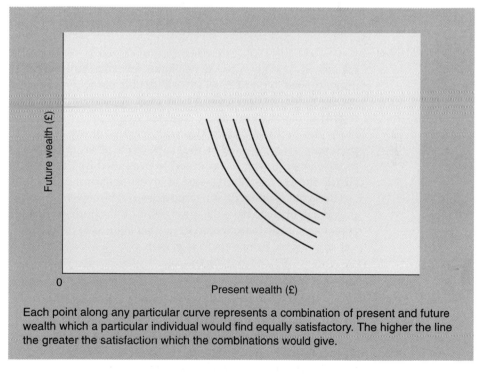

Each point along any particular curve represents a combination of present and future wealth which a particular individual would find equally satisfactory. The higher the line the greater the satisfaction which the combinations would give.

If we combine Figs 2.1 and 2.2, the result of which is shown in Fig. 2.3, we can see that point P is the best combination of investment/consumption for our particular investor as it gives the highest level of utility. No other point along the production curve would enable this person to achieve as high a level of satisfaction as will the investment/consumption decision implied by point P. Therefore the amount invested should be BW_0 (which will yield 0A after a year) and 0B should be

**Fig. 2.3
Utility of
consumption/
investment
for some individual**

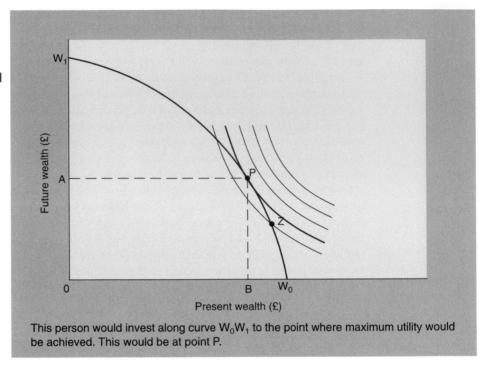

This person would invest along curve W_0W_1 to the point where maximum utility would be achieved. This would be at point P.

consumed now, giving 0A to consume next year. Suppose that our individual in fact only invested to point Z, which is a feasible possibility. While this would give some consumption, both now and next year, it does not give what this person would regard as the most satisfying combination of present and future consumption. We know this because Z coincides with a lower utility curve. Given our individual's preferences (represented by the shape of the utility curve) and the state of the world as far as investment is concerned (represented by the investment line W_0W_1), P is clearly the most satisfying level of investment for our individual.

This is not necessarily the same as would be chosen by other individuals because they are unlikely to have the same views on the trade-off between present and future consumption. So there would be *no unanimity* as to the desirable level of investment – it would vary from person to person.

The borrowing/lending opportunity

At this point let us introduce a further factor into the analysis and so make it more realistic. That factor is the opportunity available to individuals for borrowing and lending via banks and other financial institutions (the financial market).

Figure 2.4 shows another possibility which could be used alone or in conjunction with the production opportunities. If the investor were to lend all of the wealth (W_0) now, it would, with interest at rate i, become $W_0 + i\,W_0$ after a year. Thus the slope of the borrowing/lending line is $(W_0 + i\,W_0)/W_0 = 1 + i$.

The existence of borrowing/lending opportunities enables levels of investment to be undertaken in excess of the amount of wealth left after a desired level of consumption has been undertaken. This is achieved by borrowing the required

Fig. 2.4
**The borrowing/
lending opportunity
available to an
individual with
an amount of
wealth (W$_0$)**

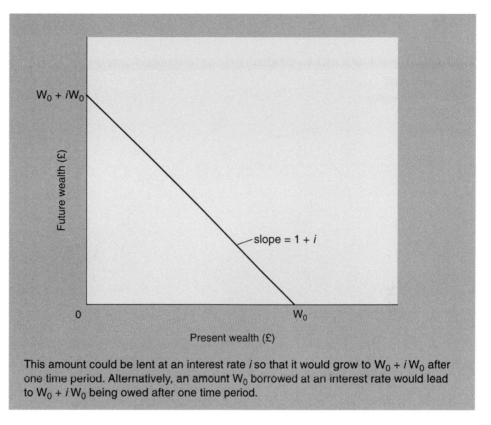

This amount could be lent at an interest rate i so that it would grow to $W_0 + i W_0$ after one time period. Alternatively, an amount W_0 borrowed at an interest rate would lead to $W_0 + i W_0$ being owed after one time period.

amount now and repaying it (with interest) next year. Similarly not all of the present wealth left after consuming the desired amount need be invested in production; some of it can be lent, to be received back (again with interest) next year. This broadening of the possibilities may well enable the investor to achieve higher levels of satisfaction (utility).

Figure 2.5 combines Figs 2.3 and 2.4, i.e. it introduces the borrowing/lending line into the investment/consumption configuration. Figure 2.5 does look rather compli-cated, but it is basically only what we have already met.

Without the borrowing/lending opportunity, point P represented the optimum consumption/investment combination for our investor, achieving utility curve $U_1 U_1$. With the introduction of borrowing/lending, a higher level of satisfaction can be achieved, moving up to utility curve $U_2 U_2$. Our individual can now invest amount EW_0 and consume amount 0D. This can be done by borrowing the shortfall (ED). Obviously this amount will have to be repaid (with interest) next year, but none-theless consumption of 0D now and 0C next year represents a more attractive (higher utility) prospect than consuming 0B now and 0A next year. Thus the intro-duction of borrowing/lending has increased utility. Note that GC (the amount which must be repaid next year out of 0G to leave the individual with 0C) is equal to ED (the amount borrowed now) plus interest on ED, i.e. ED $(1 + i)$. This is evident from Fig. 2.5 if we bear in mind that the slope of the borrowing/lending line is $(1 + i)$.

31

**Fig. 2.5
Utility of
consumption/
investment of
some individual
with the borrowing/
lending
opportunity**

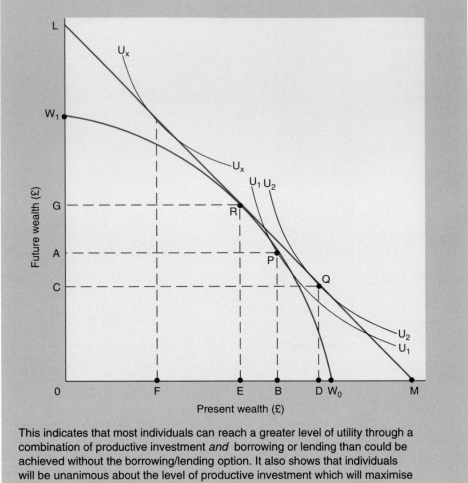

This indicates that most individuals can reach a greater level of utility through a combination of productive investment *and* borrowing or lending than could be achieved without the borrowing/lending option. It also shows that individuals will be unanimous about the level of productive investment which will maximise their utility, despite having widely differing attitudes to present and future consumption.

The separation theorem

An examination of Fig. 2.5 reveals an important point. Irrespective of the individual's time preferences (shape of utility curve), all investors faced with the productive investment opportunities depicted in Fig. 2.5 would invest up to point R and then achieve their personal highest level of utility by use of the borrowing/lending opportunity. Those investors whose highest utility curve would be tangential to the borrowing/lending line above R would invest up to R and lend that part of the remainder of their wealth which they wish not to consume. In Fig. 2.5 U_xU_x is a utility curve of a different investor from the one whose preferences are represented by U_1U_1, U_2U_2, etc. This second individual would choose to invest up to point R on the productive investment curve and then lend amount FE, leaving 0F for consumption.

An individual whose highest utility curve coincides with point R will obviously wish to invest up to that point but will not need to use the borrowing/lending opportunity.

Irrespective of the personal preferences of various investors they all agree that it is best to invest up to point R, i.e. the point where the slope of the production curve W_0W_1 is equal to that of the borrowing/lending line.

This unanimity between investors as to the optimum level of productive investment is quite interesting in the context of individuals. In the context of firms where managers should try to make investments which most benefit all their shareholders, the unanimity becomes of major importance.

The assumptions on which the above is based and their implications were each discussed in the main body of this chapter.

CHAPTER 3

Financial accounting statements and their interpretation

OBJECTIVES

In this chapter we shall deal with the following:

● the financial accounting statements published by companies

● the accounting conventions which underpin those statements

● interpretation of financial accounting statements

● the use of accounting ratios

● accounting ratios in detail

INTRODUCTION

Most UK firms which trade as limited companies are required to publish three financial statements each year. These are:

● the profit and loss account (or income statement)
● the balance sheet (or position statement)
● the cash flow statement.

These statements provide a very valuable source of information for financial managers who work within the firm and for investors, potential investors and their advisers. It is likely that managers will have access to information other than that which is made public. The nature of the additional information and the way in which it is derived, however, is probably very similar to that which is published. In this chapter we shall consider the nature of the three accounting statements, the rules which are followed in preparing them and the way they may be interpreted, so that the user is able to draw conclusions about the firm which go beyond the obvious.

It should be said that the approach to accounting which is taken in the UK is, in principle, very much the same as is taken throughout the world.

The intention of this chapter is not to provide a detailed course in accounting, but to give a broad overview of the subject. This should be useful in later chapters because reference will be made to the value of accounting information and the use of accounting ratios. If you feel that you would like to look at the subject in greater detail you could take up the suggestion for further reading which is given at the end of this chapter.

THE ACCOUNTING STATEMENTS

We shall now take a look at the accounting statements. These will be explained in the broadest way. Some of the points which will be made about the statements will be qualified in the next section when we consider the rules which underpin the statements.

Firms which trade as companies are required to produce the accounting statements annually. Most firms actually produce these statements much more frequently for their own internal, managerial purposes. The statements are often used for internal purposes as aids to financial planning in that the data which they contain will be based on plans and forecasts. The published accounts are, of course, based on past events.

The profit and loss account

This is a statement which sets out a summary of the trading events which will have affected the wealth of the firm over a particular period, the amount by which each type of event has affected the wealth and the resulting net effect on wealth. The statement also goes on to show how any net increase in the firm's wealth over the period has been deployed by the firm.

Wealth in this context is not restricted to cash. It is all the things which have economic value to the firm, net of such obligations which the firm may have to outsiders in respect of any part of its wealth. Things which have economic value to the firm (assets) include, for example, an office building owned by the firm and some money owed to the firm by a customer who has bought some of the firm's output of goods or services on credit. Outside obligations in respect of the firm's wealth might include an amount owed to a loan stockholder.

We shall now look at an example of a profit and loss account. Jackson plc is an imaginary manufacturing firm. The nature of the firm's marketing strategy is that goods are made to order so there is never any stock of finished goods. The form of accounting statements varies from one firm to the next. The layout which is shown here is broadly in line with that which UK law requires for the annual published accounts. Individual firms can and do use layouts of their own choice for accounts which are to be used for their own, internal purposes.

Jackson plc's profit and loss account shows that the firm generated wealth (earned revenues) of £837 000 by making sales to external customers. This led directly to the wealth being reduced (expenses incurred) in respect of meeting the cost of making the sales, also in distributing the goods sold and meeting the administrative costs of running the firm. This left the firm with a net increase in wealth, as a result of operating for the year, of £135 000. The interest which the firm was under a contractual obligation to pay accounted for a further £30 000.

The last part of the statement looks at how the firm deployed the wealth which it had generated. This includes after-tax profits of the current year. It also includes any profits from previous years which had not been specifically allocated. £27 000 will be paid to the Inland Revenue for Corporation Tax on the firm's profit for the year and £20 000 will be paid to the shareholders. You

Jackson plc
Profit and Loss account for the year ended 31 December 1997

	£000	£000	£000
Sales			837
Cost of sales (including depreciation £28 000 and raw materials stock usage £253 000 Raw material purchases totalled £255 000)			478
Gross profit			359
Distribution costs			
Salaries and wages	37		
Motor expenses	43		
Depreciation of motor vehicles	16		
Sundry distribution expenses	15	111	
Administrative expenses			
Salaries and wages	58		
Motor expenses	22		
Depreciation of motor vehicles	19		
Sundry administrative expenses	14	113	224
Operating profit for the year			135
Interest payable			30
Profit on ordinary activities before taxation			105
Tax on ordinary activities			27
Profit on ordinary activities after taxation			78
Retained profit brought forward from last year			151
			229
Proposed dividend on ordinary shares			20
Retained profit carried forward to next year			209

(Note that this statement does not strictly follow the layout which is required by law for published limited company accounts.)

should be clear that the £209 000 of unappropriated profit at the end of the year is that part of the firm's end-of-year wealth which has arisen from profits generated up to 31 December 1997, to the extent that it had not been paid to the Inland Revenue or to the shareholders as dividends. This is unlikely to be in the form of cash. As has already been pointed out, wealth does not just mean cash. In practice the £209 000 is probably in various forms – plant, stocks, etc.

The balance sheet

This is a statement of the manner in which the firm holds its wealth, how much of its wealth it has in each category, how much of the wealth which the firm controls is committed to outsiders and the net wealth of the firm. This net wealth obviously belongs to the shareholders. Unlike the profit and loss account which summarises the effects of various trading events on the wealth of the firm over a period, the balance sheet shows the firm's position at a specified point in time.

The balance sheet of Jackson plc, at the end of the year covered by the profit and loss account which we just considered, is as follows:

Jackson plc
Balance Sheet as at 31 December 1997

	£000 cost	£000 depreciation	£000
Fixed assets			
Freehold land	550	–	550
Plant and machinery	253	226	27
Motor vehicles	102	56	46
	905	282	623
Current assets			
Stock	43		
Trade debtors	116		
Prepaid expenses	12		
Cash	25	196	
Creditors: amounts falling due within one year			
Trade creditors	45		
Accrued expenses	18		
Taxation	27		
Dividend proposed	20	110	
Net current assets			86
Total assets less current liabilities			709
Creditors: amounts falling due after more than one year			
10% secured loan stock			300
			409
Ordinary share capital – 200 000 shares of £1 each			200
Profit and loss account			209
			409

(Note that this statement does not strictly follow the layout which is required by law.)

This balance sheet tells us that the wealth of the firm is £819 000. This is made up of fixed assets of £623 000 and current assets of £196 000. The firm has obligations to transfer part of this wealth to groups outside. £110 000 is in respect of obligations which must be met within one year, and £300 000 in respect of longer-term obligations.

The distinction between fixed and current assets is concerned with the intended use of those assets. Fixed assets are those which are intended to be used within the firm to help to generate wealth, not to be sold at a profit. Current assets are those which are acquired by the firm with the intention of turning them over in the normal course of trading. A particular fixed asset might be sold at a profit but this would not mean that it should have been treated as a current asset, provided that the primary reason for buying it was for using rather than selling it. Fixed assets can be seen as the tools of the firm.

Depreciation recognises that certain fixed assets are not worth as much at the end of their life with the firm as they cost at the beginning and, therefore, that some part of the firm's wealth will be lost. This is why depreciation appears in the profit and loss account as an expense and why the balance sheet value of depreciating fixed assets is reduced below cost. The total amount of depreciation of a particular asset is calculated by taking its cost and deducting its estimated disposal value at the end of its life with the firm. This total must then be apportioned between accounting periods in some reasonable manner. In practice in the UK this is typically accomplished by sharing the total equally between the number of accounting periods of the life of the fixed asset concerned.

It is considered useful to readers of balance sheets to deduct current (short-term) liabilities from current assets and to show the net figure of net current assets or working capital. This is because, in normal circumstances, it is out of the assets included under current assets that the current liabilities will be met. Relating current liabilities to current assets in this way highlights the extent to which the firm will find it easy to meet its short-term obligations. This is a particularly important matter since a failure of a firm to meet its short-term obligations can easily lead to financial collapse.

The bottom section of the balance sheet shows how the shareholders have contributed to the current wealth of the firm. This was by a combination of specifically putting assets, normally cash, into the firm to acquire shares, and by allowing wealth generated within the firm to remain there rather than being paid to themselves as dividends. These ploughed-back profits, shown under the heading 'profit and loss account' are known as reserves. Reserves represent part of the wealth of the shareholders just as much as dividends do.

The cash flow statement

This is simply an analysis of the cash received and paid out by the firm during a period. It is arranged in such a way that it will enable readers to derive helpful insights to the sources and uses of cash over the period. It may seem strange that one particular asset – cash – is highlighted in this way when others, e.g. stock, are not. What is so special about cash? The answer to this question is that cash tends to be at the heart of most aspects of business. A firm's ability to prosper and survive is likely to depend on its ability to generate cash. This typically is not true for other types of asset.

The cash flow statement of Jackson plc is as follows:

Jackson plc
Cash flow statement for the year ended 31 December 1997

	£000	£000
Net cash inflow from operating activities		207
Returns on investments and servicing of finance		
Interest paid	(30)	
Dividends paid	(15)	(45)
Taxation		
Corporation tax paid		(18)
Investing activities		
Payments to acquire tangible fixed assets		(33)
Net cash inflow before financing		111
Financing		–
Increase in cash		111

This statement shows that the firm generated a net cash inflow of £207 000 from its trading activities. That is to say that during the year the receipts of cash from sales exceeded payments of cash to pay wages and salaries, suppliers of goods and services, etc., by £207 000. You should be clear that this is not the same as profit. Profit is the net increase in wealth generally as a result of trading – not just cash.

The remainder of the statement shows where any other cash has come from (none in the case of Jackson plc in 1997) and gone to. In this case cash has been spent on paying the dividend which was declared in 1996, but not paid until 1997; loan interest paid in 1997; the tax which arose from the 1996 profit but was paid in 1997; and some cash was spent acquiring additional fixed assets.

Had any cash been raised through an issue of shares or loan stocks, or had any cash been paid to redeem shares or loan stocks, the effect of these would have appeared under the 'financing' heading in the statement.

DEFINITIONS AND CONVENTIONS OF ACCOUNTING

Accounting is a language which is used to store and communicate economic information about organisations. It has a set of rules, which have emerged through practice rather than as a result of an exercise to decide what is the best approach. It is particularly important that anyone trying to read accounting statements and draw conclusions from them is clear on the rules of accounting. Severe misunderstandings could arise for someone not familiar with the rules reading accounting statements.

Accounting definition of an asset

An asset has a particular meaning in accounting, which is rather more restrictive than the general one which we use in more everyday speech. To be included in a balance sheet as an asset of a particular firm, the item would need to have the following attributes:

- it is likely to produce future economic benefits to that firm
- it has arisen from some past transaction or event involving that firm
- the right of access to it by others can be restricted by that firm

The benefit of having a loyal workforce has the characteristics of an asset, to the extent of it being capable of producing probable future economic benefits, e.g. through savings in recruitment costs as a result of low labour turnover. It would not, however, be included on the firm's balance sheet because it has almost certainly not arisen as a result of any particular transaction or event. It is also the case that the firm would probably find it impossible to deny rival firms access to members of the staff to try to employ them. It can be persuasively argued that failure to take account of such assets gives accounting a limited view of reality.

Money measurement convention

Accounting defines things in terms of money and can do no other. Thus information which cannot be expressed in monetary terms cannot be included in accounting statements. This can be seen as a deficiency of accounting.

Historic cost convention

Assets are shown in the balance sheet at a value which is based on their cost to the firm when they were first acquired, not their current market value or any other basis of valuation. This means that attempts to use the balance sheet to place a value on a firm are likely to lead to misleading results. Some firms break this convention and show certain assets, particularly those relating to land and buildings, at an estimate of their current market value. Certain items of value may be omitted from the balance sheet because they do not have a cost which can be measured in money terms. Also a particular asset may have a low market value but be worth much to the firm itself. This could arise where the asset is highly specialised or specific to the firm and have little or no use to any other firm.

Adherence to the historic cost convention means that the reader of accounting statements is unable to assess the opportunity cost of using a particular asset for some purpose. For example, when the historic cost of some stock sold is included in a profit and loss account, as an expense, the reader is not able to make a judgement about how much more the wealth of the firm would have been increased had the stock been deployed in some other way.

Prudence convention

Accounting should err on the side of caution. For example, if an item of stock in trade has a sales value which is below cost, this should be reflected by reducing its value in the balance sheet to the lower figure, with the same reflection of the loss of wealth being shown in the profit and loss account. Following the same philosophy, a gain in the value of an asset is not taken into account until it is realised as a result of a disposal of the asset concerned to some person or organisation outside the firm. In this way the prudence convention tends to underpin both the historic cost and the realisation conventions.

It has been argued that adherence to the prudence convention tends to lead to a fairly consistent bias in accounting information, which could mislead a reader of accounting statements.

Going concern convention

In the absence of evidence to the contrary, it is assumed that the firm will continue indefinitely. This means, for example, that it will be assumed that a fixed asset will be capable of being used by the firm for the whole of its useful life, rather than it being assumed that the firm will be forced to dispose of the asset as a result of the firm suffering financial collapse. Thus a firm can base its depreciation policy on the cost, expected life and disposal proceeds of the particular asset, rather than on the current value of the asset at intermediate periods over its life. As a result the fact that many fixed assets have a current market value below their balance sheet value does not cause the prudence convention to be invoked.

Stable monetary unit

Accounting tends to assume that the value of the currency remains constant in terms of its ability to buy goods and services. In other words, accounting statements are prepared as if there were no inflation. The fact that inflation is a constant feature of almost every economy in the world means that this is likely to be a major cause of accounting statements giving impressions which could be misleading. Attempts have been made to agree an approach to allowing for the distortions of inflation in accounts. So far no major economy in the world has developed an approach which is consistently and widely used by its firms in their accounts.

Realisation

This convention is concerned with the point in time at which a revenue, i.e. an increase in wealth arising from trading, is recognised in the accounts. For example if a customer orders goods in one month, receives them in the next and pays for them in the third month, when should the firm supplying the goods treat the revenue (sale) as having taken place? This is not an academic question where the firm is preparing accounts for each month and comparing one month's performance with another, or where the three months do not all fall within the same accounting year.

The realisation convention says that the revenue should be recognised at the point where:

- the amount (value) of the revenue is capable of being measured with substantial accuracy;
- the necessary work to undertake the sale has substantially been completed; and
- it is reasonably certain that the cash will be received.

This point is usually taken to be the point at which the customer takes delivery, and accepts, the goods or service. Thus recognition of the revenue and receipt of the cash do not occur at the same point, except in the case of cash sales. Outside of the retail trade cash sales are rare. Thus for most firms cash receipts from sales tend to lag behind recognition of sales.

Matching

Expenses (trading events leading to reductions in wealth) are matched to the particular revenues, which they helped to generate in the same accounting period. For example, where the sale of some goods is recognised as a revenue in a particular accounting period, the cost of those goods to the supplying firm should be treated as an expense in the same period.

The objective which this convention pursues is to assess the net effect on wealth which a particular revenue generates.

Accruals

Profit or loss is concerned with net increases or decreases in wealth, not with increases or decreases in cash. Thus when deriving the amount of the expenses which are to be matched to particular revenues, the fact that cash may not yet have been paid is not relevant. For example, the cost of stock sold for inclusion in the profit and loss account will be the same, irrespective of whether payment for the stock concerned has yet been made.

PROBLEMS WITH USING ACCOUNTING INFORMATION FOR DECISION MAKING

There are significant problems in using accounting information to help to make decisions. These fall under two headings: income measurement and balance sheet values.

Income measurement

A major problem here is concerned with the costs which are matched against revenues. The costs are normally not expressed in the same terms as the revenues where there are changing prices (historic cost and stable monetary unit conventions). Since the costs tend to be incurred before the revenues are recognised, there is a tendency for costs to be understated causing profit to be overstated. Depreciation is often a particular problem here. Depreciation expenses are based on costs which may have been incurred many years earlier; also depreciation is often a significant expense. Also the fact that historic costs are used rather than opportunity costs means that only a partial impression of the effect of a particular transaction's effects on wealth is given. Again the distortion is consistently likely to overstate profit, i.e. to imply that more wealth has been created than is justified by the facts.

Balance sheet values

Adherence to the historic cost, prudence, going concern and stable monetary unit conventions, coupled with the use of a fairly restricted accounting definition of an asset, tends to cause accounts to understate the amount of wealth which is invested in the firm. This tends to be the case both asset by asset and taking the firm overall. Many assets have a greater value than is represented by the balance sheet. Some things which are of economic value to the firm may not even be included in the balance sheet at all. Many firms have goodwill, i.e. an ability to earn abnormally high profits due to some factor, like a loyal workforce or a loyal clientele. This asset is rarely included in the balance sheet since to do so would contravene one or other of the accounting rules. Yet a distorted impression of the wealth committed to the firm is given if most assets are either understated or are excluded.

It is perhaps worth noting that accounting's deficiencies for decision making purposes stem from the fact that financial accounting did not really evolve to meet the needs which decision makers currently try to satisfy. Rather it developed to provide an historical financial record of the firm. On the one hand this was a record of where funds had come from – shareholders, creditors, etc. – and how much each had contributed. On the other hand there was a record of how these funds had been deployed. So when shareholders subscribed for shares of £1 million and the firm used the cash to buy a building, this appeared on the balance sheet as share capital £1 million and freehold land £1 million. The fact that five years later the land might have a market value of £10 million is not relevant, because the balance sheet simply records the transaction. For one reason or another accountants have never really sat down with a clean sheet of paper and tried to design a system which would be more useful to decision makers. From time to time they have grafted on additional features, like the profit and loss account, but these features were always underpinned by the same approach that had been taken to the balance sheet.

Despite the deficiencies of accounting statements, they remain a very major, if not the only, source of information for many decision makers. Provided that accounting information is used with care, it should be useful, despite its limitations.

There is no reason of principle why a particular firm should not prepare accounts for its internal purposes in such a way as to correct for the distorting factors. Undoubtedly some firms do this, but probably most do not.

RATIO ANALYSIS

As well as gaining information about, and insights into, a firm's trading and position by reading the published accounts, it is also useful to calculate ratios relating particular figures to one another. It can even be useful to relate certain accounting figures to non-accounting measures, like the number of employees. One reason for calculating ratios is to attempt to summarise quite complex accounting information into a relatively small number of key indicators. An associated reason for calculating ratios is to make figures more easily comparable. For example, if firm A made a profit last year of £1 million and firm B made a profit of £2 million, what does this tell us? Clearly it tells us that firm B made the larger profit, but does it tell us that firm B was better managed or more efficient? The answer is that it does not give us any impression of relative efficiency. Firm B may be much larger than firm A. If we were to relate each firm's profit to its size a more valid comparison of efficiency can be made. The amount which the shareholders have invested (share capital plus reserves, which equals total assets less total liabilities) is a commonly used indicator of size, so we could use that.

Comparison between firms is not the only one which we may wish to make.

We may want to compare the firm's current performance with its past performance to try to identify trends, etc. We may wish to assess the firm's performance against that which was planned.

Calculating ratios from a set of accounts is a relatively easy task. A suitably primed computer will do it almost instantaneously. The hard part of interpretation of accounts lies in using skill and experience to draw valid and useful conclusions from the ratios.

Traditionally ratios are classified into five groups and we shall look at a selection of ratios under those same headings. As we proceed to consider each ratio we shall calculate each one for Jackson plc for 1997. When this is completed, to give us some basis of comparison, we shall also look at the same ratios for the firm in 1996.

Profitability ratios

These ratios are concerned with the effectiveness of the firm in generating profit.

A very popular means of assessing a firm is to assess the amount of wealth generated for the amount of wealth invested.

Return on net assets (return on capital employed)

$$\frac{\text{Net profit before long-term interest and tax}}{\text{Total assets less current liabilities}} \times 100\%$$

The ratio for Jackson plc for 1997 is $\frac{135}{709} \times 100 = 19.0\%$

This ratio looks at the return on the fixed and current assets less current liabilities (that is, creditors falling due in less than one year). The logical profit figure to use in calculating this ratio is the operating profit. This is because we are considering the effectiveness of the assets financed both by the shareholders and by the long-term creditors and, therefore, we should logically use the profit which is shared between these two groups.

Provided that short-term profit is not being generated at the expense of the long term, this ratio should probably be as high as possible. In Chapter 2 we saw that it might be open to most firms to increase current accounting earnings and, with it, the return on assets ratio, through taking actions which could adversely affect long-term profitability, or at the expense of taking on higher levels of risk.

Since this ratio goes to the heart of what most private sector firms are trying to achieve it is sometimes known as the primary ratio.

Return on equity (return on shareholders' funds)

$$\frac{\text{Net profit after long-term interest and tax}}{\text{Share capital and reserves}} \times 100\%$$

The ratio for Jackson plc for 1997 is $\frac{78}{409} \times 100 = 19.1\%$

This is quite a similar ratio to the previous one, but considers matters more specifically from the shareholders' viewpoint. For this reason the profit figure is that which is earned by the shareholders after all charges have been met.

Gross profit margin

$$\frac{\text{Gross profit}}{\text{Sales}} \times 100\%$$

The ratio for Jackson plc for 1997 is $\dfrac{359}{837} \times 100 = 42.9\%$

This shows what percentage of the sales revenue remains after the expense of making the stock available to the customers is taken into account. There is a range of pricing and output strategies which a firm can employ. At one end of the range is the strategy of charging very low prices for the output, so that customers are attracted, leading to a high sales revenue (turnover). At the other end is the strategy of offering the firm's output at a fairly high price, leading to a relatively low sales turnover. In principle neither strategy is preferable to the other. Where in the range the firm seeks to operate is a matter of managerial judgement. In making this judgement management will need to take account of the nature of the market and of the firm's own cost structure.

Net profit margin

$$\frac{\text{Net profit before long-term interest and tax}}{\text{Sales}} \times 100\%$$

The ratio for Jackson plc for 1997 is $\dfrac{135}{837} \times 100 = 16.1\%$

This ratio shows what is left of sales revenue after all of the expenses of running the firm for the period have been met. Once again it should be as large as possible, provided that the firm is not earning high profit margins at the expense of some other aspect. Again a 'short-termist' attitude to profit could lead to an apparently impressive net profit margin, but one which may not be sustainable into the future.

Activity ratios

These ratios are used to try to assess the effectiveness of a firm in using its assets.

Net asset turnover

$$\frac{\text{Sales}}{\text{Total assets less current liabilities}}$$

The ratio for Jackson plc for 1997 is $\dfrac{837}{709} = 1.18$ times

This ratio enables a judgement to be made on the extent to which the firm has generated sales. As in the return on capital employed ratio, the net assets figure is used as a measure of the size of the firm. This ratio is a measure of the effectiveness with which the firm is using its assets to generate sales. The size of this ratio will be a reflection of the firm's strategy on margins and turnover, discussed above in the context of the gross profit margin ratio. A high ratio is not necessarily beneficial if margins are so small that the net profit generated is unsatisfactory.

It is worth noting the direct relationship between return on net assets, net profit margin and net asset turnover. If you look back at the definition of each of these ratios you will see that:

$$\text{Return on net assets} = \text{net profit margin} \times \text{net asset turnover}$$

It can be quite helpful to look at sales relative to various elements of the net assets. For example, if there is a relatively small net asset turnover ratio, further analysis can be undertaken to assess fixed asset turnover, current asset turnover, etc. This may enable an analyst to make a judgement about the reason for the low net asset turnover figure. This in turn may reveal that the firm has an abnormal balance between the various elements of net assets, e.g. relatively high fixed assets.

Stockholding period

$$\frac{\text{Stock held}}{\text{Stock used}} \times 365 \text{ days}$$

Jackson is a manufacturing firm, which makes things to order and, therefore, has no stock of finished goods. Let us assume that all the stock at the year end is of raw materials (rather than work-in-progress).

The ratio for Jackson plc for 1997 is $\dfrac{43}{253} \times 365 = 62.0$ days

This ratio indicates the average number of days which stock remains in the firm before it is taken into production. Good stock management would cause this figure to be as low as possible, consistent with there being sufficient stock available to meet the firm's needs.

The stock turnover ratio is the reciprocal of this, i.e. $\dfrac{\text{Stock used}}{\text{Stock held}}$

The management of stock and the other working capital elements is discussed in some detail in Chapter 13 of this book.

Debtor collection period (Days debtors)

$$\frac{\text{Trade debtors}}{\text{Credit sales}} \times 365 \text{ days}$$

The ratio for Jackson plc for 1997 is $\dfrac{116}{837} \times 365 = 50.6$ days

(Assuming that all of the firm's sales are on credit.)

This ratio tells us how long, on average, after the sale on credit, trade debtors meet their obligation to pay. A well-managed debtor policy will lead to debtors taking as short a time as possible to pay, yet not damage good customer relations.

Creditor payment period (Days creditors)

$$\frac{\text{Trade creditors}}{\text{Credit purchases}} \times 365 \text{ days}$$

The ratio for Jackson plc for 1997 is $\dfrac{45}{255} \times 365 = 64.4 \text{ days}$

(Assuming that all of the firm's purchases are on credit and that the trade creditors only relate to purchases of raw materials stock.)

This ratio tells us how long, on average, after a purchase on credit the firm meets its obligation to pay for the goods or service bought. A well-managed creditor policy will lead to the firm taking as much 'free' credit as is possible, but at the same time preserving the goodwill of suppliers.

Liquidity ratios

These ratios are used to try to assess how well the firm is managing its working capital.

Current ratio

$$\frac{\text{Current assets}}{\text{Current liabilities}}$$

The ratio for Jackson plc for 1997 is $\dfrac{196}{110} = 1.78 : 1$

Note that this ratio is usually expressed by stating the amount of current assets per £1 of current liabilities.

This provides some measure of how the balance has been struck between the two aspects of working capital. Usually firms seek to have ratios higher than 1:1, i.e. they try to avoid having current assets financed entirely from current liabilities. In this way they hope to give the short-term creditors confidence that there are sufficient liquid assets comfortably to cover their claims.

Rule-of-thumb figures for this ratio tend to be bandied about in the literature and in financial management folklore, a popular figure being 2:1. In fact actual figures tend to vary widely but there seem to be characteristic figures for different industries. The high street supermarket chains typically seem to have ratios close to 1:1, whereas manufacturing firms have very much higher levels. The difference is almost certainly explained by the make-up of the current assets. In supermarkets they consist of cash and fast-moving stock-in-trade; supermarkets do not sell on credit (therefore they have no trade debtors) and typically stock does not gather dust on the shelves. Thus all their current assets are in a fairly liquid state, being either cash or, in the normal course of events, items

47

naturally turning into cash within a week or two. Manufacturers, by contrast, typically sell on credit and – since they do need to hold stocks of raw materials, finished goods and some amount of work in progress (WIP) – much of their current assets are perhaps several months away from turning into cash.

Quick assets (liquid or acid test) ratio

$$\frac{\text{Liquid assets}}{\text{Current liabilities}}$$

The ratio for Jackson plc for 1997 is $\dfrac{153}{110} = 1.39 : 1$

This ratio addresses itself fairly directly to the question: if short-term creditors were to demand payment of their claims more or less immediately, would there be sufficient in the way of liquid assets to meet them? What is included in *liquid assets* is a matter of judgement. For our supermarket, these would probably include all current assets since none of them is likely to be too far away from turning into cash. For a manufacturer they would probably exclude stocks and possibly some debtors.

We can probably say that, irrespective of the nature of business involved, this ratio should be about 1:1. The difference between the type of business is in effect adjusted in the definition of liquid assets.

We might ask ourselves whether it is likely that all the short-term creditors would demand their money at once. The answer is probably no, provided that they remained confident that payment would be forthcoming at the normal time. Those advancing credit without cast-iron security, which would be the position of the typical provider of short-term credit, do so for their own commercial advantage (e.g. in order to sell their wares) and they do so because they have reasonable confidence that they will be paid. Signs, including a weak acid test ratio, that the firm may not be able to pay, are likely to erode that confidence, triggering off demands for immediate payment.

No credit period

$$\frac{\text{Cash (and near cash)}}{\text{Average daily cash running costs}}$$

The ratio for Jackson plc for 1997 is $\dfrac{25}{(478 + 111 + 113 + 30 - 63)/365} = 13.6 \text{ days}$

The numerator of this is cash. The denominator is the average expenses, excluding depreciation (£63 000 for the year). Depreciation is excluded because it is not an expense which gives rise to a cash flow.

This is a more dynamic measure of liquidity than is the quick asset ratio. It asks for how many days the firm could continue to operate without any further injection of cash. In this way it relates the firm's liquid assets to its need for those liquid assets to enable it to maintain normal operations.

This ratio should be as large as possible, consistent with not having too much unproductive cash at the bank. There is some discussion of the advantages and disadvantages of holding cash in Chapter 13.

Capital gearing ratios

Capital gearing is concerned with the relative sizes of the funds provided by shareholders, on the one hand, and by loan creditors on the other. This is an important issue in business finance, about which there are various theories and a body of empirical evidence. This is discussed in some detail in Chapter 11.

For reasons which are raised in Chapter 11 loan financing tends to be cheaper than equity financing. On the other hand loan financing exposes the shareholders to greater risk than does equity financing. Ratios in this area tend to be concerned with assessing the level of capital gearing.

Debt to equity ratio

$$\frac{\text{Borrowings (long- and short-term)}}{\text{Total equity (shares plus reserves)}}$$

The ratio for Jackson plc for 1997 is $\dfrac{300}{409} = 0.73 : 1$

It is not possible to say whether a particular figure represents a high figure. 'High' is probably defined as significantly larger than is typically found in the industry in which the firm operates.

Times interest covered

$$\frac{\text{Profit before interest and tax}}{\text{Interest charges}}$$

The ratio for Jackson plc for 1997 is $\dfrac{135}{30} = 4.5$ times

This ratio looks at how many times the interest could be met from the profits. It is, therefore, some measure of how easily the firm is able to cover its interest payment obligations out of its profits.

Investors' ratios

These ratios are concerned with looking at the firm from the point of view of a shareholder, perhaps owning shares in a Stock Exchange traded firm. These ratios are of the type which appear in the financial pages of newspapers. Two of those which we shall be considering are partly based on the current market price of the shares. We shall work on the basis that Jackson plc's ordinary shares had a market value of £5.10 on 31 December 1997.

Earnings per share

$$\frac{\text{Profit after interest and tax}}{\text{Number of ordinary shares}}$$

The ratio for Jackson plc for 1997 is $\dfrac{78}{200} = £0.39$ (or 39p) per share

This is the profit attributable to each share. It is not the dividend paid per share, unless all of the profit is paid as a dividend, which would be very unusual. We should bear in mind that the profit, or at least the wealth represented by that profit belongs to the shareholders whether it is paid to them or not. In Chapter 12 we shall consider whether shareholders prefer to receive dividends or to 'plough back' their profits.

Price/earnings ratio

$$\frac{\text{Current market price per share}}{\text{Earnings per share}}$$

The ratio for Jackson plc at 31 December 1997 is $\dfrac{5.10}{0.39} = 13.1$

This ratio can be seen as the number of years that it would take, at the current share price and rate of earnings, for the earnings from the share to cover the price of the share. This has been a very popular means of assessing shares.

A share with a high PE ratio is one which has a high price compared with its recent earnings. This implies that investors are confident in future earnings of the firm. It will, of course, be on the basis of expectations of future profits that investors will assess the value of shares.

Dividend yield

$$\frac{\text{Dividend per share (grossed-up for tax)}}{\text{Current market price per share}} \times 100\%$$

The ratio for Jackson plc at 31 December 1997 is $\dfrac{(20/200) \times (100/80)}{5.10} \times 100 = 2.5\%$

This ratio seeks to assess the cash return on investment earned by the shareholders. To this extent it enables a comparison to be made with other investment opportunities available. It is necessary to 'gross up' the dividend received because it is received as if Income tax at 20 per cent had been deducted before payment. Since rates of return on investment are usually quoted in gross (pretax) terms, it makes for a more valid comparison.

Whether a high or a low figure is to be preferred for dividend yield depends greatly on the needs and investment objectives of the shareholders.

Dividend cover

$$\frac{\text{Profit after interest and tax}}{\text{Total dividend}}$$

The ratio for Jackson plc for 1997 is $\dfrac{78}{20} = 3.9$ times

This ratio indicates how comfortably the firm can meet the dividend out of current profits. The higher the ratio, the more confident shareholders can be that the dividend will be maintained, at least, at the current level, even if there were to be a downturn in profits.

We can now go on to assess Jackson plc through its accounting ratios. To give us a basis for comparison we shall assess the 1997 results against those for 1996. The profit and loss account and balance sheet of the firm, for the earlier year, are given in the appendix to this chapter. The following is a table of the 1997 ratios with their 1996 counterparts:

Jackson plc
Accounting ratios for the years ended 31 December:

	1996	1997
Profitability ratios		
Return on net assets (%)	14.9	19.0
Return on equity (%)	13.1	19.1
Gross profit margin (%)	43.8	42.9
Net profit margin (%)	13.8	16.1
Activity ratios		
Net asset turnover (times)	1.08	1.18
Stock holding period (days)	78.8	62.0
Debtor collection period (days)	64.0	50.6
Creditor payment period (days)	83.9	64.4
Liquidity ratios		
Current	0.99:1	1.78:1
Quick assets	0.76:1	1.39:1
No credit period (days)	(54.0)	13.6
Gearing ratios		
Debt to equity	1.10:1	0.73:1
Times interest covered (times)	2.9	4.5
Investors' ratios		
Earnings per share (£)	0.23	0.39
Price/earnings	15.2	13.1
Dividend yield (%)	2.7	2.5
Dividend cover (times)	3.1	3.9

Comment on the ratios

In 1997 there was a significantly higher ratio for return on net assets, which would normally be seen as desirable. This has been achieved mainly through an increased net asset turnover which more than overcame the small decrease in the gross profit margin. Thus the firm was more effective at making sales in 1997 than it was in 1996. Net profit margin rose because of the strong increase in turnover, despite an increase in the amounts spent on overheads.

Liquidity improved dramatically from a level which was probably an unhealthy one to one which would probably be considered fairly strong. This was achieved through the reduction in the amount of time for which the firm was holding stock and the time taken to collect trade debts. Creditors were more promptly paid in 1997 than they were in 1996. This represents a reduction over the year in the extent to which the firm took advantage of the availability of this theoretically cost-free form of finance. This may have been done deliberately with a view to improving relations with suppliers.

Partly as a result of the elimination of the overdraft, and partly as a result of relatively high ploughed-back profit expanding reserves, the gearing ratio dropped significantly.

The increased profit with no increase in the number of shares issued led directly to an increase in earnings per share. The price/earnings ratio diminished despite a much better profit performance by the firm in 1997. This can be explained by the fact that the share price is driven by investors' expectations of the future of the firm. Thus the price in 1996 reflected the future, rather than the 1996 profits, which were used in the calculation of the ratio. The increased profit led to an increase in the dividend cover despite the increased dividend in 1997.

Generally we have a picture of a firm which has significantly improved in most aspects of its performance and position over the year. It was more profitable which led to strong cash flows (see the cash flow statement) and, therefore, to much better liquidity and lower capital gearing.

Apart from the problems of ratio analysis which we shall consider shortly, it must be recognised that this analysis is very limited in its scope. We have only considered two years' figures. It would probably be much more instructive to have looked at ratios stretching over a number of years. We have only used another period for the same firm as our basis of comparison. It would be at least as useful to compare this firm's performance with that of other companies in the industry, perhaps the industry averages for the various ratios. We know that the debtor collection period was shorter for Jackson plc in 1997 than it had been in 1996, but this is not to say that this represented a satisfactory performance compared with the industry average, or compared with that which the firm had budgeted the debtor collection period to be.

Other ratios

There is an almost limitless number of ratios which can be calculated from one set of financial accounts. Those which we have considered only represent a sample, though these are what seem to be the more popular ratios used in practice. Certain ratios may be particularly appropriate in certain types of business. Obviously a stockholding period ratio is appropriate to a firm which deals in stock in some way. To a firm offering a service, it would be inappropriate.

Ratios need not be derived exclusively from accounting reports. The sales per employee ratio is widely used. Cost per tonne/mile (i.e. the cost of transporting a tonne of cargo for one mile) is widely used in the transport industry. Sales revenue per square metre of selling area is fairly widely used in the retail trade.

Caution in interpretation of ratios

It must be obvious from what we have seen so far that ratio analysis is not a very exact science. The choice of the ratios which are calculated, the precise definition of these ratios and the conclusions which are drawn are very much matters of judgement and conjecture. Ratios tend to raise questions rather than to answer them. Ratios can highlight areas where this year's performance was different from that of last year, or where one firm's performance was different from that of other firms in the industry. They will not tell you whether this year's performance was better than that of other years, or whether Firm A is better than the rest.

It follows that it is not appropriate to be dogmatic in interpreting ratios. For example the debtor collection period for Jackson plc was shorter for 1997 than it was for 1996. This cannot automatically be interpreted as an improvement, however. It might be that a lot of pressure has been put on debtors to pay promptly and that this has led to some loss of customer goodwill, which will, in due course, have an adverse effect on the firm's profitability.

Problems with accounting figures

Earlier in the chapter, we considered the nature of accounting information and problems with using it. In the context of accounting ratios, there are probably two particularly significant weaknesses. First there is a tendency for the profit and loss account to overstate profit, relative to a more true assessment of the amount of wealth created. Second there is a tendency for balance sheet figures to understate the amount of wealth which is tied up in the firm. This is a particular problem when we are dealing with ratios which are calculated using one figure from the profit and loss account and one from the balance sheet. A good example of this is the return on net assets ratio. For example would it be wise to conclude that Jackson plc's return on net assets of 19.0 per cent for 1997 represents a better return than bank deposit account interest of, say 8 per cent, even ignoring the disparity in the level of risk?

Another problem with using balance sheet figures is that they represent the position at a single, defined, point in time. This point in time, the firm's accounting year end, may not be typical of the firm throughout the rest of the year. This may be true by design. For example the management of a particular firm may choose a particular year end date because stocks tend to be unusually low at that time. It is quite common for firms to need to carry out a physical count of the stock at the accounting year end. Obviously this task will be made easier if stock levels are low. This problem with balance sheet figures may lead to inappropriate interpretation of ratios where balance sheet figures are involved.

Where a particular ratio relates a balance sheet figure to one from the profit and loss account there is a further problem. The balance sheet represents the position at a particular point in time, but the profit and loss account summarises a series of transactions over the period. If the balance sheet figure is not typical of the period, this can lead to distorted ratios. For example, we calculated the return on net assets for Jackson plc by relating the profit before interest and tax to net assets at the *end* of the year. Yet it is clear that at other times in the year the net assets were not the same as the year-end figure (see the 1996 balance sheet, in the Appendix to this chapter). In other words the net assets which were invested to generate the £135 000 were probably less than £709 000 for almost all the year.

An obvious solution to this problem is to average the opening and closing net assets figures and use this in the calculation of the ratio. This would give a ratio for 1997 of 19.9 per cent (i.e. [135/((651 + 709) / 2) × 100 per cent]), compared with the original figure calculated of 19.0 per cent. As we have already seen, it is not necessarily the case that the balance sheet figures are representative of the rest of the year. Here simply averaging the start-of-year and end-of-year figures may not do much to remove the distortion. This will not pose a problem to those who have access to the underlying figures because they can deduce a more representative average figure. Outsiders can do no more than average the figures which are available.

Though a combination of the law and the rules laid down by the accounting profession seek to promote the extent to which accounts are prepared on a consistent basis, from one firm to another, there are still areas where one firm may legitimately deal with the same transaction or event differently from another. This creates yet another problem for the analyst when trying to use accounting information to make inter-firm comparisons.

Other limitations of accounting ratios

Accounting ratios are derived by dividing one figure by another. As with all such indicators, information is lost. A significant reason for using ratios is to enable comparison to be made between factors which are not of the same scale. Sometimes, however, it is important to be aware of scale. For example, the size of a firm could double from one year to the next, yet ratios alone would not reveal this fact.

It can be instructive just to look at the accounting statements, trying to take a critical and enquiring approach. For example if we look back at Jackson plc's balance sheet for 1997, several points are worthy of note, none of which would be picked up from using the standard accounting ratios.

The first of these relates to fixed assets, specifically to plant and machinery. The depreciation provision, i.e. that part of the cost which has already been treated as an expense, is almost as large as the cost figure (£226 000 compared with £253 000). This implies that the plant is coming close to the end of the life which was predicted for it by the firm. This, in turn, has several implications:

● The firm is operating with old plant. This may mean it is not using the most sophisticated methods available to it. This may or may not be an important factor. Nevertheless it is something which someone trying to make an assessment of the firm might find useful to know in building up the picture.

● Perhaps, more significantly, it seems likely that there will be a need to replace various items of plant in the fairly near future. This will probably lead to a major outflow of cash. This raises the question of where the cash will come from. Has the firm got the levels of cash required or will it need to borrow or to raise new share capital?

● In a period of inflation old fixed assets implies a low annual depreciation expense charged in the profit and loss account. Thus profits may be overstated relative to that which would result if newer plant were to be used.

The next point relates to the reserves. It would be perfectly legal for the shareholders to be paid a dividend of £209 000 as at 31 December 1997, perhaps selling some of the non-cash assets to raise the necessary funds. This massive outflow of assets could have disastrous effects on the firm in terms of its ability to continue to trade. Though this large dividend is not a likely outcome, the possibility is there and it should be recognised.

A third point is that, according to the balance sheet, there is a reasonable amount of scope for further secured borrowing. The loan stock is probably secured on the freehold land. The freehold land is probably understated on the balance sheet in terms of its market value. This could mean that the firm would be able to double the amount of its secured borrowings. Since it is very much easier for a firm to borrow where it can offer the security of an asset like land, this might be a significant point. Perhaps the firm does not want to raise further loan capital. Perhaps there are separate reasons why the firm would find it difficult to borrow. On the other hand, the point about unused security might be an important one.

Similar points could be identified by further careful scrutiny of the financial statements, without even bothering to calculate any ratios.

USING ACCOUNTING RATIOS TO PREDICT FINANCIAL FAILURE

One objective of ratio analysis is to try to make a judgement about a particular firm's ability to survive and to prosper. Analysts have shown much interest in ratios which may be able to indicate firms which are in danger of getting into financial difficulties. The reason for this is that several groups who have relationships with the firm stand to suffer significantly should the firm collapse. Creditors may find that they will not receive the money they are owed, employees will probably lose their jobs, suppliers will probably lose a customer, shareholders will probably lose some or all of their investment. If these parties were able to identify 'at risk' firms, they could take steps to try to put the firm back on a sounder footing, or they could take damage limitation actions like getting their money repaid quickly, changing their jobs, finding new customers or selling their shares.

Originally interest focused on identifying individual ratios which might represent good indicators of likely financial collapse. Researchers, therefore, sought to be able to make statements such as, if the value for a particular ratio (like the acid test ratio) fell below a particular threshold figure, the firm was then significantly at risk. They attempted to do this by identifying particular ratios which might be good discriminators between potential failures and survivors.

The researchers then found a group of firms which had actually collapsed. They matched this with a second group of firms, one of which was as like one of the collapsed group as possible in size, industry, etc. This provided them with two groups of firms, as far as possible identical, except that all the members of one group had collapsed and none of the second group had. Using past data on all the firms, attempts were made to examine whether the particular ratios selected were significantly different between the two groups. Where this proved to be the case for a specific ratio, it was possible to say that a figure of above a particular figure implied that the firm was safe, whereas a figure below this benchmark implied that it was at risk.

Although researchers achieved some success at identifying ratios which were reasonably good discriminators, thoughts turned to the possibility that combining several quite good discriminator ratios might produce a Z-score (so called) which would be a very good discriminator. The most notable UK researcher in this field, Taffler, derived the following model:

$$Z = C_0 + C_1 \frac{\text{Profit before tax}}{\text{Current liabilities}} + C_2 \frac{\text{Current assets}}{\text{Total liabilities}} + C_3 \frac{\text{Current liabilities}}{\text{Total assets}} + C_4 \frac{\text{Liquid current assets}}{\text{Daily cash operating expenses}}$$

where C_0 to C_4 are constants.

According to Taffler (1995) a positive Z-score means that the firm is sound, at least in the medium term. A negative Z-score implies a relatively high risk of failure. As might be expected, the higher or lower the Z-score, the more powerful is the indication of the potential survival or failure of the firm.

The recommended reading at the end of this chapter provides some discussion on the benefits and problems of using Z-scores.

SUMMARY

Decision makers, including financial decision makers, make much use of accounting statements. Decision makers outside the firm use the annual published accounts of the firm in which they have an interest. People who work for the firm are likely to have access to other, perhaps more detailed or more frequently produced, accounting information. Accounting is based on a number of rules. It is important that anyone attempting to use accounting information is familiar with those rules.

Though the basic accounting statements, the balance sheet, the profit and loss account and the cash flow statement, are useful to the decision maker, greater insights can be gained if accounting ratios are calculated. These enable events to be summarised in key indicators.

Accounting ratios are usually classified as:

● profitability ratios
● activity ratios
● liquidity ratios
● capital gearing ratios
● investors' ratios.

The ratios which fall into each of these classes look at things from a particular perspective or are concerned with a particular facet of the firm's performance and position.

The imperfections of accounting itself, added to the particular problems of using any ratios, mean that caution must be exercised in drawing conclusions from accounting ratios. Despite this, accounting ratios are widely used and valuable tools of financial analysis.

FURTHER READING Most books on accounting provide an introduction to accounting and to accounting ratios. Many business finance books include a chapter on accounting ratios. Atrill and McLaney (1996) provides a readable and informative introduction to accounting and accounting ratios. Weston and Copeland (1988) includes a chapter on accounting ratios. Taffler (1991) describes the author's research into the use of 'Z-scores' in the identification of firms which are potential financial failures.

REVIEW QUESTIONS

Suggested answers to review questions appear in Appendix 3.

3.1 What is a balance sheet? Does the balance sheet tell us how much the firm is worth?

3.2 The first entry in the standard layout cash flow statement is 'net cash inflow/(outflow) from trading activities'. How is this figure different from the net profit before interest and tax for the same period?

3.3 People often refer to a firm as having a 'strong balance sheet'. What do they mean by this?
(Note that the answer to this question is not really provided in the chapter. However, a combination of background knowledge and common sense should enable you to come up with some relevant points.)

3.4 What does the 'matching' convention of accounting say?

3.5 The 'acid test' ratio is not included in Taffler's Z-score model for identifying potentially failing firms. Why is this?
(Note that the answer to this question is not really provided in the chapter. However, a combination of background knowledge and common sense should enable you to come up with some relevant points.)

3.6 Why is ratio analysis of financial accounts considered to be so useful? Why is a careful reading of the accounts not enough?

PROBLEMS

Sample answers to problems marked with an asterisk appear in Appendix 4.

(Note that problem questions 3.1 and 3.2 are basic level problems, while questions 3.3–3.6 are more advanced, and may contain some practical complications.)

3.1* Counterpoint plc, a wholesaler, has the following accounting ratios for last year and this year:

	last year	this year
Return on net assets (RONA) (%)	28.25	13.51
Return on equity (ROE) (%)	51.95	18.35
Gross profit margin (%)	50.00	40.00
Net profit margin (%)	20.00	10.00
Debtors collection period (days)	73	91
Creditors payment period (days)	37	46
Current ratio	1.63:1	1.37:1
Quick assets	0.72	0.60
Debt to equity (%)	128.87	141.28

On the basis of these ratios, comment on the performance of the firm this year as compared with last year.

3.2 The following are highly simplified financial statements of Duration Ltd for last year:

Profit and loss account for the year ended 31 December:

	£000
Turnover	80
Cost of sales	60
Gross profit	20
Operating expenses	10
Operating profit	10

Balance sheet as at 31 December:

	£000	£000
Fixed assets		70
Current assets	20	
Creditors: amounts falling due within one year	12	
Net current assets		8
		78
Capital and reserves		78

Calculate as many accounting ratios as the information provided will allow.

3.3* The following are the financial statements of Persona Ltd (not in the form required by the Companies Acts) for last year and this year:

Profit and loss account for the year ended 31 December:

	last year £000	this year £000
Turnover	499	602
Cost of sales	335	423
Gross profit	164	179
Operating expenses	127	148
Operating profit (before interest and taxation)	37	31
Interest payable	13	22
Profit before taxation	24	9
Taxation	8	3
Profit after taxation	16	6
Dividend paid and proposed	6	6
Retained profit for the year	10	–
Retained profit brought forward from the previous year	74	84
Retained profit carried forward	84	84

Balance sheet as at 31 December:

	last year £000	last year £000	this year £000	this year £000
Fixed assets		110		125
Current assets				
Stocks	68		83	
Debtors	80		96	
Cash	6		2	
	154		181	
Creditors: amounts falling due within one year				
Creditors	65		110	
Taxation	8		–	
Dividends	6		6	
	79		116	
Net current assets		75		65
		185		190
Creditors: amounts falling due within one year				
Loan stocks		55		60
		130		130
Capital and reserves				
Ordinary shares of £0.50 each		13		13
Capital reserves		33		33
Retained profit		84		84
		130		130

Calculate the following ratios for both years:
- return on net assets
- return on equity
- gross profit margin
- net profit margin
- current ratio
- quick assets
- stock holding period

3.4 The following is the balance sheet (in abbreviated form) of Projections Ltd for last year:

Balance sheet as at 31 December:

	£000	£000
Fixed assets		
Cost		290
Less: accumulated depreciation		110
		180
Current assets		
Stock	26	
Debtors	35	
Cash	5	
	66	
Creditors: amounts falling due within one year		
Trade creditors	21	
Taxation	15	
Dividends	12	
	48	
Net current assets		18
		198
Capital and reserves		
Share capital		150
Retained profit		48
		198

The following forecasts have been made for next year:

(i)   Sales are expected to be £350 000, all on credit. Sales will be made at a steady rate over the year and two months' credit will be allowed to customers.

(ii) £200 000 worth of stock will be bought during the year, all on credit. Purchases will be made at a steady rate over the year and one month's credit will be allowed by creditors.

(iii) New fixed assets will be bought, and paid for, during the year at a cost of £30 000. No disposals of fixed assets are planned. The depreciation expense for the year will be 10 per cent of the cost of the fixed assets owned at the end of the year.

(iv) Stock at the end of the year is expected to be double that which it was at the beginning of the year.

(v)   Operating expenses, other than depreciation, are expected to total £52 000, of which £5000 will remain unpaid at the end of the year.

(vi) During the year, the tax and dividends noted in the start of the year balance sheet will be paid.

(vii) The tax rate can be assumed to be 25 per cent and a dividend of £10 000 will be proposed for the year. Neither the tax nor the dividend for next year will be paid during the year.

Prepare a projected profit and loss account for next year and a balance sheet as at the end of next year, to the nearest £1000.

3.5* The following are the financial statements of Prospect plc (not in the form required by the Companies Acts) for last year and this year:

Profit and loss account for the year ended 31 December:

	last year £000	this year £000
Turnover	14 006	22 410
Cost of sales	7 496	11 618
Gross profit	6 510	10 792
Operating expenses	4 410	6 174
Operating profit (before interest and taxation)	2 100	4 618
Interest payable	432	912
Profit before taxation	1 668	3 706
Taxation	420	780
Profit after taxation	1 248	2 926
Dividend paid and proposed	600	800
Retained profit for the year	648	2 126
Retained profit brought forward from the previous year	722	1 370
Retained profit carried forward	1 370	3 496

Balance sheet as at 31 December:

	last year		this year	
	£000	£000	£000	£000
Fixed assets		8 600		16 470
Current assets				
Stocks	2 418		4 820	
Trade debtors	1 614		2 744	
Other debtors	268		402	
Cash	56		8	
	4 356		7 974	
Creditors: amounts falling due within one year				
Trade creditors	1 214		2 612	
Other creditors	248		402	
Taxation	420		780	
Dividends	600		800	
Bank overdraft	–		3 250	
	2 482		7 844	
Net current assets		1 874		130
		10 474		16 600
Creditors: amounts falling due within one year				
Loan stocks		3 600		7 600
		6 874		9 000
Capital and reserves				
Ordinary shares of £0.50 each		3 600		3 600
Capital reserves		1 904		1 904
Retained profit		1 370		3 496
		6 874		9 000

Calculate the following financial ratios for Prospect plc for last year and this year. (Use year end figures where balance sheet items are involved.)

- Return on net assets
- Return on equity
- Gross profit margin
- Net profit margin
- Stock turnover
- Debtors collection period (days)
- Current ratio
- Quick assets ratio
- Gearing (debt to equity) ratio

Use these ratios to comment on the performance and position of Prospect plc from the point of view of

(i)   a 10% owner of the equity, and
(ii) the firm's bank.

3.6 The following are the financial statements of High Street Enterprises plc (not in the form required by the Companies Acts) for last year and this year:

Profit and loss account for the year ended 31 December:

	last year	this year
	£000	£000
Turnover	15 600	24 160
Cost of sales	8 740	12 564
Gross profit	6 860	11 596
Operating expenses	5 296	8 572
Operating profit (before interest and taxation)	1 564	3 024
Interest payable	–	132
Profit before taxation	1 564	2 892
Taxation	316	518
Profit after taxation	1 248	2 374
Dividend paid and proposed	500	600
Retained profit for the year	748	1 774
Retained profit brought forward from the previous year	996	1 744
Retained profit carried forward	1 744	3 518

Balance sheet as at 31 December:

	last year		this year	
	£000	£000	£000	£000
Fixed assets		8 072		10 456
Current assets				
Stocks	1 850		3 166	
Trade debtors	976		1 992	
Cash	624		52	
	3 450		5 210	
Creditors: amounts falling due within one year				
Trade creditors	1 320		2 236	
Other creditors	642		834	
Taxation	316		518	
Dividends	500		600	
Bank overdraft	–		360	
	2 778		4 548	
Net current assets		672		662
		8 744		11 118
Creditors: amounts falling due within one year				
Loan stocks		–		600
		8 744		10 518
Capital and reserves				
Ordinary shares of £0.50 each		6 500		6 500
Capital reserves		500		500
Retained profit		1 744		3 518
		8 744		10 518

Calculate the suitable financial ratios for High Street Enterprises plc for last year and this year (use year end figures where balance sheet items are involved) and use the ratios to comment on the performance and position of the firm.

APPENDIX

Jackson plc
Profit and Loss account for the year ended 31 December 1996

	£000	£000	£000
Sales			701
Cost of sales (including depreciation £22 000			
and raw materials stock usage £190 000.			
Raw material purchases totalled £187 000)			394
Gross profit			307
Distribution costs			
Salaries and wages	35		
Motor expenses	41		
Depreciation of motor vehicles	16		
Sundry distribution expenses	14	106	
Administrative expenses			
Salaries and wages	53		
Motor expenses	21		
Depreciation of motor vehicles	18		
Sundry administrative expenses	12	104	210
Operating profit for the year			97
Interest payable			33
Profit on ordinary activities before taxation			64
Tax on ordinary activities			18
Profit on ordinary activities after taxation			46
Retained profit brought forward from last year			120
			166
Proposed dividend on ordinary shares			15
Retained profit carried forward to next year			151

(Note that this statement does not strictly follow the layout which is required by law.)

Jackson plc
Balance Sheet as at 31 December 1996

	£000 cost	£000 depre- ciation	£000
Fixed assets			
Freehold land	550	–	550
Plant and machinery	232	198	34
Motor vehicles	90	21	69
	872	219	653
Current assets			
Stock	41		
Trade debtors	123		
Prepaid expenses	10	174	
Creditors: amounts falling due within one year			
Bank overdraft	86		
Trade creditors	43		
Accrued expenses	14		
Taxation	18		
Dividend proposed	15	176	
Net current liabilities			(2)
Total assets less current liabilities			651
Creditors: amounts falling due after more than one year			
10% secured loan stock			300
			351
Ordinary share capital – 200 000 shares of £1 each			200
Profit and loss account			151
			351

(Note that this statement does not strictly follow the layout which is required by law.)

The market price of the ordinary £1 shares was £3.49 at 31 December 1996.

PART 2

Investment decisions

Investment decisions are at the heart of the management of all firms, except the very smallest. Errors in these decisions can, and do, prove fatal for many firms. Chapter 4 starts with an explanation of the nature and importance of investment decisions. It continues with some fairly detailed explanations of the major investment appraisal methods used in practice. It concludes with some discussion of the extent of the use of these methods in practice. Chapter 5 is concerned with some of the practical aspects of making investment decisions. These include taxation, inflation and the problem of dealing with shortages of investment finance. Chapters 6 and 7 are concerned with various approaches to trying to make investment decisions where, as is always the case in reality, the outcome of an investment is not known with certainty. Chapter 7 is particularly concerned with attempting to assess the likely effect of the risk of a particular investment on the firm's owners.

CHAPTER 4

Investment appraisal methods

OBJECTIVES

In this chapter we shall deal with the following:

- the importance of the investment decision
- the derivation of the concept of net present value
- an explanation of the meaning of net present value
- a consideration of the other approaches used to assess investment projects
- a consideration of some recent research bearing on the investment appraisal techniques used by firms in the UK and USA

INTRODUCTION

Firms operate by raising finance from various sources which is then invested in assets, usually real assets. Investment involves outflows (payments) of cash causing inflows of cash. It is in the nature of things that cash flows (out and in) do not all occur at the same time, i.e. there is some time lag, perhaps a considerable one, between them. The typical investment project opportunity with which a firm may be faced involves a relatively large outflow of cash initially, giving rise to a subsequent stream of cash inflows.

The firm's balance sheet gives, at any particular point in time and subject to the limitations of such accounting statements, the types of investment which it still has running. Balance sheets group assets by type (fixed assets, current assets, etc.) rather than by investment project. Thus it is not possible from the standard balance sheet to discern which part of the fixed and current assets relate to any particular project. Nonetheless, a glance at a firm's balance sheet would give us some idea of the scale of investment and to some extent an idea of its nature.

Selecting which investment opportunities to pursue and which to avoid is a vital matter to firms because:

(a) individual projects frequently involve relatively large and irreversible commitments of finance; and

(b) they involve this commitment for long, often very long, periods of time.

Clearly the investment decision is central to the firm. Costly and far-reaching mistakes can and probably will be made unless firms take great care in making their investment decisions. Bad decisions usually cause major financial loss and any particular firm can only make a limited number of misjudgements before collapse occurs.

In this chapter we shall consider how such decisions should best be made, after which we shall go on to consider how they appear to be made in practice.

Note that for the time being we shall continue to assume that all cash flows can be predicted with certainty and that the borrowing and lending rates of interest are equal to one another and equal between all individuals and firms.

NET PRESENT VALUE

A basis for decision making

Given the crucial importance of firms' investment decisions, managers need a logical and practical assessment procedure by which to appraise the investment opportunities which come to their notice. This procedure must promote the shareholders' wealth maximisation objective, though in the final decision other objectives may well be taken into account.

We discovered in Chapter 2 that if we assume that interest rates are equal, both as between borrowing and lending and as between firms and individuals, an investment project undertaken by the firm which will increase the spending power of all shareholders, or of any particular one of them, at one point in time, will also increase it at any other point in time. (We may remember that in the example in Chapter 2, all three of our shareholders were advantaged by acceptance of Project X, despite having different attitudes to the timing of their spending.)

It seems therefore that it does not matter whether our assessment procedure focuses on the effect on present wealth or on wealth in a year's time, or indeed at any other time. If undertaking a particular project will increase present wealth, it will also increase future wealth; that project which will most increase present wealth will most increase future wealth. Thus, both for accept/reject decisions and for ranking projects in order of desirability, it does not matter in respect of which point in time the effect on wealth is assessed, provided that consistency is maintained.

Since we are always at 'the present' when making the decision, to consider a project's effect on present wealth is probably most logical. This tends to be the approach taken in practice.

The time value of money

Suppose that a firm is offered an opportunity which involves investing £10m which will give rise to a cash receipt of £12m. Should the firm make the investment? Obviously if the cash expenditure and the cash receipt are to occur at the same time (most unlikely in real life) this represents a good investment since it will work towards the firm's assumed objective of maximising its value. It will increase the value of the firm by £2m.

Now suppose that the opportunity means investing £10m now which will give rise to a £12m cash inflow after one year. Here the decision is not so straightforward because we cannot directly compare £1 now with £1 after a year (or any other period of time). Each £1 of present expenditure is not equal in value to each £1 receipt in the future. This is for three reasons:

(a) *Interest forgone.* If the £1 is tied up in the investment for a year, the firm cannot invest it elsewhere so there is an interest *opportunity cost.*

(b) *Inflation.* Due to the loss of purchasing power of money if there is inflation in the economy (which has been the case in each post-war year in the UK), £1 will not buy as much in the way of goods and services next year as it would this year.

(c) *Risk.* The £1 paid out today is certain but the £1 anticipated receipt next year is not certain. However confident we may be of the receipt, we can never be sure of it. In many business contexts the degree of uncertainty about future receipts is profound.

At present we shall concentrate on only the first of these three, namely interest forgone, leaving issues involving inflation and risk to be dealt with in later chapters. At this point it must be clearly emphasised that even if there were no inflation and that the investment were regarded as risk free, the point would remain that £1 today is not equivalent to £1 tomorrow simply because of the opportunity cost of interest forgone.

Given that money has a 'time value' (£1 today is not equivalent to £1 after some period of time), how are we to make a comparison between the £10m now and the £12m in a year's time, and so reach a decision?

Net present value

One approach which we could take would be to add the interest forgone to the £10m, i.e. to assess the amount to which the £10m would have grown after one year, with interest, and then to compare it with the £12m. Suppose that the current rate of interest is 10 per cent, then the value of the £10m after one year would be £11m (£1m interest). In other words, if the firm were to pursue the alternative opportunity of putting the money into an interest-yielding bank deposit account, it would have £11m by the end of the year, whereas the firm will get £12m if it makes the investment under consideration. This is a totally logical and correct approach to take and the conclusion that the investment should be made because it will lead to a *net future value* of £1m (i.e. £12m – £11m) is a correct one (i.e. the firm will be £1m better off at the end of the year than had it pursued the alternative of putting the money in a bank deposit account for the year).

Another approach is to ask ourselves, if it is possible to borrow money at 10 per cent, how much could be borrowed immediately against the £12m such that the £12m would exactly repay the borrowing plus interest thereon. Put another way, if the firm could compare the £10m outflow with the present equivalent of £12m, an alternative basis for the decision could be achieved. The present value of the £12m is not necessarily a theoretical notion since it would be possible for the firm to borrow and have the present value of £12m immediately if it wanted to do so. Indeed, it could even do so to raise the finance with which to make the £10m investment (assuming that the present value of the £12m is greater than £10m).

The next question is what is the present value of £12m receivable after one year with an interest rate of 10 per cent p.a.?

If we let the amount which could be borrowed (the present value of £12m in a year's time) be B, then,

$$£12\text{m} = B + \left(B \times \frac{10}{100} \right)$$

(i.e. the borrowing plus the interest for one year)

$$\text{i.e. } £12\text{m} = B\left(1 + \frac{10}{100} \right) = B \times 1.10$$

$$B = \frac{£12\text{m}}{1.10}$$

$$= £10.9\text{m}$$

If we now compare the present value of the future receipt with the initial investment , we have an investment whose *net present value* (NPV) is £0.9m (i.e. £10.9m – £10m). Since this is positive, the investment should be undertaken assuming that there is not a mutually exclusive alternative with a higher positive NPV.

What the £0.9m NPV tells us is that the firm can invest £10m immediately to gain a benefit whose present value is £10.9m, i.e. a £0.9m increase in the value of the firm.

More generally we can say that the NPV of an investment opportunity lasting for one year is

$$\text{NPV} = C_0 + \frac{C_1}{1+i}$$

where

C_0 is the cash flow immediately (time 0) (usually negative, i.e. an outflow of cash);

C_1 is the cash flow after one year;

i is the interest rate.

In practice we tend to use the NPV approach to investment decision making (i.e. we *discount* future cash flows) rather than the net future value approach (*compounding* present cash flows), though in essence neither is superior to the other.

The reasons for favouring NPV are:

(a) When comparing investment opportunities (choosing between one and the other), if net future value is to be used a decision must be made on when in the future the value should be assessed (i.e. how many years compounding). If the opportunities are of unequal length (e.g. one lasts three years, the other five years) this can cause difficulties.

(b) If the opportunity is to be assessed by looking at its effect on the value of the firm it seems more logical to look at the present effect rather than the future effect.

Investment opportunities lasting for more than one year

In reality, few investment opportunities last for only one year. Suppose that an investment opportunity involves an immediate cash outflow C_0 which will give rise to inflows C_1 and C_2 after one and two years respectively. We already know that the present value of C_1 (effect on the value of the firm) is

$$\frac{C_1}{(1+i)}$$

By the same logic that we used to derive this, we could borrow an amount, say A, which would exactly be repaid with interest compounded annually out of C_2. Then

$$C_2 = A + Ai + (A + Ai)i$$

(i.e. the original borrowing plus interest on that amount for the first year plus interest on these two during the second year).

This expression expands to:

$$C_2 = A + Ai + Ai + Ai^2$$

Taking A outside brackets,

$$C_2 = A(1 + 2i + i^2)$$
$$C_2 = A(1+i)^2$$
$$A = \frac{C_2}{(1+i)^2}$$

Following this logic, it can be shown that the present value of any amount of cash receivable after n years (C_n) would be

$$\frac{C_n}{(1+i)^n}$$

Thus the NPV of any investment opportunity is given by:

$$\text{NPV} = \sum_{n=0}^{t} \frac{C_n}{(1+i)^n}$$

where t is the life of the opportunity in years, i.e. the NPV of an opportunity is the sum, taking account of plus and minus signs, of each of the annual cash flows discounted according to how far into the future each one will occur.

EXAMPLE

Seagull plc has identified that it could make operating cost savings in production by buying an automatic press. There are two suitable such presses on the market, the Zenith and the Super. The relevant data relating to each of these are as follows:

	Zenith £	Super £
Cost (payable immediately)	20 000	25 000
Annual savings:		
Year 1	4 000	8 000
2	6 000	6 000
3	6 000	5 000
4	7 000	6 000
5	6 000	8 000

The annual savings are, in effect, opportunity cash inflows in that they represent savings from the cash outflows which would occur if the investment were not undertaken.

Which, if either, of these machines should be bought if the borrowing/lending cost is 12 per cent p.a.?

SOLUTION

The NPV of each machine is as follows:

	Zenith £	Super £
Present value of cash flows:		
Year 0	(20 000)	(25 000)

Year 1

$$\frac{4000}{1+0.12} = 3\ 572 \qquad \frac{8000}{1+0.12} = 7\ 143$$

Year 2

$$\frac{6000}{(1+0.12)^2} = 4\ 783 \qquad \frac{6000}{(1+0.12)^2} = 4\ 783$$

Year 3

$$\frac{6000}{(1+0.12)^3} = 4\ 271 \qquad \frac{5000}{(1+0.12)^3} = 3\ 559$$

Year 4

$$\frac{7000}{(1+0.12)^4} = 4\ 449 \qquad \frac{6000}{(1+0.12)^4} = 3\ 813$$

Year 5

$$\frac{6000}{(1+0.12)^5} = 3\ 404 \qquad \frac{8000}{(1+0.12)^5} = 4\ 539$$

£479 £(1 163)

(This process of converting future cash flows to their present value is known as *discounting*.)

The firm should therefore buy the Zenith as this would have a positive effect on its wealth, whereas the Super would have a negative effect. The firm would not be prepared to buy the Super even if it were the only such machine on the market, as to do so would be to the firm's detriment. The value of the firm would, theoretically, fall as a result of buying the Super. Only if it were possible to negotiate a price lower than £23 837 (i.e. the sum of the discounted savings) would the value of the annual savings justify the cost of that machine, given the financing cost. Similarly up to £20 479 could be paid for a Zenith and it would continue to be a profitable investment.

It is important to recognise that the size of the initial investment is not of any direct relevance to the decision (except to the extent that it is used in the calculation of the NPV); only the NPV is important. Thus if the Super had a positive NPV of £480 it would be selected in preference to the Zenith. The only occasion where we would need to consider the size of the NPV in relation to the amount of investment is when there is some shortage of investment finance and projects need to compete for it. This is an aspect which we shall consider in Chapter 5.

The use of tables and annuity factors

Tables are readily available which will give the discount factor $1/(1 + i)^n$ for a range of values of i and n. Such a table appears in Appendix 1 to this book. Note that it is not necessary to use the table for discounting; the calculation can easily be done from first principles.

Sometimes an investment involves a series of identical annual cash flows. In these circumstances there is a short cut to the present value of those cash flows.

EXAMPLE

A firm is faced with an investment opportunity which involves an initial investment of £35 000 which is expected to generate annual inflows of £10 000 at the end of each of the next five years. The firm's borrowing/lending rate is 10 per cent per annum. What is the NPV of this opportunity?

SOLUTION

If we discounted the cash inflows using the table of discount factors in Appendix 1, the calculation would be as follows:

(10 000 x 0.909) + (10 000 x 0.826) + (10 000 x 0.751) + (10 000 x 0.683) + (10 000 x 0.621)

This could be rewritten as:

10 000 (0.909 + 0.826 + 0.751 + 0.683 + 0.621)

where the figures in brackets are the discount factors at 10 per cent for a series of annual cash flows of £1 for five years. In cases like this the calculation is made easier for us in that tables giving the sum of discount factors, for specified periods of years and discount rates, is readily available. There is one shown in Appendix 2 to this book. Such tables are usually known as *annuity* tables. Even if such a table is not available, you can easily deduce the appropriate annuity factor. It is

$$\sum_{n=1}^{t} \frac{1}{(1+i)^n}$$

If we look up the annuity factor for five years and 10 per cent, we find that the factor is 3.791. (This only differs from the sum of the five discount factors through rounding.)

Thus the NPV of the investment opportunity is:

− £35 000 + (£10 000 x 3.791) = + £2910

It is probably fair to say that situations where there is a steady stream of cash flows are, in real life, relatively rare.

How a positive NPV leads to an increase in shareholder wealth

It has been said, quite reasonably, that the essence of good investment is to buy assets for less than they are worth. Clearly, doing this will enhance the value of the firm. When assessing an investment opportunity like the Zenith, it comes down to the question of how much the estimated future benefits of owning the Zenith are worth to Seagull plc. The future benefits obviously are the potential operating cost savings (£4000 in year 1, £6000 in year 2, etc.).

In order to know whether the value of these future benefits exceeds the cost of the asset (£20 000), it is necessary to place some value on them. The only logical way to value them is to discount each one according to how far into the future the benefit will occur, and to sum the discounted values. Thus NPV is an entirely logical approach to investment decision making, assuming that enhancing the value of the shareholders' wealth is the objective being pursued.

Discounting – a slightly different view

Staying with the example, a superficial assessment of the Zenith might be that it should be bought because it cost £20 000 but would yield total savings of £29 000 (the sum of the annual savings), i.e. a benefit of £9000. A second look reveals however that this cannot be a correct assessment as no rational investor regards all of the £s in the question as equivalent to one another. We should all prefer £1 today to £1 next year and we should prefer it still more to £1 in five years' time, even if we assume no erosion of value through inflation. This is because if we have the £1 today we could, if we wished, lend it so that after a year we should have not only the £1 but the interest on it as well.

Simply adding the annual savings and comparing the total with the initial outlay would be illogical. It would be like saying that a certain item is more expensive to buy in France than in the UK because it costs 50 in France and only 5 in the UK, without mentioning that the 50 is francs whereas the 5 is pounds (£s). To make a sensible price comparison we should need to convert the francs to pounds (£s) or vice versa.

Similarly, it is necessary to undertake a conversion exercise to make the various cash flows associated with the Zenith comparable. In fact we usually convert the future cash flows to their present value and then make the comparison. The conversion exercise is, of course, achieved by discounting, by multiplying each of the cash flows by

$$\frac{1}{(1 + i)^n}$$

NPV can thus be viewed as a *time adjusted* measure of financial benefit.

Conclusions on NPV

We have seen that NPV is a totally logical way of assessing investment opportunities. It is logical and potentially useful, because it possesses the following attributes.

- It is directly related to the objective of maximisation of shareholders' wealth (value of the firm).
- It takes full account of the timing of the investment outlay and of the benefits, i.e. the time value of money is properly reflected. Put another way, we can say that NPV properly takes the cost of financing the investment into account.
- All relevant, measurable financial information concerning the decision is taken into account.
- It is practical and easy to use (once the anticipated cash flows have been identified) and it gives clear and unambiguous signals to the decision maker. It should be emphasised that identifying future cash flows is usually very difficult to do in reality.

INTERNAL RATE OF RETURN

This approach seeks to identify the rate of return that an investment project yields on the basis of the amount of the original investment remaining outstanding during any period, compounding interest annually. Identifying this internal rate of return (IRR), at least by hand, can be laborious.

EXAMPLE

What is the IRR of a project where an initial investment of £120 is followed a year later by a cash inflow of £138 with no further inflows?

SOLUTION

Obviously it is:

$$\frac{138 - 120}{120}(\times 100) = 15\%$$

What though if the project were £120 initial outlay, followed by inflows of £69 at the end of each of the following two years?

Despite the total inflows still being £138, the IRR is not 15 per cent because it now runs over two years. Nor is it 7.5 per cent (i.e. 15 divided by 2) because much of the £120 is repaid in year 1 and so is not outstanding for both years. In fact the first £69 represents a payment of the *interest* on the investment during the first year plus a repayment of part of the *capital*. By the same token the second £69 represents interest on the remaining capital outstanding after the end of year 1, plus a second instalment of capital such that this second instalment will exactly repay the £120 initial outlay.

A moment's reflection should lead us to conclude that the IRR is closely related to the NPV discount rate. In fact the IRR of a project is the discount rate which if applied to the project yields a zero NPV. For this example it is the solution for i to the following expression

$$-120 + \frac{69}{(1+i)} + \frac{69}{(1+i)^2} = 0$$

which could be solved using the standard solution to a quadratic equation, not a difficult matter. (The answer incidentally is $i = 0.099$, or 9.9 per cent.)

When we look at, say, the Zenith from our earlier example the equation from which we must solve for i is:

$$-20\,000 + \frac{4000}{(1+i)} + \frac{6000}{(1+i)^2} + \frac{6000}{(1+i)^3} + \frac{7000}{(1+i)^4} + \frac{6000}{(1+i)^5} = 0$$

Solving for i here is not so easy and in fact some iterative (trial and error) approach becomes the only practical one. One such method (involving differential calculus), *Newton's approximation*, could be used. In practice however, we usually solve for i by trying various values of i until we find one which satisfies or almost satisfies the equation. On p. 74, we calculated that the Zenith has an NPV of +£479 when discounted at 12 per cent. This tells us that it must have an IRR of above 12 per cent, because the higher the discount rate, the lower the present value of each cash flow. How much above 12 per cent lies the Zenith's IRR we do not know, so some higher discount rate needs to be tried, say 14 per cent.

Referring to the 14 per cent column of the NPV table in Appendix 1 we can deduce the following:

Time	Cash flow £	Discount factor	Present value £
Year 0	(20 000)	1.000	(20 000)
1	4 000	0.877	3 508
2	6 000	0.769	4 614
3	6 000	0.675	4 050
4	7 000	0.592	4 144
5	6 000	0.519	3 114
		NPV	£(570)

As the NPV when the cash flows are discounted at 14 per cent is negative, we know that the discount rate which gives this project a zero NPV lies below 14 per cent and apparently close to the mid-point between 14 and 12 per cent. We can prove this by discounting at 13 per cent.

Time	Cash flow £	Discount factor	Present value £
Year 0	(20 000)	1.000	(20 000)
1	4 000	0.885	3 540
2	6 000	0.783	4 698
3	6 000	0.693	4 158
4	7 000	0.613	4 291
5	6 000	0.543	3 258
		NPV	£(55)

Given the scale of the investment, an NPV of –£55 is not significantly different from zero, so we can conclude that for practical purposes the IRR is 13 per cent.

Where IRR is used to assess projects, the decision rule is that only those with an IRR above a predetermined hurdle rate would be accepted; where projects are competing, the project with the higher IRR is selected.

The IRR approach so closely resembles the NPV method that at first glance it appears that they are completely interchangeable. This might lead us to assume that they will always come to similar conclusions on any particular decision. This is not true, as can be seen by the following comparison of methods.

(a) IRR is *not* directly related to the value of the firm maximisation criterion. If the hurdle rate used in conjunction with IRR is the cost of finance then in most cases the two methods will give identical results. Certainly this will tend to be the case on straightforward accept/reject decisions (i.e. those where the decision is either to invest or not to invest). With competing projects the two methods sometimes give conflicting signals. This can happen where two mutually exclusive projects involve a different scale of investment.

EXAMPLE

Two mutually exclusive projects have the following features.

		Cash flows	
Time		Project A	Project B
		£	£
Year	0	(10 000)	(6 000)
	1	6 000	3 650
	2	6 000	3 650
NPV @ 10%		413	334
IRR (approximately)		13%	14%

If the cost of finance to support the project is 10 per cent p.a., which of these two projects should the firm pursue (assuming no shortage of finance)?

SOLUTION

There is obviously a conflict here. Both NPV and IRR are based on discounting cash flows, both have IRRs in excess of 10 per cent, yet there are different signals coming from the NPVs and the IRRs. Figure 4.1 shows a graph of NPV against discount rate for these two projects. Not surprisingly, as the discount rate is increased the NPV falls. The points where the curves cross the horizontal axis are the respective IRRs for each of the two projects.

It is possible to read off, for each project, the NPV for any particular discount rate. For example, at an 8 per cent discount rate the NPV for Project A is about £700 and for Project B about £500. At discount rates up to about 11.3 per cent Project A has the higher NPV. Beyond 11.3 per cent, Project B has the higher NPV.

Going back to the question as to which project should be selected, the correct answer (from a wealth maximisation viewpoint) is Project A. Although Project B would be more attractive if the cost of finance were over 11.3 per cent, the fact of the matter is that in this example it is 10 per cent and, since we are pursuing wealth maximisation, Project A is the one which should be selected. The conflict arises because of an incorrect implicit assumption of the IRR model. The discount rate used

**Fig. 4.1
Graph of the
NPV against the
discount rate for
two projects
(A and B)**

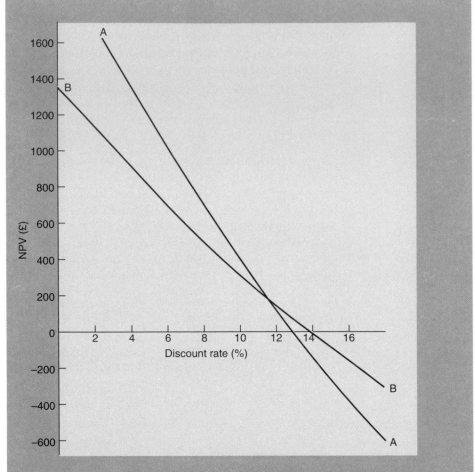

As the discount rate increases, NPV decreases. The discount rate at zero NPV is the IRR. The rate at which NPV decreases differs from one project to another. Whereas project A has the higher NPV where the discount rate is below about 11.3%, Project B has the higher NPV where the discount rate is higher than 11.3%. This leads to a conflict between the signals given by NPV and IRR, where the discount rate is less than 11.3%.

with NPV should be the *opportunity* cost of finance. That is, it is the cost of funds raised to support the project or, if funds are available already, it is the rate which they could alternatively earn. According to the basic principles of NPV, referred to earlier in this chapter, this is the borrowing/lending rate. IRR, on the other hand, makes the assumption that the opportunity cost of finance is equal to the IRR, so that funds generated by the project could either be used to repay finance raised at the IRR or they could be reinvested at that rate. Clearly this is illogical; why should it be the case in our present example that if Project A is undertaken the opportunity cost of finance is 13 per cent, whereas if Project B is pursued it suddenly becomes 14 per cent? The choice by a particular firm of specific projects would not alter the economic environment so that either the cost of finance or the investment alternatives change with the firm's decision.

What IRR fails to recognise in the above example is that if finance is available at 10 per cent the firm's wealth would be more greatly increased by earning 13 per cent on a £10 000 investment than 14 per cent on a £6000 one. IRR fails to recognise this because it does not consider value, it is only concerned with percentage returns.

(b) Like NPV, IRR takes full account both of the cash flows and of the time value of money.

(c) All relevant information about the decision is taken into account by IRR, but it also takes into account the irrelevant, or perhaps more strictly the incorrect, namely the wrong assumption (which we discussed in (a) above) made by IRR.

(d) IRR can be an unwieldy method to use, if done by hand. This is not a practical problem, however, since computer software, which will derive IRRs is widely available; many spreadsheet packages are able to perform this function. The trial and error process, which is the only way to arrive at IRRs, can be very time-consuming, especially where long projects are involved, if it is done by hand. Computers also try and err, but they can do it much more quickly than humans so deriving IRRs is not usually a great difficulty in practice.

(e) IRR cannot cope with differing required rates of return (hurdle rates). IRR provides an average rate of return for a particular investment project. This rate is normally compared with a required rate of return to make a judgement on the investment. If financing costs are expected to alter over the life of the project, this comparison might cause difficulties. The reasons why the required rate may differ from one year to another include the possibility that market interest rates might alter over time. If the IRR for a particular project is consistently above or below all of the different annual required rates of return, there is no difficulty in making the decision. Where, however, the IRR lies above the required rate in some years but below it in others, the decision maker has a virtually insoluble problem. This situation poses no problem for NPV because it is perfectly logical to use different discount rates for each year's cash flows.

(f) The IRR model does not always produce clear and unambiguous results. As we have seen, the IRR for a particular project is the solution to an equation containing only one unknown factor. This unknown factor is, however, raised to as many powers as there are time periods in the project. Any project therefore which goes beyond one time period (in practice one year) will usually have as many IRRs as there are time periods. In practice this is not very often a problem because all but one of the roots (IRRs) will either be unreal (e.g. the square root of a negative number) or negative themselves and, therefore, of no economic significance. Sometimes, though, all of the roots can be unreal so that there is no IRR for some projects. Sometimes a project can have more than one real root (IRR).

These problems of multiple and no IRRs can arise with projects which have *unconventional* cash flows. Projects A and B in the previous example have conventional cash flows in that chronologically a negative cash flow is followed by positive ones, i.e. there is only one change of sign in the cumulative cash flow total (from negative to positive between years 1 and 2 in both projects).

However, now consider the following two projects:

| | Cash flows | |
Time	Project C £	Project D £
Year 0	(10 000)	10 000
1	33 000	(16 000)
2	(24 000)	12 000

Both of these are unconventional in that they each have two changes of sign. Project C changes from negative to positive between years 0 and 1 and from positive to negative between years 1 and 2. Project D does precisely the opposite.

The graphs of NPV against discount rate for each of these unconventional projects are shown in Figs 4.2 and 4.3. Project C has two IRRs (8 per cent and 122 per cent), both of which are equally correct. Which of these should be taken as being the appropriate one for investment decisions? There is no answer to this question and so here IRR gives an ambiguous result. NPV can be used though: with any cost of finance between 8 per cent and 122 per cent the project is favourable; if the firm's cost of finance is below 8 per cent or above 122 per cent the project should be rejected.

**Fig. 4.2
Graph of the
NPV against the
discount rate for
Project C**

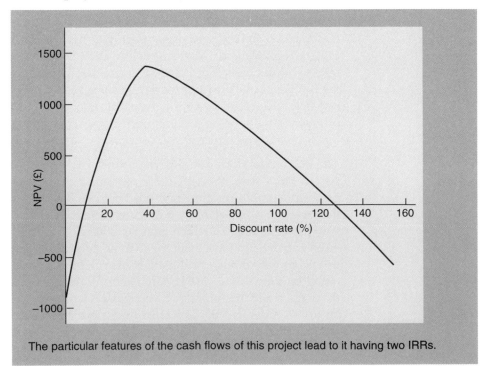

The particular features of the cash flows of this project lead to it having two IRRs.

Fig. 4.3
Graph of the
NPV against the
discount rate for
Project D

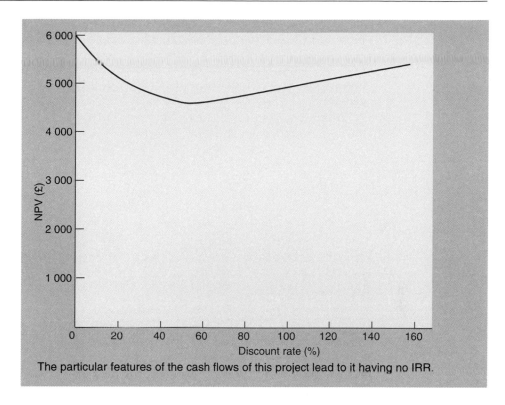

The particular features of the cash flows of this project lead to it having no IRR.

Trying to find the IRR of Project D by trial and error would be a frustrating experience because there simply is not one, not at least a real one. The graph shows there to be no intercept between the horizontal axis and the curve. Once again IRR is incapable of assessing the project despite the fact that it has a large NPV at all discount rates.

It would be wrong to imagine that projects with unconventional cash flow profiles do not really happen in practice. Probably they form a minority of the total of all projects, but nonetheless they do exist. For example, many projects involving mineral extraction would show something like the cash flow characteristics of Project C. Such projects frequently involve large commitments of cash in order to restore the land to its original contours after the mine or quarry has been fully exploited.

Generally, on IRR, we can conclude that if the opportunity cost of finance is used as the hurdle rate, it will usually give the same signals as the NPV model. Sometimes, though, IRR will give false, ambiguous or incoherent signals, which if heeded could lead to sub-optimal decisions being made. It seems that IRR is a mathematical result rather than a reliable decision-making technique. Usually, by coincidence, it will give the right signal but not always. There are means of modifying IRR to overcome some of these problems, but is there any point in our doing so? NPV always gives logical and clear signals and so we might as well use it as the primary assessment method all the time.

PAYBACK PERIOD

This technique asks the simple question, how long will it take for the investment to pay for itself out of the cash inflows which it is expected to generate?

Continuing to assess the investment opportunity in the example from p. 74, the cash flows for which were:

		Zenith £	Super £
Year	0	(20 000)	(25 000)
	1	4 000	8 000
	2	6 000	6 000
	3	6 000	5 000
	4	7 000	6 000
	5	6 000	8 000

**Fig. 4.4
Payback period for
the Zenith
machine**

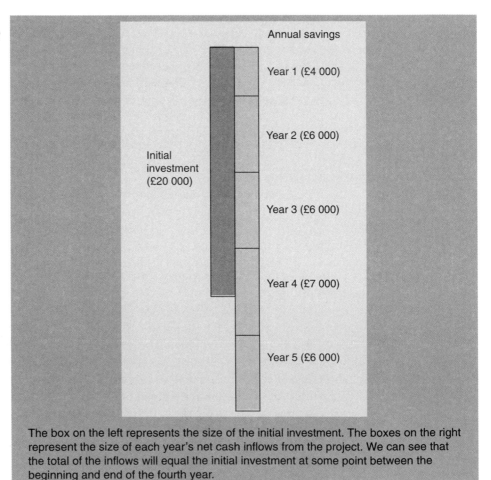

The box on the left represents the size of the initial investment. The boxes on the right represent the size of each year's net cash inflows from the project. We can see that the total of the inflows will equal the initial investment at some point between the beginning and end of the fourth year.

we should find that the anticipated paybacks would be:

	Zenith	*Super*
4 years (assuming that the cash flows occur at year ends),		4 years

or 3½ years (assuming that the cash flows occur evenly over the year)

The payback period (PBP) for the Zenith is represented in Fig. 4.4.

The decision rule for PBP is that projects will only be selected if they pay for themselves within a predetermined period. Competing projects would be assessed by selecting the one with the shorter PBP (provided it was within the predetermined maximum). Thus PBP favours the Zenith over the Super (if cash flows are assumed to occur evenly).

Let us now consider PBP's attributes against those of NPV.

(a) PBP is badly flawed to the extent that it does *not* relate to the wealth maximisation criterion. It promotes the acceptance of shorter-term projects and thus promotes liquidity rather than increased value.

(b) PBP takes account of the timing of the cash flows only in the most perfunctory way. The method divides the life of the project into two portions, the payback period and the period beyond it. PBP does not therefore really treat cash flows differently depending on when they arise. It merely puts any particular cash flow into one of two categories, the relevant category and the irrelevant one. We can see this incompleteness of consideration of the timing of cash flows by reference to the example. With the Super, the payback period would be identical (four years) if there were no savings in each of the first three years but a £25 000 saving in year 4. Clearly these two situations would not be regarded as equally desirable by any rational investor, yet PBP is incapable of distinguishing between them. Some firms use a refinement to the PBP method which to some extent overcomes this weakness. These firms look at the discounted figures when assessing the payback period. Taking the discounted figures for the Zenith from p. 74 we can see that the discounted payback period is $4^{2925}/_{3404}$ years (about 4.86 years), assuming that the cash flows occur evenly over the year; otherwise it is 5 years. The Super does not have a discounted payback period, i.e. its discounted inflows never sum to its initial investment.

(c) Not all relevant information is considered by PBP. The method completely ignores anything which occurs beyond the payback period. For example, PBP is incapable of discriminating between the anticipated cash flows for the Super and those of some other project with identical outflows and inflows until year 4 and then annual savings of £20 000 each year for the next ten years.

(d) PBP is very easy to use and it will almost always give very clear results. How those results are interpreted is not so straightforward though. How does the firm decide what is the minimum acceptable payback period? Inevitably this is a pretty arbitrary decision, which means that the PBP method itself will tend to lead to arbitrariness of decision making, unless the project with the shortest PBP is always selected. Even then it would promote quick returns rather than wealth maximisation.

Advocates of PBP argue that it will tend to identify the less risky projects, i.e. those for which the investment is at risk for least time. Even so, PBP takes a very limited view of risk. It only concerns itself with the risk that the project will end prematurely. It ignores such risks as sales being less than anticipated or costs being greater than planned.

We may generally conclude that PBP is not a very good method for selecting investment projects and its use is likely to lead to suboptimal decisions. It can, however, give insights into projects which NPV fails to provide, particularly on the question of liquidity. Thus PBP can be seen as a useful complement to NPV.

ACCOUNTING (UNADJUSTED) RATE OF RETURN

This method compares the average annual profit increase, after taking the cost of making the initial investment into account, with the amount of the initial investment. The outcome is usually expressed as a percentage.

For the two opportunities in the example, the accounting rates of return (ARR) would be:

Zenith

$$\frac{[(4000 + 6000 + 6000 + 7000 + 6000) - 20\,000]}{5} \text{ divided by } 20\,000 = 9.0\%$$

(The £20 000 is deducted from the total annual savings to take account of the cost of the depreciation of the machine over the five years.)

Super

$$\frac{[(8000 + 6000 + 5000 + 6000 + 8000) - 25\,000]}{5} \text{ divided by } 25\,000 = 6.4\%$$

The decision rule would be that projects would only be accepted where they are expected to yield an ARR higher than some predetermined rate. With competing projects the one with the higher ARR (the Zenith in this case) would be selected. It should be noted particularly that ARR deals with accounting flows, *not* with cash flows. This is to say that ARR looks at the effect on future reported profits which a particular project will cause.

Though in the example it has been assumed that cash flows and accounting flows arising from the purchase of either of the presses (Zenith or Super) are the same for the years concerned, this will not always be the case for all projects to be assessed, as is explained shortly.

ARR is also known as *Return on Investment* (ROI).

Comparing ARR with NPV

(a) ARR does not relate directly to value maximisation but pursues maximisation of a rate of return measured by accounting profits.

(b) ARR almost completely ignores the timing of the cash flows and hence the financing cost. The above ARRs for the Zenith and the Super would be identical irrespective of when within the five years they fell, provided that they had the same totals. With the Zenith, for example, the alternative cash flows shown below would give the same ARR as the original ones.

	Original	Alternative
	£	£
Year 0	(20 000)	(20 000)
1	4 000	25 000
2	6 000	1 000
3	6 000	1 000
4	7 000	1 000
5	6 000	1 000

Any rational investor would prefer the alternative, yet ARR cannot distinguish between them. The method makes no attempt to adjust the cash flows to reflect their timing.

(c) Typically all relevant information on the cash flows (except their timing) is used in arriving at the ARR of an investment prospect. However, ARR often picks up some irrelevant data as well. This is because accounting profit is calculated on a basis which, for example, apportions a share of overheads to a particular project, even where the overheads do not vary according to whether or not the project is undertaken. In practice, it can be very misleading to use accounting information to make decisions about the future in the way that the ARR approach does. This is not to say that measuring accounting profit is not a useful activity, simply that it is not a useful approach to assessing future real investment opportunities.

(d) ARR is simple and easy to use, easier than NPV.

Like PBP, ARR seems likely to lead to poor decisions. Also like PBP, there is the question of how the firm arrives at a minimum ARR which it is prepared to accept. One of its features is the fact that it does not reflect repayments of the original investment. Take for example the 'alternative' cash flows for the Zenith given above. Here all of the original investment would be repaid in the first year and it is thus a very attractive investment with a very high rate of return. Yet despite this, if the devotee of ARR decided to use the cost of borrowing (say 12 per cent) as the hurdle rate, the project would be rejected because its ARR is only 9 per cent! Perhaps more logically, the net profit to net assets rate taken from recent profit and loss accounts and balance sheets would be used as this is the approach that ARR uses (hence its name). This would still be an arbitrary approach though, for why should past accounting returns on assets be felt to be a useful basis for decisions relating to the future? In any case maximisation of accounting rates of return will not, except by coincidence, promote value maximisation.

It is possible to overcome a major problem of ARR, that is the timing problem, by using accounting profits which take full account of the finance cost involved with investment. In practice, however, this can be very unwieldy.

Table 4.1 summarises the relative merits of investment appraisal techniques.

Table 4.1 Summary of the relative merits of the four investment appraisal techniques

	NPV	IRR	PBP	ARR
Directly related to the wealth maximisation objective	Yes	No	No	No
Fully accounts for timing of cash flows and the time value of money	Yes	Yes	No	No
Takes account of all relevant information (other than timing)	Yes	Yes	No	Yes
Practical, easy to use and provides clear signals	Yes	Usually	Yes	Yes

INVESTMENT APPRAISAL METHODS USED IN PRACTICE

Having considered the attributes and the theoretical strengths and weaknesses of the methods found in practice, it seems appropriate to consider the extent to which these methods are actually used by firms.

The past 30 years have seen a large volume of research into the methods of investment appraisal actually used by firms. The more relevant of these for UK firms were conducted by Pike (1982 and 1992), by Pike and Wolfe (1988) (P&W), by McIntyre and Coulthurst (1985) (M&C) and by Drury, Braund, Osborne and Tayles (1993) (DBOT).

Pike and P&W concentrated on very large firms, in fact 100 of the largest 300 UK firms. M&C looked at a sample of 141 firms which fell within the Companies Act 1985 definition of a 'medium-sized' company. These are firms which satisfy two of the three criteria; annual turnover between £1.4m and £5.75m, gross assets between £0.7m and £2.8m and total number of employees between 50 and 250 people. Compared with the largest UK firms, the firms in the M&C study would be rather small ones, whatever the formal legal designation of their size. The DBOT survey was of 260 UK manufacturing firms of various sizes.

The results of these studies may be summarised as shown in Table 4.2.

Table 4.2 Investment appraisal methods used in practice in the UK

	Large firms				Smaller firms	Manufacturing firms (various sizes)
	1975 %	1981 %	1986 %	1992 %	1985 %	1993 %
Net present value	32	39	68	74	36	91
Internal rate of return	44	57	75	81	28	80
Payback period	73	81	92	94	82	86
Accounting rate of return	51	49	56	50	37	77
Other methods					4	
Totals	200	226	291	299	187	334

Appraisal methods and corporate objectives

These results suggest a number of factors which we shall go on to consider. An important point which we should bear in mind as we do this is that the choice of investment appraisal methods can quite logically be seen as evidence of the financial objective which firms are following. This is because, when making investment decisions, firms are frequently making judgements which will have the most profound effect on their future welfare and success.

We have already seen in this chapter that NPV's major theoretical justification stems from an assumption that firms pursue the objective of shareholder wealth maximisation. If this is the objective which firms pursue in fact, we should expect to find strong adherence to NPV as the primary appraisal technique in practice.

It would probably be wrong, however, to conclude that, since NPV is not used by all firms, shareholder wealth maximisation is not the primary objective. Indeed, Pike and Ooi (1988) found that there was no significant association between the importance to a particular firm of shareholder wealth maximisation and the use of NPV. It may be that there is a lack of sophistication among some financial decision makers which causes them not to relate a particular objective to the appraisal method which will, in theory, promote it. The fact that NPV is much less popular with the smaller firms, where less sophistication would be expected, may provide evidence for this point. On the other hand the disparity in the use of NPV between the larger and the smaller firms may be explained by a difference between the objectives followed by the typical large firm as compared with the typical smaller one.

Multiple appraisal methods

The fact that the totals in Table 4.2 are all greater than 100 per cent reveals that there is a large element of the use of more than one method. This does not necessarily mean that more than one method is consistently being used by a particular firm in respect of each decision. It seems that firms vary their approach according to the nature of the capital investment decision concerned. For example, Pike found that, although 74 per cent of his 1986 respondents used NPV, only a bit less than one-half of those firms used it for all decisions and about one-sixth of that 74 per cent rarely used it. It seems likely, however, that many firms use more than one method concurrently to assess a particular investment project. The extent of the use of multiple methods seems to be greater among the large firms than among the smaller ones. Its incidence also seems to be increasing over time. M&C found that almost half of their sample used only one method, and that only 13 per cent of that group used a discounting technique (NPV or IRR); 74 per cent of the single-method firms relied entirely on the payback method.

The fact that the use of multiple appraisal methods is so widespread may provide evidence that firms pursue multiple financial objectives. On the other hand, as was suggested above, a lack of managerial sophistication may be the reason for this phenomenon.

Discounting techniques

Both NPV and IRR have shown strong growth in popularity over time with the large firms. Though the Pike and P&W studies show increasing popularity for all four methods, it is the discounting methods, particularly NPV, which have made the greatest progress. It seems likely that all, or all but a few, of the large firms now use a discounting method in respect of most investment decisions. By contrast only 44 per cent of the smaller firms surveyed by M&C used a discounting method.

The increasing popularity of the discounting techniques with the large firms is comforting to the theorists who have long argued the merits of NPV and, to a lesser extent, IRR. Why IRR remains the more popular of the discounting methods, despite its theoretical weaknesses, is not clear. It is felt by some observers that financial decision makers respond more readily to a percentage result than to an NPV expressed in £s.

It is also felt by some that decision makers prefer to leave the question of the 'hurdle rate' (minimum acceptable IRR) until after the analysis, something which NPV will not allow since the NPV cannot be deduced without selecting a discount rate. Since most discounted cash flow analysis will now be done using a computer 'spreadsheet' or similar device, this point does not seem totally valid. This is because it is very easy to enter the predicted cash flows for a particular project and then to try various discount rates to see their effect on the NPV figure.

The suggestion has also been made that some firms may prefer to keep the minimum acceptable IRR as information confidential to senior management and by leaving it out of the quantitative analysis it need not become accessible to less senior staff who may be involved in deducing the IRR for particular projects.

From the popularity of NPV and the fact that, in most circumstances, IRR will give exactly the same decision as NPV, there is some evidence that firms do, in fact, pursue shareholder wealth maximisation as a primary objective.

Payback period

The continued popularity of PBP has confounded academics in this area for decades. As we have seen, it has serious theoretical flaws; perhaps most significantly it ignores the shareholder wealth maximisation objective. Despite these flaws it is very widely used by both large and smaller UK firms. For 50 firms (74 per cent) out of the 68 firms in the M&C study of smaller firms which used only one method of investment appraisal, PBP was that method. It is also very popular with the large firms.

There has been much conjecture among academics as to why PBP remains so popular. Some have suggested that it provides evidence that firms do not pursue shareholder wealth maximisation or at least that they couple it with 'short-termism', a point which was discussed in Chapter 2. Pike (1985) conducted some research, the results of which suggested that firms whose objectives emphasise shareholders' interests place less reliance on PBP. Others (e.g.

Boardman, Reinhart and Celec (1982)) have suggested that PBP may fit into a strategic framework involving matching returns from investments with the need to repay a term loan of some description. Another possible reason for its continued popularity may lie with its simplicity and therefore usefulness as a means of one manager arguing the case for a particular project when confronted by opposition to that project from other managers who do not have a financial background. Perhaps it is used in conjunction with a discounting method or is only used for relatively minor decisions. Another possibility is that PBP is used as an initial 'screening' device through which all project proposals must pass before the detailed analysis is conducted.

This point is somewhat undermined, however, by the fact that both PBP and the discounting methods use the same basic inputs (predicted cash flows). Having identified these inputs it is little additional effort to apply discount factors to them.

Chen and Clark (1994) undertook a survey of US manufacturing firms and found that the use of PBP is strongly linked to the extent to which managers believe that accounting profits are important to the way in which their performance is assessed, particularly where their remuneration is linked to accounting profit. PBP tends to favour projects which will generate fairly high operating cash flows and, therefore, profits in the short term.

A further, and perhaps more likely reason, for PBP's continued popularity may lie in the fact that the discounting methods whose theoretical development mostly occurred during the 1960s have not yet fully established themselves. This may be particularly so with non-financial managers. The popularity of PBP may stem from a lack of managerial sophistication. This point is supported by the fact that PBP is overwhelmingly the most popular approach taken by the smaller firms, according to M&C. It would be expected that there would be a narrower range of financial management skills in the smaller firms than in the larger ones.

Accounting rate of return

Despite its almost complete lack of theoretical justification ARR continues to be widely used. As with PBP, this fact could call into question whether firms do actually seek a shareholder wealth maximisation objective. The widespread use of ARR may indicate that firms are in fact pursuing some accounting return objective, possibly in conjunction with some wealth-enhancing one (also discussed in Chapter 2). However, as with PBP, use of ARR may imply a lack of managerial sophistication. Most managements are fairly used to accounting statements, profit and loss accounts, etc. It may be that they prefer to think in accounting terms rather than in discounted cash flow terms, despite the fact that accounting measures are inappropriate for assessing individual investment opportunities, certainly where shareholder wealth maximisation is the goal.

The United States experience

Survey research evidence undertaken in the USA shows that the same broad usage of the investment appraisal methods applies there as in the UK (Moore and Reichert, 1983; Scapens, Sale and Tikkas, 1982; Levy and Sarnat, 1988). There seems to be a greater incidence of the use of discounting methods than in the UK but, in contrast with the UK, NPV is more popular than IRR with US firms. Interestingly PBP seems to be as popular in the USA as it is in the UK.

SUMMARY

Firms may in one sense be regarded as investment agencies. As such, one of their most important decision-making areas is in choosing between possible investment projects in real assets. In practice firms tend to use one or more of these methods:

(a) net present value;
(b) payback period;
(c) accounting rate of return; and
(d) internal rate of return.

Of these NPV is much the most conceptually correct, mainly because it is the only one of the four which is directly related to the generally accepted criterion of wealth maximisation. In fact IRR will in most cases give similar results but it can in some circumstances be problematical. Recent research in the UK and USA shows that the conceptual arguments in favour of NPV, and to a lesser extent of IRR, seem not yet to be fully reflected in practice. The reasons for this are difficult to discern, though the increasing popularity of the discounting method suggests that it might be a lack of sophistication in firms' assessment procedures.

FURTHER READING There are literally dozens of good texts covering topics discussed within this chapter, including those by Brealey and Myers (1991), Davis and Pointon (1994), Drury (1996) and Lumby (1994), all of which clearly and thoroughly deal with the basic principles of the investment appraisal techniques. The reports by Pike and Wolfe (1988), Drury, Braund, Osborne and Tayles (1993), and the article by McIntyre and Coulthurst (1985) all provide very readable and interesting accounts of the research evidence on investment appraisal methods used in the UK which was cited in this chapter. Mills (1988) gives a useful summary of the results of a number of surveys of appraisal methods used in both the UK and the USA.

REVIEW QUESTIONS

Suggested answers to review questions appear in Appendix 3.

4.1 Is the objective of discounting to take account of inflation? Explain.

4.2 When we say that future cash flows should be discounted at a rate which takes account of the *opportunity* cost of finance, what do we mean by *opportunity*?

4.3 What is the key point about the net present value approach to investment decision making which makes it the most correct method, in theory?

4.4 The payback period method of assessing potential investment projects is badly flawed, but it is widely used nonetheless. Why is it so widely used?

4.5 What is the fundamental flaw of using the internal rate of return method? Is it a problem in practice?

4.6 Evidence shows that many firms use more than one of the four methods of investment appraisal found in practice. What could be the reason for this?

PROBLEMS

Sample answers to problems marked with an asterisk appear in Appendix 4.

(Note that problem questions 4.1–4.4 are basic level problems, while questions 4.5 and 4.6 are more advanced, and may contain some practical complications.)

4.1* Barclay plc is assessing an investment project. The estimated cash flows are as follows:

		£m	
Year	0	10	outflow
	1	5	inflow
	2	4	inflow
	3	3	inflow
	4	2	Inflow

The firm's cost of finance is 15 per cent per annum and it seeks projects with a three year maximum discounted payback period.

Should the project be undertaken on the basis of NPV and discounted PBP?

4.2 Branton & Co. Ltd is choosing between two mutually exclusive investment opportunities, Project A and Project B. The estimated cash flows for the two projects are as follows:

	Project A £000	Project B £000
Investment (immediate cash outflow)	50	60
Net annual cash flow (inflow/outflow)		
Year 1	39	28
2	9	8
3	12	14
Cash inflow from residual value Year 3	7	6

The firm's cost of finance is estimated at 10 per cent.

Calculate:
(a) the net present value for both projects.
(b) the approximate internal rate of return for Project A.
(c) the payback period for both projects.

4.3 Turners Ltd is considering the purchase of a new machine which is expected to save labour on an existing project. The estimated data for the two machines available on the market are as follows:

	Machine A £000	Machine B £000
Initial cost (Year 0)	120	120
Residual value of machines (Year 5)	20	30
Annual labour cost savings:		
Year 1	40	20
2	40	30
3	40	50
4	20	70
5	20	20

Which machine will be selected under the following criteria;

(a) NPV, assuming a cost of finance of 10 per cent per annum?
(b) IRR?
(c) ARR?
(d) PBP?

Ignore taxation throughout, and treat the savings as if they will occur at the end of the relevant year.

4.4 RTB plc has recently assessed a potential project to make and sell a newly developed product. Two possible alternative systems have been identified either one of which could be used to make the product. The results of the assessment can be summarised as follows:

	NPV (£m)	IRR (%)	Initial investment (£m)
Using system A	4.0	16	4.0
Using system B	6.0	13	6.0

The firms cost of capital (finance cost) is 10 per cent per annum.

Which system should the firm select?

Explain what assumptions you have made about the firm and your reasons for the selection made.

4.5* Cantelevellers plc's primary financial objective is to maximise the wealth of its shareholders. The firm specialises in the development and assembly of high quality television sets. It normally subcontracts manufacture of the components of each set, carrying out the final assembly itself.

   Recently the firm has developed a new TV set which has been named 'Flatview', and a decision now needs to be taken as to whether to take it into production. The following data are available:

(1) If the decision is taken to go into production with the Flatview, production and sales will start on 1 January 19X4 and end in 19X8. It is estimated that each set will be sold for £2 000. It is also estimated that the annual production and sales of Flatview televisions will be a steady 1 500 units for each of the five years.

(2) Development and market research in relation to the Flatview were undertaken during 19X3. The cost of these totalled £3 million. It is the firm's policy to write off all such costs against profits as they are incurred. Of the £3 million, £1.8 million was an apportionment of development department overheads. The remaining £1.2 million was spent on materials and services, including a market survey, which were purchased specifically in respect of the Flatview project.

(3) Assembly of the Flatview would take place in premises leased specifically for the assembly work, separate from the firm's main premises. The directors believe that suitable premises could be leased at an annual rent of £450 000, payable annually in advance.

(4) Labour for the Flatview project is available from the firm's existing staff. If the project is not undertaken the staff involved will be declared redundant on 31 December 19X3 and paid a total of £250 000 in compensation at that time. If the project goes ahead the total incremental cost of employing the staff concerned is estimated at £200 000 per annum throughout the duration of the project. At the end of the project the staff concerned will all be made redundant, with estimated total compensation cost of £300 000, payable at that point.

(5) Assembly of each Flatview set requires the use of a number of different bought-in components. Tenders have been obtained from the firm's normal suppliers, and the lowest total purchase cost of all of the components necessary to make one Flatview is £380. This figure includes £120 for component F451. This component is the only one of which the firm already has a stock since 500 units of F451 are held in stock as the result of a surplus from a previous project. These originally cost £80 each. If the Flatview project does not proceed, the only possible use for these stock items has been identified as selling them back to the original manufacturer at a price of £100 each, with the buyer bearing transport costs. Since the manufacturer cannot use these items until the end of 19X5, delivery and payment will not take place before that time. There are no incremental storage costs involved with retaining this stock until 19X5.

Each Flatview set requires the use of one component F451.

(6) Incremental overheads associated with the Flatview project are expected to cost £200 000 for each year of production.

(7) Plant and machinery will have to be bought and paid for on 1 January 19X4. The total cost will be £5 million, which includes all installation costs. It is estimated that at the end of the Flatview manufacturing project (19X8) the plant will have a disposal value of £1 million.

(8) The directors judge that the Flatview project will cost 15 per cent per annum to finance.

Prepare a schedule which derives the annual net relevant cash flows arising from the Flatview project and use this to assess the project on the basis of its net present value.

Ignore any factors (like taxation) which are not referred to in the question.

4.6 Cool Ltd is a firm whose main financial objective is to maximise the wealth of its shareholders. Cool specialises in providing a service for its clients. All of the work undertaken by the firm is of a similar type for similar clients.

Cool's management is contemplating offering a new service. This will require the acquisition of an item of plant on 1 June 19X4.

Cool intends to buy the plant for £300 000, payable on the date of acquisition. It is estimated that the asset will have a negligible market value by 31 May 19X8 and will be scrapped on that date.

A study of likely sales demand for the new service suggests that it will be as follows:

Year ending 31 May:	£000
19X5	220
19X6	250
19X7	300
19X8	260

Variable operating costs associated with the new service are estimated at 30 per cent of the sales figure.

The introduction of the new service is planned to coincide with the discontinuance of an existing activity. This discontinuance will release labour. If the new service is introduced, the staff currently employed on the existing activity can all be fully employed throughout the four years at a total salary bill of £45 000 p.a.

If the new service is not introduced, it is estimated that the existing activity could be kept going until 31 May 19X7, generating revenues as follows:

Year ending 31 May:	£000
19X5	100
19X6	80
19X7	80

Variable operating costs associated with the existing service are also estimated at 30 per cent of the sales figure.

If the new service is not introduced, it is envisaged that the staff will be made redundant and paid total redundancy pay of £20 000 on 31 May 19X7. This item was taken into account in the analysis, on which the original decision to start the existing service was based, several years ago. If the new service *is* introduced, staff will be made redundant upon its conclusion on 31 May 19X8, and paid total redundancy pay of £22 000.

Labour is a fixed cost (i.e. it does not vary with the level of output). Exactly the same staff will be employed in the provision of either service.

Apart from those which have already been mentioned, there are estimated to be no incremental operating costs involved with offering these services.

The cost of finance to support the project is expected to be 10 per cent per annum.

(a) *Prepare a schedule which derives the annual net relevant cash flows associated with the decision as to whether Cool should acquire the plant and offer the new service, based on the information provided above, and use it to draw a conclusion about this decision on the basis of the project's net present value.*

(b) *Estimate the internal rate of return for the project.*

(c) *Discuss the factors which Cool needs to take into account in respect of the decision, other than the NPV and IRR.*

CHAPTER 5

Practical aspects of investment appraisal

OBJECTIVES

In this chapter we shall deal with the following:

● the importance of cash flows rather than accounting flows for investment decision making

● the relationship between cash flows and accounting flows

● the importance of assessing the timing as well as the magnitude of cash flows

● the necessity of identifying only those cash flows which differ according to the decision and to identify all of them even where they are not very obvious

● the treatment of inflation in the investment decision

● how the basic NPV rule must be adapted to deal with situations where there are shortages of investment finance

● replacement decisions

● the importance of establishing routines to try to identify possible projects

● the link between strategic planning and investment decision making

INTRODUCTION

In the last chapter we established that the most theoretically correct approach to assessing investment opportunities is on the basis of their net present values. This involves identifying the cash flows and their timing and then discounting by an appropriate factor.

In this chapter we shall examine how the firm should go about identifying the cash flows and assessing them, particularly in the NPV context. We shall also consider some other practical problems, including how the company should deal with a situation of having insufficient finance to support all of the projects which appear desirable. While we shall mainly be concerned with the more practical aspects of using NPV, many of the points relate equally well to the other techniques for assessing investment projects, particularly to IRR.

CASH FLOWS OR ACCOUNTING FLOWS?

When assessing a particular business investment opportunity, should the firm identify and discount cash payments and receipts or should it discount profits arising from the project? This is an important question as the cash flows from a particular project in a particular time period will rarely equal the accounting profit for the project during the same period.

If we go back to the principles on which the concept of NPV is based (discussed in Chapter 4), we see that discounting takes account of the opportunity cost of making the investment. It is not until cash needs to be expended in the project that the opportunity for it to produce interest will be lost. Only when cash flows back from the project, can the firm use it to pay dividends, repay borrowings, to lend it or to reinvest it in another project.

Over the life of a project the accounting profits will equal the net cash flows (undiscounted) in total; it is the timing which will be different. Why should this be the case?

The roles of financial accounting and investment appraisal

In the context of income measurement, financial accounting sets out to assess the profit (increase in wealth) for a period, perhaps a year. In doing so it needs to treat each period as a self-contained unit. This is despite the fact that most of the firm's investment projects will not be self-contained within that same period. Fixed assets, perhaps acquired in a previous period, may be used in the period and continue to be owned and used by the firm into future periods. Stock in trade acquired in the previous period may be sold in the current one. Sales made (on credit) in the current period may be paid for by customers in the following period. Financial accounting tends to ignore the timing of payments and receipts of cash but to concentrate on wealth generated and extinguished during the period. Costs, less anticipated disposal proceeds, of fixed assets are spread in some equitable way (depreciated) over their lives so that each period gets a share of the cost, irrespective of whether or not any cash is actually paid out to suppliers of fixed assets in the particular accounting period under consideration. Sales are usually recognised and credit taken for them by the selling firm when the goods change hands even though the cash receipt may lag some weeks behind. The reduction in wealth suffered by using up stock in trade in making sales is recognised when the sale is made – and not when the stock is purchased or when it is paid for.

These points are not weaknesses of financial accounting. Its role is to seek to measure income (profit) over time periods so that interested parties can obtain a periodic assessment of the firm's progress. As projects will not usually be self-contained within time periods as short as a year, it is necessary for financial accounting to take some consistent approach as to how to deal with the problem; the approach taken seems a very logical one.

Investment appraisal has a somewhat different objective from that of financial accounting, however. This is to assess a project over its entire life, not to assess it for a particular portion of that life. This difference of purpose is represented graphically in Fig. 5.1. This shows a firm with six investment projects (A to F), each of which starts and ends at a different time. Financial accounting seeks to assess the profit for a period such as p. During this period one project ends (Project E), one starts (Project B), whilst the other four run

Fig. 5.1
Six investment
projects of a firm.
All of these
projects operate
during at least
two accounting
periods

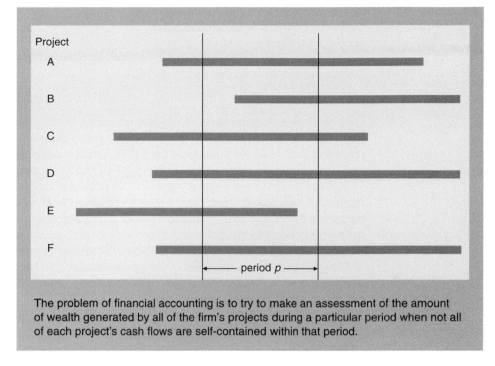

The problem of financial accounting is to try to make an assessment of the amount of wealth generated by all of the firm's projects during a particular period when not all of each project's cash flows are self-contained within that period.

throughout period p. Investment appraisal seeks to assess whether any particular project is a viable one, before it starts. Profit measurement tends to be cross-sectional, investment appraisal longitudinal.

Converting accounting flows to cash flows

We know from Chapter 4 that when using the NPV approach it is cash flows, not accounting profits, which should be discounted, yet frequently when projects are being assessed in advance of possible implementation they are expressed in terms of anticipated profit. As regards the operating items, i.e. those concerned with sales and material, labour and overhead costs, the differences between the accounting flows and the cash flows will be concerned principally with timing differences. The adjustment to convert accounting flows to cash flows can be done by taking account of the working capital requirement of the project.

EXAMPLE

A project to manufacture widgets, if undertaken, will start on 1 January with the purchase of (and payment for) a widget-making machine. Materials for use in the manufacture of widgets will be bought in January and paid for in February and these will be used in production in February. February's production will be sold in that month, on credit, and customers will pay in April. If the monthly purchase of raw materials is £10 000 and the monthly sales revenue from widgets £20 000, then once the project gets under way the working capital investment at any given moment will be:

	£
Debtors (two months at £20 000 p.m.)	40 000
Stocks (one month at £10 000 p.m.)	10 000
	50 000
Less: Creditors (one month at £10 000 p.m.)	10 000
	£40 000

(This assumes that the level of activity, the stock holding and the credit periods remain the same.) So to take account of the difference between operating accounting flows and cash flows we could treat the £40 000, which is the magnitude of the difference between accounting and cash flows, as an initial investment of the project. We should also need to treat it as a receipt of the project at its end. During the last few months of the project more cash would be received from sales than sales made; debtors will continue to pay after the end of the project for two months. Stocks will not be bought during the last month of production, though creditors for stocks bought the previous month will need to be paid during that last month.

Provided that this recognition of the timing difference which the £40 000 represents is correctly adjusted for, operating accounting flows can be used as a surrogate for the (more strictly correct) cash flows.

Failure to make this adjustment to accounting flows will tend to cause a bias in the appraisal, usually giving a more favourable impression than justified by the facts. It will tend to give this more favourable impression because accounting flows do not reflect the fact that sales are usually made on credit so that the cash inflows may lag some time behind the sale. While it is true that an opposite effect is caused by the fact that the firm is likely to be buying its raw materials on credit, this opposite effect is itself likely to be offset by the fact that the firm probably holds stocks of raw materials and perhaps finished goods as well.

In any case, for projects which are likely to be favourably considered by the firm, the sales revenues will tend to be larger than the operating costs. Also sales are usually made on credit whereas some significant operating costs (e.g. wages) are payable more or less immediately.

With the initial capital expenditure, its level and more particularly the timing difference between recognition of the expenditure in accounting flows and cash flows, make it vital to adjust the accounting flows to get the cash flows.

EXAMPLE

A project involving an initial outlay of £20 000 is expected to generate annual profits of £6000 (after deducting depreciation) each year for four years. Depreciation is calculated on an even (straight line) basis, assuming that disposal proceeds of the original investment will be £4000 receivable at the end of year 4. If it is assumed that there are no significant time differences between accounting recognition and cash payment or receipt in respect of operating revenues and costs then the cash flows may be taken to be:

		£	
Year	0	(20 000)	
	1	10 000	(i.e. pre-depreciation profit £6000 + £4000)
	2	10 000	
	3	10 000	
	4	14 000	

and it is these figures which should be discounted, using an appropriate rate, to arrive at the NPV. The figures are arrived at by adding back the annual depreciation figure of £4000 (i.e. [£20 000 – £4000]/4) and treating the initial cost as an outflow in year 0 (immediately) and the disposal proceeds as an additional inflow in year 4.

Discounting cash flows rather than profits does not really mean that depreciation is ignored. It is in effect taken into account by treating the initial investment as an outflow of cash and the disposal proceeds as an inflow, thus effectively charging the difference between these amounts to the project.

DO CASH FLOWS REALLY OCCUR AT YEAR ENDS?

In the examples which we have considered so far, all of the cash flows have occurred exact numbers of years after the start of the project. This obviously is not very representative of real life.

Most investments undertaken by firms are in land, buildings, plant, machinery, trading stocks, etc. The returns from these are in the form of sales revenues against which have to be set costs of labour, materials and overheads. Clearly these cash flows are not likely to occur at year ends. They tend to be spread throughout the year, perhaps fairly evenly or perhaps more concentrated at some parts of the year than at others, reflecting a seasonal aspect of certain trades.

Strictly the precise timing of the cash flows should be identified and they should be discounted accordingly. The discount factor $1/(1 + i)^n$ would be the same; however, the n would not necessarily be a whole number.

In practice, whilst the precise timing of cash flows could be recognised, it seems not usual to do so. The simplifying assumption that cash flows occurring within a year occur at the year end is thought to be popular in practice. Making this assumption tends to introduce an element of bias in that it usually treats cash flows as occurring a few months later than they actually do. This tends to have the effect of systematically understating NPVs. It is probably best in practice to identify the forecast cash flows month by month and to discount them according to when they actually are expected to occur.

WHICH CASH FLOWS?

As we saw in Chapter 2, only those cash flows relevant to the decision should be brought into the appraisal. Cash flows will be relevant only where they will be different, depending upon the decision under review. Items which will occur in any case should be ignored.

For example, where a decision involving a choice as to whether or not to make a new product would not have an effect on the fixed overheads of the firm, the fixed overheads should be disregarded when making the decision. They will be unaffected by the decision and so must be ignored when making it.

Similarly, past costs are irrelevant as they will inevitably be the same whatever happens in the future. For example, where a machine costing £50 000 one year ago is under review as to whether or not it should be replaced, the decision should not take the £50 000 into account. All that should be considered are the future benefits which could be derived from the machine, in terms of either proceeds of disposal or cash flow benefits of its retention. The present decision is not whether or not to buy the machine a year ago; that decision was made over twelve months ago and was either a good decision or a bad one. In either case it is not something which can now be altered.

Opportunity cash flows

It is not only cash flows which are expected to occur physically which should correctly be taken into account. Opportunity cash flows are as important as physical cash flows. In the above example, if the machine has a current market value of £10 000 then one of the cash flows associated with retaining the machine will be a £10 000 outflow at whatever time it would be disposed of if the alternative action (disposal) were followed. Obviously if the machine is retained this cash flow will not actually occur, nonetheless it should be taken into account because retention of the machine deprives the firm of the opportunity to dispose of it. The £10 000 represents a difference arising from the decision. Some opportunity cash flows may be fairly remote from the project under review and so can quite easily be overlooked unless care is taken. An example of such opportunity cash flows are losses of sales (and variable costs) of one of the firm's existing activities as a result of introducing a new one. For example, a chain store contemplating opening a new branch should not just assess the cash flows of that branch. It should also consider cash flow changes which might occur in other branches in the locality as a result. Sales might be lost at existing branches if a new one is opened.

Forecasting cash flows

We are, of course, dealing here with forecasts of future cash flows. Forecasting the cash flows associated with particular courses of action is likely to be difficult and subject to error. The techniques and problems of forecasting go beyond the scope of this book. These techniques include such approaches as the use of statistical data on past events (generated inside and outside the firm), market research projects and soliciting the opinions of experts.

Financing costs

One type of cash flow which should not be included in the appraisal is the cost of finance (interest) to support the project. Discounting deals with the financing cost in a complete and logical manner in that future cash flows are reduced (discounted) to take account of the time that finance will be tied up and the relevant interest rate.

TAXATION

Cash flows associated with taxation must be brought into the assessment of the project. Most projects will cause differences in Corporation Tax. This may be because of capital expenditure attracting relief (capital allowances), profits from the project attracting additional tax, or losses attracting tax relief. As tax is not assessed by the Inland Revenue project by project but for the company as a whole, then the tax cash flows which must be considered are differences between the tax cash flows that would exist without the project under review and those which will occur if it is undertaken.

The taxable profit

Basically companies are taxed on the basis of the profit shown by a profit and loss account (income statement) drawn up following the generally accepted accounting rules and conventions. This profit figure is, however, subject to some adjustment. There are certain items of expense and revenue which though legitimately appearing in the profit and loss account have been singled out by statute as being illegitimate for tax purposes.

Most of these items are fairly unusual in occurrence or relatively insignificant in effect, though there is one which is neither of these. This is depreciation, the accounting device for spreading capital costs of long-term (fixed) assets over their useful lives. Depreciation must be added back to the profit revealed by the profit and loss account, to be replaced by capital allowances.

Capital allowances

These are allowances which are set against the taxable profit in order to relieve expenditure on fixed assets. There are several categories of asset into which statute has placed the various types of business fixed asset. Each of these has its own rules and basis for granting the allowance. In practice two of these, dealing with plant and machinery and with industrial buildings, are by far the most important to the typical firm.

(a) Plant and machinery

This includes a wide range of assets, from industrial machinery to the reference books of a lawyer, and includes motor vehicles. For expenditure on plant and machinery, companies are allowed to deduct 25 per cent of the cost of the asset from the (otherwise taxable) profit of the period during which the asset was acquired. In each subsequent year of ownership of the asset, 25 per cent of the balance brought forward may be deducted.

EXAMPLE

In 1997 Carriers Ltd buys a delivery lorry for £12 000. The capital allowances would be claimable as follows:

Year	Balance £	Capital allowance £	
1997	12 000	3 000	(25% of £12 000)
1998	9 000	2 250	(25% of (£12 000–£3000))
1999	6 750	1 688	etc.
2000	5 062	1 266	
	etc.		

This pattern will continue until the asset is sold or scrapped.

When the asset is disposed of, in broad effect, any unrelieved expenditure is relieved, and any excess of relief is 'clawed back' by the taxman.

For example if Carriers Ltd (above) disposed of the lorry for £6000 in the year 2000, tax would be charged on £938 (i.e. £6 000 – £5 062). On the other hand, were the disposal proceeds to be £4 000, additional relief of £1 062 (i.e. £5 062 – £4 000) would be given to the company.

The broad effect of capital allowances is to give tax relief on the difference between the acquisition cost of the asset and its disposal proceeds (if this is a lower figure), spread over the life of the asset.

(b) Industrial buildings

These are buildings used directly or indirectly in manufacturing, the transport industry and other restricted purposes. Not included in the definition are shops and offices.

Relief is granted by allowing companies to deduct 4 per cent of the cost of the building from the taxable profit in each year of its ownership and use. On disposal the proceeds will cause a claw-back of excess allowances or an additional allowance, if the difference between cost and the disposal proceeds has not already been fully relieved.

Other types of asset which attract capital allowances are:

- Hotels
- Agricultural buildings and works
- Patents
- Scientific research
- Mines, oil wells, etc.
- Know-how
- Expenditure on dredging
- Cemeteries and crematoria.

Having considered the basis on which company profits are taxed in the UK, it will be useful to proceed to an example.

EXAMPLE

The profit and loss account of Amalgamated Retailers plc, for the year ended 31 March 1997, showed a net profit of £1 640 000. In arriving at this figure depreciation was charged as follows:

	£
Shop premises	120 000
Shop equipment and fittings	85 000

During the year the company purchased new computerised cash registers for all its branches at a total cost of £500 000 and spent £350 000 on acquiring the freeholds of several new shops, all of which commenced trading during the year. The tax written down values of the company's fixed assets at 1 April 1996 were as follows:

	£
Shop premises	280 000
Shop equipment	210 000

The company always claims all possible allowances and reliefs at the earliest opportunity.

The taxable profit of the company would be as follows:

		£
Net profit (from the profit and loss)		1 640 000
Add: Depreciation:		
Premises	120 000	
Equipment	85 000	205 000
		1 845 000
Less: Capital allowances		
(see below)		177 500
Taxable profit		£1 667 500

Capital allowances – shop equipment	
	£
Written down value at 1.4.96	210 000
Add: Additions	500 000
	710 000
Less: Allowance @ 25%	177 500
Written down value at 31.3.97	£532 500

No capital allowances would be given on the acquisition of the freeholds as they do not fall within the definition of any of the classes of asset for which capital allowances are given.

Rates of tax and dates of payment

The taxable profit is taxed at 33 per cent where the annual figure exceeds £1 500 000 (as above) and 23 per cent where it is less than £300 000. Between these levels of profit the rate is on a sliding scale, so that profits of just over £300 000 will be taxed at just over 23 per cent and profits of just under £1 500 000 at nearly 33 per cent. Companies whose taxable profit fluctuates from year to year will pay at different rates from year to year, unless their profits are always over £1 500 000 or under £300 000.

Thus the liability of Amalgamated Retailers in the above example will be:

$$33\% \times £1\ 667\ 500 = \underline{£550\ 275}$$

Tax will be payable on 1 January 1998, nine months after the end of the company's accounting year.

Where the company has paid any dividends to its members during the accounting period concerned, part of the total liability is paid shortly after the dividend payout date.

As is evident from the above, the tax cash flows frequently lag well behind the cash flow events giving rise to them. It is important to recognise this time lag, particularly as the cash flows concerned are likely to be large.

INFLATION

Throughout almost the whole of the twentieth century the UK has experienced erosion of the purchasing power of the pound. Much has been written on the causes of and possible cures for it, neither of which falls within the scope of this book. The effects of inflation, the problem which it causes to capital investment decision makers, and how they might cope with the problem are our concern here, however.

Even with relatively low levels of inflation (say, less than 5 per cent), over long periods prices will be greatly affected. An item costing £100 today would cost £127.6 after five years if its price increased by 5 per cent each year. In the UK our recent history tends to cause us to regard even a 5 per cent rate of inflation as pretty modest.

The principal problem facing the decision maker is whether to forecast future cash flows associated with an investment project in real terms or in money terms. Real terms here means in terms of today's (the date of the decision) price levels; money terms refers to price levels which are forecast to obtain at the date of the future cash flow.

Seeking to forecast in real terms is probably going to be easier because it does not require any estimation of rates of inflation. Forecasting in money terms is not simply taking the real terms forecasts and adjusting for the rate of inflation because different types of cash flows will be differently affected by inflation. We tend to view inflation as operating at one rate across all commodities; this is incorrect. Inflation acts differentially. An index such as the Retail Price Index (RPI) by which inflation is quite often assessed is simply a weighted average of the inflation rates of commodities bought by a 'typical' household. Within that, some commodities may have static or even declining prices though the average may still be increasing.

Assessing projects in money terms requires forecasts of future price levels for each element of the decision. In many instances, however, it probably will not materially affect the issue if prices of all elements are assumed to grow equally. In other cases this simplifying assumption may cause unreasonable distortions.

The other element of the decision which inflation will affect in the discount rate. Interest and finance costs generally reflect expectations of the general level of inflation rates. Suppliers of finance require compensation for being prepared to delay consumption. They tend to require additional compensation where they not only delay consumption by lending, but reduce the amount which they can ultimately consume as a result of commodity price rises during the period of the loan. The relationship is

$$1 + i_m = (1 + i_r)(1 + h)$$

where i_m is the money rate of interest (the actual rate of interest payable by borrowers), i_r is the real rate of interest (the rate that would be payable if the inflation rate were zero) and h the expected rate of inflation in the economy generally. Where no inflation is expected i_m will equal i_r.

Consistency of approach

In principle it does not matter whether money cash flows or real ones are used in the NPV analysis, provided each is used in conjunction with the appropriate discount rate.

Where the cash flows are estimated in money terms (i.e. incorporating the forecast effects of inflation), then the discount rate should also reflect inflation expectations. Therefore the discount rate should be based on the money interest rate.

If the cash flows are to be assessed in real terms, then the discount rate should be based on the real interest rate.

It is important that there is consistency of approach. To use real cash flows in conjunction with a money discount rate would be to understate the NPV of the project, which could quite easily lead to desirable projects being rejected. A survey conducted in the UK during the 1970s by Carsberg and Hope (1976) suggested that this rejection of desirable projects, resulting from wrongly dealing with inflation, was indeed a problem.

Drury, Braund, Osborne and Tayles (1993), in their survey of 260 UK manufacturing firms, found that only 27 per cent of those firms dealt correctly with inflation, 13 per cent of the firms surveyed made an error which was probably not very significant, but this left 60 per cent of firms dealing with inflation in such a manner as to give a significantly misleading result.

Dealing with cash flows and discount rate in real terms does not completely avoid forecasting the rate of inflation. Real rates of interest are not directly identifiable in the way that money rates are. Money rates on government stocks, for example, are quoted daily in several national newspapers. Money rates can be converted into real rates by adjusting for expectation of future inflation rates which are incorporated in them. In order to identify inflation rate expectations we probably could not improve on taking some average or consensus view from the various economic forecasts which are published regularly by a number of commercial and academic institutions.

The central point regarding inflation in investment decisions is that it cannot be ignored, not as long as inflation runs at significant rates. Not only must it be confronted but consistency of approach must apply. Money cash flows must be discounted at money discount rates and real cash flows at real discount rates.

AN EXAMPLE OF AN INVESTMENT APPRAISAL

Having considered the practical aspects of applying the NPV rule in principle, we shall now go on to see how it would be applied to a practical example.

EXAMPLE

Kitchen Appliances plc is assessing an investment project which involves the production and marketing of a sophisticated household food mixer, the Rapido. Annual sales are expected to run at 10 000 Rapidos for five years.

The development department has produced the following estimate of annual profit from the project:

	£000
Sales	1000
Raw materials	300
Labour	300
Depreciation	120
Rent	30
Overheads	100
Interest	50
	900
Annual net profit	100

The following additional information is relevant:

(a) The production will require the purchase of a new machine at a cost of £600 000, payable on delivery. The machine will be depreciated on a straight line basis over the five years. It is not expected to have any second-hand value at the end of that time.

(b) Production of Rapidos will take place in a building presently used for storage. Apportioning the rent of the entire site occupied by the firm on the basis of area, the building has a rental cost of £30 000. If production goes ahead the firm can rent a small warehouse, which will be adequate for storage purposes, for £5000 p.a. payable annually in arrears.

  If Rapido production is not undertaken there are plans to sublet the building to a neighbouring firm at a rent of £20 000 p.a. payable annually in arrears and to rent the small warehouse for £5000 p.a.

(c) £18 000 has been spent on developing the Rapido and £5000 on a market survey to assess demand.

(d) The overheads of £100 000 p.a. represent an apportionment of the entire firm's overheads on the basis of labour hours. The operating overheads of the firm will be increased by £45 000 p.a. as a result of Rapido manufacture. This includes £15 000 p.a. salary to a manager who is due to retire immediately on a firm's pension of £5000 p.a. If Rapido manufacture goes ahead he will not retire for another five years. Staying on for the additional period will not affect the pension which the manager concerned will ultimately receive. Pensions are paid by the firm and the amounts charged to non-operating overheads.

The remaining £30 000 represents salaries payable to two managers who will be taken on for the duration of the project, should it go ahead.

(e) If Rapidos come on to the market there is expected to be a reduction in anticipated demand for the existing food mixer, the Whizzo, which the firm manufactures.

The reduction in sales of Whizzos would be expected to be:

		Units
Year	1	10 000
	2	10 000
	3	5 000
	4	5 000
	5	5 000

Whizzos sell at £40 each with variable costs of £20 each. Lower Whizzo sales would not be expected to affect overhead costs, which are fixed.

(f) The firm's Corporation Tax rate is 33 per cent with payment date falling one year after the event giving rise to it.

(g) The expenditure on the new machine would attract capital allowances at the rate of 25 per cent p.a. with any unrelieved expenditure being allowed on disposal.

(h) All of the data given are expressed in current terms. Inflation is expected to run at about 5 per cent p.a. over the next decade. All of the relevant cash flows are expected to increase at this annual rate.

(i) The firm's after tax financing cost is (and is expected to remain at) 12 per cent p.a. in money terms.

(j) Working capital of £50 000 will be required from the start of the project and will be returned at the end of year 5.

(All of the above cash flows have been expressed in real terms, i.e. in terms of prices at the date of the start of the project.)

On the basis of NPV should the project be undertaken or not?

SOLUTION

Kitchen Appliances plc
Assessment of Rapido project

Despite the fact that using either a 'real' or a 'money' approach will give identical results if they are correctly applied, in practice the money approach tends to be a lot easier to use. We shall, therefore, use the money approach.

In the assessment of the project our guiding principles must be:

● to identify the cash flows relevant to the decision (i.e. differences between the cash flows which will occur if the project is undertaken and those which will take place without the project) and convert them into money terms
● to identify the timing of those relevant cash flows
● to discover the NPV of the project by applying the adjustment for the time value of money to the relevant cash flows according to when it is anticipated that they will occur

Annual operating cash flows

	£000	
Sales	1000	
Raw materials	300	
Labour	300	
Rent	20	
Overheads	40	
Contributions lost from Whizzo sales	200	
	860	
Annual net operating cash flow (in real terms)	140	(240 for years 3, 4 and 5)

Notes

(a) *Depreciation.* This is irrelevant as it does not represent a cash flow.

(b) *Rent.* The appropriate figure here is the difference, which is the rent from the subtenant should the project not go ahead. Irrespective of the decision, both the rent of the entire site (of which £30 000 is part) and the £5000 rent of the outside warehouse will be paid; thus they are irrelevant to the decision.

(c) *Overheads.* The retiring manager's salary makes a difference of £10 000 p.a. dependent on the decision. Irrespective of the decision the manager will be paid £5000 p.a. so it is the £10 000 which is relevant. The other £30 000 is also relevant. The apportionment of overheads is not relevant as this is not the amount of the difference in overheads associated with rejection or acceptance of the project.

(d) *Interest.* This will be taken into account by discounting.

(e) *Contributions from lost Whizzo sales.* These amount to £200 000 (i.e. 10 000 x £(40–20)) for years 1 and 2, and £100 000 (i.e. 5000 x £(40–20)) for years 3, 4 and 5.

Since lost Whizzo sales do not affect overheads, only sales revenue lost (£40 per unit) and variable costs saved (£20 per unit) are relevant to the decision.

This aspect must be accounted for, as accepting the project will affect Whizzo sales.

Corporation Tax cash flows

The relevant operating cash flows will also be the basis of the differential tax charges.

Capital allowances on the initial investment will be as follows:

	Balance	Allowance claimed	Tax savings (at 33%)
	£000	£000	£000
Year 1 Acquisition	600		
Writing down allowance (25%)	150	150	50
	450		
2 WDA (25%)	113	113	37
	337		
3 WDA (25%)	85	85	28
	252		
4 WDA (25%)	63	63	21
	189		
5 Balancing allowance (nil proceeds)	189	189	62

The tax payable will be as follows:

	Operating cash flow surplus	Tax payable (at 33%)
	£000	£000
Year 1	140	46
2	140	46
3	240	79
4	240	79
5	240	79

Notes

(a) Each of these payments will lag one year (strictly, nine months) behind the year to which it relates.

(b) The tax payable amounts represent the difference between the tax which would be payable if the project is accepted and that which would be payable if it is rejected. It is not necessary for us to know what the tax payable would be in total; we only need know the difference.

Discounting

	Initial investment	Working capital	Operating profit	Tax on operating profit	Capital allowance tax reliefs	Net cash flows	Discount factor	Discounted cash flows
	£000	£000	£000	£000	£000	£000	@ 12%	£000
Year 0	(600)	(50)				(650)	1.000	(650)
1		(3)	147			144	0.893	129
2		(2)	154	(49)	50	153	0.797	122
3		(3)	278	(51)	37	261	0.712	186
4		(4)	292	(92)	28	224	0.636	142
5		62	306	(96)	21	293	0.567	166
6				(101)	62	(39)	0.507	(20)
							Net present value	75
See Note		(b)	(c)	(d)	(e)		(f)	(g)

As the NPV is positive and significant, from a financial viewpoint, the production of the Rapido should be undertaken.

Notes

(a) The costs of developing the product and of the market survey will not vary with the present decision and must therefore be ignored. They exist irrespective of the decision.

(b) Treating the working capital commitment in the way shown takes account, in a broadly correct way, of the timing difference between operating cash flows and accounting flows. In 'money' terms, the investment in working capital will increase as inflation increases the prices of stock and sales prices. Each of the outflows of years 1 to 4 (inclusive) comprises the additional amount necessary to invest to bring the working capital up to the higher level. In each case the figure is 5 per cent of the previous year's working capital figure.

(c) The operating profits are simply the 'real' figures, adjusted for inflation at 5 per cent, for as many years into the future as is relevant.

(d) The tax figures are simply the operating profits multiplied by 33 per cent (the CT rate).

(e) The CA tax reliefs are taken directly from the table showing capital allowances on the initial investment. (*See* p. 111.)

(f) The discount factor reflects the 'money' cost of capital. Quite how the discount rate is established (i.e. where the 12 per cent came from) is a question which we shall consider in some detail later in the book.

(g) Note that the NPV via 'real' cash flows is identical to that via 'money' cash flows. Note also that each year's present value is identical, no matter whether 'real' or 'money' cash flows are used.

(h) All the calculations in this example have been rounded to the nearest £1000. Whilst this is not strictly correct, the accuracy to which cash flows, timings and discount rates can be predicted is such that this rounding is not out of place. It could be argued that doing other than this in such calculations would give the result an air of precision not justified by the levels of possible (probable?) inaccuracy of the input data.

(i) This example (except to the extent of the rounding mentioned in point (h) above) has completely ignored the question of risk.

How reliable are the predictions of labour costs? What if the bottom fell out of the domestic food mixer market? Would the increased level of activity which this project engenders prove too much for the competence of the firm's management?

These and many other matters are present with this project and similar ones with any other project. These risks should be formally assessed and their effect built into the decision-making process. How this may be done will be addressed in the next two chapters.

(j) The net cash flows figures in the example could be used as the basis of an IRR or a PBP assessment of the project without modification. IRR and PBP would simply use them differently.

CAPITAL RATIONING

In Chapter 4 we saw that firms will maximise the wealth of their shareholders by undertaking all investment opportunities which have a positive NPV when discounted at the borrowing/lending interest rate.

In some circumstances the firm may be unable or unwilling to undertake all such opportunities because it cannot or does not wish to raise finance to the level required. Where it cannot raise the finance because sources of supply are limited, the situation is known as *hard capital rationing*. Where the constraint is self-imposed because, for example, the firm feels that it does not have a sufficient volume of management talent to expand beyond a certain point, it is referred to as *soft capital rationing*. Research evidence (Pike and Ooi (1988)) suggests that in real life hard capital rationing is relatively rare, finance seeming to be available for viable projects. Most instances of capital rationing seem to be of the soft variety. One way or another, capital rationing means that there are more calls on finance than there is finance available.

Irrespective of whether there are hard or soft constraints, capital rationing requires that the basic NPV rule cannot be applied without modification. The modification depends on whether the constraint is to operate for one year only or is to persist over several years.

Single-period capital rationing

Where there is single-period capital rationing, projects should be ranked according to the NPV per £ of scarce initial investment capital.

EXAMPLE

A firm is unable or unprepared to invest more than £500 000 in the current year, but has the following projects available to it:

Project	Initial investment £	NVP £
A	100 000	15 000
B	150 000	29 000
C	140 000	31 000
D	210 000	22 000
E	180 000	36 000

SOLUTION

The NPV per £ of investment and thus the ranking of the projects is as follows:

Project	NPV/£ of investment	Ranking
A	0.15	4
B	0.19	3
C	0.22	1
D	0.10	5
E	0.20	2

The firm should therefore take on the projects in the order shown until the capital is exhausted. This would mean taking on projects as follows:

Project	£
C	140 000
E	180 000
B	150 000
A (30/100 thereof)	30 000
	500 000

This solution assumes that it is possible to take on 30/100 of Project A and that the cash flows of that project will simply be reduced to 30 per cent of their original figures, giving an NPV of 30 per cent of the original NPV. In reality this assumption may well be without foundation. If this is the case the decision maker would have to look at the various combinations of the projects which have total initial investment outlays of £500 000; that combination with the highest total NPV would be selected. Some trial and error is likely to be involved with finding this combination. Obviously use of the NPV per £ of investment approach (usually known as the *profitability index*), will cause NPV to be maximised for the level of investment finance involved.

Multiple-period capital rationing

Where the constraint operates for more than one time period, a more sophisticated approach needs to be adopted. Linear programming (LP) is such an approach.

EXAMPLE

Listed below are the cash flow characteristics of four investment projects. Investment finance is rationed at years 0 and 1 to £100 000 at each time. Projects cannot be delayed nor can they be brought forward. The cost of finance is 10 per cent.

Project	Year 0	Year 1	Year 2	Year 3	NPV (at 10%)
	£000	£000	£000	£000	£000
W	(70)	(20)	60	60	6.44
X	–	(90)	60	50	5.30
Y	(80)	10	60	30	1.18
Z	–	(50)	30	30	1.86

(Note that the NPVs are as at year 0 (now) even for projects X and Z which, even if selected, will not commence until year 1. Also note that project W requires cash outflows both in year 0 and in year 1.)

SOLUTION

We should seek to undertake such a combination of the four projects as would give the highest possible total NPV, subject to the capital constraints at years 0 and 1. Letting w, x, y and z be the proportions of the four projects which it is desirable to undertake, we are seeking to maximise the function:

$$NPV = 6.44w + 5.30x + 1.18y + 1.86z$$

subject to $70w + 80y \leq 100$, i.e. the total outlays at year 0 on W and Y being £100 000 or less; and

$$20w + 90x - 10y + 50z \leq 100$$

i.e. the total outlays on projects W, X and Z, less the inflow from project Y at year 1, must not exceed £100 000.

In fact further constraints will have to be applied, since each of the proportions must be positive or zero and cannot (presumably) exceed 1.
i.e.

$$1 \geq w \geq 0$$
$$1 \geq x \geq 0$$
$$1 \geq y \geq 0$$
$$1 \geq z \geq 0$$

There is no mathematical reason why the optimal solution should not completely exclude one of the projects. Note that the above formulation assumes that any uninvested funds cannot be carried forward from one year to be invested in the next, but it does assume that inflows from existing projects can be reinvested. It need not make these assumptions, however.

The optimal solution can be derived manually or by computer through the LP technique, finding the maximum value of the objective function subject to the various constraints. In addition to providing the proportion of each project which should be undertaken to achieve the maximum NPV, the LP output will also show, directly or indirectly, the following:

● the value of the maximum NPV
● how much it is worth paying for additional investment funds in order to increase the NPV
● how much funds would be needed in each year before that year's shortage of investment funds ceased to be a constraint.

LP will give results which assume that the projects can be partially undertaken. As with the profitability index approach to single-period constraints, this will not be practical to apply in many real life situations because many business investments cannot be made in part. Real life instances of firms going into partnership on large projects (e.g. the financing of Eurotunnel) can be found. These may provide examples of firms undertaking only part of a project, because capital is rationed.

An alternative technique, integer programming, can be applied which derives the optimal combination of complete projects.

Most texts on operations research and quantitative methods in business explain how to arrive at a solution to the above example through linear programming.

REPLACEMENT DECISIONS

A particular type of investment decision in which the decision maker may be involved is deciding when to replace an existing asset with an identical one.

EXAMPLE

A firm owns a fleet of identical motor vehicles. The firm wishes to replace these vehicles after either three or four years. Each one costs £10 000 to replace with a new vehicle. If the firm replaces the vehicles after three years it can trade in the old vehicle for £5000. If it retains the vehicle for a further year the trade-in price falls to £4000. Assuming that the firm regards a 15 per cent discount rate as appropriate, which trade-in policy will be cheaper for the firm?

Assuming that the running costs of the vehicles, ignoring depreciation, are identical each year, the relevant cost of owning one vehicle, expressed in present value terms, as at the date of buying a new vehicle, is:

	Replace after 3 years	*Replace after 4 years*
	£	£
Cost of the vehicle	(10 000)	(10 000)
Present value of the disposal proceeds:		
£5000 x $[1/(1.00 + 0.15)^3]$	3 288	
£4000 x $[1/(1.00 + 0.15)^4]$		2 287
Net present cost of owning the vehicle	£6 712	£7 713

For a wealth-maximising firm, it would appear at first glance that the three-year replacement cycle offers the better option. These two figures cannot, however, be directly compared because one of them is the net present capital cost of owning a vehicle for three years, which is naturally cheaper than the other which is the net present capital cost of owning the vehicle for four years.

One solution to this problem is to look at the position over 12 years. This is because whichever of the two replacement periods (after three years or after four years) is selected, after 12 years the firm would be on the point of replacing the vehicle and would have had continual use of a vehicle throughout this period. In other words we should be comparing two costs which have both led to a similar provision.

Time		Replace after 3 years £	Replace after 4 years £
0	Cost of a new vehicle	(10 000)	(10 000)
1		–	–
2		–	–
3	PV of the disposal proceeds:		
	£5000 x [1/(1.00 + 0.15)^3]	3 288	
	PV of the cost of a new vehicle		
	£10 000 x [1/(1.00 + 0.15)^3]	(6 575)	
4	PV of the disposal proceeds:		
	£4000 x [1/(1.00 + 0.15)^4]		2 287
	PV of the cost of a new vehicle		
	£10 000 x [1/(1.00 + 0.15)^4]		(5 718)
5		–	–
6	PV of the disposal proceeds:		
	£5000 x [1/(1.00 + 0.15)^6]	2 162	
	PV of the cost of a new vehicle		
	£10 000 x [1/(1.00 + 0.15)^6]	(4 323)	
7		–	–
8	PV of the disposal proceeds:		
	£4000 x [1/(1.00 + 0.15)^8]		1 308
	PV of the cost of a new vehicle		
	£10 000 x [1/(1.00 + 0.15)^8]		(3 269)
9	PV of the disposal proceeds:		
	£5000 x [1/(1.00 + 0.15)^9]	1 421	
	PV of the cost of a new vehicle		
	£10 000 x [1/(1.00 + 0.15)^9]	(2 843)	
10		–	–
11		–	–
12	PV of the disposal proceeds:		
	£5000 x [1/(1.00 + 0.15)^{12}]	935	
	£4000 x [1/(1.00 + 0.15)^{12}]		748
Net present cost of owning the vehicles		£15 935	£14 644

Now that we are able to make a valid comparison we can see that it is less costly to replace the vehicles after four years.

In this case using this approach was not too laborious because the lowest common multiple (LCM) is only 12 years. Suppose, however, that we were considering replacement after either eight or nine years? Here the LCM is 72 years. If we were also considering a seven-year possibility, the LCM would be 504 years! Clearly we need a more practical approach.

An alternative approach is to imagine that we were able to rent a vehicle, either to be replaced with a new one after three years or after four years. In either case let us also imagine that the rent is of a fixed annual amount and that payment is made at the end of each year. If we could deduce the annual rent which would represent the equivalent cost, in NPV terms, to £6712 (three-year replacement) and £7713 (four-year replacement) (see above), we could make a valid comparison between the two replacement policies.

One way to do this is by trial and error. We could try to find an amount such that the NPV of three payments of that amount, one at the end of each of the next three years, equals £6712. Fortunately there is a quicker way, using the annuity table (Appendix 2 of this book). You may care to look back to p. 75 for an explanation of the annuity table.

Looking at the annuity table for 15 per cent and 3 years we find an annuity factor of 2.283. This means that the present value of £1 receivable at the end of this year and of the next two years totals £2.283. Thus the amount payable at the end of this year and of the next two years, which has an NPV of £6712, totals £6712/2.283 = £2940.

The four-year annuity factor (from the table) is 2.855. Thus the equivalent annual cost of replacing the vehicle after four years is £7713/2.855 = £2702.

Again we find that the four-year replacement cycle is the less costly option. Note that the equivalent annual cost approach gives the same signal as the LCM approach because they follow exactly the same principles, even though the two approaches seem quite different.

The example we have used is a very basic one. In reality there would probably be a tax aspect, different running costs of the vehicle in each of the four years and the effects of inflation. All these can be incorporated without any great difficulty. There may well also be non-quantifiable factors like the effect on the image of the firm of having its staff driving relatively new vehicles.

ROUTINES FOR IDENTIFYING, ASSESSING, IMPLEMENTING AND REVIEWING INVESTMENT PROJECTS

In Chapter 2 we saw how the decision making process involves six steps; these are:

- Identifying the firm's objectives
- Identifying possible courses of action
- Assembling data relevant to the decision
- Assessing the data and reaching a decision
- Implementing the decision
- Monitoring the effects of decisions.

Accepting that wealth maximisation is the principal financial objective for all decisions, we can now look at the other five of these in the context of investment decisions.

Identifying possible investment opportunities

The assessment of possible investment projects is only one step in a process of the search for opportunities. This process should not be regarded as one which should be undertaken, say at five-yearly intervals, but as one which should be part of the routine of the firm. Good investment opportunities do not tend to beat a path to the firm's door; they must be sought out. Business tends to be highly competitive, so opportunities overlooked by one firm will probably be taken up by another. Any firm which regularly overlooks opportunities must sooner or later fall by the wayside.

Staff need to be encouraged to identify new products, new markets, new ways of supplying those markets and new approaches to production. Technical help should be available to help staff to develop ideas into formal investment proposals.

Assembling the relevant data for an investment proposal

Estimates of the relevant costs associated with the proposal must be made. This probably needs to be carried out by a financial manager. Care must be taken to gather all relevant costs and benefits. There is a danger that bias can influence some of the cost estimates, particularly where a particular manager has a strong commitment for or against the proposal. If an independent finance manager can carry out this task, it may help to promote freedom from bias.

Assessing the data and reaching a decision

The data must be fed into the decision-making model which the firm is using. Assuming that the firm is a wealth maximiser this model should be NPV. Once again this process demands certain technical skill and freedom from bias, so it is best carried out by someone who has those attributes, like an independent financial manager.

Implementing the decision

Action needs to be taken to get the project under way. A project team may well be established to take the necessary steps.

Monitoring the effects of the decision

Reviews, sometimes known as post audits, need to be carried out to try to assess the effectiveness of the project. One of the reasons for this is to assess the quality of the decision making process, so that improvements in this process can be sought in respect of future decisions. Perhaps it is discovered that some factor which has caused the original decision to be a bad one was ignored when the original decision was taken. In this case steps can be taken to ensure that that factor has account taken of it in all future decisions of the same type. Pike and Wolfe (1988) found that 63 per cent of the 100 large UK firms surveyed by them carried out a post-audit on 'most major projects'. Given the size and sophistication of the large firms in the survey, it seems likely that post audits are not a feature of the majority of investment decisions in the majority of firms, despite the compelling arguments in favour of their use.

The progress of the project must also be monitored to assess whether or not it is economic to continue with it. Periodically over the life of the project the question as to whether the project should be abandoned needs to be raised. The project will not be able to continue indefinitely – plant wears out, markets decline, etc. – so identifying the economically optimum moment for its abandonment is important. For the wealth maximising firm, this process logically involves an NPV analysis of the relevant costs and benefits of continuation relative to those associated with abandonment.

Some criticism has been made of researchers in capital investment appraisal implying that they have tended to concentrate on the minutiae of the quantitative assessment of projects, leaving largely untouched questions surrounding the search for possible projects.

The quantitative assessment is a purely technical process, even though a complicated one at times. The real test of management talent is not whether they are able to assess projects but whether they can identify good projects which will promote the achievement of the firm's objectives.

INVESTMENT APPRAISAL AND STRATEGIC PLANNING

So far, we have tended to view investment opportunities as if they are, more or less, unconnected independent entities which follow no particular pattern. It seems that in practice, however, successful firms are those which establish some framework for the selection of projects. Without such a framework it may be difficult to identify projects where the firm is sufficiently well placed for the project to be beneficial, i.e. to have a positive NPV. Such beneficial projects can only exist where a combination of the firm's internal strengths (e.g. skills, experience, access to finance, etc.) match the opportunities available and, probably, match them better than those of its competitors. In areas where this match does not exist, other firms, for whom the match does exist, are likely to have a distinct competitive advantage. This advantage means that they are likely to be able to provide the product or service more cheaply and/or of a better quality.

Establishing what is the best area or areas of activity and style of approach for the firm is popularly known as strategic planning. In essence strategic planning tries to identify the direction in which the firm needs to go, in terms of products, markets, financing etc., to best place it to generate profitable investment opportunities. In practice, strategic plans seem to have a time span of around five years and generally tend to ask the question 'where do we want the firm to be in five year's time and how can we get there?'

Strategic planning is typically seen to follow a series of steps which are set out diagrammatically in Fig. 5.2.

Establish mission and objectives

The mission is a broad statement of the general direction and aspirations of the firm. It tends to identify what the firm is trying to do, in the broadest

Fig. 5.2
The strategic
planning
framework

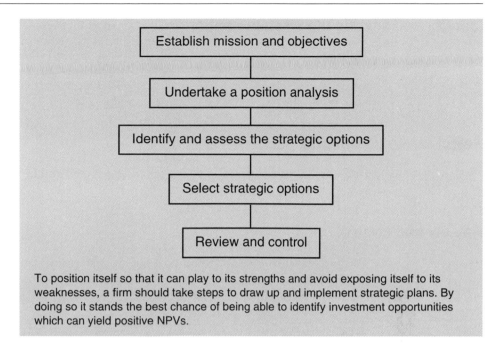

To position itself so that it can play to its strengths and avoid exposing itself to its weaknesses, a firm should take steps to draw up and implement strategic plans. By doing so it stands the best chance of being able to identify investment opportunities which can yield positive NPVs.

terms, usually identifying the business which the firm wants to be involved in.

Objectives are much more precise and operational. We reviewed possible objectives in Chapter 2 and concluded that for most firms, maximisation of wealth seems to be a major objective, if perhaps not the only one. The essential feature of objectives is that courses of action must be capable of being assessed against them. In other words, identifying objectives is not helpful unless the firm can distinguish between meeting them and failing to meet them.

Undertake a position analysis

This step seeks to identify how the firm is placed relative to its environment (competitors, markets, technology, the economy, political climate, etc.), in the context of the firm's mission and objectives. This is often formally approached through an analysis of strengths, weaknesses, opportunities and threats (a *SWOT analysis*). The first two of these are factors which are internal to the firm. Strengths might include such matters as technical expertise, strong finances, and access to markets. Weaknesses are such things as lack of experience, lack of access to new finance, and lack of access to raw materials. Opportunities and threats are external factors. Opportunities might include a new market opening, some new technology developing or a competitor leaving the market. Threats could be factors like a new competitor entering the market, the decline of a market or a change in the law which will make it harder for the firm to operate.

It is not essential that the position analysis is carried out in the SWOT framework, though this seems to be a popular approach.

Identify and assess the strategic options

This step is concerned with pursuing the firm's mission and objectives by trying to identify courses of action which use the firm's strengths to exploit opportunities, at the same time avoid, so far as possible, the firm's weaknesses being exposed to the environmental threats.

Select strategic options

Here the best strategic option or options are selected and formed into a strategic plan.

Review and control

The performance of the firm should be measured against the strategic plan. This is rather like the post-audit for an individual investment project, but for the entire strategy rather than just for one of its building blocks.

SUMMARY

When applying the NPV rule to investment decisions, it is cash flows rather than accounting flows which must be discounted. Often, accounting flows are used as a surrogate for cash flows; this is acceptable provided adjustments for working capital and depreciation are made. Accounting and investment appraisal have different objectives. All cash flows which vary with the decision, including opportunity cash flows, must be taken into account in the investment appraisal. In practice cash flows are often discounted as if they occurred at year ends, a simplifying assumption which should not necessarily be followed blindly.

Inflation must be considered; in doing so it is important to take a consistent view. Money cash flows must be discounted using a money discount rate, real cash flows using a real discount rate.

Where there is capital rationing a variation to the usual NPV rule must be followed. For single-period rationing, projects can be ranked on the basis of their NPV per £ of investment. Where the constraint is to last for more than one period some mathematical programming technique must be used in finding the optimal use of the capital.

Where the investment decision involves replacing one asset with a similar one on a continuing basis, special techniques can be used.

The quantitative assessment of projects is just the culmination of a process of identifying possible projects. The earlier stages of this process are aspects which require considerable management talent. Routine systems should be established to seek out possible investment opportunities. Failure to identify possible projects will sooner or later result in the demise of a firm.

Investment opportunities worth pursuing will only emerge if the firm plans to place itself in a strong strategic position.

FURTHER READING Most texts on business finance and capital investment appraisal deal to a greater or lesser extent with the practical aspects. The following tend to deal with those aspects to a greater extent: Weston and Copeland (1988), Brealey and Myers (1991), Samuels, Wilkes and Brayshaw (1995). Harper (1982) gives clear coverage of linear programming. Bowman and Asch (1987) provides a very readable introduction to strategic planning.

REVIEW QUESTIONS

Suggested answers to review questions appear in Appendix 3.

5.1 'Depreciation is taken into account when deducing profit (in the profit and loss account), but ignored in NPV assessments. If both accounting profit and NPV are meant to be decision making tools, this difference is illogical.'

Is it illogical?

(Note that the answer to this question is not really provided in the chapter. A combination of background knowledge and common sense should enable you to come up with some relevant points, however.)

5.2 Is it logical to include interest payments on cash borrowed to finance a project as cash outflows of the project in an NPV assessment?

Explain your answer.

5.3 Is it true that the 'money' rate of interest is equal to the 'real' rate, plus the rate of inflation?

Explain your answer.

5.4 When inflation is predicted over the life of a project under assessment, there are two approaches to dealing with inflation. What are these? Which is the better one to use?

5.5 How can it be argued that 'hard' capital rationing does not exist in real life?

5.6 What is meant by a 'profitability index'?

Is it a helpful approach to dealing with multi-period capital rationing problems?

PROBLEMS

Sample answers to problems marked with an asterisk appear in Appendix 4.

(Note that problem questions 5.1–5.4 are basic level problems, while questions 5.5 and 5.6 are more advanced and may contain some practical complications.)

5.1* Dodd Ltd is assessing a business investment opportunity, Project X, the estimated cash flows for which are as follows:

	£000
Investment (cash outflow on 1 January 19X2)	250
Net annual cash flow inflow (arising on the last day of the year)	
19X2	160
19X3	160
19X4	100
Cash inflow from residual value 31 December 19X4	50

All of the above figures are expressed at 1 January 19X2 prices. Inflation is expected to operate at 5 per cent p.a. throughout the project life.

123

The firm's 'real' (i.e. not taking account of inflation) cost of finance is estimated at 10 per cent p.a.

Corporation tax is charged on profits at the rate of 25 per cent, payable one year after the year in which the profit is earned (assume that the taxable profit equals the net operating cash flow). The asset, which will be bought in 19X2 and disposed of in 19X4 is of a type which does not give rise to any tax relief on its cost nor a tax charge on its disposal.

Calculate (using 'money' cash flows), the net present value of Project X.

5.2 Lateral plc has a limit of £10 million of investment finance available to it this year and it has the following investment opportunities available to it:

Project	Investment required this year (£ million)	Net present value (£ million)
U	8.0	3.3
V	3.2	0.9
W	5.3	1.2
X	2.0	0.5
Y	4.5	2.0
Z	0.5	0.4

Assuming that the capital shortage only relates to the current year and that each project can be undertaken in part, with the NPV scaled down in direct proportion to the proportion undertaken, which projects should Lateral plc undertake?

5.3 The management of Roach plc is currently assessing the possibility of manufacturing and selling a new product. Two possible approaches have been proposed.

Approach A
This involves making an immediate payment of £60 000 to buy a new machine. It is estimated that the machine can be used effectively for three years, at the end of which time it will be scrapped for zero proceeds.

Approach B
This involves using an existing machine which cost £150 000 two years ago, since when it has been depreciated at the rate of 25 per cent p.a., on cost. The firm has no use for the machine, other than in the manufacture of the new product, so if it is not used for that purpose it will be sold. It could be sold immediately for £48 000. Alternatively there is a potential buyer who will pay £60 000 and take delivery of the machine in one year's time. There are no additional costs of retaining the machine for another year.

If the machine is retained for manufacturing the new product, it will be scrapped (zero proceeds) in two years' time.

The staff required under Approach B will be transferred from within the firm. The total labour cost involved is £25 000 for each of the next two years. The employees concerned will need to be replaced for two years at a total cost of £20 000 for each of those years. The operating profit estimates, given below, are based on the labour cost of the staff who will actually be working on the new product.

The estimated operating profits, before depreciation, from the new product are as follows:

	Year 1 £'000	Year 2 £'000	Year 3 £'000
Approach A	30	50	60
Approach B	60	40	–

The new production will require additional working capital. This is estimated at 10 per cent of the relevant year's operating profit, before depreciation. It is required by the beginning of the relevant year.

The firm's cost of finance to support this investment is 20 per cent p.a.

On the basis of NPV which, if either, of the two approaches should the firm adopt?

(Hint: You will need to make the decision about what to do with the old machine if Approach B is adopted, before you can go on to compare the two approaches.)

5.4* Livelong Ltd has the continuing need for a cutting machine to perform a particular function vital to the firm's activities. There are two machines on the market, the Alpha and the Beta. Investigations show that the data relating to costs and life expectancy of each machine are as follows:

	Alpha	Beta
Acquisition cost	£50 000	£90 000
Residual value at the end of the machine's useful life	£5 000	£7 000
Annual running cost	£10 000	£8 000
Useful life	4 years	7 years

The two machines are identical in terms of capacity and quality of work.
The relevant cost of finance is 10 per cent p.a.

Produce workings which show which machine is the most economical.

By how much, and in which direction, would the acquisition cost of an Alpha need to alter in order that the two machines were equally economical?

Ignore taxation and inflation.

5.5* Mega Builders plc (Mega), a civil engineering contractor, has been invited to tender for a major contract. Work on the contract must start in January 19X6 and be completed by 31 December 19X7. The contract price will be receivable in three equal annual instalments, on 31 December 19X6, 19X7 and 19X8. Mega's management has reason to believe that a tender price in excess of £13.5 million will probably not be accepted by the client.

It is estimated that the contract will require 500 000 hours of non-management labour, in each of the two years 19X6 and 19X7, paid at an hourly rate of £5 and hired for the duration of the contract.

Management of the contract would be undertaken by staff who would be hired only for the duration of the contract. Employment costs of the management staff (including travel and subsistence) would be £250 000, in each of 19X6 and 19X7.

Materials for the contract will be bought at an estimated cost of £1.3 million, in each of the two years 19X6 and 19X7.

The contract would follow on from an existing contract which will be completed at the end of 19X5. The new contract requires the use of an item of plant which is being used on the existing contract and could be moved for the new contract. This item of plant was bought in May 19X4 for £6 million. Were it not to be used on the new contract it would be sold on 31 December 19X5 for an estimated £2.5 million (in 'money' terms), payable on that date. Transporting the plant to the new site would cost an estimated £100 000, payable on 31 December 19X5. This cost would be expected to be treated as part of the capital cost of the plant for tax purposes. It is estimated that at the end of the new contract this plant would be disposed of for a zero net realisable value.

Full writing down allowances (at the rate of 25 per cent reducing balance) have in the past been claimed at the earliest opportunity. This is expected to be continued in the future.

For taxation purposes, it is the firm's normal practice to recognise revenues in the accounting periods in which it receives the cash. Mega matches the costs of contracts with the revenues on a pro-rata basis. This is done by taking the total known and expected future costs of the contract (excluding financing costs and capital allowances) and allocating this to accounting years, as the contract price is received. This approach is accepted by the Inland Revenue. Capital allowances are given in the normal way. Mega's accounting year ends on 31 December.

Mega's corporation tax rate is expected to be 33 per cent. Assume that tax will be payable twelve months after the end of the accounting year to which it relates.

Mega's management regards the 'real' cost of capital for the new contract to be 10 per cent p.a. (after tax).

There are not thought to be any other incremental costs associated with the new contract.

Forecasts of the general rate of inflation are 3 per cent for 19X6, 4 per cent for 19X7 and 5 per cent for both 19X8 and 19X9. It is estimated that the labour (both management and non-management) and material costs will increase in line with the general rate of inflation.

Would the new contract be financially advantageous to Mega at a tender price of £13.5 million? (Use a 'money', rather than a 'real' approach to your analysis.)

What is the minimum price at which Mega should tender for the contract?

What other factors should be taken into account in deriving the tender price?

(Assume that all cash flows occur on 31 December of the relevant year, unless another date is specified in the question.)

5.6 Marine Products Ltd has identified three possible investment projects. Two of these would have to be started very shortly (year 0), the third in a year's time (year 1). None of these projects can be brought forward, delayed or repeated.

The estimated cash flows for the possible projects, none of which will generate cash flows beyond year 5, are as follows:

Project	A	B	C
	£ million	£ million	£ million
Year 0	(1.6)	(2.3)	–
1	(0.8)	0.6	(2.5)
2	0.7	0.9	0.8
3	1.5	0.9	1.5
4	1.5	0.5	1.4
5	0.4	–	0.5

All of these projects are typical of projects which the firm has undertaken in the past. The firm's cost of capital is 15 per cent p.a.

The entire cash flows of project A for years 0 and 1, of project B for year 0 and of project C for year 1, are capital expenditure. The subsequent net cash inflows are net operating cash surpluses.

The firm is not able to raise more than £2 million of investment finance in years 0 and 1. However, to the extent that the firm does not invest its full £2 million in year 0, it will be allowed to use it in year 1. The firm can also use any operating cash surpluses from previously undertaken investments as new investment finance.

In past years the firm has used all of its investment finance. It is expected that past investments will produce operating cash surpluses as follows:

	£ million
Year 1	0.5
2	0.5
3	0.3
4	0.2
5	0.1
6 and thereafter	zero

Set out the various statements (equations and/or inequalities) which can be subjected to linear programming to provide the management of the division with guidance on best investment strategy for years 0 and 1.

NOTE: *The solution to the linear programming problem is **not** required.*
Work to the nearest £100 000.
Assume that all cash flows occur on 31 December of the relevant year.
Ignore inflation.
Ignore taxation.

Risk in investment appraisal

In this chapter we shall deal with the following:

- the importance of risk and of its formal consideration in the decision-making process
- the use of sensitivity analysis to try to assess the riskiness of a particular project
- the use of statistical probabilities to try to assess risk
- expected value and its deficiencies in the treatment of risk
- systematic and specific risk
- utility theory
- risk aversion
- the logic of the expected value/variance criterion for selecting risky investments in some circumstances
- the particular risks of making overseas investments
- evidence on dealing with risk by firms in practice

INTRODUCTION

Until this point in the book we have all but ignored questions of risk. We are now going to start to confront the issue and though this is the only chapter with the word 'risk' in its title, much of the remainder of the book is concerned with problems of making decisions about a future in which we just do not know what is going to happen. Some events we can predict fairly confidently (e.g. the population of the UK in five years' time, give or take a million). Other matters (e.g. how many of that population will buy our firm's product) are rather more difficult to predict. None of the input data for decisions is known with absolute certainty, so risk is a constant problem to decision makers.

Despite this awkward environment, decisions must still be made. Delaying decisions until the mist of doubt lifts will not be a very fruitful approach, since it never will lift. In the context of a particular decision, it might be that delay may remove some major uncertainties but it will never remove them all. For example, a firm manufacturing armaments might await an expected major policy statement by the government on the future of UK defence policy before making a decision on a significant investment in its own manufacturing capacity.

Risk and uncertainty

Some observers have sought to distinguish between risk and uncertainty. Risk is seen as the phenomenon which arises from circumstances where we are able to identify the possible outcomes and even their likelihood of occurrence without being sure which will actually occur. The outcome of throwing a true die is an example of risk. We know that the outcome must be a number from 1 to 6 (inclusive) and we know that each number has an equal (1 in 6) chance of occurrence, but we are not sure which one will actually occur on any particular throw.

Uncertainty describes the position where we simply are not able to identify all, or perhaps not even any, of the possible outcomes, and we are still less able to assess their likelihood of occurrence. Probably most business decisions are characterised by uncertainty to some extent.

Since no one has yet suggested any way of dealing with uncertainty, it represents a particularly difficult area. Perhaps the best that decision makers can do is to try to identify as many as possible of the feasible outcomes of their decision and to attempt to assess each outcome's likelihood of occurrence.

The importance of taking account of risk

It is vital we take account of risk. This should be done in the most formal possible way, not as an afterthought. The level of risk fundamentally affects a decision. We should view very differently the opportunity to wager on a throw of a die and to wager on the spin of a coin. If on payment of £1 we could either guess which face of the die would land upward or which face of a coin would land upward, in either case the prize for a correct guess being £5, which would we choose? Most people would probably be happy to enter the coin spinning wager but few would be eager to go in for the die throwing. This is because the level of risk attaching to each wager would cause us to view them differently, even though they both only have two possible outcomes (lose £1 or gain £5). It is the likelihood of each possible occurrence which would cause us to distinguish between them.

We shall now go on to consider some ways in which risk in investment decisions can be dealt with.

SENSITIVITY ANALYSIS

All business investment decisions have to be made on the basis of predictions of the various inputs. One approach is to assess the decision on the basis of the 'best estimate' of each of the input factors. Assuming that this assessment is favourable, the risk of the project can be assessed by taking each input factor and asking by how much the estimate of that factor could prove to be incorrect before it would have the effect of making the decision a bad one. This approach is known as *sensitivity analysis*.

EXAMPLE

Greene plc has the opportunity to invest in plant for the manufacture of a new product, the demand for which is estimated to be 5000 units a year for five years. The following data relate to the decision:

- The machine is estimated to cost £50 000 (payable immediately) and to have no residual value.
- The selling price per unit is planned to be £10.
- Labour and material costs are estimated to be £4 and £3 per unit respectively.
- Overhead costs are not expected to be affected by the decision.
- The firm's cost of finance for such a project is estimated to be 10 per cent.
- The project is not expected to require any additional working capital.
- In the interests of simplicity taxation will be ignored.
- Assume, also in the interests of simplicity, that all cash flows occur at year ends.

Required:

(a) an assessment of the project (via NPV) on the basis of the above estimates; and
(b) a sensitivity analysis of the above estimates.

SOLUTION

The annual cash flows will be: 5000 x £[10 − (4 + 3)] = £15 000 each year. Thus the project's cash flows are estimated to be:

		£
Year	0	(50 000)
	1	15 000
	2	15 000
	3	15 000
	4	15 000
	5	15 000

The annuity factor for five years at 10 per cent is 3.791 (*see* Appendix 2, p. 378). The NPV is therefore:

$$-50\ 000 + (15\ 000 \times 3.791) = +£6865$$

Thus on the basis of the estimates the project is favourable (it has a positive NPV) and should be undertaken.

The estimates are not certain however, so we shall now go on to look at each of the input factors one by one to see how sensitive the decision is to each factor, i.e. to see by how much each one could vary from the original estimate before the project would become unfavourable (negative NPV). While we consider each factor we shall assume that the others will all be as originally estimated.

The factors whose estimates were used in calculating the NPV were as follows:

Original investment	I
Annual sales volume	V
Sales revenue/unit	S
Labour cost/unit	L
Material cost/unit	M
Cost of capital	r
Life of the project	n

We can represent the project as

$$-I + [V \times (S - (L + M))] \, A_r^n = NPV$$

where A_r^n is the annuity factor for period n years at discount rate r per cent.

To carry out the sensitivity analysis in respect of each of the input factors we shall equate the NPV to zero (the lowest NPV value for which the project could still be accepted) and put in the original estimates for all factors except the particular one under consideration. The value of the factor under consideration which satisfies the equation is the value at which that factor alone will cause the project to be marginal.

(1) Original investment:

$$-I + 5000 \, [10 - (4 + 3)] \, 3.791 = 0$$
$$I = £56 \, 865$$

Thus the initial investment could increase by £6865 before the project would become marginal.

(2) Annual sales volume:

$$-50 \, 000 + V \, [10 - (4 + 3)] \, 3.791 = 0$$

$$V = \frac{50 \, 000}{(10 - 7) \times 3.791}$$

$$= 4396 \text{ units}$$

(3) Sales revenue/unit:

$$-50 \, 000 + 5000 \, [S - (4 + 3)] \, 3.791 = 0$$

$$S = \frac{50 \, 000}{5000 \times 3.791} + 7$$

$$= £9.64$$

(4) Labour cost/unit:

$$-50 \, 000 + 5000 \, [10 - (L + 3)] \, 3.791 = 0$$

$$L = 7 - \frac{50 \, 000}{5000 \times 3.791}$$

$$= -\frac{10}{3.791} + 7$$

$$= £4.36$$

(5) Material cost/unit:

$$-50\,000 + 5000\,[10 - (4 + M)]\,3.791 = 0$$

$$M = 6 - \frac{50\,000}{5000 \times 3.791}$$

$$= £3.36$$

(6) Cost of capital:

$$-50\,000 + 5000\,[10 - (4 + 3)]\,A_r^n = 0$$

$$A_r^n = \frac{50\,000}{5000 \times 3}$$

$$= 3.333$$

It is now a question of looking at the annuity table to find the discount rate for which the annuity factor over five years is 3.333.

At 15 per cent the annuity factor is 3.352 and at 16 per cent it is 3.274. Interpolating between these two we can say that the rate is

$$15\% + \left(\frac{3.352 - 3.333}{3.352 - 3.274}\right)\% = 15.24\%$$

(7) Life of the project:

Once again we shall look at the annuity table for 3.333 but this time we are looking in the 10 per cent column to find the year. At four years the factor is 3.170 and at five years it is 3.791. Once again we can interpolate between these. The life will be

$$4 \text{ years} + \left(\frac{3.333 - 3.170}{3.791 - 3.170}\right) \text{ years} = 4.26 \text{ years}$$

(Note that linear interpolation to find the cost of finance and the life is not a strictly correct approach as the relationship between these factors (cost of capital and time) and the annuity factor is not linear. It is however fairly close to linear over small ranges so the above figures are a reasonable approximation.)

We can now tabulate our results as follows:

Factor	Original estimate	Value to give zero NPV	Difference as percentage of original estimate for the particular factor %
Original investment	£50 000	£56 865	13.7
Annual sales volume	5000 units	4396 units	12.1
Sales revenue/unit	£10	£9.64	3.6
Labour cost/unit	£4	£4.36	9.0
Material cost/unit	£3	£3.36	12.0
Cost of capital	10%	15.24%	52.4
Life of the project	5 years	4.26 years	14.8

From this we can see at a glance how sensitive the NPV calculated on the basis of the original estimates, is to changes in the variables in the decision. This gives us some basis on which to assess the riskiness of the project. If we can look at the table confident that all of the actual figures will fall within a reasonable safety margin, then we should regard the project as very much less risky than if this were not the case. If, on the other hand, we felt that all other factors seemed safe but that we were doubtful about, say, labour costs, the fact that only a 9 per cent rise would cause the project to become unfavourable might reduce our confidence in the investment.

Sensitivity analysis is a type of breakeven analysis where, in respect of each factor, we can assess the *breakeven point* and the *margin of safety*.

If the essentials of the project being assessed can be put into a computer, which is usually a pretty straightforward matter, the decision maker can, fairly effortlessly, take the analysis rather further than we have just done. A series of assumptions can be made about the variables and the effect on the project's NPV of each combination of assumptions can be assessed. This approach is known as *scenario building*.

Since it is most unlikely that all but one of the variables will turn out as estimated, the rather static approach taken in our example gives a very limited perspective on the project. Without the aid of a computer, however, doing much more than this would tend to be so laborious that it would be unreasonable to attempt. Commercial spreadsheet packages capable of undertaking sensitivity analysis are cheap and readily available.

Irrespective of the depth to which sensitivity analysis/scenario building is taken, it enables the decision maker to 'get inside' a project, see which are the crucial estimates and get a feel for its riskiness. It is clear that sensitivity analysis can be a very useful approach to gaining an impression of a project.

Knowledge of the more sensitive factors might enable us to reassess those factors or even take steps to reduce or eliminate their riskiness. In the above example we discovered that the project's success, in NPV terms, is very sensitive to the estimates both of sales volume and of sales revenue per unit. We may feel that undertaking additional market research would be a way either of reinforcing our confidence in the original estimates or of changing our view of the project.

The results from a sensitivity analysis might cause us to take more positive steps to deal with particularly sensitive factors. The analysis in the example shows the project's success to be fairly sensitive to material costs. It would be quite possible to place orders at fixed prices for the raw material or to take out insurance cover against the possibility of a material price increase. Alternatively, it might be possible to purchase an option to buy the material at a set price on a future date. This is an example of a *derivative*.

Clearly these approaches to risk reduction are not without cost. Market research costs money. A supplier who is required to be committed to a fixed price contract, or option, would need that fixed price, or price of the option, to take account of the risk that its own costs might increase. Insurance companies do not cover risks for nothing. We may feel, however, that these are prices worth paying to reduce the risk to a point where the project would become acceptable.

Despite its benefits to the decision maker, the technique does have its weaknesses:

(a) Sensitivity analysis does not provide us with any rule as to how to interpret the results. We could carry out more market research and possibly reinforce our confidence in the original estimate. If we could not, we have no formal basis on which to proceed to a decision.

(b) The sensitivities are not directly comparable from one factor to the next. In our example, it might seem that the life of the project (14.8 per cent sensitive) is less of a problem than the amount of the original investment (13.7 per cent sensitive). However, this is not true. The original investment is to be made immediately and for that reason alone is likely to be known with more certainty than the life reaching well into the future. Also, if it is found that the cost of making the original investment creeps to above £56 865, the project could be cancelled. Only when the project has been undertaken and large amounts of finance committed to it would we discover whether or not the estimate of the project's life was over-optimistic.

USE OF PROBABILITIES

Perhaps more useful than looking at the amount by which a particular factor may vary from its estimate before it renders a project unprofitable, is to look at how likely it is to do so. If the whole range of possible outcomes for each factor can be estimated together with each one's statistical probability of occurrence, a much fuller picture would be obtained. These could be combined to discover the range of possibilities and probabilities for the NPV of the project as a whole. Before we go on to look at how this could be done, it should be pointed out that reliably identifying possible outcomes and their probabilities is very difficult to achieve in practice.

In ascribing probabilities to various aspects, decision makers might use:

(a) *Objective probabilities*, based on past experience of the outcomes and their likelihood of occurrence. For example, if we know what the annual demand for a particular product has been over the years, we could assume that this would define the possible outcomes and their probabilities for next year. Suppose that during each of six of the past ten years the demand for the product had been 2 million units and it had been 3 million for each of the other four years, we could conclude that next year's demand will either be 2m or 3m with a 0.6 and 0.4 probability respectively. If we have reason to believe that the past is not a good guide to the future because, for example, the product has just been superseded by a more technologically advanced version, this approach could not be justified.

(b) *Subjective probabilities*, based on opinions, preferably of experts, on the possibilities and on their probability of occurrence.

However ascribed, the use of probabilities enables a fuller picture of the range of outcomes to be considered.

EXAMPLE

Using the data from the sensitivity analysis example (Greene plc) let us assume that all the factors are known with certainty (impossible in real life) except sales volume. Extensive market research suggests that annual demand will be:

 (a) 4000 units (0.2 probable)
or (b) 4500 units (0.5 probable)
or (c) 5000 units (0.3 probable)

What are the possible outcomes?

SOLUTION

NPV at 4000 units p.a.
      $= -50\,000 + 4000\,(10 - 7)\,3.791$
      $= -£4\,508$ (probability 0.2)

NPV at 4500 units p.a.
      $= -50\,000 + 4500\,(10 - 7)\,3.791$
      $= +£1\,179$ (probability 0.5)

NPV at 5000 units p.a.
      $= -50\,000 + 5000\,(10 - 7)\,3.791$
      $= +£6\,865$ (probability 0.3)

Thus we have a description of the range and probabilities of the outcomes.

This example vastly oversimplifies the situation both by assuming that there are only three possible outcomes for sales volume and by assuming that there is only one possible outcome for each of the other factors. Let us, however, take one more small step towards reality.

EXAMPLE

Still staying with the same data, let us assume not only that the sales volume has the same three possible outcomes, but that, independent of the sales volume, the cost of labour will either be:

(a) £3/unit (0.1 probable)
(b) £4/unit (0.7 probable)
(c) £5/unit (0.2 probable)

What are the possible outcomes and how likely is each one?

(Note that the word 'independent' in the above context means that the actual outcome as regards sales volume implies nothing about which labour cost is most likely.)

SOLUTION

This situation is rather more complicated in that there are now nine possible outcomes. Each of the three possible sales volume outcomes could occur in conjunction with each of the three possible labour costs.

The outcomes might usefully be represented in a diagram (see Fig. 6.1). For ease of reference the nine possible outcomes are labelled A to I inclusive. Outcome

Fig. 6.1
**Possible outcomes
of Greene plc's
investment
opportunity**

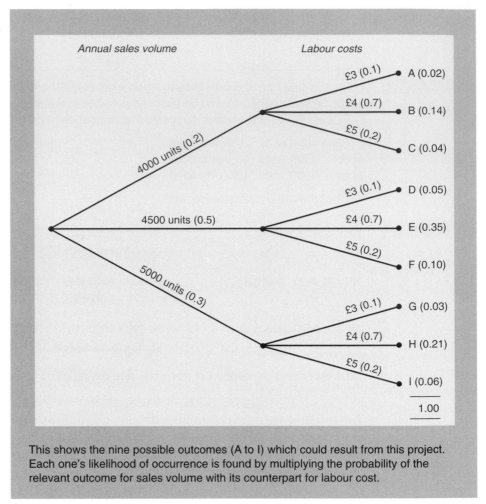

This shows the nine possible outcomes (A to I) which could result from this project.
Each one's likelihood of occurrence is found by multiplying the probability of the
relevant outcome for sales volume with its counterpart for labour cost.

F, say, will occur if 4500 units p.a. are sold and the labour cost is £5/unit. As the
probability of the first is 0.5 and of the second 0.2 then the joint probability is the
product of these, which is 0.10.

Note that the sum of the probabilities of all the nine possibilities is 1.00, i.e. one
of them is certain to occur.

The NPVs of each possibility are:

A: NPV = −50 000 + 4000 [10 − (3 + 3)] 3.791
= +£10 656

B: NPV = −50 000 + 4000 [10 − (4 + 3)] 3.791
= −£4508

C: NPV = −50 000 + 4000 [10 − (5 + 3)] 3.791
= −£19 672

D: NPV = −50 000 + 4500 [10 − (3 + 3)] 3.791
= +£18 238

E: NPV   = −50 000 + 4500 [10 − (4 + 3)] 3.791
                = +£1179

F: NPV   = −50 000 + 4500 [10 − (5 + 3)] 3.791
                = −£15 881

G: NPV   = −50 000 + 5000 [10 − (3 + 3)] 3.791
                = +£25 820

H: NPV   = −50 000 + 5000 [10 − (4 + 3)] 3.791
                = +£6865

I: NPV   = −50 000 + 5000 [10 − (5 + 3)] 3.791
                = −£12 090

Listing these in order of size, we get:

Possible outcome	NPV £	Probability
C	−19 672	0.04
F	−15 881	0.10
I	−12 090	0.06
B	−4 508	0.14
E	+1 179	0.35
H	+6 865	0.21
A	+10 656	0.02
D	+18 238	0.05
G	+25 820	0.03
		1.00

Note that, given the data from the question, one of the above nine outcomes must occur, and only one can occur.

As we have seen, a very modest attempt at reality causes complications. We can well imagine the number of possible outcomes were we to explore a more realistic set of possibilities for each of the input factors, even with our simple example.

How useful to us is the array of nine outcomes and probabilities shown above? The NPV rule is to accept projects with positive NPVs and reject those with negative ones. Here we know that four of the nine possible outcomes will yield a negative NPV, yet the other five give positive ones. One of these nine possibilities will occur, but which one? One way forward on the problem of the vast array of possible outcomes and the problem of making the decision once we have them is through the notion of 'expected value'.

EXPECTED VALUE

As ever, when we are confronted by a mass of data, it can be useful if we can find some way of summarising it so that we can more readily absorb and use it.

One way of summarising is to calculate a weighted average or *expected* value. This involves multiplying each possible outcome by its probability of occurrence. Taking the array of outcomes from the example gives us the following result.

Possible outcome	NPV £	Probability (p)	NPV × p
C	−19 672	0.04	−787
F	−15 881	0.10	−1588
I	−12 090	0.06	−725
B	−4 508	0.14	−631
E	+1 179	0.35	+413
H	+6 865	0.21	+1442
A	+10 656	0.02	+213
D	+18 238	0.05	+912
G	+25 820	0.03	+775
		Expected value	+24

Incidentally, if the decision maker were not interested in the individual outcomes (A to I) there is a much more direct approach to arriving at the expected value. This is to calculate the expected value of the risky factors and then to calculate the NPV, incorporating these expected values.

$$\text{Expected sales volume} = (4000 \times 0.2) + (4500 \times 0.5) + (5000 \times 0.3)$$
$$= 4550 \text{ units}$$
$$\text{Expected labour cost} = (£3 \times 0.1) + (£4 \times 0.7) + (£5 \times 0.2)$$
$$= £4.1$$
$$\text{NPV} = -50\,000 + 4550\,[10 - (4.1 + 3)]\,3.791 = +£22$$

The difference between this figure and the original expected NPV (+£24) is entirely due to rounding errors in the original calculation.

We now have one single factor to which we could apply the NPV rule. (In this case the expected NPV is very close to zero and thus the project would be on the margin between acceptance and rejection if ENPV is the decision criterion.)

There are some obvious weaknesses in the ENPV approach.

(a) As with all averaging, information is lost. The figure of +£24 for the ENPV of the project in the example does not tell us that there is a 4 per cent chance of the project yielding a negative NPV of £19 672. It also fails to tell us that the single most likely outcome, outcome E, gives a positive NPV of £1179.

How could we distinguish between this project and one with a certain NPV of +£24? We need some measure of dispersion, such as range or standard deviation.

(b) The ENPV may well represent a value that could not possibly exist. In our example an NPV of +£24 is certain not to occur. The possible outcomes are A to I, one of which must occur, and +£24 is not amongst them. In this sense expected value is a misnomer as it could not possibly occur (not in this example at least), let alone be expected in the normal meaning of the word. Does this invalidate ENPV as a decision-making criterion?

We know that the probability of a fair coin landing heads up is 0.5. If we are offered a wager such that we should gain £1 if a coin lands heads up and nothing if it lands tails up, one such throw would have an expected value of £0.50 (despite the fact that the outcome could only be £1 or nothing). If the wager were repeated say 100 times we should be very surprised if the expected value (£50) and the actual outcome differed by much. In other words, where there is a large number of projects, the expected value and the actual outcome are likely to be close, provided that the projects are independent.

Firms typically hold *portfolios* of investment projects; they have a number, perhaps a large number, of projects in operation at any given time. They do this, amongst other reasons, to diversify risk, i.e. to seek actually to achieve the expected value of the sum of the projects. Managers know that the expected value of each project probably will not (probably cannot) actually occur but that 'swings and roundabouts' will cause the sum of the expected values to be the outcome. Greene plc (in the example) may well have many other projects and it expects that the unlikely event of outcome C occurring will be matched by an unexpectedly favourable outcome in another project. The firm would expect this in the same way as a coin landing heads up five times in a row is possible (a 1 in 32 chance) but, over a reasonably large number of throws, chance will even out so that heads will face upwards in only about 50 per cent of the total number of throws.

Diversification

This holding of a portfolio of investment projects in order to seek risk reduction is known as 'diversification'.

EXAMPLE

A firm has two investment opportunities in each of which it can invest any amount up to £2m. The firm has £2m to invest. The characteristics of the two opportunities are as follows:

Project	Outcome (NPV as % of investment)	Probability
A	(i) +20%	0.5
	(ii) −10%	0.5
B	(i) +20%	0.5
	(ii) −10%	0.5

SOLUTION

If all of the £2m is invested in either project the outcome will either be +£0.4m or −£0.2m. However, if part, say half, is invested in each project then there are four possible outcomes for the firm:

A(i) and B(i): Total NPV = (£1.0m x 20%) + (£1.0m x 20%)
                          = £0.4m
            Probability = 0.5 x 0.5 = 0.25

A(i) and B(ii):   Total NPV = (£1.0m x 20%) + (£1.0m x −10%)
                                 = +£0.1m

                       Probability = 0.5 x 0.5 = 0.25

A(ii) and B(i):   Total NPV = (£1.0m x −10%) + (£1.0m x 20%)
                                 = +£0.1m

                       Probability = 0.5 x 0.5 = 0.25

A(ii) and B(ii):   Total NPV = (£1.0m x −10%) + (£1.0m x −10%)
                                 = −£0.2m

                       Probability = 0.5 x 0.5 = 0.25

As both projects have identical possible returns, diversification does not change the highest or lowest outcome (still +£0.4m or −£0.2m). Diversification does however introduce two new possibilities, both of which would combine a favourable outcome from one project with an unfavourable one from the other. These two possibilities, between them, are 0.5 probable.

The expected NPV of either or both of the projects with a total investment of £2.0m is:

$$(£2.0m \times 20\% \times 0.5) + (£2.0m \times -10\% \times 0.5) = +£0.1m$$

We can see that, as far as this example is concerned, diversification means that the expected value starts to become a likely outcome. Diversification has also reduced the chance of the best outcome occurring, the worst outcome is also less likely (in both cases down from 0.5 to 0.25 probability).

We shall see a little further on that most investors will readily accept a reduction of expectations of high returns in order to reduce the likelihood of low ones.

Systematic and specific risk

How likely in real life is it that a firm's investment projects are independent of one another in the way that spins of a fair coin are? Is it not quite likely that the very factors which will cause one project to turn out unfavourable will similarly affect each of the others? In the last example is it not true that outcome (ii) occurring with project A in real life, implies outcome (ii) occurring to project B as well, meaning that there would be no advantage from diversification?

The answer to these questions seems to be that whilst there are factors specific to each individual investment such that they will affect only its outcome, there are also underlying factors which will affect just about all projects.

Specific risk is the expression used to describe the part of the risk which relates to the particular project. This portion of the risk can be eliminated by diversification, in the way that the example suggests, because specific risk factors for separate projects are independent of each other.

Consider the perhaps unlikely example of a firm whose investments are diversified between making light bulbs and making chocolate. Project X might fail if a new means of making light bulbs is discovered by a rival, Project Y might fail if there is a world shortage of cocoa. These are specific risk factors for separate projects which are independent of each other. There is no reason to believe that the world market for cocoa could possibly affect light-bulb making.

That part of the risk which cannot be diversified away because it is caused by factors common to all activities is known as *systematic risk*. Such factors would include the general level of demand in the economy, interest rates, inflation rates, labour costs. Few, if any, activities are unaffected by these factors so diversification will not remove the risk. These factors seem likely to affect both light bulb and chocolate manufacture.

Clearly firms eager to eliminate specific risk by diversifying between industries must have more than half an eye on the fact that this is likely to have the effect of taking the firm into areas in which it has no expertise or experience.

The existence of systematic risk means that expected value is not the whole answer to dealing with risk. Not all of the risk is susceptible to elimination through diversification. Systematic factors mean that expected value may well not occur for the firm as a whole, even though forecast assessments of financial effect and probability of occurrence of the various possible outcomes may be impeccable.

Before going on to consider another reason why expected value may not be a complete way of dealing with risk, let us take a brief look at a useful way of expressing attitudes towards risk.

UTILITY THEORY

The notion of utility provides a means of expressing individual tastes and preferences. This is an important aspect of business finance and something to which we shall return on several occasions in this book. Utility is the level of satisfaction which an individual derives from some desirable factor, e.g. going away on holiday, having drinking water available, eating caviar or having wealth. Utility and differing levels of it are frequently represented graphically by *indifference curves*, each one showing a constant level of utility or satisfaction for differing combinations of related factors.

UU in Fig. 6.2 represents the utility curve of the attitude of some individual towards holidays and how much money the person is prepared to devote to them. 0S represents the total of the person's cash resources, all of which could be spent on going away on holiday this year. Alternatively all or part of them could be retained for other purposes. The curve suggests that this particular individual is prepared to spend some money to go on holiday. In fact the person is prepared to spend a lot of savings in order to go for a short time (the curve is fairly close to being horizontal at the bottom right). As we move up the curve (bottom right to top left) less and less utility is derived from each extra day of holiday so that the individual is prepared to give up less and less money to it. In fact this individual reaches a point towards the top of the curve where there is a reluctance to spend any more money to get extra days of holiday (the curve becomes vertical). This suggests that once this person has had a certain amount of holiday there is an unwillingness to spend more money on extra days. It is important to recognise that the curve depicted applies only to this individual and reflects his or her personal tastes; any other individual may see things very

**Fig. 6.2
Utility of going
away on holiday
for some individual**

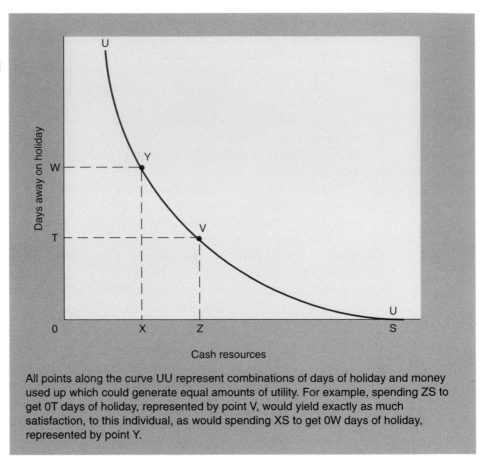

All points along the curve UU represent combinations of days of holiday and money used up which could generate equal amounts of utility. For example, spending ZS to get 0T days of holiday, represented by point V, would yield exactly as much satisfaction, to this individual, as would spending XS to get 0W days of holiday, represented by point Y.

differently – perhaps even not liking being away from home very much and so being unwilling to devote any money to it.

For the individual whose preferences are depicted in Fig. 6.2, all points along the curve UU represent combinations of days away on holiday and money retained which will give equal satisfaction. Thus points V and Y on curve UU represent just two of the many combinations of days of holiday and money retained which would be of equal satisfaction or utility to our individual. This person would view having 0T days of holidays and retaining 0Z of money as equally satisfying to going on holiday for 0W days, leaving only 0X of money. The person would be indifferent to which of these two combinations, or indeed of any other combinations lying along curve UU, were to be taken.

Figure 6.3 shows the same combinations of days of holiday and money retained but at varying levels. Each of the curves U_1U_1, U_2U_2, U_3U_3 and U_4U_4 of themselves show combinations which yield equal satisfaction or utility but the higher the curve, the higher the level of utility. For example, any point along U_2U_2 is more satisfactory than any point along U_1U_1 for our individual. This is because, at any level of spending, more days of holiday could be taken; or, at any number of days of holiday, the inroads into the person's cash resources would be less. For example, if PS of money were devoted to paying for a holiday

Fig. 6.3
Various levels of utility of going away on holiday for some individual

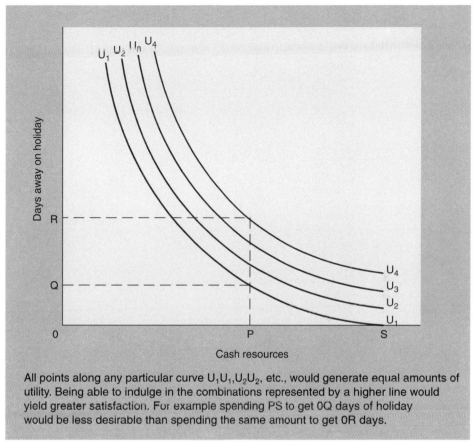

All points along any particular curve U_1U_1, U_2U_2, etc., would generate equal amounts of utility. Being able to indulge in the combinations represented by a higher line would yield greater satisfaction. For example spending PS to get 0Q days of holiday would be less desirable than spending the same amount to get 0R days.

(leaving 0P to save or spend other than on holidays), 0Q days of holiday would be obtained if the state of the world implied curve U_1U_1, but the much larger 0R days if it implied curve U_4U_4. Different levels of utility imply different states of the world, e.g. U_4U_4 implies that holidays are cheaper and/or our individual can get the first few days of holiday without cost as compared with the U_1U_1 position. Thus the individual would prefer the range of possibilities portrayed by U_2U_2 over those shown on U_1U_1. To be on U_3U_3 would be even better and on U_4U_4 even better still. Thus whilst the individual is indifferent to where he or she is on any particular curve there is a clear preference to be on the highest possible curve (i.e. the one furthest to the top right) as this gives the maximum possible level of satisfaction or utility.

Figure 6.3 represents just four of an infinite number of similarly shaped curves, parallel to the curves shown. Note that the shape of these curves is determined by our individual's preferences; which curve actually applies is decreed by the state of the world (e.g. price of holidays). This example concerning the trade-off between money spent and days away on holiday illustrates a phenomenon which seems to apply generally to human behaviour. The more individuals have of a particular factor which they might find desirable (e.g. going away on holiday) the less they are willing to pay for additional amounts of it. Thus

**Fig. 6.4
The utility function
of some individual
for going away on
holiday**

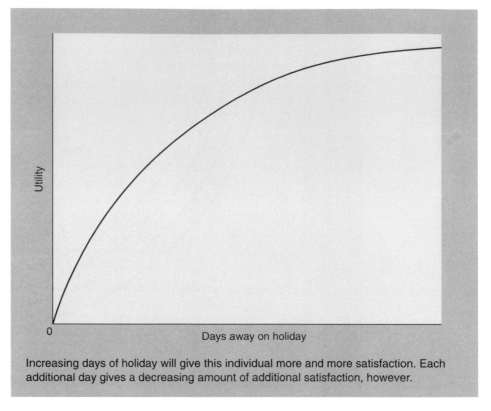

Utility

0   Days away on holiday

Increasing days of holiday will give this individual more and more satisfaction. Each
additional day gives a decreasing amount of additional satisfaction, however.

the worth (in financial terms) of an additional day of holiday not only varies
from individual to individual; it probably also depends on how much holiday
the individual already has.

An alternative way in which we could represent this individual's attitude
to holidays is shown in Fig. 6.4. Here utility itself is plotted against days of
holiday. We can see from Fig. 6.4 that our individual derives great utility from
increases in days of holiday at the lower end but, as more days are obtained,
the additional utility given by each extra day diminishes. Figure 6.4 raises the
question of how utility is measured, and how we actually draw such a graph
in practice. In fact utility is not a readily measurable factor and therefore
graphs of it are difficult to construct. Utility is in the mind of the individual.

Utility theory has been criticised for the fact that utility is difficult to measure.
Most observers agree, however, that the notions represented in the theory have
an inexorable logic. For our present purposes it is sufficient that we accept these
notions; we shall not need to concern ourselves further than that.

ATTITUDES TO RISK AND EXPECTED VALUE

Let us now go back to expected value and the other reason why it is not apparently as useful as it might be to decision makers in firms.

Like the attitude of our individual to holidays, depicted in Fig. 6.4, most people's attitude to wealth varies with the amount of it that they have. On the face of it, the expected value of a risky venture is what a rational person would pay for it. For example, the expected value of a wager on the spin of a fair coin which pays out £200 for a head and nothing for a tail is £100 (i.e. (£200 × 0.5) + (0 × 0.5)). We might expect that a rational person would be prepared to pay £100 to take part in the wager. In fact it would appear that only a minority of people would be prepared to risk losing £100 in order to stand a one in two chance of winning £200. This is because most of us are risk-averse.

Figure 6.5 shows the utility of wealth curve for a risk-averse individual. Utility, as we saw in the previous section, is a level of satisfaction. W on the horizontal axis represents the present level of wealth of an individual. To this individual, increasing wealth by £100 would increase personal satisfaction (utility) by CB, but losing £100 would reduce that satisfaction by CD, a rather larger amount. This individual would only become indifferent to the wager if the potential gain were x, so that the increase in utility from the gain (should it arise) would equal the potential loss of utility from the loss of the money (i.e. CA = CD). The risk-averse person would need the prize for the coin landing heads to be in excess of £200 to make the wager attractive.

Fig. 6.5
A graph of the utility of wealth against wealth for some risk-averse individual

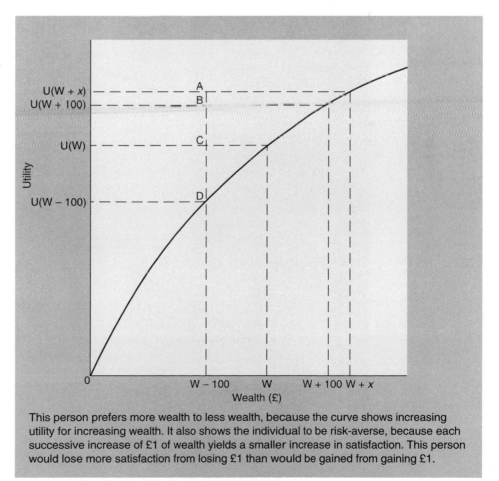

This person prefers more wealth to less wealth, because the curve shows increasing utility for increasing wealth. It also shows the individual to be risk-averse, because each successive increase of £1 of wealth yields a smaller increase in satisfaction. This person would lose more satisfaction from losing £1 than would be gained from gaining £1.

**Fig. 6.6
Graphs of the
utility of wealth
against wealth for
individuals with
different attitudes
towards risk**

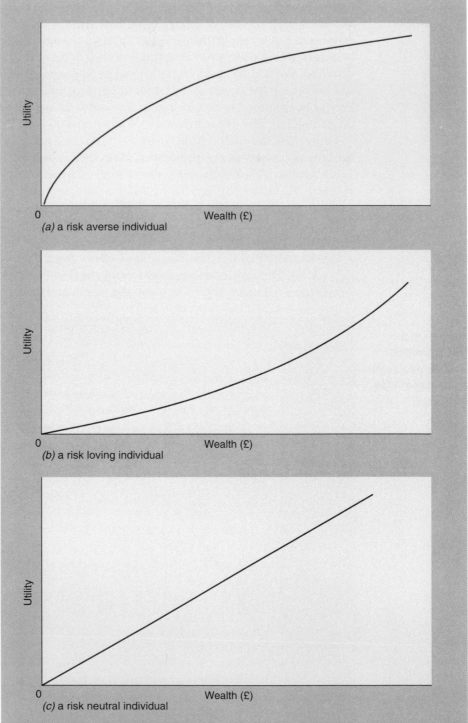

(a) a risk averse individual

(b) a risk loving individual

(c) a risk neutral individual

The risk-averse individual (graph (a)) would gain less satisfaction from having an additional £1, than the satisfaction which would be lost from having £1 less. The risk-loving individual (graph (b)) would gain more satisfaction from having an additional £1, than would be lost from having £1 less. To the risk-neutral individual (graph (c)), the gain in satisfaction from having an additional £1 is equal to the loss in satisfaction of having £1 less.

The precise shape of a utility curve (and thus how much the prize in the above wager needs to be) depends on the personal preferences of the individual concerned. The curve in Fig. 6.5 represents the preferences of just one hypothetical individual, though all risk-averse individuals will have a curve of roughly the same shape. Note that how much the prize in the wager would need to be, to tempt any particular individual, depends both on that person's utility curve and the level of wealth of that individual at the time when the wager is on offer.

Figure 6.6 shows the general shapes of the utility curves of (a) a risk-averse investor, (b) a risk-loving investor, and (c) a risk-neutral investor. A risk-neutral investor views equally entering a wager whose expected value is zero, and doing nothing.

There might well be some individuals in the world who are risk-lovers. Such an individual might, for example, be prepared to enter a coin-spinning wager standing to lose £100 but to gain only £190. Such might be the desire to be exposed to risk that he or she would be willing to take on wagers with negative expected value. Most of us are not.

There is quite a lot of evidence around us to support the assertion that most people are risk-averse. People's general desire to cover potential disasters by insurance is an example. Most house-owners, with no legal compulsion, choose to insure their property against destruction by fire. Clearly, taking account of the potential financial loss and the risk of fire, the premium must be more than the expected value of the loss, otherwise the fire insurance companies would consistently lose money. For example, if the potential damage from a fire for a particular house is £30 000 and the probability of a serious fire during a year is 1 in 1000 (i.e. 0.001 probability), the expected value of the loss is £30 (i.e. £30 000 × 0.001). Unless the house-owner is prepared to pay a premium higher than £30 p.a. the insurance company would not accept the risk, yet most house-owners seem to insure their houses at a premium, presumably more than the expected value of the potential loss. They are prepared to do this because the loss of utility caused by paying the premium is less than the anticipated loss of utility caused by the cost of a fire (if the house is uninsured) multiplied by its probability of occurrence. This arises from the fact that for risk-averse individuals utility of wealth curves are not straight lines, i.e. there is not a linear relationship between wealth and utility of wealth.

Figure 6.7 shows the range of possible outcomes for two investment projects A and B. Both have expected values of £15 000 (the outcomes of each are symmetrically arrayed around this value); in fact £15 000 is the single most likely outcome (the mode) in each case.

Both of these projects would be acceptable to the investor as they both have positive NPV, irrespective of where in the range the actual outcome falls. Since most of the human race seems to be risk-averse, project A would be most people's first choice if they had to choose between the projects. This is despite the fact that project B holds the possibility of an NPV as high as £30 000 whereas project A's maximum is only £21 000. The risk-averse investor's eyes would be drawn to the lower end of the scale where that person would note that project A gives a guaranteed minimum NPV of £9000 whereas project B's outcome

**Fig. 6.7
A graph of the
probabilities of
the NPV for two
projects each
having equal
expected NPVs**

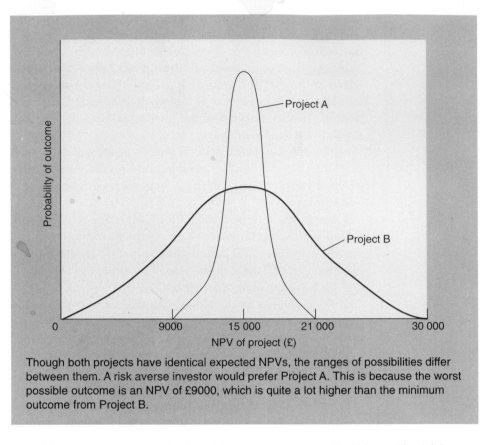

Though both projects have identical expected NPVs, the ranges of possibilities differ
between them. A risk averse investor would prefer Project A. This is because the worst
possible outcome is an NPV of £9000, which is quite a lot higher than the minimum
outcome from Project B.

could be as low as zero. To the risk-averse, the so called *downside risk* looms
larger than the *upside potential*. By contrast a risk-lover would be more attracted
to project B. A risk-neutral investor would be unable to distinguish between
these two projects.

Expected value and firm's investment decisions

From what we have seen (above), in deciding on risky investment projects we
cannot directly translate the wealth maximisation rule into one of expected
wealth maximisation, i.e. we cannot simply take on all available projects with a
positive expected NPV. The reason for this is that shareholders are probably all
risk-averse. The situation is complicated still further by the fact that they
probably show different degrees of risk aversion (different shaped utility curves
and levels of wealth). An investment whose risk/return profile might be acceptable to one shareholder may not be acceptable to another.

This potential lack of unanimity may seem familiar. It is, of course, analogous
to the investment decision without the borrowing/lending facility (a matter
which we discussed in Chapter 2), and it poses the same problem. How do
managers make their investment decisions when shareholders take different
attitudes to risk? As before, it is really the utility, or satisfaction of wealth, that
shareholders want maximised, but shareholders will not necessarily all

agree on what satisfies them most. Maximisation of the utility of wealth involves some consideration of the range of possible outcomes (as is evident from Fig. 6.5).

In the next section we shall look at a partial solution to management's problem.

THE EXPECTED VALUE/VARIANCE (OR MEAN /VARIANCE) CRITERION

A popular statistical measure of dispersion is the variance (or its square root, the standard deviation). The variance (σ^2) is defined as follows:

$$\sigma^2 = \sum_{i=1}^{n} p_i [x_i - E(x)]^2$$

where p_i is the probability of outcome x_i, $E(x)$ its expected value or mean, and there are n possible outcomes.

EXAMPLE

A project will yield one of three NPVs whose amount and probabilities of occurrence are as follows:

NPV £	Probability
−1000	0.2
+1000	0.5
+2000	0.3

What is the expected NPV of the project and its variance?

SOLUTION

$$
\begin{aligned}
\text{ENPV} &= (0.2 \times -1000) + (0.5 \times 1000) + (0.3 \times 2000) \\
&= \underline{\underline{£900}} \\
\sigma^2 &= 0.2(-1000 - 900)^2 + 0.5(1000 - 900)^2 + 0.3(2000 - 900)^2 \\
&= (0.2 \times 3\,610\,000) + (0.5 \times 10\,000) + (0.3 \times 1\,210\,000) \\
\sigma^2 &= \underline{\underline{1\,090\,000}} \text{ (in £}^2)
\end{aligned}
$$

The variance is a particularly useful device for our present purposes. It can be shown (Levy & Sarnat, 1988) that if we assume that the range of possible outcomes from a decision is distributed normally around the expected value, then knowledge of the expected value and the variance (or standard deviation) is all that risk-averse investors need, to enable them to select between two risky investments.

In other words, provided that the investor is risk-averse and that the dispersion of possible outcomes is normal, then selecting investments on the basis of their expected (or mean) value and variance will cause a maximisation of the investor's utility of wealth.

EXAMPLE

A risk-averse investor is faced with two competing investment projects, dispersions of both of whose possible outcomes are *normal* about their expected values. Which should the investor select?

Project	A	B
Expected value (£)	20 000	20 000
Variance (£^{2})	10 000	12 000

SOLUTION

Project A would be selected since this offers an equal expected value to Project B but with less risk. By selecting Project A, maximisation of the utility of wealth of the risk-averse investor will be promoted.

The expected value/variance criterion (EVC) may be summarised as

(a) where the expected value of Project A is equal to or greater than that of Project B, A should be preferred to B if A has a lower variance; and

(b) where the variance of Project A is equal to or smaller than that of Project B, A should be preferred to B if A has a higher expected value.

What EVC does not tell us is how to choose between two investments where both the expected value and the variance of Project A are greater than those of Project B. We shall look at how this dilemma can be addressed in the next chapter.

PARTICULAR RISKS ASSOCIATED WITH MAKING INVESTMENTS OVERSEAS

In principle, investing in a project based overseas is the same as investing in a similar one in the UK. There are several respects in which the overseas project is likely to be more risky. These include:

(a) Lack of local knowledge

There is the danger that the decision makers may have insufficient knowledge of the political and financial environment in which the investment is to be made. The obvious means of eliminating this risk is by using expert consultants to advise on factors which represent gaps in the knowledge of the managers making the decision.

(b) Foreign exchange risk

Where the investment is being made at one time and the rewards are expected to occur at another, there is the risk that the exchange rate, between the home currency and the currency in which the investment is to be made, may move in a manner adverse to the project. Where the shareholders predominantly spend their wealth in the home country, this is important. For example, a firm makes an investment overseas. At that point the project has a positive NPV. Shortly after converting the required amount of the home currency into the local currency and making the investment, the home currency strengthens against the local currency. This means that the benefits of the investment, when converted into the home currency, are now less, possibly by an amount large enough to render the project adverse, from an NPV perspective.

This is a very real and significant risk. Any overseas investor who entered a project in the UK just before 16 September 1992, the day that the UK left the

European Monetary System and devalued by about 15 per cent, may well have made an adverse investment. This means that the wealth of the shareholders of that overseas company could be less as a result of making the investment.

There are ways of avoiding the exchange rate risk. They amount, in effect, to passing this risk on to someone else. One way is to use the foreign exchange market to sell the overseas currency, expected to be derived from the project, for the home currency (i.e. convert the overseas currency into the home currency) with delivery of both currencies to take place at a future time, but at the current exchange rate. This means that outflows and inflows of the project will be converted at the same exchange rate.

A disadvantage with forward sales of currency is that if the exchange rate moves in a manner favourable to the investment, the advantage will go to the other party to the forward transaction. This can be overcome through a currency options deal. Here the investing firm can buy the right to sell the overseas currency at a particular time in the future (a put option). The rate at which the sale will be made will be specified in the option contract. It could be the rate at which the investment finance was converted. If, at the time when the overseas currency needs to be converted, the exchange rate has moved in a manner adverse to the project, the investing firm can exercise its option. Otherwise, the firm will allow the option to lapse and simply use the normal (spot) currency market to carry out the conversion.

Both of these hedging strategies remove the exchange rate risk, but they cost money. Generally future exchange rates are not as favourable as are the spot rates. Similarly, currency options sellers need to be rewarded for providing their service. Currency futures and options are examples of derivatives.

(c) Political risk Investing overseas exposes the investing firm to risks associated with the overseas country concerned. These include dangers of war, civil unrest, unexpected increases in taxes on the revenues from the project, restrictions on the extent to which the cash outflows can be remitted to the home country. These risks may be no more or even less than those to which the firm is exposed at home. The problem is that they are likely to be in addition to those which are faced at home. Clearly one way of avoiding political risk is to avoid investing in high political risk countries. There are commercial services which provide information on political risk, country by country. Another way of avoiding the risk is by passing it on to others through insurance. It is not uncommon for firms to insure their overseas investments.

SOME EVIDENCE ON RISK ANALYSIS IN PRACTICE

To gain some insight into the extent to which, and how, risk is taken into account, in practical investment decision making we shall rely on the researches of Ho and Pike (1991), whose findings are consistent with other, similar studies conducted recently. This evidence relates to a survey of 146 of the largest firms in the UK, conducted in 1987.

The evidence seems to suggest that:

(a) Formal consideration of risk is not a universal practice. Of the firms questioned 87 per cent formally considered risk in relation to their capital investment decisions. Earlier research by Pike and Woolf (1988) suggests that it is unlikely that many of the firms surveyed formally assessed risk in respect of every investment decision. It might be reasonable to suppose that among the firms who do not formally assess risk all the time, there is a greater tendency to assess it in respect of larger investment decisions.

A reason suggested for the popularity of the use of the payback method of investment appraisal (see Chapter 4) is that it provides an assessment of the riskiness of the project. Though the validity of using this method of investment appraisal as a means of dealing with risk is theoretically somewhat dubious, its widespread use by firms of all sizes may imply that consideration of risk is also widespread. It is difficult to believe that many firms completely ignore the question of risk in investment decision making, even though it may be done on an informal basis in many cases.

(b) There is an increasing tendency formally to take account of risk. As we have seen, 87 per cent of the firms surveyed by Ho and Pike in 1987 formally accounted for risk. However, Pike (1982) found (with a similar survey sample) that in 1975 there were only 26 per cent of firms which formally accounted for risk, a figure which had grown to 38 per cent by 1981.

(c) Some of the firms which formally take account of risk use more than one approach to dealing with it.

(d) There are two main approaches to assessing the riskiness of projects:
    (1) sensitivity analysis, used by 85 per cent of Ho and Pike's respondents; and
    (2) use of probabilities, used by 51 per cent.

(e) There are also two main approaches to distinguishing between projects on the basis of their riskiness:
    (1) shortening the payback period for riskier projects (used by 75 per cent);
    (2) requiring higher rates of return (presumably discount rate or IRR hurdle rate) for riskier projects (used by 77 per cent).

Both of these methods seem fairly popular among those who tackle the problem of risk in a formal way.

Conclusions on practice in risk analysis

It is perhaps surprising how small a proportion of firms formally account for risk. If we bear in mind that the evidence relates to large firms, it seems likely that little consideration of it will occur in the smaller firms.

It is not clear why the risk-adjusted rate of return has become so popular (speaking relatively, of course). Perhaps it is intuition based partly on observation that high risk seems to engender high returns.

In the next chapter we shall go on to see that the practice of requiring higher rates (discount rates) for riskier projects can be seen as a rational way of taking account of risk and of selecting investments. We shall also see that there is a theoretically correct way for management to make decisions on risky investment projects with which all the firm's shareholders will agree.

SUMMARY

Risk is ever-present in decision making as decisions only concern the future and the future is not known with certainty. Risk must formally be considered in each decision taken.

One approach to dealing with risk is to assess the decision using the best estimate for each of the data inputs and then to carry out a sensitivity analysis to test how sensitive the particular decision would be to estimation errors in each input. This approach has several defects, not least of which is the fact that having discovered how sensitive the decision is, we do not really know quite what to do about it.

Identifying the possible outcomes and ascribing probabilities to each one can be enlightening, though possibly mind-boggling, due to the large number of outcomes which a project would have in the real world. A range of possible outcomes does not really provide us with the basis of a clear decision rule.

Expected value, a weighted average of the possible outcomes, reduces the volume and gives us one figure which can form the basis for the decision. Expected value also has several problems. That firms typically, at any given moment, have a number of projects operating partially overcomes these problems. The fact that all firms and all industries are subject to an economy-wide systematic risk means that expected value remains incomplete. Expected value also fails to consider risk aversion, a phenomenon which characterises the human race.

Utility theory provides a useful means of representing personal attitudes of individuals to factors which they find desirable or undesirable. The concept of utility can be a useful one in the context of the attitude of individuals to risk. A risk-averse person is one who derives a decreasing amount of satisfaction from each additional increment of wealth.

Provided that the dispersion of possible returns is normal about the expected value, the expected value/variance criterion provides a useful decision rule for all risk-averse investors.

Overseas investments raise additional risk problems, which need to be addressed.

In practice, risk seems to be formally considered by most very large UK firms. It seems unlikely that this is the case with smaller firms. Sensitivity analysis and assessment of probabilities are fairly popular in assessing risk. Reduced payback periods and increased discount rates seem fairly popular responses to perceived risk.

FURTHER READING Risk generally is dealt with very thoroughly in a number of texts, including those by Bierman and Smidt (1988) and Levy and Sarnat (1994). The subject of probabilities is well explained by Harper (1982), who also deals with expected values. The research studies of Ho and Pike (1991) and of Pike and Wolfe (1988), both of which were cited in the chapter, are well worth reading.

REVIEW QUESTIONS

Suggested answers
to review questions
appear in Appendix 3.

6.1 What are the limitations of the results of a sensitivity analysis such as the one carried out in the example relating to Greene plc, early in the chapter?

6.2 When deducing the expected NPV of a project, you can:
(i) identify all possible outcomes (and their individual NPVs) and deduce the expected NPV from them; or
(ii) you can deduce the expected value of each of the inputs and use these to deduce the expected NPV directly.
What are the advantages and disadvantages of each of these two approaches?

6.3 What is the difference between the 'specific' and 'systematic risk' of a project? Why might it be helpful to distinguish between these two?

6.4 What does the word 'utility' mean in the context of utility theory?

6.5 What is a risk averse person? Are most of us risk averse?

6.6 What risks, additional to those risks normally borne by firms, are associated with investments in foreign countries?

PROBLEMS

Sample answers to
problems marked with
an asterisk appear in
Appendix 4.

(Note that problem questions 6.1–6.3 are basic level problems, while questions 6.4–6.6 are more advanced, and may contain some practical complications.)

6.1* Easton Ltd needs to purchase a machine to manufacture a new product. The choice lies between two machines (A and B). Each machine has an estimated life of three years with no expected scrap value.

Machine A will cost £15 000 and machine B will cost £20 000, payable immediately in each case. The total variable costs of manufacture of each unit are £1 if made on machine A, but only £0.50 if made on machine B. This is because machine B is more sophisticated and requires less labour to operate it.

The product will sell for £4 each.

The demand for the product is uncertain but is estimated at 2000 units for each year, 3000 units for each year or 5000 units for each year. (Note that whatever sales level actually occurs, that level will apply to each year.)

The sales manager has placed probabilities on the level of demand as follows:

Annual demand	Probability of occurrence
2000	0.2
3000	0.6
5000	0.2

Presume that both taxation and fixed costs will be unaffected by any decision made.

Easton Ltd's cost of capital is 6 per cent p.a.

You are required:
(a) to calculate the NPV for each of the three activity levels for each machine A and B and state your conclusion.
(b) to calculate the *expected* NPV for each machine and state your conclusion.

6.2* In Problem 6.1, assume that the 2000 level is the 'best estimate' of annual demand for Easton Ltd, and that only machine A is available.

(a) Should the firm acquire machine A on the basis of its NPV?
(b) Carry out a sensitivity analysis on the decision recommended in (a).

6.3 Plaything plc has just developed a new mechanical toy, the 'Nipper'. The development costs totalled £300 000. To assess the commercial viability of the Nipper a market survey has been undertaken at a cost of £35 000. The survey suggests that the Nipper will have a market life of four years and can be sold by Plaything plc for £20 per Nipper. Demand for the Nipper for each of the four years has been estimated as follows:

Number of Nippers	Probability of occurrence
11 000	0.3
14 000	0.6
16 000	0.1

If the decision is made to go ahead with the Nipper, production and sales will begin immediately. Production will require the use of machinery which the firm already owns, having bought it for £200 000 three years ago. If Nipper production does not go ahead the machinery will be sold for £85 000, the firm having no other use for it. If it is used in Nipper production, the machinery will be sold for an estimated £35 000 at the end of the fourth year.

Each Nipper will take two hours labour of staff who will be taken on specifically for the work at a rate of £4.00 per hour. The firm will incur an estimated £10 000 in redundancy costs relating to these employees at the end of the four years.

Materials will cost an estimated £6.00 per Nipper. Nipper production will give rise to an additional fixed cost of £15 000 p.a.

It is believed that if the firm decides not to go ahead with producing the Nipper, the rights to the product could be sold to another firm for £125 000, receivable immediately.

Plaything plc has a cost of capital of 12 per cent p.a.

On the basis of the expected net present value, should the firm go ahead with production and sales of the Nipper? (Ignore taxation and inflation.)

Assess the expected net present value approach to investment decision making.

6.4 Block plc has £6 million of cash available for investment. Four possible projects have been identified. Each involves an immediate outflow of cash and is seen as having two possible outcomes as regards the NPV. The required initial investment, possible NPVs and probabilities of each project are as follows:

Project	Initial outlay £ million	NPV £ million	Probability
A	6.0	3.0 (positive)	0.5
		1.5 (negative)	0.5
B	2.0	1.0 (positive)	0.5
		0.5 (negative)	0.5
C	2.0	1.0 (positive)	0.5
		0.5 (negative)	0.5
D	2.0	1.0 (positive)	0.5
		0.5 (negative)	0.5

The outcomes of each project are completely uncorrelated.

The firm has decided to adopt one of two strategies.

- Strategy 1   Invest all of the cash in Project A; or
- Strategy 2   Invest one-third of the cash in each of Projects B, C and D.

Deduce as much information as you can on the effective outcome of following each strategy.

Which of the two investment strategies would you recommend to the directors? Why?

What assumptions have you made about the directors and the shareholders in making your recommendation?

Would your recommendation have been different had more or less finance been involved in the decision?

6.5* Hi Fido plc, a company financed by a mixture of equity and debt capital, manufactures high fidelity sound reproduction equipment for the household market, principally in the UK. It has recently incurred £500 000 developing a new loud speaker, called the 'Tracker'.

A decision now needs to be taken as to whether to go ahead with producing and marketing Trackers. This is to be based on the expected net present value of the relevant cash flows, discounted at the company's estimate of the 1996 weighted average cost of capital of 8 per cent (after tax). The company's management believes that a three year planning horizon is appropriate for this decision, so it will be assumed that sales will not continue beyond 1999.

Manufacture of Trackers would require acquisition of some plant costing £1 million, payable on installation, on 31 December 1996. This cost would attract the normal capital allowances for plant and machinery. If the company makes the investment, it would elect for the plant to be treated as a 'non-pool' asset. [This means that, for tax purposes, the plant will be depreciated on a reducing balance basis at 25 per cent p.a., starting in the year of acquisition irrespective of the exact date of acquisition during the year. In the year of disposal, no tax depreciation is charged, but the difference between the written down value and the disposal proceeds is either given as an additional tax allowance or charged to tax depending whether the written down value exceeds the disposal proceeds or vice versa.]

For the purposes of assessing the viability of the Tracker, it will be assumed that the plant would not have any disposal value on 31 December 1999.

The first sales of Trackers would be expected to be made during the year ending 31 December 1997. There is uncertainty as to the level of sales which could be expected, so a market survey has been undertaken at a cost of £100 000.

The survey suggests that, at the company's target ex-works price of £200 per pair of Trackers, there would be a 60 per cent chance of selling 10 000 pairs and a 40 per cent chance of selling 12 000 pairs during 1997.

If the 1997 sales were to be at the lower level, 1998 sales would be either 8 000 pairs of Trackers (30 per cent chance) or 10 000 pairs (70 per cent chance). If 1997 sales were to be at the higher level, 1998 sales would be estimated at 12 000 pairs of Trackers (50 per cent chance) or 15 000 pairs (50 per cent chance).

In 1999 sales would be expected to be 50 per cent of whatever level of sales actually occur in 1998.

Sales of Trackers would be expected to have an adverse effect on sales of Repros, a less sophisticated loud speaker produced by the company, to the extent that for each two pairs of Trackers sold, one less pair of Repros would be sold. This effect would be expected to continue throughout the three years.

Materials and components would be bought in at a cost of £70 per pair of Trackers.

Manufacture of each pair of Trackers would require three hours of labour. This labour would come from staff released by the lost Repro production. To the extent that this would provide insufficient hours, staff would work overtime, paid at a premium of 50 per cent over the basic pay of £6 an hour.

The Repro has the following cost structure:

	Per pair £
Selling price (ex-works)	100
Materials	20
Labour (four hours)	24
Fixed overheads (on a labour hour basis)	33

The management team currently employed by the company would be able to manage the Tracker project, except that, should the project go ahead, four managers, who had accepted voluntary redundancy from the company, would be asked to stay on until the end of 1999. These managers were due to leave the company on 31 December 1996 and to receive lump sums of £30 000 each at that time. They were also due to receive an annual fee of £8 000 each for consultancy work, which the company would require of them from time to time. If they were to agree to stay on, they would receive an annual salary of £20 000 each, to include the consultancy fee. They would also receive lump sums of £35 000 each on 31 December 1999. It is envisaged that the managers would be able to fit any consultancy requirements round their work managing the Tracker project. These payments would all be borne by the company and would qualify for full tax relief.

Tracker production and sales would not be expected to give rise to any additional operating costs beyond those mentioned above.

Working capital to support both Tracker and Repro production and sales would be expected to run at a rate of 15 per cent of the ex-works sales value. The working capital would need to be in place by the beginning of each year concerned. There would be no tax effects of changes in the level of working capital.

The company's accounting year end is 31 December. Sales should be assumed to occur on the last day of the relevant year. The company's corporation tax rate is expected to be 33 per cent throughout the planning period.

On the basis of expected NPV, should the firm go ahead with the Tracker project?

6.6 Focus plc has several wholly-owned subsidiaries engaged in activities which are outside the firm's core business. A decision has recently been taken to concentrate exclusively on the core business and to divest itself of its other activities.

One of the non-core subsidiaries is Kane Ltd, which operated in an activity which the board of Focus believed to be in a fast declining business. Senior managers at Kane disagreed with this view of Kane's potential. It seemed likely that it would be difficult to find a buyer for the subsidiary as a going concern, and its break-up value was considered to be small. In view of these points it had been decided to retain Kane, allowing it to run down gradually over the next three years as its product demand waned. Shortly after the announcement of Focus's intentions for Kane, the Focus board was approached by some of Kane's managers with a view to looking at the possibility of an immediate management buy-out, to be achieved by the managers buying the entire share capital of Kane from Focus. The managers had taken steps to find possible financial backers and believed that they could find the necessary support and produce cash at relatively short notice. The board of Focus was asked to suggest a price for Kane as a going concern.

The Focus board was sympathetic to the Kane managers' proposal and decided to set the offer price for the buy-out at the economic value of Kane to the group, on the assumption that Kane remains a group member until its proposed close down in three years' time. The economic value would be based on the expected present value of Kane's projected cash flows, Focus's tax position and Focus's cost of capital.

Estimates of the various factors relating to Kane, assuming that it continues to be a subsidiary of Focus, have been made and these are shown in notes 1 to 8 below. All of the cash flows are expressed in terms of current (i.e. beginning of year 1) prices. The years referred to are the accounting years of Focus (and Kane).

(1) Sales for year 1 are estimated at either £6 million (60 per cent probable) or £5 million (40 per cent probable). If sales in year 1 are at the higher level, year 2 sales are estimated at either £4 million (80 per cent probable) or £3 million (20 per cent probable). If year 1 sales are at the lower level, year 2 sales are estimated at either £3 million (20 per cent probable) or £2 million (80 per cent probable). If Year 2 sales are at the £4 million level, year 3 sales are estimated at either £3 million (50 per cent probable) or £2 million (50 per cent probable). At any other level of year 2 sales, year 3 sales are estimated at £2 million (100 per cent probable).

(2) Variable costs are expected to be 25 per cent of the sales revenue.

(3) Avoidable fixed costs are estimated at £1 million p.a. This does not include depreciation.

(4) It is expected that Kane will operate throughout the relevant period with zero working capital.

(5) When the close-down occurs at the end of year 3, there will be close-down costs (including redundancy payments to certain staff) estimated at £0.5 million, payable immediately on closure. The premises will be put on the market immediately. The premises can be sold during year 4 for an estimated £2 million and the cash would be received at the end of year 4. This is not expected to give rise to any tax effect. The plant is old and would not be expected to yield any significant amount. The tax effects of the plant disposal are expected to be negligible.

(6) The corporation tax rate for Focus is expected to be 33 per cent over the relevant period. You should assume that tax will be payable twelve months after the end of the accounting year to which it relates.

(7) Focus's cost of capital is estimated for the next few years at 14 per cent p.a., in 'money' terms.

(8) The rate of inflation is expected to average about 5 per cent p.a. during the relevant period. All of Kane's cash flows are expected to increase in line with this average rate.

How much will the Kane managers be asked to pay for the firm's shares?
(NOTE: Work in 'money' terms)

Assuming that the estimates are correct, does this seem a logical price from Focus's point of view? Why?

What factors may cause the managers of Kane to place a different value on the firm? Why? What direction (higher or lower) is the difference likely to be?
NOTE: Assume that all cash flows occur at year ends.

CHAPTER 7

The pricing of securities and its relevance to real investment decisions

OBJECTIVES

In this chapter we shall deal with the following:

● the effect on risk and return of holding risky assets in portfolios

● efficient portfolios and the efficient frontier

● the risk-free rate and two-fund separation

● the relationship between the risk and expected return on individual assets

● the implications of this relationship, particularly on the discount rate which must be applied to expected cash flows to assess real investment projects through NPV

● the arbitrage pricing model

INTRODUCTION

The relevance of security prices

Most of the developed countries of the world have a market in which the owners of shares in particular local and international companies may be bought and sold. These capital markets, known typically (in English) as stock markets or stock exchanges, also provide a forum for the purchase and sale of loan stock, both of private sector companies and of governments and public utilities. Research evidence shows that in many of these markets (including the UK one), the market forces which set the prices of individual securities (shares and loan stocks) cause pricing efficiency to occur. 'Efficiency' in this context means that all available information concerning a particular security's future prospects is at all times fully and rationally reflected in the security's price. In Chapter 9 we shall take a more detailed look at the workings of the UK capital market and at the evidence for the efficiency of its pricing. At present it is sufficient that we appreciate that such a market does exist and that its pricing mechanism tends to be efficient.

In this chapter we are going to consider how securities traded in capital markets seem to be priced. We might feel that this is at most only of passing interest to us in the study of business finance since our main concern is that of firms' investment and financing decisions. That would, however, be an incorrect view of the topic, since:

(a) Financial managers are concerned with the way in which their firm's securities are priced in the free market as this might well have some impact on their financing decisions, e.g. at what price to issue new securities.

(b) Financial managers are also concerned with the relationship between how securities are priced in the capital market and firms' investment decisions. Firms make decisions concerning investment in real assets on the basis of anticipated returns and of the risk attaching to those returns. The capital market is a free market which deals in precisely those two commodities: return and risk. Thus we have a free and apparently efficient market which sets prices for return and risk. A lot of historical data is available on security prices and dividends, so we can readily observe what has happened in the past and draw conclusions on how return and risk seem to be related. In other words we can see how risk is dealt with in the pricing mechanism of a free market. This should be useful to financial managers since there seems no logical reason why they should take a different view of return and risk from that taken by investors in the capital market.

The market's pricing mechanism for securities becomes even more relevant to us when we remind ourselves that managers are seeking through their investment decisions to increase the wealth of the shareholders, partly through the firm's value on the capital market. It seems even more logical, therefore, that managers should take a similar attitude to risk and return to that of the security investors in the market.

If we can come to some sensible conclusion on the way in which risk and return are priced in the capital market, this should provide us with a very useful basis for the firm to assess real investment opportunities.

A reminder

In the last chapter we saw that diversification can reduce investment risk. We also saw that, given the assumption that possible returns are 'normally' distributed around the expected value and that investors are risk-averse, then the mean (or expected value) and the variance (or its square root, the standard deviation) are valid and practical, though sometimes incomplete, bases on which to assess and rank investment opportunities.

SECURITY INVESTMENT AND RISK

If we were to select a number of marketable securities at random, form them into portfolios of varying sizes, measure the expected returns and standard deviation of returns from each of our various-sized portfolios and then plot standard deviation against size of portfolio, we should obtain a graph similar to that in Fig. 7.1.

Before we go on to consider the implications of Fig. 7.1, just a word of explanation on its derivation. The expected returns referred to are the monthly returns of a security or a portfolio of securities. This is calculated as:

$$r_t = \frac{P_t - P_{t-1} + d_t}{P_{t-1}}$$

Where P_t is the market value of the security or portfolio at the end of month t, P_{t-1} the value at the start of the month and d_t the dividend (if any) arising from the security or portfolio during the month. The expected value of returns for a security or portfolio is based on past experience, say of returns over the past 60 months. Thus the expected value could be the average (mean) of the monthly returns for the past five years.

Fig. 7.1
The risk of various-sized, randomly selected portfolios

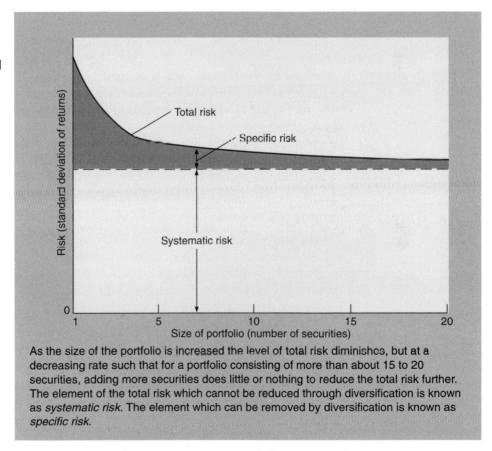

As the size of the portfolio is increased the level of total risk diminishes, but at a decreasing rate such that for a portfolio consisting of more than about 15 to 20 securities, adding more securities does little or nothing to reduce the total risk further. The element of the total risk which cannot be reduced through diversification is known as *systematic risk*. The element which can be removed by diversification is known as *specific risk*.

The various-sized portfolios are constructed randomly. Several portfolios of each size are constructed, and the standard deviation depicted in Fig. 7.1 is the average of the standard deviations of all of the portfolios for each size (see Evans and Archer, 1968).

As standard deviation of returns around the mean is a reasonable measure of risk, Fig. 7.1 suggests that large reduction in risk can be achieved merely by randomly combining securities in portfolios. This provides empirical support for the maxim 'Do not put all your eggs in one basket' which is often applied to investment in securities.

Two features might surprise adherents to the eggs and baskets maxim, however. These are:

(a) Very limited diversification yields large reductions in the level of risk. Even spreading the investment funds available into a couple of different securities successfully eliminates a large amount of risk. Each additional different security added to the portfolio yields successively less by way of risk reduction.

(b) Once the portfolio contains about 15 to 20 securities there is little to be gained by way of risk reduction from further increases in its size. There seems to be part of the risk which is impervious to attempts to reduce it through diversification.

That part of the risk which is susceptible to removal by diversification is of course specific risk; the stubborn part is systematic risk. Total risk is the sum of these two.

As we saw in the last chapter, specific (or unsystematic) risk arises from factors which are random as between one firm's securities and those of another. As these factors are random, a reasonably small amount of diversification will cause them to cancel one another.

The systematic (or portfolio) risk is concerned with economy-wide (macro-economic) factors which affect all firms.

The implications of the phenomenon represented in Fig. 7.1 are:

(a) investors should hold securities in portfolios as, by doing so, risk can be reduced at little cost; and

(b) there is limited point in diversifying into many more than 15 to 20 different securities as nearly all the benefits of diversification have been exhausted at that size of portfolio. Further diversification means that the investor will have to pay higher dealing charges to establish the portfolio and then will have more cost and/or work in managing it.

If systematic risk must be borne by investors because it is caused by economy-wide factors, it seems likely that some securities are more susceptible to these factors than are others. For example, a high street food supermarket would seem likely to suffer less than would a manufacturer of capital goods, say, as a result of economic recession.

Is the level of risk attaching to the returns from all securities the same, even though no one is forced to bear any specific risk? This question and several others relating to it will now be examined.

PORTFOLIO THEORY

If we assume both that security returns are normally distributed about their expected value and that investors are risk-averse then we can completely

Fig. 7.2
The risk/return
profiles of three
securities

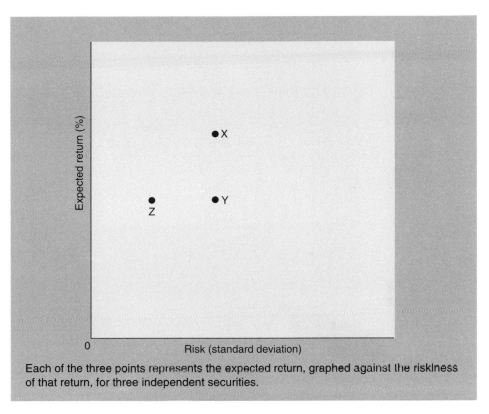

Each of the three points represents the expected return, graphed against the riskiness of that return, for three independent securities.

describe securities by their means and standard deviations and so represent them graphically, as in Fig. 7.2.

In Fig. 7.2 all investors would prefer investment X to investment Y as it has a higher expected value for the same level of risk. All risk-averse investors would prefer investment Z to investment Y as it has lower risk for the same level of expected return. Thus both X and Z are said to dominate Y. The choice between X and Z, however, depends upon the personal attitude to risk of the investor making the decision (i.e. on the shape of the particular investor's utility curve).

Points A and B in Fig. 7.3 are securities whose positions on the graph are defined by their expected values and standard deviations. B is expected to yield higher returns than A (14 per cent as against 10 per cent) but it is also expected to be more risky (standard deviation of 12 per cent as against 10 per cent). Assuming that all investors have similar expectations of these and other securities, then they would all see these securities as occupying the same position on the graph depicted in Fig. 7.3.

Suppose that we were to form a portfolio containing a proportion (α) of each of A and B. (Note that since the entire portfolio consists only of securities A and B, $\alpha_B = 1 - \alpha_A$.) The expected return from that portfolio would be:

$$r_p = \alpha_A r_A + \alpha_B r_B$$

where r_p, r_A and r_B are the expected returns from the portfolio, security A and security B respectively, i.e. the returns of the portfolio is simply the weighted

Fig. 7.3
The risk/return
profiles of two
securities, A and B

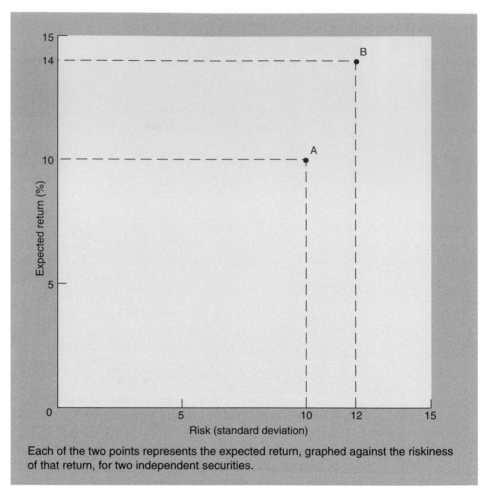

Each of the two points represents the expected return, graphed against the riskiness of that return, for two independent securities.

average of the returns of the constituent securities. The standard deviation of the portfolio would be:

$$\sigma_P = \sqrt{\alpha_A^2 \sigma_A^2 + \alpha_B^2 \sigma_B^2 + 2\alpha_A \alpha_B R \sigma_A \sigma_B}$$

where σ_P, σ_A and σ_B are respectively the standard deviation of the expected returns of the portfolio, security A and security B. R is the coefficient of correlation between the expected returns of the two securities.* If R were +1 it would mean that the expected returns would be perfectly correlated one with the other, e.g. an increase of x per cent in the returns of A would always imply a y per cent increase in the returns of B and vice versa. If R were –1 it would imply as close a relationship but a negative one, e.g. an x per cent increase in the returns of A would always mean a y per cent decrease in the returns from B. R of value

* $R = \dfrac{\text{Covariance (A, B)}}{\sigma_A \sigma_B}$

Readers who are not too confident with these statistical measures should refer to Harper (1991) or one of the other texts which cover the ground.

between −1 and +1 means less direct relationships with a value of zero meaning that there is no relationship between the returns of the two securities. (Note that there would be a separate R for any two variables. The particular value of R for A and B would be peculiar to A and B and not the same, except by coincidence, for any other two securities C and D nor even A and C.)

Table 7.1 Risk and expected returns for various portfolios of securities A and B with differing assumptions as to the correlation coefficient

Proportion of security A in portfolio %	Expected returns of portfolio (r_p) %	Standard deviation for various correlation coefficients (R)				
		−1.0 %	−0.5 %	0.0 %	+0.5 %	+1.0 %
0	14	12.0	12.0	12.0	12.0	12.0
25	13	6.5	8.0	9.3	10.5	11.5
50	12	1.0	5.6	7.8	9.5	11.0
75	11	4.5	6.5	8.1	9.4	10.5
100	10	10.0	10.0	10.0	10.0	10.0

Table 7.1 shows the expected returns and standard deviations for a selection of possible portfolios of A and B for a range of hypothetical correlation coefficients (R).

The expected return/risk profiles of each of these portfolios are mapped out in Fig. 7.4. Here we can see that the greatest risk reduction possibilities occur with negatively correlated securities. In fact there is a combination* of A and B which has no risk when the correlation coefficient is assumed to be −1. In reality such perfectly negatively correlated securities would be impossible to find. Their existence would imply that it would be possible to form portfolios possessing no risk at all, which is not likely to be the case. It is probably equally unlikely that securities whose expected returns are perfectly positively correlated exist in the real world. If they did, forming portfolios of them would do nothing to

* This is discoverable by finding the minimum value for σ_P by means of differential calculus, viz. :

$$\sigma_P^2 = \alpha_A^2 \sigma_A^2 + (1 - \alpha_A)^2 \sigma_B^2 + 2\alpha_A(1 - \alpha_A)R\sigma_A\sigma_B$$

(this is because $\alpha_B = 1 - \alpha_A$)

$$\frac{d\sigma_P^2}{d\alpha_A} = 2\alpha_A\sigma_A^2 + 2\alpha_A\sigma_B^2 - 2\sigma_B^2 + 2R\sigma_A\sigma_B - 4\alpha_A R\sigma_A\sigma_B$$

Setting this equal to zero and putting in the actual values for σ_A and σ_B and assuming $R = -1$ we get :

$$(2\alpha_A \times 100) + (2\alpha_A \times 144) - (2 \times 144) - (2 \times 10 \times 12) + (4\alpha_A \times 120) = 0$$

$$200\alpha_A + 288\alpha_A + 480\alpha_A = 288 + 240$$

$$\alpha_A = \frac{528}{968}$$

reduce risk, since the risk of the portfolio is simply a linear combination of the risks of the constituent securities. This is evidenced by the straight line connecting A and B representing the profile of expected return/risk for $R= +1$ in Fig. 7.4. In reality securities with positive, but less than perfect positive, correlation are what we tend to find. To that extent the second-from-right column of Table 7.1 is the most realistic. Here the correlation coefficient is +0.5 and combining A and B provides some reduction in the total risk but by no means total elimination of it.

Fig. 7.4
The risk/return profiles of various portfolios of securities A and B, with differing assumptions regarding the correlation coefficient

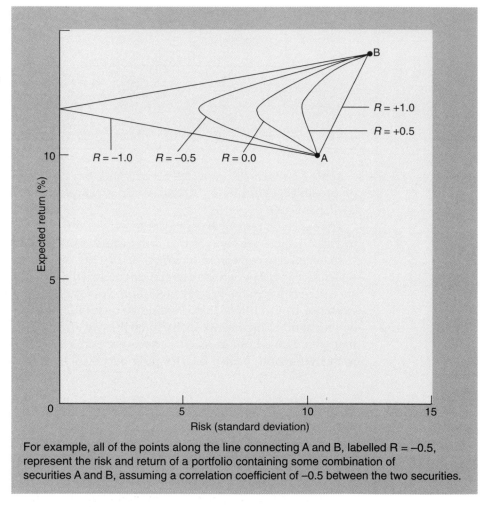

For example, all of the points along the line connecting A and B, labelled R = –0.5, represent the risk and return of a portfolio containing some combination of securities A and B, assuming a correlation coefficient of –0.5 between the two securities.

That part of the risk which reduces when A and B are combined in a portfolio is of course specific risk. As we saw from Fig. 7.1, combining two securities far from exhausts the possibilities of specific risk reduction. Introducing further securities in appropriate combinations into the portfolio would reduce the risk still further.

Figure 7.5 shows three more securities C, D, and E brought into the reckoning. The various curved lines show the expected return/risk profiles of various combinations of any two of the five securities. The line XB furthest to the top

Fig. 7.5
The risk/return
profiles of various
portfolios of
securities A, B, C,
D and E

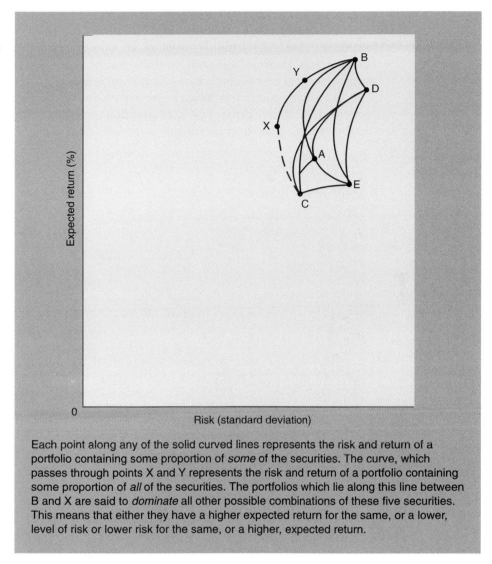

Each point along any of the solid curved lines represents the risk and return of a portfolio containing some proportion of *some* of the securities. The curve, which passes through points X and Y represents the risk and return of a portfolio containing some proportion of *all* of the securities. The portfolios which lie along this line between B and X are said to *dominate* all other possible combinations of these five securities. This means that either they have a higher expected return for the same, or a lower, level of risk or lower risk for the same, or a higher, expected return.

left of the graph shows the expected risk/return profile of a portfolio containing various proportions of each of these five securities. Note that every combination of expected return and risk along this line 'dominates' any other position in which the investor could be with these five securities. Take point X along this line, for example. No other combination available will yield higher expected return for X's level of risk, nor less risk for X's expected return. Consider the portfolio represented by point Y; although this has a higher expected return than X, it also has higher risk. Thus X does not dominate Y, nor does Y dominate X.

Efficiency

Of course these five securities do not represent the total of financial investment opportunities nor, therefore, the maximum specific risk reduction opportunities available. There is an efficient frontier for securities as a whole. This is represented in Fig. 7.6. Each point on the line EE represents some portfolio constructed from some or all of the securities available in the economy as a whole. 'Efficient' in this context means that there is no specific (unsystematic) risk present; it has all been diversified away.

None of the many portfolios represented by the efficient frontier has any specific risk; if they did, it would be possible to diversify further and get rid of it, thus pushing the frontier further to the top left.

Fig. 7.6
The efficient frontier

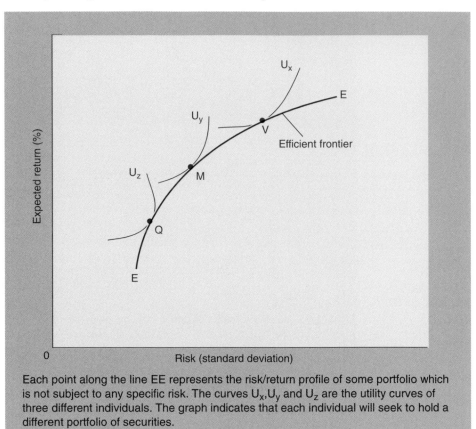

Each point along the line EE represents the risk/return profile of some portfolio which is not subject to any specific risk. The curves U_x, U_y and U_z are the utility curves of three different individuals. The graph indicates that each individual will seek to hold a different portfolio of securities.

Utility

Let us remind ourselves of what we discussed in Chapter 6 on the subject of utility. It is possible (in theory at least), in respect of any particular individual and of any two related factors, to represent that individual's preferences as regards the trade-off between the factors by a set of utility curves. If we assume both that investors are risk-averse and that they are expected utility of wealth maximisers, then they would have utility curves similar to those depicted in Fig. 7.6 (U_x, U_y and U_z).

Note that each of these utility curves (U_x, U_y and U_z) relate to different individuals all of whom are prepared to take on some risk, but require compensation in the form of increased expected returns for doing so. In each case the investors depicted require increasingly large increments in expected return for each successive increment of risk which they are prepared to accept. This is why each of these curves slopes upwards to the right.

The individual whose risk/expected return preferences are represented by U_z is rather more risk-averse than the individual represented by U_x. The latter is prepared to accept much more risk to achieve any given level of expected return than is the former. The U_x individual is still risk-averse and therefore needs increasing amounts of expected return for each additional increment of risk, but less so than the U_z individual.

Irrespective of their personal preferences, each of the investors whose attitudes are represented in Fig. 7.6 would reach the highest level of utility (satisfaction) by investing in some portfolio which lies along the efficient frontier (EE). No one would want to invest in individual securities or portfolios lying below or to the right of the efficient frontier because these all have some specific risk.

A risk-free asset

We now make another assumption which is that there is a financial market which will lend to and borrow from all investors unlimited amounts of money, at an equal, risk-free rate (r_f). This would transform the position from that shown in Fig. 7.6 to that of Fig. 7.7. Now all investors would locate on the straight line r_fS.

**Fig. 7.7
The efficient frontier with borrowing and lending**

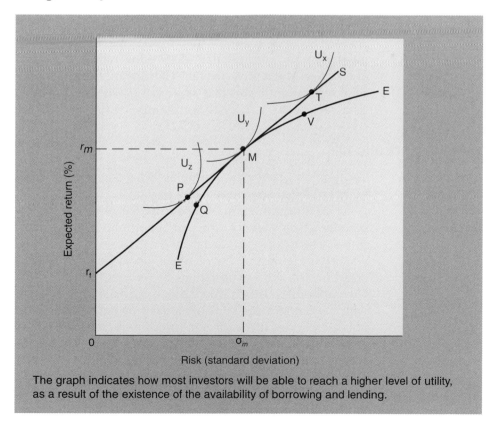

The graph indicates how most investors will be able to reach a higher level of utility, as a result of the existence of the availability of borrowing and lending.

An investor whose preferences are represented by a utility curve such as U_z in Figs 7.6 and 7.7 would choose to put some wealth into risky securities and lend the remainder at the risk-free rate. U_y is the utility curve of an investor who would invest entirely in risky securities despite the existence of the risk-free asset. This is because this person's utility curve is tangential to r_fS where r_fS itself is tangential to EE. The investor whose preferences are depicted in curve U_x (who is the least risk-averse of the three) would choose to borrow at rate r_f so that an amount even greater than that individual's wealth can be invested in risky securities.

Note that two of our investors will achieve a higher level of utility (a higher level of expected return for a given level of risk, or lower level of risk for a given level of expected return) through the existence of the risk-free borrowing/lending opportunity. Compare point P with point Q, or point T with point V in Fig. 7.7. For the third investor the position is unchanged. Only investors who happen to have preferences which cause their highest level of utility to be tangential with r_fS at M will be unaffected by the existence of the risk-free borrowing/lending opportunity. Every other investor will be better off.

Two-fund separation

The result of this is what is known as *two-fund separation*. Irrespective of the personal preferences of individuals they will all choose to invest their wealth in some combination of the portfolio M and the risk-free asset. This state of affairs is somewhat analogous to Fisher separation, which we encountered in Chapter 2. Fisher separation implies that irrespective of personal preferences as regards investment and consumption, all investors will concur about the optimum level of real investment provided that a borrowing/lending opportunity exists. Two-fund separation means that all investors will concur on the same portfolio of risky securities if a risk-free borrowing/lending opportunity exists.

What is portfolio M?

The foregoing raises the questions, 'What is this portfolio in which we all want to invest? What securities does it contain?'

Let us attack these questions from the other position. What happens to a security which does not form part of portfolio M? If we all want portfolio M, the prices of securities excluded from it will be zero. Any commodity which no one wants has a zero price (in a free market, at least). This means that there would be securities, with expectations of returns, which we can buy for nothing. Obviously this position would be too good to be true. Capital market efficiency, which we know at least broadly to exist, demands that such anomalies just could not occur in real life; such zero-priced or merely underpriced securities would offer superior returns for their risk and would enhance the portfolio M. Thus they would be bought until their price, relative to the prices of securities generally, was a reasonable one. The only logical conclusion from this is that the portfolio M strictly must contain a proportion of all securities on the market, i.e. it is the market portfolio.

More strictly still, since the capital market for securities is not a self-contained, sealed entity, the market portfolio should contain a proportion of all capital assets in existence. It is possible and often practical to sell securities and use the proceeds to buy (for instance) gold, land, a painting, some vintage wine, and thus such assets must be regarded as possible substitutes for securities and logically they must form part of the market portfolio.

Clearly, no one can hold the strict market portfolio. Most of what we know of capital market efficiency (and which we shall review in Chapter 9) suggests however that securities are priced logically one against another. To that extent they are substitutes for one another and so failure strictly to hold the market portfolio may not invalidate the principles so far established.

The capital market line

The line $r_f S$ in Fig. 7.7 is known as the capital market line (CML). The CML defines the relationship between risk and return for efficient portfolios of risky securities. Note that this line will shift up and down, closer to or further from the horizontal, as interest rates change over time.

We can see from Fig. 7.7 that the expected return available to an investor is:

$$r_f + \text{risk premium}$$

The amount of the risk premium is dependent on how much of the investment is in the portfolio of risky securities.

CAPITAL ASSET PRICING MODEL

The CML defines the risk return trade-off for efficient portfolios. What is probably of more interest and value to us is the relationship between expected return and risk for individual securities. In fact this is:

$$E(r_i) = r_f + (E(r_m) - r_f)\frac{\text{Cov}(i, M)}{\sigma_m^2}$$

where $E(r_i)$ is the expected return from i, a particular individual security, r_f is the risk-free borrowing/lending rate, $E(r_m)$ the expected return on the market portfolio, $\text{Cov}(i,M)$ the covariance of returns of security i with those of the market portfolio and σ_m^2 the variance (square of the standard deviation) of the market returns.

This statement, known as the capital asset pricing model (CAPM), can be derived directly from what is known about the CML. (The Appendix to this chapter gives the detailed derivation of CAPM.)

Note that in using CAPM to discover the expected return for any particular security i, we only use one factor which refers specifically to i. This is $\text{Cov}(i,M)$. All of the other factors ($E(r_m)$, r_f and σ_m^2) are general to all securities. The only factor which distinguishes the expected returns of one security from those of another is the extent to which the expected returns from the particular security covary with the expected returns from the market portfolio.

This ties in pretty well with what we have discovered so far about specific and systematic risk. We know that specific risk can easily be avoided; it is not therefore surprising to find that the returns which we expect to get from a particular security bear no relation to specific risk. Even though higher risk usually engenders higher expectations of returns it is entirely logical that no higher return should be expected by someone who is needlessly exposed to specific risk.

Suppose that an office block window cleaner went to his employer to demand higher wages on the grounds that by choosing not to wear the safety harness provided by the employer, the window cleaner was exposed to greater risk than the other employees who wear the harness. No doubt the employer would answer emphatically that the window cleaner was not being asked to bear this risk and that it was unnecessary to bear it, since by the simple expedient of wearing the safety harness it could be completely avoided. In effect the capital market says the same to the misguided bearer of specific risk; consequently it will not compensate that investor for bearing that risk.*

CAPM tells us that expectations of returns will be enhanced by the extent of the covariance of expected returns from the particular security with those of the market portfolio. Again this ties in with what we already know in that systematic risk, which the investor is forced to bear, relates to factors which tend to affect all securities. The greater their effect on a particular security, the greater the systematic risk, and logically, the greater the returns expected from that security. It is not surprising that covariance with the generality of securities is a measure of systematic risk.

β: a measure of risk

CAPM tells us that the capital market prices securities so that no higher returns are expected for bearing specific risk. Bearing systematic risk is expected to be rewarded by a risk premium (over the risk-free rate) of

$$(E(r_m) - r_f) \times \mathrm{Cov}(i, M)/\sigma_m^2$$

The last term is usually known as β (beta) so CAPM is typically written as $E(r_i) = r_f + (E(r_m) - r_f)\beta_i$; the greater the β which characterises a particular security, the higher are that security's expected returns.

Securities with high βs are by no means guaranteed high returns. It is in the nature of risk that nothing is guaranteed. However, before the event, high-β securities lead to expectations of higher returns than those from low-β ones.

---

* Some readers might be mystified as to how the capital market sets the returns from a particular security.

Remember that return in this context is dividend (if any) plus appreciation in value of the security over a period divided by the value of the security at the start of the period. The capital market, through the actions of buyers and sellers, sets the current market price of each security. If investors feel that 15 per cent p.a. is the appropriate level of return for the level of risk involved, the capital market will set the price of the security accordingly.

After the event, the actual return may prove to be other than 15 per cent. This difference is in the nature of risk; what is anticipated may not occur.

If the generality of investment in securities (the market portfolio) does well, then portfolios containing high-β securities will prosper – the higher the β, the more that they will prosper. On the other hand, should securities generally fare badly, high-β securities will fare particularly badly. In other words, β is a measure of volatility of returns relative to those of the market portfolio. βs above unity are regarded as high and those below unity as low. High-β securities are sometimes referred to as *aggressive* and low-β ones as *defensive*. In real life, equity shares can be found having βs of up to about 2.0; they can also be found with βs as low as around 0.4.

There is no reason of principle why some securities should not have a negative β. Systematic risk is caused by a number of macro-economic factors, such as the level of interest rates, the price of fuel, etc. Some securities are greatly affected by most of these in an adverse way (high-β securities). Other securities are little affected by those factors (low-β securities). There could be some securities which are favourably affected by these factors, at a time when the factors are adversely affecting most securities; such securities would have a negative β.

Probably most firms are adversely affected by high interest rates and high fuel prices. However, banks and fuel-producing firms, respectively, might tend to be favoured by high levels of those two factors. This does not necessarily mean that the securities of banks and fuel producers have a negative β. A security's β is related to all of the macro-economic factors affecting it. In the case of a particular security, whilst there may be one or two of these factors which have the opposite effect to the one they have on the majority of securities, most factors will have a similar effect to their effect on the majority. The bank may be favoured by high interest rates, but it is still adversely affected by high fuel costs, high labour costs, trade recession, etc. In practice, negative-β securities seem not to exist.

It should be particularly noted that βs only indicate the effect of a particular security on a well diversified portfolio. A security with a low β may be very risky, but much of its risk may be specific risk.

Figure 7.8 shows CAPM represented diagrammatically. Here risk is measured by β. The risk/return profile of all assets should lie somewhere along the line r$_f$T, which is known as the security market line (SML).

It is important to recognise the difference between the capital market line and the security market line. The CML shows expected returns plotted against risk, where risk is measured in terms of standard deviation of returns. This is appropriate because the CML represents the risk/return trade-off for efficient portfolios, i.e. the risk is all systematic risk. The SML on the other hand shows the risk/return trade-off where risk is measured by β, i.e. only by the systematic risk element of the individual security. No individual security's risk/return profile is shown by the CML because all individual securities have an element of specific risk, i.e. they are inefficient. Thus all individual securities (and indeed all inefficient portfolios) lie to the bottom-right of the efficient frontier (Fig. 7.6).

CAPM was developed by Sharpe (1963), though others independently reached similar conclusions.

Fig. 7.8
The graphical
representation
of CAPM – the
security market
line

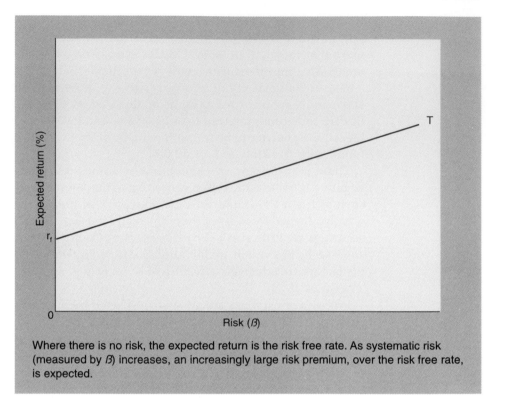

Where there is no risk, the expected return is the risk free rate. As systematic risk (measured by β) increases, an increasingly large risk premium, over the risk free rate, is expected.

CAPM: AN EXAMPLE OF BETA ESTIMATION

EXAMPLE

The year end level of a representative Stock Exchange index and of the price of an ordinary share of Ace plc were as follows:

Year	Index	Ace plc (£)
1987	218	1.09
1988	230	1.20
1989	248	1.33
1990	250	1.40
1991	282	1.80
1992	297	1.99
1993	288	1.81
1994	290	1.98
1995	320	2.25
1996	356	2.55
1997	371	2.80

You are required on the basis of the above to calculate β. (Ignore dividends throughout.)

SOLUTION

Estimation of market factors

Year (1)	Index (2)	Return (3)	Return deviation (4)	Return variance (5)
	p_{mt}	$r_{mt} = \dfrac{p_{mt} - p_{mt-1}}{p_{mt-1}}$	$r_{mt} - \bar{r}_m$	$(r_{mt} - \bar{r}_m)^2$
1987	218			
1988	230	0.055	(0.001)	0.0000
1989	248	0.078	0.022	0.0005
1990	250	0.008	(0.048)	0.0023
1991	282	0.128	0.072	0.0052
1992	297	0.053	(0.003)	0.0000
1993	288	(0.030)	(0.086)	0.0074
1994	290	0.007	(0.049)	0.0024
1995	320	0.103	0.047	0.0022
1996	356	0.113	0.057	0.0032
1997	371	0.042	(0.014)	0.0002
		0.557		0.0234

$$\bar{r}_m = \frac{0.557}{10} = 0.056, \ \text{var} \ r_m = \frac{0.0234}{9} = 0.0026$$

(Note that to find the var r_m we divide by 9 as there are 10 readings but one *degree of freedom* has been lost in the calculation of the mean.)

Estimation of β of Ace plc

Year (1)	Share price (2)	Return (3)	Return deviation (4)	Covariance with market (5)
	$£ p_{it}$	$\dfrac{p_{it} - p_{it-1}}{p_{it-1}}$	$r_{it} - \bar{r}_{it}$	$(r_{it} - \bar{r}_{it})(r_{mt} - \bar{r}_{mt})$
1987	1.09			
1988	1.20	0.101	(0.002)	0.0000
1989	1.33	0.108	0.005	0.0001
1990	1.40	0.053	(0.050)	0.0024
1991	1.80	0.286	0.183	0.0132
1992	1.99	0.106	0.003	(0.0000)
1993	1.81	(0.090)	(0.193)	0.0166
1994	1.98	0.094	(0.009)	0.0004
1995	2.25	0.136	0.033	0.0016
1996	2.55	0.133	0.030	0.0017
1997	2.80	0.098	(0.005)	0.0001
		1.025		0.0361

$$\bar{r}_i = \frac{1.025}{10} = 0.103, \ \text{Cov}(i, M) = \frac{0.0361}{9} = 0.0040$$

(Here again we divide by 9 to find the covariance, since one degree of freedom has been lost in the calculation of r_{it} and r_{mt}. If the reader is confused by this, reference should be made to a statistics text such as Harper, 1991).

$$\text{Since } \beta_i = \frac{\text{Cov}(i, M)}{\text{Var } r_m}$$

$$\text{Then } \beta_{Ace} = \frac{0.0040}{0.0026} = 1.54$$

Thus Ace plc equity has a fairly high β.

The explanation of the calculation of the market factors shown on p. 175 is as follows:

- p_{mt} is the value for the index used as a surrogate for the market and is shown in column (2).
- r_{mt} is the return for the year on the market. It is calculated as the gain during the year, i.e. the end of year value (p_{mt}) less the start of year value (p_{mt-1}) divided by the start of the year value (p_{mt-1}). For example the return during 1990 was the increase in the index from 1989 to 1990 (i.e. 12) divided by the value at the start of 1990 (i.e. 218).
- r_m is the mean of the annual returns, i.e. the sum of them divided by the number of returns (i.e. 10).
- Column (4) is deduced by deducting the mean annual return (0.056) from each year's return (column (3)).
- Column (5) is column (4) squared.

The figures in the table relating to Ace plc are similarly derived.

ASSUMPTIONS OF CAPM

In developing CAPM several assumptions need to be made. These are:

(a) investors are risk-averse, and maximise expected utility of wealth;

(b) the capital market is not dominated by any individual investors;

(c) investors are only interested in two features of a security, its expected returns and its variance (or standard deviation);

(d) the existence of a risk-free rate at which all investors may borrow or lend without limit at the same rate;

(e) the absence of dealing charges, taxes, and other imperfections;

(f) all investors have identical perceptions of each security.

Let us briefly consider these in terms of their validity: (a) seems to be true; certainly most people seem to prefer more wealth to less (all things being equal) and most of us are risk-averse. (b) also is broadly true, with investors, even the large ones, not usually dominating the market in any one security. There has been much discussion of the validity of the *mean variance* criterion in the literature (e.g. Levy and Sarnat, 1988) and it seems that in the context of security returns, assumption (c) is probably not too far-fetched. Fama (1972) discusses evidence which suggests that while security returns are not strictly 'normal' in their distribution, they are roughly so.

Clearly (d), (e) and (f) are invalid. Whether or not their invalidity seriously weakens the model is probably only discernible by looking at how well CAPM works in practice.

TESTS OF CAPM

For most of us, certainly for most financial managers, the only important feature of a theoretical derivation like CAPM is how well it explains, and more particularly how well it predicts, real events.

β as an explainer of past events

CAPM has been subjected to a large number of empirical tests. Most of these have sought to calculate the β for a security by regressing the monthly returns (capital gain plus dividend expressed as a fraction of the security price at the beginning of the month) against returns from the *market portfolio*. Since the market portfolio is strictly unobservable (it contains some of every possible capital investment), a surrogate is used. Typically this is some representative capital market index (in the UK the 'Financial Times Actuaries Index' is sometimes used for this purpose). βs tend to be calculated on the basis of monthly returns over fairly protracted periods such as five years (60 months). The tests have then gone on to assess whether or not CAPM explains the returns for securities over the period observed.

Until recently it was possible to say that the various tests had broadly supported CAPM. Doubts had been expressed about the validity of using short-term bills of stable governments, like that of the UK and USA, as a risk-free rate, since it did not really fit with the evidence. Researchers found, however, β to be a valid and fairly complete measure of risk. Despite the fact that CAPM deals with expected returns (which are impossible to test) and tests had, of necessity, dealt with actual past events, it was concluded that CAPM was broadly valid as a useful explainer of what happened.

Recently, however, evidence has emerged which calls the validity of CAPM into question. Fama and French (1992) carried out a major study of US stocks covering the period 1962 to 1989. They found that β is not a useful explainer of investment returns. They found a correlation between β and returns, but they discovered that this was due to a correlation of both β and returns with other factors, such as the size of the firm whose shares were being considered. Thus, for example, they found a clear link between firm size and investment returns. The shares of large firms tend to give lower returns than those of smaller firms. Fama and French concluded that once they allowed for the effect of firm size and other such factors, the relationship between β and returns was, at best, weak.

It is probably too soon after publication of this research to conclude that CAPM is invalid. Indeed, Ross, Westerfield and Jaffe (1996) make a number of points which call the Fama and French conclusion into question. Other studies may cast more light on the subject. Meanwhile CAPM retains a fair degree of practical credibility.

β as a predictor of future events

An important issue, as regards the usefulness of CAPM to financial managers, concerns how well the β of a particular security calculated from past data predicts that security's β for a future period – in other words, how stable are βs over time.

The evidence suggests that βs of individual securities calculated over one time period are not very good predictors of the β for those individual securities over the following and subsequent periods. On the other hand, where securities are combined into portfolios, the β of the portfolio for one period seems a reasonable predictor of that portfolio's β during the next period. (Incidentally, the β of a portfolio is the weighted average of the βs of the constituent securities, i.e.

$$\beta_P = \sum_{i=1}^{n} \alpha_i \beta_i$$

where security i represents proportion α_i, by market value, of the portfolio.)

The stability of portfolio βs is particularly of interest to financial managers when it is considered that the portfolios concerned could be made up entirely of ordinary shares of firms in some particular industry. That is to say, there is a characteristic β for each industry which remains fairly stable over time.

Why should it be the case that βs of individual securities are not very stable, whilst those for a portfolio tend to be? There are perhaps two reasons for this:

(a) Measurement errors – the β calculated for a security may well not be the 'true' β for that security due to errors in estimating the β including, for example, using a capital market index as a surrogate for the market portfolio; and

(b) Actual changes in the security's risk profile over time – there is absolutely no reason why the capital market's perceptions of a security should remain constant when the firm concerned may, for example, be changing its real investment patterns. As we shall see in Chapter 11, the extent to which the particular firm is reliant on long-term borrowings also affects its securities' β, so changes in the extent of this reliance over time will tend to make the β look unstable.

Each of these factors will probably tend to be fairly random in nature (from one security to another), so that combining securities in portfolios would tend to give a more stable picture.

IMPLICATIONS OF CAPM

For security investors

These seem to be that:

(a) Investors should diversify sufficiently to eliminate most of the specific risk from their portfolios. There seem to be no rewards for bearing specific risk.

(b) They should decide whether they wish to invest in high-risk $(\beta > 1)$, medium-risk $(\beta \approx 1)$ or low-risk $(\beta < 1)$ securities. There is a list of βs of the leading Stock Exchange quoted equities published regularly by the London Business School which subscribers may use to help them to construct portfolios, reflecting their personal risk/return preferences. The published βs are updated quarterly and are believed to be derived from comparing monthly returns of the immediately preceding five years with those of a representative Stock Exchange index, acting as a surrogate for the market portfolio. (Several commercial organisations in the USA offer a similar service in relation to US securities.)

Whilst the evidence on capital market efficiency indicates that it is impossible to spot winners systematically, this does not mean that one firm's securities are much the same as those of another. The evidence on CAPM suggests that it is possible to distinguish between those securities which will perform better than average if the market does well – and worse if the market does badly – on the one hand, and less volatile, less risky securities on the other. Thus investors are able to select the level of risk which suits their situation and personality and to expect returns commensurate with that risk level.

The instability of βs for individual securities is probably not too significant here since investors are well advised to hold portfolios in any case.

For financial managers in deriving the discount rate for real investment projects

At this point it might be useful to ask ourselves how firms should select the rate at which to discount the expected cash flows of prospective real investment projects, in order to discover their NPVs.

In our discussion of shareholder wealth maximisation in Chapter 2, we introduced the idea that the appropriate discount rate is the borrowing/lending interest rate. In the real world such an approach is not tenable because the comparable alternative to real investment is not risk-free lending. The opportunity with which the project under consideration must logically be compared is one of equal risk to that project.

Let us remind ourselves of three factors which bear on the discount rate decision.

(a) The value of a firm is the sum of the NPVs of all of the projects which it currently has in operation, so that undertaking a new project with a positive

NPV should increase the value of the firm by the amount of the positive NPV (*see* Chapter 4).

(b) Capital market efficiency research suggests that events of economic significance occurring within the firm reflect in the firm's share price so that taking on projects with positive NPVs should actually increase the market value of the firm's securities (*see* Chapter 9).

(c) CAPM tells us that expected return is directly proportional to the level of risk for each individual investment. Furthermore, the only part of risk which matters (assuming investors hold efficient portfolios) is systematic risk (measured by β).

Between them, these three lead to the assertion that the logical discount rate for an individual real (and inevitably risky) investment project should be derived from CAPM. The β value to be used would reflect the covariance of expected returns from the project with those from the generality of risky investments (the 'market' portfolio).

After all, the capital market is one where the commodities traded are risk and expected return, and to use a market-derived price of risk (which is what CAPM does) seems a reasonable way of pricing individual real investments. This is particularly logical where shareholder wealth maximisation is the firm's goal.

Whether it is very practical actually to seek to assess βs of individual real investment projects is less certain. It is difficult enough trying to estimate the cash flows, without trying to assess the degree of covariance these might have with the market portfolio.

A more practical approach probably is to try to use characteristic (average) βs for the industry in which the real investment is to be made, to derive the discount rate for the project. This might, at first sight, appear to be too much of a broad brush approach in that there are risks attaching to any particular project which may not apply to the area of activity more generally. A brief reflection, however, will reveal that the non-general factors relate, of course, to specific risk which the individual investor can diversify away.

For example, a firm, most of whose real investments are in newspaper publishing, intends to make a real investment in the manufacture of kitchen furniture. To derive the appropriate discount rate for the project it should use the average β of firms which are completely engaged in the same activity. By doing so the discount rate would reflect the capital market's perceptions of the systematic risk attaching to kitchen furniture manufacture.

Since the firm is seeking to enhance its shareholders' wealth, presumably, mainly through the market value of the shares, the perceptions of the market are all-important.

We should note that by advocating a capital market derived discount rate, we are saying that we should use an opportunity cost discount rate in the same way as the cash flows to be discounted are the opportunity cash flows. This is true since an investment alternative of equal systematic risk to the real investment under consideration is buying shares of another firm of equal β to that of the project. Thus we should only be prepared to make the real investment where we expect a positive NPV when expected cash flows are discounted at the expected rate of return from the security investment alternative.

LACK OF SHAREHOLDER UNANIMITY ON RISKY INVESTMENT

In the last chapter we identified a problem facing firms' managements in respect of selecting risky investment projects. The problem is that individual shareholders may not all see a particular risky project in the same light; while a project may increase the utility of one shareholder, it may reduce that of another. This simply reflects different levels of risk aversion among shareholders.

Theoretically, discounting the expected cash flows (Σ[possible cash flows $\times$ each one's probability of occurrence]) using a discount rate derived from CAPM will overcome this problem. All shareholders, irrespective of their individual attitude to risk (provided that they are risk-averse), will be unanimous that projects having a positive NPV when expected cash flows are discounted at a CAPM-derived rate will increase their utility of wealth, and therefore should be undertaken. Note that this theoretical unanimity depends on the assumption that all shareholders hold the shares of the firm under consideration, as part of a well diversified portfolio.

USING CAPM TO DERIVE DISCOUNT RATES FOR REAL INVESTMENTS – THE PRACTICAL PROBLEMS

There are three factors which need to be estimated for the future in order that the logic of using CAPM to derive the discount rate can be carried into practice. We shall now take a look at each in turn to try to assess the difficulty of arriving at reasonable estimates for them. Really what we shall need to ask ourselves is whether the past is likely to be a useful guide to the future in respect of each of them and if it seems that it is not, what, if anything, can we use as an alternative?

The risk measure (β)

This is perhaps the least problematical of the three factors in that the average βs for ordinary shares of firms in particular industries do seem to be reasonably stable over time. It certainly seems that the β of a portfolio, calculated over a five-year period, is a fairly good predictor of the β of that same portfolio over the subsequent five years, although Gregory-Allen, Impson and Kavafiath (1994) have cast doubt on this.

In practical terms, a reasonable approach seems to be to estimate, or better still, to use some commercial β service's estimate of the βs for several firms whose principal activity is similar to that in which the particular real investment under consideration lies. These individual βs should then be averaged.

The risk-free rate (r_f)

Here we should need to identify a risk-free asset and to make some estimation of its likely future value. Whilst there is strictly no such thing as a risk-free asset, short-dated UK Government bills probably are as safe an asset as we can find in the real world. The historical interest rates on these is readily accessible to us. Our problem remains one of estimating likely future rates. Fortunately Government bill rates are fairly stable from year to year and seem to be predicted with a fair degree of accuracy by the leading economic forecasters.

The expected return on the market portfolio ($E(r_m)$)

This is something of a problem area. This factor tends to be pretty volatile from year to year and difficult to forecast accurately. We could use an average of returns for the immediate past periods as a surrogate for future expectations but, as was shown by Ibbotson and Sinquefield (1979) on the basis of US data, vastly differing results could be obtained depending on which starting point is selected, e.g. annual rates of 6.5 per cent in the period 1960–78, 4.5 per cent for 1970–78 and 0.9 per cent for 1973–78.

Dimson (1996) cites evidence that the average excess of equity returns over that from treasury bills (the risk premium) was between 8 and 9 per cent p.a. in the UK during the period 1918 to 1994. Interestingly the figures for the US are very similar.

Probably the best approach to the problem of estimating the risk premium for the market is to base it on this long term average of 8 to 9 per cent p.a.

CAPM and tax

The point emerged clearly in Chapter 5, that, in practice, we should predict after-corporation tax cash flows and discount them at an after-corporation tax cost of capital. This raises the crucial question, in the context of using CAPM to derive the discount rate: is the CAPM derived rate before corporation tax or after corporation tax? The answer is that, as it is normally derived, it is after tax. This is because the expected return on the market portfolio $E(r_m)$, which is directly used in CAPM, is an after-corporation tax return. Returns on individual securities, and on portfolios of securities, are calculated using dividends (which are paid out of post-corporation tax income) and capital gains (which are based on future expectations of dividends). Thus the $E(r_m)$ is a post-corporation tax rate. It is essential that the risk-free rate (r_f) is also expressed in after-corporation tax terms.

CAPM and real life

Nothing that we have discussed so far in this chapter should lead us to the conclusion that CAPM is a perfect description of the real relationship between risk and return in the context of marketable securities. Tests of CAPM have found some inconsistency between fact and theory which seems unlikely completely, if at all, to be accounted for by inadequacies in the testing methods.

At the same time the logic of the derivation of CAPM and the reasonableness of the major assumptions on which that derivation is based, plus the general tendency of the evidence to support it, strongly suggest that its basic tenets are justified. It does seem reasonable for us to believe that risk is divided into that which is specific and susceptible to elimination, and that which is systematic and unavoidable. Furthermore, there does seem to be a clear relationship between risk as measured by β and return.

Even if CAPM is less than perfect, its broad approach seems well worth taking into account.

When we come to consider how useful CAPM can be to us in the real investment appraisal context, it is then that our problems arise. As we have just seen, reliably estimating the three factors to plug into the model to obtain the expected return from an asset is rather difficult. This seems particularly problematical with the expected return on the market portfolio, or at least its proxy, a representative market index.

This probably means that CAPM is severely limited in its operational usefulness to financial managers when they are making real investment decisions. It is not easy to use it in practice to derive the discount rate. However, what is the alternative? If we are not to use CAPM, warts and all, what are we to do? The answer must be to make some guess at a discount rate, a guess based on no particular logic. In the face of this situation an approach which is logical, even if problematical, must be preferable.

ARBITRAGE PRICING MODEL

The fact that tests of CAPM have shown β not to be a perfect explanation of the relationship between the level of risk and the expected risk premium, caused researchers to look at other approaches. One such approach led to the development of the Arbitrage Pricing Model (APM). The logic of this model is that there is not a unique explanation of the risk/risk premium relationship, as is suggested by CAPM, but a number of them. The APM, which was developed by Ross (1976), holds that there are four factors which explain the risk/risk premium relationship of a particular security.

Basically, CAPM says that:

$$E(r_i) = r_f + \lambda \beta_i$$

where λ is the average risk premium $(E(r_m) - r_f)$.

However, APM holds that:

$$E(r_i) = r_f + \lambda_1 \beta_{i1} + \lambda_2 \beta_{i2} + \lambda_3 \beta_{i3} + \lambda_4 \beta_{i4}$$

where $\lambda_1, \lambda_2, \lambda_3$ and λ_4 are the average risk premiums for each of the four factors in the model and $\beta_{i1}, \beta_{i2}, \beta_{i3}$ and β_{i4} are measures of the sensitivity of the particular security i to each of the four factors.

The four factors in the APM relate to future macroeconomic factors, including industrial output and levels of inflation.

Tests conducted on APM appear to show it superior to CAPM as an explainer of historical security returns. However, because it contains four factors, rather than one, its practical usefulness in deriving a discount rate to be applied in NPV analyses is even more questionable than is that of CAPM.

DIVERSIFICATION WITHIN THE FIRM

CAPM and the principles from which it is derived tell us that specific risk may be eliminated by the investor holding securities in efficient portfolios. The same is true of APM. Evidence suggests that investors typically hold fairly well diversified portfolios.

As the typical individual or institutional investor in securities is diversified (not too exposed to specific risk), there seems no advantage to the shareholder in firms diversifying their own real investments across industries. Indeed it has been argued that firms should take on real investments which they know best how to manage (i.e. within their own area of expertise) and leave the diversification to their shareholders.

The fact that firms diversified across industries are very common may arise for one or both of two reasons.

(a) Managers are unfamiliar with the principles of modern portfolio theory and believe that the interests of shareholders are best served by inter-industry diversification.

(b) Managers are, not unnaturally, concerned with how risk affects themselves. Whereas shareholders tend to hold securities in portfolios this is not very practical for managers as regards their employments. They usually only have one employment at a time and are thus exposed to both the specific and the systematic risks of their firms. To individual shareholders the demise of the firm will be unfortunate but not fatal, to the extent that they each hold only perhaps 5 per cent of their wealth in that firm. To managers the failure of their employer firm will probably be something of a disaster, to the extent of loss of employment.

This second point identifies a possible area of conflict between the best interests of the shareholders and those of the managers.

SUMMARY

Risks associated with investment in marketable securities consist of two types, specific risk and systematic risk. Most of the specific risk can be diversified away by holding diversified portfolios. Relatively little random diversification will eliminate nearly all specific risk, leaving a rump of systematic risk which is impervious to diversification.

Systematic risk affects securities differentially and the extent of particular securities' risk depends on the level of covariance with risky investments generally.

By making several simplifying assumptions it can be shown that all investors will choose to hold exactly the same portfolio of risky assets in conjunction with borrowing or lending at a risk-free rate. From this it is possible to derive a model relating expected returns to the level of systematic risk for individual securities. The capital asset pricing model, which is fairly robust to empirical testing, asserts that the expected returns from an asset are directly proportional to the level of covariance between those expected returns and those from a market portfolio. CAPM provides some insights into the risk/return *trade-off* relating to investment in risky assets, including real investment by firms. CAPM therefore provides a basis for the derivation of the appropriate discount rate to apply to the expected cash flows when assessing the potential NPV of real investment opportunities, though applying it in real life has its practical problems.

The arbitrage pricing model also shows insights on the risk/return relationship and has generally shown greater robustness to empirical testing than has CAPM. APM poses even greater problems than CAPM in the derivation of investment project discount rates.

FURTHER READING Levy and Sarnat (1988) give a clear explanation of the derivation of CAPM and its implications for real investment appraisal. This is also clearly covered by Sharpe (1995). Puxty and Dodds (1991) are also worth reading on the derivation of CAPM and empirical tests of the model. Copeland and Weston (1988) give a rigorous coverage of CAPM and APM and discuss empirical tests of them. For an interesting and fairly detailed account of how one firm (Bowater–Scott Corporation Ltd) used CAPM to derive a discount rate, see Sizer and Coulthurst (1984).

REVIEW QUESTIONS

Suggested answers to review questions appear in Appendix 3.

7.1 'Modern portfolio theory' tends to define risky investments in terms of just two factors – expected returns and variance (or standard deviation) of those expected returns.

What assumptions needs to be made about investors and the expected investment returns (one assumption in each case) to justify this 'two factor' approach?

Are these assumptions justified in real life?

7.2 'The expected return from a portfolio of securities is the average of the expected returns of the individual securities which make up the portfolio, weighted by the value of the securities in the portfolio.'

'The expected standard deviation of returns from a portfolio of securities is the average of the standard deviations of returns of the individual securities which make up the portfolio, weighted by the value of the securities in the portfolio.'

Are these statements correct?

7.3 What can be said about the portfolio which is represented by any point along the efficient frontier of risky investment portfolios?

7.4 What is meant by 'two fund separation'?

7.5 'The capital asset pricing model tells us that a security with a β of 2 will be expected to yield a return twice that of a security whose β is 1.'
Is this statement true?

7.6 What justification can there be for using the rate of return derived from capital (stock) market returns as the discount rate to be applied in the appraisal of a real investment project within a firm?

PROBLEMS

Sample answers to problems marked with an asterisk appear in Appendix 4.

(Note that problem questions 7.1–7.3 are basic level problems, while question 7.4 is more advanced, and may contain some practical complications.)

7.1* What sort of factors relating to a firm specialising in operating ferries crossing the English Channel would tend to give rise to:

(a) specific risk; and
(b) systematic risk?

7.2 You have overheard the following statement:

'If an investor holds shares in about 20 different firms all of the risk is eliminated and the portfolio will give a return equal to the risk free rate.'

Is this statement correct? Explain.

7.3 You have overheard the following statement:

'According to modern portfolio theory, shares are priced on the basis of their systematic riskiness. This means, therefore, that a piece of bad news relating only to a particular firm will not affect the market price of the shares in that firm.'

Is this statement correct? Explain.

7.4* The following are the annual returns for the ordinary shares of Court plc and for a representative equity price index:

		Court plc	Index
		%	%
Year	1	19	13
	2	(8)	(7)
	3	(12)	(13)
	4	3	4
	5	8	8
	6	17	10
	7	14	15
	8	14	16
	9	14	16
	10	1	(2)

(The bracketed figures are negative returns.)

(a) *What is the β for Court plc's ordinary shares?*
(b) *If the risk-free rate is 6 per cent p.a., what would be the expected return on Court plc's ordinary shares if the expected return for equities generally was 12 per cent p.a.?*

APPENDIX – DERIVATION OF CAPM

Fig. 7.9
The relationship of an individual security *i* with the market portfolio M and the capital market line

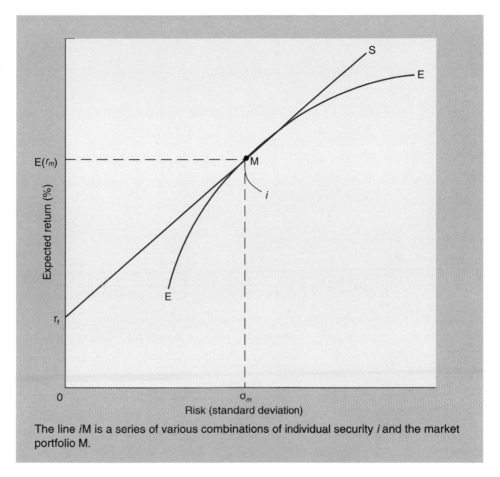

The line *i*M is a series of various combinations of individual security *i* and the market portfolio M.

In Fig. 7.9:

(a) EE is the *efficient frontier* of risky assets.

(b) r_f is the risk-free rate.

(c) r_fS is the efficient frontier of possibilities once the risk-free asset is introduced.

(d) *i*M is the risk return profile of various portfolios containing proportions of an individual *inefficient* asset *i* and the *market* portfolio M.

Let α be the proportion of *i* in the portfolio (p) of *i* and M. Then,

$$E(r_p) = \alpha\, E(r_i) + (1 - \alpha)E(r_m) \tag{1}$$

and

$$\sigma_p = \sqrt{(\alpha^2 \sigma_i^2 + (1 - \alpha)^2 \sigma_m^2 + 2\alpha(1 - \alpha)\mathrm{Cov}(i, M))} \tag{2}$$

The slope of iM at any point is given by

$$\frac{dE(r_p)}{d\sigma_p}, \text{ which equals } \frac{dE(r_p)}{d\alpha} \times \frac{d\alpha}{d\sigma_p}$$

$$\frac{dE(r_p)}{d\alpha} = E(r_i) - E(r_m)$$

If we let x = the expression within the square root sign in equation (2), then

$$\frac{d\sigma_p}{d\alpha} = \frac{dx}{d\alpha} \times \frac{d\sigma_p}{dx}$$

and $\qquad \sigma_p = x^{1/2}$

$$\frac{d\sigma_p}{dx} = \tfrac{1}{2} x^{-1/2}$$

or $\qquad \tfrac{1}{2} \times \dfrac{1}{\sqrt{[\alpha^2 \sigma_i^2 + (1-\alpha)^2 \sigma_m^2 + 2\alpha(1-\alpha)\text{Cov}(i, M)]}}$

$$\frac{dx}{d\alpha} = 2\alpha\sigma_i^2 + 2\alpha\sigma_m^2 - 2\sigma_m + 2\text{Cov}(i, M) - 4\alpha\text{Cov}(i, M)$$

so $\qquad \dfrac{dE(r_p)}{d\sigma_p} = [E(r_i) - E(r_m)]$

$$\times \frac{2\sqrt{[\alpha^2 \sigma_i^2 + (1-\alpha)^2 \sigma_m^2 + 2\alpha(1-\alpha)\text{Cov}(i, M)]}}{2\alpha\sigma_i^2 + 2\alpha\sigma_m^2 - 2\sigma_m^2 + 2\text{Cov}(i, M) - 4\alpha\text{Cov}(i, M)}$$

If the market is in equilibrium, then M will already contain the appropriate proportion of i and so the portfolio of i and M will contain no excess i. Thus the only point on iM which would be expected to occur will be M, i.e. the point where $\alpha = 0$.

When $\alpha = 0$, $\dfrac{dE(r_p)}{d\sigma_p}$ (above) reduces to :

$$(E(r_i) - (E(r_m)) \times \frac{\sigma_m}{\text{Cov}(i, M) - \sigma_m^2} \qquad (3)$$

At M the cord iM is tangential to (has the same slope as) the capital market line $r_f S$.

The slope of $r_f S$ is $\dfrac{E(r_m) - r_f}{\sigma_m}$

Equating this with (3) above and simplifying gives

$$F(r_i) = r_i + (F(r_{iii}) - r_i)\frac{Cov(i, M)}{\sigma_m^2}$$

or $\quad E(r_i) = r_f + (E(r_m) - r_f)\beta \text{ where } \beta = \dfrac{Cov(i, M)}{\sigma_m^2}$

This is the CAPM which says, in effect, that the expected return from a risky asset depends on the risk-free rate of interest, the expected returns from the market portfolio and the degree of correlation between the risky asset's returns and those of the market portfolio.

PART 3

Financing decisions

Investment requires finance and there are many sources available. This part of the book considers how decisions are made on the most appropriate sources to finance particular investments. Chapter 8 reviews the principal sources of finance and their particular features. The role and effectiveness of the market for finance is discussed in Chapter 9. The theory that share prices always reflect the economic reality is examined in some detail. In Chapter 10, assessing the cost of finance is examined. The relationship between the investment and the financing decision is also considered. Chapter 11 is concerned with the extent to which it is likely to be beneficial for firms to borrow funds as an alternative to raising them from shareholders. Raising funds from shareholders can be done in broadly two possible ways. These are 'ploughing back' past profits, instead of paying them to shareholders as dividends, and raising fresh money from shareholders by asking them to buy new shares. Chapter 12 considers which of these two approaches, if either, is likely to be the most appropriate.

CHAPTER 8

Sources of long-term finance

OBJECTIVES

In this chapter we shall deal with the following:

- the major issues to consider in respect of each type of financing
- equity financing
- methods of raising equity finance
- preference shares
- loan stocks and debentures
- convertible loan stocks
- warrants
- term loans
- the use of financial leasing
- financial grants from public funds and their importance
- the attitude that firms should take to deciding on their financing method

INTRODUCTION

In previous chapters we have seen that firms raise their long-term finance either from equity shareholders or from borrowings. Within each type of financing (equity or borrowing) are several sub-types. In fact one fairly important financing method (convertible loan stock) has elements of both equity and borrowing.

In this chapter we shall consider the various sub-types. Given the financial objective of maximisation of shareholders' wealth we shall consider each of them in the context of how they will affect the interests of existing equity shareholders. We shall also try to assess their attractions to potential investors.

The primary capital market

We shall in fact be considering the capital market in its primary function, as a market for *new* capital. The primary capital market does not reside in a single location. It is a somewhat nebulous market; in fact any point of contact between a supplier and a user of capital is part of the primary capital market. In the UK this includes the International Stock Exchange of the UK and the Republic of Ireland which, as well as its more familiar role as probably the most important part of the secondary market, is also a very important sector of the primary market. However, the primary market also includes a large number of other institutions and organisations.

An important financial source in the modern UK is grants given by the government and the European Union. We shall therefore be considering these in broad terms.

The factors

From the point of view of the firm and its existing shareholders there are several important factors relating to any particular source of new finance. These include:

(a) the administrative and legal costs of actually raising the finance;
(b) the cost of servicing the finance, e.g. interest payments;
(c) the level of obligation to make interest or similar payments;
(d) the level of obligation to repay the finance;
(e) the tax deductibility of costs related to the finance;
(f) the effect of the new finance on the level of control of the firm by its existing shareholders and on their freedom of action.

To the supplier of new finance to the firm the following are likely to be important factors:

(a) the level of return which is expected by investors;
(b) the level of risk attaching to the expected returns;
(c) the potential for liquidating the investment either through direct repayment by the firm or via the secondary market;
(d) the personal tax position of investors in relation to returns from their investment;
(e) the degree of control or influence over the firm's affairs which the investor is likely to acquire as a consequence of investing.

In this chapter we shall assess each of the financial sources reviewed in the context of these factors. We should note that those relating to suppliers of finance are of more than passing interest to the firm's financial managers and existing shareholders. Those factors have a considerable bearing on the attractiveness of any particular type of finance and therefore on the likely success of an attempt to raise new finance in that particular way.

Risk and return

Both intuition and the results of several studies suggest that investors expect and actually get, on average, higher returns where higher risk is involved. The relationship appears to be something like that depicted in Fig. 8.1.

To the firm the position is the corollary of that of the investors; sources of finance which are relatively risky to the firm tend to be cheap in terms of servicing cost, safe sources tend to be expensive. The level of returns required by secured lenders is relatively low but the existence of such loans represents,

Fig. 8.1
The risk/return relationship for various types of security

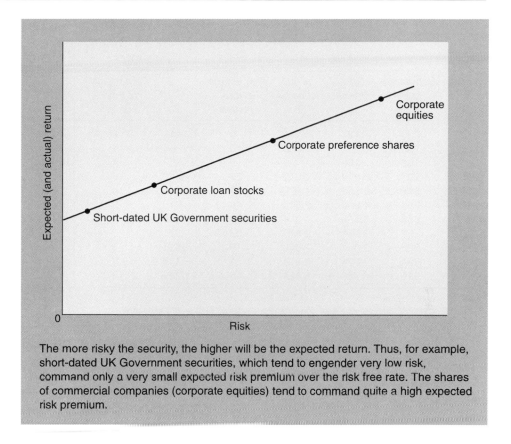

The more risky the security, the higher will be the expected return. Thus, for example, short-dated UK Government securities, which tend to engender very low risk, command only a very small expected risk premium over the risk free rate. The shares of commercial companies (corporate equities) tend to command quite a high expected risk premium.

as we shall see, a potential threat to the welfare of the shareholders. Equity investors expect high returns, but issuing additional ordinary shares does not tend greatly to increase the risk borne by the original shareholders.

ORDINARY OR EQUITY CAPITAL

Equity financing is overwhelmingly the most important in the UK corporate private sector. Both as regards the cumulative financing arrangements and the raising of new capital, equity finance is by far the largest source (*see* Table 8.1). Equities seem to attract a wide range of investors, both private and institutional.

The nature of equity

The ordinary shareholders are the owners of the firm, who, through the voting rights attaching to their shares, exercise ultimate control over the firm.

As owners of the firm the ordinary shareholders bear the gretest risk. If the firm trades unsuccessfully, the ordinary shareholders are the first to suffer in terms of lack of dividends and, probably, falls in the market value of their shares. If the firm collapses (it is put into liquidation) it is the ordinary shareholders who will be at the bottom of the list with a claim for repayment of their investment.

Table 8.1 New security issues, net of redemptions, by UK firms (by type of security)*

| Year | Loan stocks | | | | Preference | | Ordinary | | Total issues |
	Convertible loans £m	Other loans £m	Total loans £m	Percentage of total issues	£m	Percentage of total issues	£m	Percentage of total issues	£m
1985	320	121	441	9	414	8	4 211	83	5 066
1986	55	851	906	10	65	1	7 751	89	8 722
1987	186	(186)	0	0	659	4	14 717	96	15 376
1988	707	2 312	3019	38	612	8	4 352	54	7 983
1989	1 580	2 952	4 532	61	1 016	14	1 883	25	7 431
1990	1 763	1 046	2 809	46	515	8	2 852	46	6 176
1991	858	3 486	4 344	30	485	3	9 741	67	14 570
1992	97	2 782	2 879	35	271	3	5 089	62	8 239
1993	998	2 047	3 045	19	515	3	12 723	78	16 283
1994	894	2 024	2 918	22	438	3	9 904	75	13 260
1995	915	5 780	6 695	46	1 245	9	6 584	45	14 524

Source: Bank of England
* This table gives information on issues to UK investors by Stock Exchange listed firms.

On the other hand, the fruits of the firm's success principally benefit ordinary shareholders; other participants in the firm – labour, lenders, suppliers, etc. – tend to earn returns not related to the firm's success. Thus once the claims of these other claimants are met the balance accrues to the ordinary shareholders.

Nominal values

When the firm is first established, a decision would have been made about how much equity finance (the law requires that there is some) it wishes to raise and into how many shares this is to be divided. If, for example, the decision is that £1m needs to be raised, it could be in the form of two shares of nominal value £500 000 each, 1m shares of £1 each, 200 000 shares of £5 each, or (more likely) 2m shares of £0.50 each. Which of these, or any one of the almost infinite number of other possibilities, is decided upon, is a matter of the judgement of the promoters of the firm.

In making this decision, probably the major factor is marketability. Most investors would not find shares of very large nominal value very attractive as this would make it difficult to set aside an amount of money to be exactly invested in the firm. If the shares were of nominal value £50, an investor who wishes to invest £275 in the firm could not do so. The choice would be between five or six shares. Even if the shares were £10 nominal value the investor could get fairly close to the target of £275 (27 or 28 shares). It seems to be believed that large nominal value shares are not as readily marketable as those of smaller denomination. Certainly large-denomination shares are very rare in practice. Few ordinary shares have nominal values larger than £1 each.

Once the firm has invested its capital and has started to trade, the market value of its ordinary shares will probably move away from the nominal value, as a result of market forces. Further issues of ordinary shares will normally be priced by reference to current market prices, i.e. firms will seek to issue further ordinary shares at the highest price which the market will bear. In fact nominal values cease to have much significance once the firm has started trading. This is evidenced by the fact that in the USA, which has similar corporate financing arrangements to those encountered in the UK, shares of no par (or nominal) value are not unusual.

The decision on nominal value is not irrevocable; firms may subsequently *split* or *consolidate* nominal values. For example a firm whose ordinary shares have a nominal value of £1 each may split them into shares of £0.50 each. In practice this is easily accomplished and culminates in each ordinary shareholder being sent a replacement share certificate showing twice as many £0.50 shares as the investor previously had £1 ones. As we have seen, the objective of such a move seems to be to reduce the unit price to make the shares more marketable.*

Investment ratios

Several ratios are used by, or at least made available to, investors which give measures of some aspects of the ordinary shares' performance. These are published daily, together with the daily share price, by most of the more serious national newspapers. These ratios (which were introduced in Chapter 3) are:

(a) Price/earnings ratio (PE)

Here the current price per share is expressed as a multiple of the earnings per share (net profit available for ordinary shares divided by the number of ordinary shares which the firm has issued). The profit figure used in the calculation of the ratio is that for the most recently reported year.

Shares with large PEs are those which are highly priced for their historical earnings level, indicating the market's faith in the future of the firm and its ability to grow.

(b) Dividend yield (DY)

This expresses the gross equivalent of dividends per share paid in the most recent year as a percentage of the current market price. It gives some idea of the rate of return which the dividend represents. This may be compared with returns from other investments to try to assess the particular share. To the extent that over a period capital gains and losses are much more important in amount per share than dividends, DY is (to say the least) an incomplete measure of the benefits of ownership of the share.

(c) Dividend cover (DC)

This expresses the earnings per share, after prior claims have been satisfied, as a multiple of the actual dividend per share paid from those earnings. It gives some indication of the extent to which the firm pays its profits out as dividends and to what extent they are ploughed back.

* If the shares are in fact rendered more attractive by splitting, logically the market value of a particular investor's holding would be increased by the split. The evidence seems to indicate that this does not actually happen in practice. See Copeland and Weston (1988) for a discussion of some tests relating to this point.

Much of what we have already discussed in this book on such matters as the importance of risk calls into question the value of relying on the above ratios. It must be said, however, that such ratios are widely available to investors and therefore, are probably used by them. We shall discuss the issues relating to the choice of dividend levels in Chapter 12.

Factors for the firm to consider on equity financing

Issue costs

These vary considerably according to the method used to raise the new equity and the finance raised; ranging from virtually nothing up to about 15 per cent of the new finance raised (Jenkinson, 1990). We shall consider this in more detail when dealing with the various methods in the following section.

Servicing costs

Equity holders expect relatively high returns in terms of capital appreciation and dividends. Dividends represent an explicit cost. The capital appreciation results from the fact that sooner or later profits not paid out as dividends are expected to end up in the hands of the shareholders, even if they have to wait until the firm is liquidated before this happens. Thus one way or another, the entire profits will eventually be paid out to shareholders.

Obligation to pay dividends

Dividend levels are a question of the discretion of directors and financial managers. As we saw under 'Servicing costs' above, ultimately the dividend must be paid, but shareholders cannot directly force payment of a particular level of dividend in a particular year.

Obligation to redeem the investment

There is no such obligation unless (or until) the firm is liquidated. Because of this and to some extent because of the flexibility on dividend levels, finance provided by ordinary shareholders does not impose much by way of cash flow obligation on the firm.

Tax deductibility of dividends

In contrast with the servicing of virtually all other types of finance, dividends are not tax-deductible in arriving at the firm's Corporation Tax liability. This tends to make dividends more expensive than a similar gross equivalent loan interest rate (see the Appendix to this chapter for more details). In fact the advent of UK corporate tax rates close to the basic personal tax rate means that this point is not necessarily of great significance.

Effect on control and freedom of action

Where new equity finance is raised from other than the existing shareholders in the same proportions as their original investment, voting power will shift to some extent, perhaps to a large extent, and possibly with it control of the firm. This is not neccessarily a feature of all increases in equity financing. In fact the two most important means of raising equity finance for most firms, retained profits and rights issues (each discussed below), generally avoid this problem.

It is somewhat doubtful whether this is really of much concern to typical ordinary shareholders, since they seem not to use their votes in any case. Most firms' annual general meetings are characterised by a distinct absence of most of those entitled to be present and to vote. Control is a factor which is more likely to be of concern to ordinary shareholders in small firms, a point which we shall discuss in Chapter 15.

Factors for the potential investor to consider on equity financing

Level of return

This would be expected to be higher than the level of return associated with 'safe' investments such as UK Government securities. This has historically been the case with real returns from UK equities averaging around 11 per cent p.a. since 1918, contrasting with an average real return from Government securities of about 3 per cent p.a. over the same period (Dimson 1996). Compared with other types of security, ordinary shares have on average provided the best, though nonetheless often an incomplete, hedge against inflation.

Equities provide an opportunity to make investments where returns are related fairly directly to commercial success. Most investment opportunities of this type require investors to spend time managing the assets in which their money is invested; they also expose investors to unlimited liability. However, equities enable delegation of day-to-day management to the directors and protect the investors' other assets.

Riskiness of returns

Returns both in terms of capital gains and of dividends are not certain by any means. Negative returns are very common over periods of a year or two (or less), though historically above-average positive returns compensate for these. A period of adverse trading could cause the value of a particular firm's ordinary shares to fall to zero, losing the shareholder the entire amount invested in those shares.

Ease of liquidating the investment

Typically, when investors take up part of an issue of new equity of a firm, they have no particular thoughts of the firm ever repaying that investment. However, the average investor would be reluctant to take up equities unless it were clear that there would be the opportunity to liquidate the investment, in some other way. This is where the secondary capital market comes in. It is clearly in the interest of the firm to have its ordinary shares regularly traded on a recognised stock exchange so that the facility to liquidate the investment exists.

Equities and personal tax

In the UK, dividends are taxed as *income* in the hands of the shareholder, at marginal rates up to 40 per cent. Capital appreciation is subject to the rather less severe Capital Gains Tax at rates similar to those applied to income.

Degree of control

Ordinary shares typically carry voting rights. This tends not to be too important to the typical shareholder but it does put him or her in a position, perhaps in concert with other shareholders, to apply pressure to the firm's senior management on any matter of concern.

METHODS OF RAISING ADDITIONAL EQUITY FINANCE

There are broadly three ways of raising new equity finance. These are retaining profits rather than paying them out as dividends, making issues of new shares to existing shareholders and making new share issues to the public. Evidence shows, despite some fluctuation from year to year, the clear dominance of retained profits over other methods. With new shares, over recent years, those issued to existing shareholders as rights issues have tended to be more important than issues to the general public (Bank of England).

Retained profit

It may seem surprising to mention retained profits as a source of new equity finance. However, profits certainly lead to a net increase in funds and retaining these, or part of them, rather than paying them out as dividends, is effectively a way of raising finance. After all, if the full profit were paid out as dividends and then shareholders bought new shares with their dividend money, this would have much the same effect as retaining the funds in the first place.

In fact retained profits are a very important source of finance, probably accounting for about half of all the long-term finance raised by UK firms over recent years.

A free source of finance?

At first sight, retained profits seem to be a source which costs nothing to service. A moment's reflection however shows this *not* to be true. From the ordinary shareholder's point of view, there is a clear opportunity cost in that, if cash dividends were paid, that cash could be invested in some income-yielding way. As the obvious comparison is an investment in equities of similar risk to those of the firm under consideration, retained profits logically have a cost similar to that of the original ordinary shares.

Bonus shares

In much the same way as firms can and do split nominal values, firms can convert retained profits into ordinary shares which are then distributed to existing shareholders free of charge.

EXAMPLE

The following is a highly abbreviated balance sheet of a firm which has been trading for some period of time and which has retained at least some of its profits.

Balance sheet as at 30 June 1997

Sources of finance (claims)	£m	Uses of finance (investments)	£m
Ordinary shares of £1 each	4	Fixed assets	5
Retained profits	3		
Total equity	7	Working capital	4
Long-term loan	2		
	9		9

It is open to the firm, with only the minimum of administrative difficulty, to convert all or part of the £3m retained profit to shares which may be issued pro rata to the ordinary shareholders. Let us assume for our example that £2m of the £3m retained profit is so converted. The revised balance sheet would be:

Balance sheet as at 30 June 1997

Sources of finance (claims)	£m	Uses of finance (investments)	£m
Ordinary shares of £1 each	6	Fixed assets	5
Retained profits	1		
Total equity	7	Working capital	4
Long-term loan	2		
	9		9

Note that the conversion of retained profits into shares leaves the uses of funds totally unaffected. It also leaves completely untouched the total equity figure, i.e. the contribution of the ordinary shareholders is not altered by the bonus issue. All that will occur is that for every two shares held before the bonus issue, the shareholder will hold three after it. As with splitting, the economic effect of a bonus issue should logically be zero. If in this example the price of an ordinary share were £1.80 before the issue, it should be £1.20 (i.e. £1.80 × ⅔) afterwards.

If they have no economic consequences, why do firms make bonus issues? Do managements believe that shareholders will be fooled into thinking that they have got something for nothing? If so, the evidence (discussed in Chapter 9) suggests that they are wrong. Possibly bonus issues are intended to transmit information. Bonus issues are sometimes thought to indicate a confidence on the part of management in the investments which it has made. A third possible reason, as with splits, is simply to reduce the unit price of the shares to (what management may regard as) a more marketable size.

Factors to consider in respect of raising finance by retention of profits

Does dividend policy affect the net wealth of the shareholder?
If it does then retaining one proportion of the profit, rather than another proportion, will have some effect on the sum of the dividend paid and the ex-dividend price of the share. We shall review the debate and evidence on this topic in some detail in Chapter 12.

No issue costs
Other means of raising additional equity have explicit issue costs not applicable to retained profits.

Profits are uncertain
Once the need for raising further finance has been identified there is no guarantee that sufficiently large profits will subsequently be made to meet the requirements. On the other hand, once the funds have been generated from profits, their existence is certain and their retention just a matter of a management decision. This latter point contrasts with other methods of raising equity finance.

No dilution of control

Retaining profits does not alter the voting strength of any individual shareholder.

Rights issues

These are offers to existing ordinary shareholders to take up additional shares, for cash, at a price usually significantly below that at which the shares already issued trade in the capital market at the time.

Rights issues have generally represented by far the most important method of raising new equity finance in the UK, after retained profits, over recent years. In fact, the law requires, in normal circumstances, that any new equity issue must be offered first to existing shareholders in proportion to their individual shareholdings. Shareholders can agree to waive these 'pre-emption rights'. The existence of this point of law is sometimes seen as a restriction on the ability of directors to take advantage of some other source of equity finance.

Once the firm has decided on the amount of finance it needs and has set a price, it simply offers shares to existing shareholders. The number of new shares which any individual shareholder has the *right* to take up depends on the number of shares which he or she already owns.

If the shareholder wishes not to take up this entitlement, the rights may be sold to someone who does wish to take them up (irrespective of whether or not that someone is an existing shareholder). Usually rights may be sold in the capital market. Their buyer acquires the same right to take up the shares as did the shareholder to whom they were originally granted.

EXAMPLE

A firm has in existence 4m ordinary £1 shares whose current market price is £1.80 each. The firm wishes to raise £1.2m by a rights issue at £1.50 per share. The number of shares to be issued will be £1.2m/£1.5m, i.e. 800 000 shares. These will be offered on a 1 for 5 basis to existing ordinary shareholders. For example, a shareholder owning 200 shares will therefore be given the right to buy an additional 40 shares.

In the above example, the value of the entire equity of the firm immediately before the rights issue was £7.2m (i.e. 4m × £1.80). Immediately following the issue, this should rise by £1.2m (the amount of *new* money raised). The total value of the equity should now be £8.4m or £1.75 per share (i.e. £8.4m/4.8m).

This is the price at which the shares should trade immediately following the rights issue, assuming that everything else remains equal. Thus the value of the right to buy one share is likely to be £0.25 (i.e. the difference between the rights issue price, and the ex-rights price). Market forces would tend to ensure that this is broadly true since if it were not, it would imply that it would be possible either to make abnormal gains by buying rights on the one hand, or no one would be prepared to buy them on the other.

Let us consider a shareholder who starts with 100 ordinary shares and as a result is offered 20 new shares in the rights issue. This person has three choices:

(a) Pay £30 (i.e. 20 × £1.50) to the firm and take up the entitlement. If this is done the value of the shareholding will go up from £180 (i.e. 100 × £1.80) to £210 (i.e. 120 × £1.75). This increase of £30 is exactly the amount which has just been paid to take up the rights, so the rights issue leaves the shareholder neither richer nor poorer than before.

(b) Sell the rights presumably for £5 (i.e. 20 × £0.25). This would leave a shareholding worth £175 (i.e. 100 × £1.75) and £5 in cash, a total value of £180, once again leaving the shareholder neither better nor worse off.

(c) Allow the rights to lapse, in which case the value of the shareholding will fall from £180 to £175. Thus the shareholder will lose wealth by failing to act either to take up the rights or to sell them within the time allowed by the firm to do so.

The importance of the rights issue price

How important is it that the firm gets the price right? In the above example, would existing ordinary shareholders be worse off, better off or unaffected if the rights issue price had been, say, £1 per share instead of £1.50?

Obviously to raise £1.2m would require issuing 1.2m shares if the issue price were to be £1 each. The value of the equity immediately following the issue would still be £8.4m but the market price per share would be £1.615 (i.e. £8.4m/5.2m). This would put the value of the rights at £0.615 per share. Let us again consider the position of a holder of 100 of the original ordinary shares who chooses to take up the entitlement of 30 new shares (remember that 1.2m new shares will now have to be offered to the holders of the original 4.0m shares, i.e. 3 for 10).

The value of our shareholder's increased holding will be £210. Again the increase from the original value of the holding (£180) is entirely accounted for by the cash which our shareholder has had to pay. Thus the wealth of the shareholder is not affected by the price at which the rights issue is made. It can equally well be shown that the shareholder who chooses to sell the rights will similarly be unaffected.

Firms typically price rights issues at about 20 per cent below the current pre-rights share price. As we have seen, doing this should not really advantage the shareholder. However, since allowing the rights to lapse disadvantages shareholders, a rights issue priced at a discount puts pressure on them either to take up the issue or to sell the rights. In either case this is likely to lead to the issue being successful in terms of all of the shares being taken up and the desired amount of money raised.

Another reason for pricing rights issues at a discount is to try to ensure that any fall in the market price of the shares already issued, between the date of the announcement of the rights issue (and of the rights issue price) and the date of the issue, still leaves the rights issue price below the market price. If, on the issue date, shares were cheaper to buy in the capital market than by taking up the rights, the issue would almost certainly fail.

Factors to consider in respect of rights issues

Rights issues are a relatively cheap way of raising equity finance

It is estimated that an issue of £2m costs about 4 per cent of that amount (Wilson Committee report 1980). Note that since many of these costs are fixed, the cost will be proportionately more or less for smaller or larger issues respectively.

Pricing of issues is not a critical factor

As we have seen shareholders who either sell or take up their rights are left in more or less the same position as regards wealth irrespective of the issue price.

Rights issues are fairly certain

It is relatively rare in practice for a rights issue to fail. This is an important factor since many of the issue costs are committed in advance and are lost if the issue fails.

Existing shareholders are forced either to increase or to liquidate part of their shareholding

To shareholders given rights to take up additional shares, doing nothing is not a sensible option. In order to preserve their wealth they must either take up the shares and so increase their investment in the firm or sell the rights thus effectively liquidating part of their investment in the firm. Neither of these may be attractive to some shareholders which could cause the shares of firms which make frequent rights issues to become unpopular, thus adversely affecting their market value.

It is of course always open to an individual shareholder to sell some of the rights to obtain sufficient cash to take up the rest. This still requires action on the shareholder's part. In practice the vast majority of rights are taken up by existing shareholders (90 per cent according to the Wilson Committee, 1980).

Dilution of control

This need not occur with rights issues as existing shareholders are given the opportunity, usually accepted, to retain the same voting power after the issue as they had before.

Equity issues to the public

Such issues are relatively rare in practice and do not account for a very large proportion of total equity fund raising – probably less than 10 per cent of all new equity finance in the UK over recent years. Whilst there are not many such issues, those which do occur tend to be large in size. They seem to occur most with firms which have newly been listed by the Stock Exchange for a quotation and dealing, i.e. firms which are making their first significant public issue of ordinary shares.

Technically there are two ways of making public issues:

(a) The issuing firm can sell the shares to an *issuing house*, usually a merchant bank which specialises in such work. The issuing house then sells the shares to the public. This is known as an *offer for sale*.

(b) The issuing firm sells the shares direct to the public. Often such firms are advised by a merchant bank on such matters as the pricing of the issue. Here the offer is known as an *offer by prospectus*.

Irrespective of which of these methods is used, the general procedure is the same. Basically the shares are advertised in newspapers and/or elsewhere. The advertisement is required by law and by the regulations of the Stock Exchange to give a large volume of detailed information. This is very expensive to prepare, including as it does reports from independent accountants, etc. The objective of including such voluminous and detailed information is to protect the public from the type of sloppy and sometimes fraudulent claims which were made by firms' managements in the earlier days of the Stock Exchange.

Smaller firms may not wish to be subjected to the rigours, and the accompanying cost, of obtaining a full Stock Exchange listing for their shares. For such firms the Stock Exchange provides a separate market in which shares may be traded. This is the *Alternative Investment Market (AIM)*, which tends to cater for firms whose shares have a total market value of around £20 million.

The fact that a particular firm's securities are traded in the AIM should warn potential investors that the requirements for the firm to obtain a full listing for its shares have not been met, though less rigorous ones will have been complied with. This implies that such securities represent a more hazardous investment than would those of a similar firm which had obtained a full listing.

Pricing of issues to the public

In contrast with the position with rights issues, the pricing of issues of ordinary shares to the public is of vital importance to existing shareholders.

If the new shares are priced at a discount on the value of the existing shares, unless existing holders were to take up such a number of new shares as would retain for them the same proportion of the total as they had before, it would be the equivalent of a shareholder allowing all or some of the allotment in a rights issue to lapse (see the example on p. 202 for the effect of this).

Since issues to the public tend to occur where a firm is significantly extending its equity base, it is most unlikely that an existing shareholder will be able to take up sufficient new shares to avoid being penalised by an issue at a discount.

It is a matter of judgement as to how well the issue price strikes the balance between attracting the maximum amount of cash per share on the one hand, and avoiding a very costly failure to raise the required funds, after spending large amounts on promoting the issue, on the other. There are two ways in which the pricing problem can be mitigated. One is to have the shares underwritten. For a fee, underwriters will guarantee to take up shares for which the public do not subscribe. This ensures the success of the issue. The underwriters' fee or commission is fixed by them according to how many shares they are underwriting, the offer price and naturally, how high the underwriter believes the possibility to be that some shares will not be taken up by the public. Underwriters are in effect insurers. Most issues to the public are underwritten. Underwriting costs tend to be in the order of 2 per cent of the capital raised.

The second way of dealing with the pricing problem is for the shares to be open to tender. This is much like an auction where the shares are sold to the highest bidders, usually subject to a pre-stated reserve price (i.e. a price below which offers will not be accepted). When all of the offers have been received (the closing date for offers has been reached), the firm or the issuing house assesses what is the highest price at which all of the shares could be issued. This can probably best be explained with a simple example.

EXAMPLE

Suppose that a firm wishes to issue 10m shares by tender. After publishing the advertisement in the required form it receives offers as follows:

1m	shares at £5.00 each
1m	shares at £4.50 each
2m	shares at £4.00 each
2m	shares at £3.50 each
3m	shares at £3.00 each
5m	shares at £2.50 each
10m	shares at £2.00 each

The highest price at which all of the 10m shares could be issued yet each offerer be required to pay the same price per share is £2.50. This is known as the striking price, i.e. the price at which all 10m shares will be issued, 9m to those who offered above £2.50 and the other 1m to some of those who offered £2.50 exactly. Note that all of the 10m shares are issued at £2.50 each.

Issues by tender seem to be increasingly popular, the late 1980s having seen several of them.

Share issues in depressed markets

It is argued by some observers that it would be unfair to sell new shares to the public when either capital market prices generally, or the firm's shares in particular, are depressed. This is because it would allow outsiders to buy shares 'on the cheap' at the expense of the existing shareholders. If a rights issue is made under such circumstances, it is claimed, this advantage would only go to existing shareholders.

This seems an illogical view in the light of the evidence on capital market efficiency, which will be reviewed in the next chapter. Such evidence strongly supports the hypothesis that the current market price of a share is the consensus view of its value at the time. There is no reason to believe that because it has recently fallen in value it is about to increase, any more than it should cause us to feel that it is about to suffer a further decrease in value or to remain static.

Factors to consider in respect of equity issues to the public

Issue costs

These are very large, estimated at 12½ per cent of the proceeds for a £5m issue (Jenkinson, 1990). This compares with 2 per cent for a rights issue and zero cost for retained profits. This probably explains the small number of public issues and why they tend mainly to occur in cases where there is not the rights or retained profits option.

Uncertainty of public issues The relative certainty of success associated with rights issues does not exist with issues to the public. As we have discussed already, the use of underwriters and/or issuing by tender can overcome the problem to some extent, but at a cost.

Pricing of issues is critical If the interests of existing ordinary shareholders are to be protected, the pricing question is one of vital importance. Issuing by tender does, to some extent, overcome the problem. Capital market efficiency suggests that offers will rationally and fairly price the issue.

Dilution of control Clearly this is going to occur with issues to the public. It is probably the price which the original shareholders have to pay to obtain access to additional equity finance when rights issues and retained profits are not possibilities.

PREFERENCE SHARES

Preference shares form part of the risk-bearing ownership of the firm but since preference shareholders usually have the right to the first slice (of predetermined size) of any dividend paid, they bear less risk than do ordinary shares. Investors' expectations of returns from preference shares are therefore lower than expectations from ordinary shares in the same firm. Historically preference shares have been a significant source of corporate finance.

More recently they seem to have fallen from favour and have tended to be of very little importance though they saw a revival in 1995 (*see* Table 8.1, p. 196).

Preference shares may be, and usually are, *cumulative*. This means that if the preference dividend is not met in full in any particular year, ordinary shareholders are not entitled to dividends in any future year until preference share dividends have been brought up to date.

Nominal value

Preference shares have a nominal value but, as with ordinary shares, its size is not usually of much importance. However, the preference dividend is usually expressed as a percentage of the nominal value (though it need not be).

Investment ratios

Dividend yield and dividend cover are important ratios to the preference shareholder. Dividends would normally be by far the most important part of the preference shares' returns, so the effective rate and its security are important matters.

Factors for the firm to consider on preference share financing

Issue costs These are likely to be rather similar to those associated with raising new equity finance and similarly variable with the method used.

Servicing costs These would tend to be somewhat lower than those relating to ordinary shares, since preference shares expose their holder to rather less risk.

Obligation to pay dividends Preference shares do not impose on the firm the legal obligation to pay a dividend. They do, however, impose the obligation to meet the preference dividend before any dividend may be paid to ordinary shareholders. Where preference shares are cumulative, arrears of unpaid preference dividends must also be made good before ordinary shareholders may participate in dividends. In practice, despite the lack of legal obligation, firms seem reluctant to miss paying a preference dividend.

Obligation to redeem preference shares Some preference shares are expressly issued as redeemable and where this is the case the firm must be mindful of the necessity to finance this redemption. By no means are all preference shares redeemable and where they are not, the position is similar to that of ordinary shares. Where preference shareholders cannot demand redemption, this type of financing is a relatively safe one from the ordinary shareholders' viewpoint.

Tax deductibility of preference share dividends The UK tax system does not distinguish between ordinary and preference dividends so they, like ordinary share dividends, are not deductible from the firm's profit for Corporation Tax purposes (see the Appendix to this chapter on p. 220).

Effect on control and on freedom of action Normally preference shares do not impose much by way of restriction on the ordinary shareholders. Many firms' preference shares give the holders the right to vote only where their dividends are in arrears. Generally preference shareholders have no voting rights.

Factors for the potential investor to consider on preference shareholding

Level of return This tends to be low, significantly below that of equities of the same firm. It all tends to be in the form of dividends since preference shares do not normally experience significant changes in values.

Riskiness of returns Typically this risk lies between that attaching to ordinary shares and to loan stocks. This is mainly because preference dividends have priority over ordinary ones.

Ease of liquidating the investment Where preference shares are redeemable and/or traded in the capital market, liquidation is possible. Failure for at least one of these to be the case will usually make investors reluctant to take up preference share issues.

Preference shares and personal tax Dividends are taxed as income.

Degree of control Unless dividends are in arrears preference shareholders typically have no voting rights and hence no real power.

Methods of raising preference share capital

These are more or less identical to the options available with ordinary shares, including bonus issues to ordinary shareholders created from retained profits. In practice, rights issues seem to be the most popular methods of issuing preference shares.

LOAN STOCKS AND DEBENTURES

Many firms borrow by issuing securities with a fixed interest rate (known as the *coupon rate*) and a pre-stated redemption date. They are typically issued for periods within the range of 10 to 25 years, though some are issued for periods outside that range. Indeed, perpetual loan stocks (no redemption date) do exist.

The popularity of loan stocks to firms as a means of raising long-term finance seems to fluctuate rather wildly from year to year. In 1989, 61 per cent of the value of all securities issued by UK firms (net of redemptions) were loan stocks of some description or another, yet as recently as 1987, net of redemptions, the figure was zero (*see* Table 8.1, p. 196).

Most loan stocks are secured either on specified assets of the borrowing firm, or on the assets generally. Alternatively, the loan stock holder may simply have the security which the law of contract gives any unsecured creditor to enforce payment of interest or capital if the firm defaults. Whether a loan stock is secured or not determines where in the queue for payment the loan stock holder will stand in the event of the liquidation of the borrowing firm.

Since it is not usually practical for individual loan stock holders to monitor their security at all times, trustees are often appointed by the firm to do this for them. Firms will be prepared to do this so that the issue will attract lenders.

Many firms seek and obtain a capital market quotation for their loan stocks so that potential lenders can *buy* a firm's borrowings from a previous lender. The new owner of the loan stock will, from the date of acquiring it, receive interest payments as well as the capital repayment if the stock is held until the redemption date.

Loan stocks attract all types of investors who seek relatively low-risk returns. Institutional investors are particularly attracted by them, especially those institutions which need regular cash receipts to meet recurring payment obligations, e.g. pension funds.

Investment ratios

Since profitability *per se* is of no direct interest to loan stock holders, ratios dealing with the effective rate of interest (yield) are likely to be of more concern to them.

Two ratios which tend to be widely reported (in newspapers etc.) are:

(a) *Flat yield*. This is simply the gross interest receivable expressed as a percentage of the current market value of the relevant amount of loan.

(b) *Redemption yield*. Where, as is usually the case, the loan stock is redeemable, the effective return from owning it may include some capital gain or even loss. (A capital loss would arise where the current market price is above the redemption value. This would tend to occur where prevailing rates of interest are below the coupon rate for the loan stock.)

The redemption yield (r) would be given by the following expression:

$$\text{Current market value} = \sum_{t=1}^{n} I/(1+r)^t + RV/(1+r)^n$$

where I is the annual gross interest payment, RV is the redemption value and n is the remaining life (in years) of loan stock.

Examples of calculations involving this equation are given in Chapter 10.

Methods of issuing loan stocks

Loan stocks can be issued in several ways, including direct issues to the public by newspaper advertisement etc. Quite often firms wishing to issue loan stocks will approach a stockbroking firm and ask it to try to place part of the issue with its clients, often institutional ones.

Factors for the firm to consider on loan stock financing

Issue costs

These tend to be relatively low; they have been estimated at about $2\frac{1}{2}$ per cent of the value of the cash raised on a £2m issue (Wilson Committee, 1980).

Servicing costs

Since loan stock represents a relatively low-risk investment to investors, expected returns tend to be low compared with those typically sought by equity holders. Historically this has been reflected in actual returns.

Obligation to pay interest

Loan stock holders have the basic right under the law of contract to take action to enforce payment of interest and repayment of capital on the due dates, should they not be forthcoming. Fairly typically, loan stock holders have the contractual right to take some more direct action (e.g. effective seizure of an asset on which their loan is secured), should the borrowing firm default on payments.

This clear obligation to pay interest, with potentially dire results for defaulting, can make servicing the loan stock finance a considerable millstone around the neck of the borrowing firm.

Obligation to redeem loan stocks

Irrespective of whether loan stocks are issued as redeemable or not, it is always open to the firm to buy its own loan stock, in the open market, and to cancel what it buys. Thus loan stocks offer a level of flexibility not so readily available with ordinary and preference shares. On the other hand, if loan stocks are issued as redeemable with a stated redemption date, which will usually be the case, the firm is under a contractual obligation to redeem. This could put the firm into a difficult cash flow position as the due date for redemption approaches.

Tax deductibility of loan stock interest	Interest is fully deductible from the firm's profit for Corporation Tax purposes. This has tended in the past to make loan interest payments cheaper, £ for £, than ordinary and preference share dividends. This is now considerably less the case in the light of the recent downward movement of UK Corporation Tax rates.
Effect on control and on freedom of action	The severity of the consequences of failing to meet interest payments and capital repayments can considerably limit the freedom of action of the firm. Whilst control in the sense of voting rights is not usually involved with loan stock financing, control in the sense of being able to manage affairs without impediment may well be seriously eroded by the issuing of loan stocks.

It is common for those who lend money to a firm to impose conditions or covenants on the firm. Failure to meet these covenants could, depending on the precise contract between the lenders and the firm, give the lenders the right to immediate repayment of the loan. Typical covenants include:

- a restriction on dividend levels
- maintenance of a minimum current asset/current liability ratio
- a restriction on the right of the firm to dispose of its fixed assets.

We shall go more fully into the effect on the position of the ordinary shareholders as borrowings increase, in Chapter 11.

Factors for the potential investor to consider on loan stocks

Level of returns	These tend to be relatively low, compared with those expected from equities and preference shares.
Riskiness of returns	Though the level of risk associated with default by the borrowing firm tends to be low, the loan stock holder is usually exposed to another risk, namely *interest rate risk*. This is the risk of capital losses caused by changes in the general level of interest rates.

EXAMPLE	An investor has £100 nominal value of perpetual (irredeemable) loan stock which has a coupon rate (the rate which the borrowing firm is contracted to pay on the nominal value of the stock) of 10 per cent. The prevailing interest rates and the level of risk attaching to the particular loan stock cause the capital market to seek a 10 per cent return from it. Since the loan stock's return on its nominal value is 10 per cent, the capital market would value the holding at £100 (i.e. the nominal value).

If the general level of interest rates were to increase so that the capital market now sought a 12½ per cent return from this loan stock, its value would fall to £80 (i.e. the amount on which the 10 per cent interest on £100 represents a 12½ per cent return). Thus our loan stock holder would be poorer by £20.

If the loan stock were not perpetual but redeemable at £100 at some date in the future, the price would probably not drop as low as £80 on the interest rate change. The closer the redemption date, the smaller the fall, but irrespective of the redemption position some loss of value would occur. Clearly the investor would gain similarly from a general fall in prevailing interest rates but a risk-averse investor (and most investors seem to be risk-averse) would be more concerned with the potential loss than with the potential gain.

The relatively lower interest rate risk associated with *short-dated* loan stocks tends to mean that lower returns are available from them, compared with those from stocks not due for redemption for some time.

Ease of liquidating the investment
Firms that wish to make public issues of loan stocks must seek a capital market quotation for them if they are to have any serious hopes of success. Thus publicly issued loan stocks can be liquidated by sale in the market.

Loan stocks and personal tax
Interest is subject to Income Tax in the hands of individual loan stock holders. Capital gains are also taxed. Since all or almost all of the returns from loan stocks are in the form of interest, capital gains tend not to be significant.

Degree of control
Loan stocks do not give their holders any control over the firm, except that which is necessary to enforce payment of their dues in the event of the firm defaulting.

Eurobonds

These are unsecured loan stocks denominated in a currency other than the home currency of the firm which made the issue. They are foreign currency loans. Firms are prompted to make Eurobond issues to exploit the availability of loan finance in an overseas country. Also Eurobonds can offer innovative features making them more attractive, both to the lenders and to the issuing firm. This latter point arises from the fact that the bonds are traded in an unregulated market.

Interest rate swaps

A firm may have borrowed money where the contract specified a floating interest rate, i.e. an interest rate which varies with the general level of interest rates in the economy. The firm may prefer to have a loan with a fixed rate, but was unable to negotiate such an arrangement.

Under these circumstances, it may be possible for the firm to find another firm with exactly the opposite problem, i.e. a fixed rate loan but a preference for a floating rate loan. Having identified one another, each of the firms might agree to service the loan of the other one. In practice the firms would probably make contact first and then issue the loan stock or undertake the borrowing in some other form.

Interest rate swaps have practical relevance because different firms have differing credit ratings. One may be able to negotiate a floating rate loan at a reasonable rate, but not a fixed rate one. The other firm may find itself in the opposite position. Swaps are another example of a derivative.

CONVERTIBLE LOAN STOCKS

These are securities which bear all of the features of loan stocks, which we have just discussed, except that at a pre-stated date they may be converted by the holders, at their discretion, into ordinary shares of the same firm. The conversion rate is usually expressed as so many ordinary shares in exchange for £100 nominal value of loan stock. If there are any splits or bonus issues of ordinary shares during the life of the loan stock, the conversion rights are usually adjusted to take account of them.

Convertible issues have wavered somewhat in their popularity recently. They accounted for as much as $28\frac{1}{2}$ per cent of total long-term securities issued in 1990, yet they have been insignificant in other years (*see* Table 8.1, p. 196).

Since convertibles are a hybrid of loan stocks and equities, the factors important both to the issuing firm and to potential investors will basically be those which we have already considered. However, a couple of features of convertibles are worth mentioning.

Issue costs

The fact that loan stocks are cheaper to issue than are equities means that convertibles may be a cheap way to issue ordinary shares, particularly where the firm is keen to have some loan finance in any case.

Loans are self-liquidating

There is no need for the firm to find cash to redeem the loan stock since it is redeemed with ordinary shares. This does not, of course, make it free. Issuing shares to redeem loan stock represents an opportunity cost to the firm.

WARRANTS

Warrrants are loan stocks which give the holder the right to subscribe for ordinary shares at some time and price, in some pre-determined quantity. They differ from convertible loan stocks only in the fact that the warrant is not exchanged for equity as in the case of convertibles; the warrant holder continues to own the warrant after having exercised the right to take up the equity. Thus, unlike convertibles, warrants are not self-liquidating.

However, in most ways warrants so resemble convertibles that the important factors are much the same.

TERM LOANS

Term loans are negotiated between the borrowing firm and some financial institution including clearing banks, insurance companies and merchant banks. This sort of finance is extremely important, perhaps accounting for as much as 25 per cent of new finance raised by firms other than through retained profits.

In many ways term loans are like loan stocks in that security is usually given to the lender and loans are made for up to 20 years. They differ from loan stocks in that they are not usually transferred from lender to lender in the way that loan stocks typically are. They are not traded in the capital market. Some term loans are repayable in instalments so that each monthly or annual payment consists of part interest, part capital repayment, in a similar manner to mortgage loan payments made by private house purchasers.

Term loans tend to be very cheap to negotiate, i.e. *issue costs* are very low since the borrowing firm deals with only one lender (at least in respect of each loan) and there is room for very much more flexibility in the conditions of the loan than is usually possible with an issue of loan stock.

Clearly, term loans so closely resemble loan stocks that, with the exception of the points concerning transferability and the possible spreading of capital repayment, the factors concerning both borrower and lender are much the same as those which we reviewed in respect of loan stocks.

LEASING

It may seem strange to see leasing appearing in a chapter dealing with sources of long-term finance, but in fact it is very close to being secured lending, which certainly justifies its place here.

Leases may be divided into two types:

(a) *Operating leases* It is often possible to hire an asset, say an item of plant, which is perhaps required only occasionally, rather than purchasing it. Usually the owner carries out any maintenance necessary. The decision whether to buy the asset or to lease it will perhaps be affected by financing considerations. Basically, though, it is an operating decision which would be made according to which approach would be cheaper.

(b) *Financial leases.* Here the potential user identifies an asset in which it wishes to invest, negotiates price, delivery, etc., and then seeks a supplier of finance to buy it. Having arranged for the asset to be purchased the user leases it from the purchaser. Naturally the lease payments will need to be sufficient to justify the owner's expenditure, both in terms of capital repayment and of interest.

It is financial leases which concern us here since they are effectively term loans with capital repayable by instalments. This is an important source of finance which has been estimated as providing as much as 20 per cent of the total finance for new capital expenditure by firms over recent years (Drury and Braund, 1990).

In the past, financial leasing has been believed to be popular with users partly because, whilst it is tantamount to borrowing, neither the asset nor the obligation to the owner appeared on the balance sheet of the user firm. Such a source of *off balance sheet* finance could be overlooked by those trying to assess the financial position of the firm. However, a combination of changes in the law and in accounting practice has now put leasing *on the balance sheet*. Firms are now required to show both the leased assets and the capital value of the obligation to the owner on the face of the balance sheet.

Another feature of financial leasing, which was apparently a major reason for the growth in its popularity during the late 1970s and early 1980s in the UK, was its considerable *tax efficiency* in some circumstances. Lease payments are fully deductible for Corporation Tax purposes by the borrowing firm. This includes the capital portion of the payment.

Until 1984, the capital cost of items of plant attracted 100 per cent first-year capital allowance in their year of acquisition. As far as the borrowing firm was concerned, leasing rather than buying a fixed asset would deny it the opportunity to claim the first-year allowance. On the other hand, leasing would still enable the firm to claim 100 per cent of the cost of the asset, but over its life, rather than in the first year. In many cases, however, even where firms were to buy the asset, raising finance, say from a term loan, profits were insufficient for the full benefit to be gained from the large first-year allowance. This was particularly true where recession restricted profitability.

With leasing, the right to claim capital allowance passed to the 'lender'. If the profits from leasing and other activities, were such as to put the 'lender' in a position to take full advantage of them, some of this advantage could be passed on to the 'borrower' in lower lease payments. Thus the 'borrower' could give up some of the advantage of the first-year allowance in exchange for a lower lease charge.

The advent in the mid-1980s of lower Corporation Tax rates and the abolition of the 100 per cent first-year allowance greatly reduced the benefit of financial leasing. This, taken together with the requirement for the 'borrower' firm to disclose in its annual accounts the extent of its indulgence in this source of finance seemed likely to reduce the level of use of financial leasing.

In fact, far from decreasing in popularity since the accounting and tax changes of the mid-1980s, financial leasing has expanded massively in popularity since the late 1980s. The reasons for this fact are not obvious. Drury and Braund (1990) conducted a survey of UK firms of various sizes on the reasons why firms frequently prefer to acquire assets on financial leases, rather than buying them. There were two principal reasons given by firms for the popularity of leasing. The first was that the interest rate implied in leasing contracts was lower than the rate which the firms would have to pay to raise finance to buy the assets themselves. The other main reason given was that firms believed it still to be more tax-efficient to lease rather than to buy, despite the changes in the tax treatment of fixed assets.

Though in the case of some firms one or both of the principal reasons given in the survey could be valid, for the majority of firms this seems unlikely to be so. Drury and Braund discovered one factor which could cast some light on the subject. This was an alarmingly high incidence of mishandling of the analysis of the decision whether to lease, on the one hand, or to borrow and purchase, on the other. Even among larger, and presumably more financially sophisticated firms, about 30 per cent were taking an incorrect approach to the analysis such as to bias the results in favour of a decision to lease.

Though it would be unreasonable to conclude that the continued popularity of financial leasing is based on wholesale mishandling of the decision data, it remains far from clear as to why leasing is so popular.

To lease or not to lease – a financing decision

When a firm is considering the acquisition of an asset, it should estimate the cash flows which are expected to arise from its ownership. These should then be discounted at a rate which reflects the level of risk associated with those cash flows. If the NPV is positive the asset should be acquired, if negative it should not, at least from a financial viewpoint.

Whether the asset should be financed by a financial lease or by some other means is a completely separate decision. The first is an investment decision, the second a financing one.

Only by coincidence will the appropriate discount rate be equal to the rate inherent in the financial lease. This latter rate will tend to reflect the relative risk-free nature of lease financing from the lenders' point of view. To the user of the asset the level of risk is likely to be rather greater than that borne by the lender. It would therefore be illogical to discount the cash flows from the asset at the rate implicit in the financial lease.

We shall consider more fully the importance of separating the investment and the financing decision in Chapter 11.

Financial leasing is so similar in practical effect to secured borrowing that the factors which both *borrower* and *lender* need consider are pretty similar in respect of each of them.

GRANTS FROM PUBLIC FUNDS

In the UK there is a large number of different grants or sources of finance which are given at little or no direct cost to firms. The bulk of such finance emanates either from UK Government sources or from the European Union.

Each of the grants available is only available to encourage firms to act in a particular way. Examples of such action include:

- investment in new plant
- development of the microelectronics industry
- training and retraining staff
- energy conservation
- research and development

Many of the grants available apply only or particularly to businesses located in specified parts of the UK.

Since there are so many different schemes and since they tend to alter quite frequently, it is probably not worth our looking at any individual ones here. It must be emphasised, however, that the amounts which individual firms may claim can be highly significant and that every effort should be made by financial managers to familiarise themselves with the grants available and how to claim them. The Department of Trade and Industry will provide information on most sources of grant finance. Local authorities, particularly County Councils, tend to produce guides to grants available in their own neighbourhood.

CONCLUSIONS ON LONG-TERM FINANCE

The apparent existence of an efficient capital market, coupled with the evidence on the relationship between risk and expected return, suggest that firms are unlikely to be advantaged significantly by selecting one type of finance rather than another.

Increases in equity financing, which does not expose existing ordinary shareholders to increased risk, tend to be expensive. Secured loan finance which does expose them to increased risk tends to be cheap. This suggests that there is no advantage or disadvantage to existing ordinary shareholders in raising further finance in one way rather than another. One method may increase expected returns of existing ordinary shareholders but it is also likely to increase their risk commensurately.

However, the situation in real life is probably not quite as suggested by Fig. 8.1, p. 196. There are anomalies in the primary capital market which can mean that using one form of financing rather than another can be to the advantage of equity holders. For example, loan finance attracts tax relief in a way that equity finance does not. Convertibles are probably a cheaper way of issuing ordinary shares than is a direct offer of equities to the public.

These points and those which will be discussed in the context of the gearing and dividend debates later in the book perhaps explain why we find that firms seem to devote much effort to deciding on the most appropriate means of raising long-term finance.

Perhaps we could generally conclude that firms should assess all possible methods of raising long-term finance. They should look for anomalies like the ones mentioned above and then seek to exploit them as far as is practical, given the particular circumstances of the firm.

SUMMARY

Firms obtain long-term finance from various sources, most of which are either in some form of equities or loans. All firms must have some equity finance but when considering increasing their long-term financing base they must assess the merits of the options open to them.

Equity finance has the advantage of not putting a financial millstone around the necks of existing equity holders but it tends to be expensive in terms of returns expected by investors. The cheapest method of raising equity finance (in terms of the issue costs) is by retaining profits; rights issues are relatively cheap, with issues to the public relatively costly.

Loan finance in the form of marketable (transferable) loan stocks tends to be relatively cheap to issue and can give a degree of flexibility. The existence of loan finance does however increase the risks attached to the returns to equity holders.

Term loans from financial institutions are a popular and relatively flexible financing method.

Convertible loan stocks, i.e. loan stocks which are exchanged for equities at some time after their original issue, can give a type of investment which could attract interest from potential investors. Warrants are, in effect, quite similar to convertibles.

Financial leases are in effect another type of loan finance. They used to be able to, and to some extent still can, exploit the tax system by transferring reliefs available to, but not usable by, one firm to another firm which can use them.

Grants from public funds can be an important source of finance to eligible firms. Financial managers should seek to exploit this source of free finance to the greatest extent possible.

Broadly (with the exception of grants), there is the usual risk/return trade-off in the cost of finance. Financing methods which are cheap are those which increase risk. Theoretically there is nothing to be gained by raising *cheap* finance, not at least from the viewpoint of the ordinary shareholders. However, anomalies exist which cut across this theory so managers should seek to exploit these as far as seems practical.

FURTHER READING Weston and Copeland (1988) and Samuels, Wilkes and Brayshaw (1995) give full treatment, from both a theoretical and practical perspective, of corporate financing. Rutterford and Carter (1993) is a comprehensive collection of articles on various types of corporate finance sources. Drury and Braund (1990) give an account of their survey of financial leasing and a general discussion of the subject.

REVIEW QUESTIONS

Suggested answers to review questions appear in Appendix 3.

8.1 From the point of view of the borrowing firm, loan capital tends to be cheap, but risky. In what sense is it risky?

8.2 Why are retained profits not a free source of finance?

8.3 If retained profits are not a free source of finance, why are they nonetheless such a popular source of finance?

8.4 A loan stock, quoted on the stock market, has a 'coupon' rate (interest rate specified in the contract between the firm and the lenders) of 10 per cent. Does this necessarily mean that the current pre-tax cost of the loan stock is 10 per cent.

8.5 What factors tend to affect the market value of a particular convertible loan stock? (NOTE that the answer to this question is not really provided in the chapter. A combination of background knowledge and common sense should enable you to come up with some relevant points, however.)

8.6 In what way can it be said that financial leasing is a source of long-term finance?

PROBLEMS

Sample answers to problems marked with an asterisk appear in Appendix 4.

(Note that problem questions 8.1–8.3 are basic level problems, while questions 8.4 and 8.5 are more advanced, and may contain some practical complications.)

8.1* Many firms issue loan stocks which carry the right for holders to convert them into ordinary shares in the same firm at a later date.

Why might a firm choose to issue convertible loan stocks rather than make an issue of equity in the first place?

8.2* Most firms, particularly larger ones, have outstanding claims (financial obligations) of a wide variety of types from a wide variety of claimants at any given moment.

Why is there this diversity?

8.3 Polecat plc has 18 million £0.50 ordinary shares in issue. The current Stock Exchange value of these is £1.70 per share. The directors have decided to make a one for three rights issue at £1.25 each.
Julie owns 3 000 Polecat ordinary shares.

Assuming that the rights issue will be the only influence on the share price:

(a) What, in theory, will be the ex-rights price of the shares (i.e. the price which the shares will be worth once the rights issue has taken place)?

(b) For how much, in theory, could Julie sell the 'right' to buy one share?

(c) Will it matter to Julie if she allows the rights to lapse (i.e. she does nothing)?

8.4* Memphis plc has 20 million £0.10 ordinary shares in issue. On 7 June 19X6 the Stock Exchange closing price of the shares was £1.20. Early on the morning of 7 June 19X6, the firm publicly announced that it had just secured a new contract to build some hospitals in the Middle East. To the firm, the contract had a net present value of £4 million. On 29 June 1996 the firm announced its intention to raise the necessary money to finance the work, totalling £10 million, through a rights issue priced at £0.80 per share.

Assuming that the events described above were the only influence on the share price, for how much, in theory, could a shareholder sell the right to buy one of the new shares?

8.5 The management of Memphis plc (Problem 8.4) is reconsidering its decision on the rights issue price. It is now contemplating an issue price of £1 per new share. One of its concerns is the effect which the issue price will have on the wealth of its existing shareholders. You have been asked to advise.

Calculate the effect on the wealth of a person who owns 200 shares in Memphis plc before the rights issue, assuming in turn a rights issue price of £0.80 and £1.00. In each case make your calculations both on the basis that the shareholder takes up the rights, and that the shareholder sells the rights.

Taking account of all of the factors, what would you advise the firm to do about the rights issue price?

APPENDIX – THE TAX POSITION OF DIVIDEND AND INTEREST PAYMENTS

Dividends

When a dividend is paid by a company to its shareholders (ordinary or preference) it is treated from a tax viewpoint as being paid out of the after-tax profit of the company for the accounting year in which the dividend payment is made. Arising from the dividend payment the company must pay an instalment towards its eventual Corporation Tax liability for the year concerned. This *Advance Corporation Tax (ACT)* is calculated by reference to the amount of the dividend paid; in fact it is $\frac{20}{80}$ of the dividend paid. ACT must be accounted for and paid to the Inland Revenue on a quarterly basis with payment being made on the 14th of the month following the end of the quarter.

For example, if a company paid a dividend on its shares in August 1996 of £16 000, then the ACT would amount to £4000 (£16 000 × $\frac{20}{80}$), due to be paid on 14 October 1996, unless the company's financial year end is 31 August, when a dividend paid in August 1996 will have to pay its ACT on 14 September 1996.

To the shareholders, the dividend receipt represents an amount received under deduction of the lower rate of Income Tax. A dividend receipt of, say, £80 represents to the shareholder a gross amount of £100 to which attaches an Income Tax credit of £20. To the recipients whose marginal rate of Income Tax is 20 per cent or 23 per cent the liability is completely discharged by the credit. Shareholders whose marginal rate is 40 per cent will subsequently have to pay an additional amount; if their marginal rate is zero (for example where a recipient is a registered charity) the tax credit can be claimed from the Inland Revenue and a repayment made.

Loan interest

Unlike dividends, payments of interest to the company's loan creditors are deducted in arriving at the Corporation Tax liability.

CHAPTER 9

The secondary capital market (the Stock Exchange) and its efficiency

In this chapter we shall deal with the following:

- the role of the capital markets in their secondary function
- the mechanisms of the British Stock Exchange
- efficiency of the secondary capital market
- tests of efficiency
- the implications of capital market efficiency

INTRODUCTION

The capital market is a title given to the market where long-term finance is raised by firms and by local and national governments. Firms raise this type of finance through the issue of equity (shares) and debt (loan stocks) to members of the public and to investing institutions (unit trusts, insurance companies, etc.), usually in exchange for cash. It is also a market where holdings of equity or debt (securities) may be transferred from one investor to another. The new finance market is known as the *primary capital market* whilst the market in which second-hand securities are traded is referred to as the *secondary capital market*. We have already considered this primary role in Chapter 8. In this chapter we shall confine ourselves to consideration of the secondary aspect.

The most important secondary capital markets throughout the world tend to be the official stock exchanges or stockmarkets. They are not the whole of the secondary capital market however – certainly not in the UK as we shall see later in the chapter, nor indeed in the USA. Nonetheless, the world's official stock exchanges are the major forums for trading local, and increasingly international, securities. Most of these official stock exchanges fulfil a primary function as well as a secondary one.

The existence of a secondary capital market is vital to firms wishing to raise long-term finance. Potential long-term investors will not generally be prepared to take up issues of shares or loan stocks, unless the opportunity exists to liquidate their investment at any time. Since it is not practical for firms themselves constantly to hold cash in readiness to redeem the securities, it is necessary for there to be a secondary capital market where security holders may sell their investments. The absence of secondary market facilities tends to make the raising of long-term finance impossible or, at best, very expensive in terms of returns demanded by investors. It is thought by some observers that under-developed countries are often restrained in their industrial and commercial development by the lack of an established secondary capital market and there-fore by the lack of long-term investment finance.

Potential investors will not only require the existence of the opportunity to liquidate their securities as and when they wish, they will also be interested in whether their investment is *efficiently* priced. Efficiency in the context of pricing implies that, at all times, all available information about a firm's prospects is fully and rationally reflected in that firm's security prices. That is to say, the market price of a particular security is the present (discounted) value of the future economic benefits which ownership of the security will bestow on its owner. This will interest investors as they would generally prefer that the price at any particular moment is set rationally and not a matter of sheer chance. Perhaps more important is the fact that, as the capital market is the interface between managers and investors, efficiency means that financial decisions made by managers will reflect in the firms' security prices and so have a direct effect on shareholders' wealth. As maximisation of shareholders' wealth is generally accepted as one of the criteria for management decisions, this reflection of management action is a significant matter, with several implications.

In this chapter we shall look briefly at the mechanisms of the International Stock Exchange (the Stock Exchange) in its secondary role before going on to consider whether or not it seems to be efficient. Lastly we shall consider the implications for investors and for financial managers of the efficiency (or other-wise) of the Stock Exchange.

THE INTERNATIONAL STOCK EXCHANGE (OF THE UK AND THE REPUBLIC OF IRELAND)

As with all capital markets in their secondary role, the Stock Exchange is basically a marketplace where securities of private firms and public bodies may be bought and sold.

Stock Exchange members

Whereas in many types of markets members of the public may directly buy and sell on their own behalf, in the Stock Exchange they are barred from entry. Only members of the Stock Exchange have direct access to buy and sell securities. When members of the public wish to buy or sell securities through the Stock Exchange they can only do so by using a member as an agent.

The rules governing the conduct of the members are laid down and enforced by a Council elected by the membership. One of the functions of the Council is to authorise specific securities as suitable to be dealt on the Stock Exchange. Authorised securities are those which satisfy a number of criteria established by the Council. The object of screening securities before authorising them is to try to avoid members of the investing public from losing money by buying very hazardous securities.

Stock Exchange members have two roles:

(a) As market makers or dealers, equivalent in principle to a trader in a street market. Each dealing firm specialises in a particular group of securities in much the same way as traders in street markets tend to specialise in fruit, or meat, or fish, etc.

(b) As agents of the public who wish to buy or sell through the Stock Exchange (stockbrokers).

Dealing on the Stock Exchange

Dealers will usually be prepared to buy or sell irrespective of whether they are immediately able to *close the deal*. Thus dealers will normally be ready to sell securities which they do not at the time possess or to buy those for which they have no immediate customer. It is only with very rarely traded securities and with exceptionally large orders that dealers may not be prepared to deal either as a buyer or seller. Any unwillingness on a dealing firm's part to make a market in a particular security on a particular occasion may damage its reputation. This could have an adverse effect on the future trade of that dealer. There is therefore a sanction against dealers who fail properly to fulfil their function as market makers.

At any given time a particular firm of dealers will typically hold a *trading* stock, either a positive or a negative one, of some of the securities in which it deals. Where the stock is a positive one it is said to hold a *bull position* in that security, and where securities have been sold which the dealer has yet to buy in it is said to hold a *bear position*.

Dealers are risk-taking market makers. When dealers buy some securities they judge that they can subsequently sell them at a higher price. Similarly, when they sell securities which they do not possess (where they take a bear position), their judgement is that they can buy the securities which they have an obligation to deliver, at a lower price. If they are wrong in this judgement it could be an expensive mistake as they may have to offer a very high price to encourage a seller into the market. Member firms who act only as dealers make their living through profits from trading.

Until the mid-1980s virtually all Stock Exchange transactions were conducted on the floor of the Exchange. Here each dealer firm would have its own 'stall' to which stockbrokers could go to deal on their clients' behalf. To deal at the most advantageous prices it would be necessary for the stockbroker to call at the stalls of all, or at least a good sample of, dealers who dealt in the particular security concerned, in order to compare prices. Now the 'floor' of the Stock Exchange is, in effect, a computerised dealing system, though essentially the system remains the same as it used to be. The Stock Exchange Automated Quotations system (SEAQ) allows dealers to display their prices to interested parties and constantly to update those prices. It also enables members of the Stock Exchange to deal directly using a terminal linked to SEAQ, without leaving their offices.

When members of the investing public wish to buy or to sell a particular security, they would typically telephone their firm of stockbrokers, or possibly visit the firm's premises. The stockbroker can immediately display the prices at which all dealers are prepared to trade. These prices will normally vary from one dealer to another. This is because estimates of the value of the particular security concerned will vary from dealer to dealer. The 'stockholding' position of the particular dealer at that particular moment will also influence the prices on offer. A dealer with a bear position may well be prepared to pay a higher price to buy the particular securities than one with bull position. In respect of a particular security and a particular dealer, the SEAQ screen will display two prices. At the lower of these the dealer is prepared to buy and at the higher one to sell. The same information is available to all member firms and to others who wish to subscribe. The stockbroker can tell the client what is the best price in the security according to whether the client is a potential buyer or a potential seller. The client can then immediately instruct the stockbroker to execute the trade at this best price or to do nothing. If the client wishes to go ahead with the deal the stockbroker, using the SEAQ terminal, executes the transaction immediately and without any direct contact with the relevant dealer firm. The effective contact between the stockbroker and the dealer is through SEAQ. The system automatically informs the dealer concerned that the trade has taken place and provides a record of the details of the transaction. Although anyone can be provided with the SEAQ information, only members of the Stock Exchange can use that information directly to trade through SEAQ.

Stockbroking firms charge their clients a commission, which is the brokers' source of income. These dealing costs tend to be significant, particularly on small transactions, though they typically become proportionately cheaper on larger ones.

Stockbrokers offer their clients a range of professional services related to investment, rarely viewing their role in the narrow sense of buying and selling agents. They are, of course, in a competitive position one with another for investors' business. Those giving the best service, in terms of advice and guidance, are likely to attract most dealing commissions.

Options

Not only can investors buy and sell securities, they may also, through the Stock Exchange, buy the right (but not the obligation) to buy or sell specified securities at predetermined prices before a stated date. Where, for example, an investor believes that Trafalgar House shares are due to rise, an option to buy a certain quantity at a specified price before a stated date can be bought. This would be known as a 'call' option and the price of such an option would depend on the quantity, the call price and the exercise date. If, by the exercise date, the market price of Trafalgar House is above the call price, the investor would take up the option to buy the shares. An option giving the right to sell is known as a 'put' option. In certain securities the option itself may even be bought and sold (traded options). Share options are another example of derivatives (see Chapter 1).

The place of the Stock Exchange in the UK secondary market

There is no legal requirement in the UK that all secondary market activities must be carried out through the Stock Exchange. Whilst it has long been and still remains the case that the Stock Exchange dominates the UK secondary market in terms of business transacted, there are other markets, albeit limited ones.

There are for example commercial organisations which operate an *over the counter (OTC)* market, where the organisations act as a market maker in a range of securities. Securities are bought from and sold to the investing public, in much the same way as dealers in second-hand furniture do with their wares, without an agent being involved.

Whilst the Stock Exchange has been and still is regarded as pre-eminent in the UK secondary market, there is no special reason why it should continue to hold that position. There is some evidence – for example the recent emergence of the OTC market – which suggests that members of the investing public will readily look elsewhere if they feel that the Stock Exchange is not providing the service they need, at a price they are prepared to pay.

CAPITAL MARKET EFFICIENCY

When security prices at all times rationally reflect all available, relevant information, the market in which they are traded is said to be *efficient*. This implies that any new information coming to light which bears on a particular firm will be incorporated into the market price of the security,

(a) quickly, and
(b) rationally, in terms of size and direction of security price movement.

To say that a secondary capital market is efficient is not necessarily to imply that the market is 'perfect' in the economists' sense, though to be efficient the market has to display most of the features of the perfect market to some degree. It is also important to note that efficiency does not mean perfect powers of prediction on the part of investors. All that it means is that the current price of a security is the best estimate of its economic value on the basis of the available evidence.

Why should capital markets be efficient?

Prices are set in capital markets by the forces of supply and demand. If the consensus view of those active in the market is that a security is underpriced, demand will force the price up.

In a secondary capital market such as the Stock Exchange, security prices are observed by large numbers of people, many of them skilled and experienced, nearly all of them moved to do so by that great motivator – financial gain.

Information on the firm comes to these observers in a variety of ways. From the firm itself come accounting statements, press releases and leaks (deliberate or otherwise). Information on the industry and economy in which the firm operates will also be germane to assessment of the value of a particular security and this will emerge from a variety of sources.

Where observers spot what they consider to be an irrational price, they tend to seek to take advantage of it or to advise others to do so. For example, an investment analyst employed by a unit trust assesses the worth of a share in Marks and Spencer plc at £5.50 but notes that the current share price is £4.90. The analyst might then contact the investment manager to advise the purchase of some of these shares on the basis that they are currently under-priced and there are gains to be made. The increase in demand which some large-scale buying would engender would put up the price of the shares. Our analyst is just one of a large number of pundits constantly comparing the market price of Marks and Spencer shares with their own assessment of their worth. Most of these pundits will take action themselves or cause it to be taken by those whom they advise if they spot some disparity. The market price of the shares at all times represents the consensus view. If people feel strongly that this price is irrational they will take steps to gain from their beliefs; the greater they perceive the irrationality to be, the more dramatic the steps that they will take.

Efficiency and the consensus

Efficiency has been interpreted by some people as requiring that there is at least one person active in the market who has great knowledge, skill and judgement. This need not be the case. Beaver (1989) points out that all that is needed for efficiency is many observers with most having some rational perceptions even if their other perceptions about the security are misguided. He argues that the misguided perceptions will be random and probably not held by others. The rational perceptions, on the other hand, will be common, perhaps not to all, but nonetheless to a large number of observers. As the security price reflects a *weighted average* of the perceptions of all those active in the market for that particular security, the misconceptions, because they are random, will tend to cancel each other out and so have no overall effect on the price. The correct perceptions will not be random and so will not cancel each other and will therefore be reflected in the share price.

Beaver illustrates and supports this point with what is at first sight an irrelevant account of some predictions of results (win, lose or draw) of American football games. The *Chicago Daily News*, on each Friday over the period 1966 to 1968, reported the predictions of each of its 14 or 15 sports staff of the outcome of the games to be played over the forthcoming weekend. The newspaper also published the consensus view of the sports staff, i.e. the majority view on each game. When the success of the predictions was summarised for the three years the results were as shown in Table 9.1.

Table 9.1 Performance of forecasters of American football games

	1966	1967	1968
Number of forecasters (including the consensus)	15	15	16
Number of forecasts per forecaster	180	220	219
Rank of leading forecasters:			
J. Carmichael	1 (tie)	8	16
D. Nightingale	1 (tie)	11	5
A. Biondo	7	1	6
H. Duck	8	10	1
Rank of the consensus	1 (tie)	2	2

Source: Chicago Daily News

It is interesting to note that the consensus view outperforms all *individuals* over the three years and indeed outperforms all but one or two in any particular year (it tied with two individuals in 1966 and was beaten by one individual in 1967 and 1968). It is clear from the Table that the performance of the successful individuals is inconsistent, suggesting some element of luck in their successful year. Luck may not be the only reason for the success, since Biondo performed better than average in all three years. Yet despite the possible presence of skill in one individual, over the three years the consensus easily beat them all.

It would appear that some forecasters are more skilled than others. It also seems that the consensus performs even better than the best individual. This is despite the fact that the consensus combines the forecasts of all the individuals, skilled and not so skilled. Far from having the effect of dragging down the quality of the forecasts of the best individuals, combining the forecasts, to find the consensus, actually improves the quality of forecasting. Beaver suggests that this is because idiosyncratic factors (e.g. personal loyalties to a particular football team, which might influence the forecasts of even the best forecaster) tend to cancel out when a reasonably large number of different individuals is involved in forming the consensus. Thus the consensus represents a rather more clear-sighted and objective forecast than any individual can provide, on a consistent basis.

Efficiency and speed of reaction

Efficiency requires not only that prices react rationally to new information, but that they react speedily. Certainly the rate at which data can be transmitted, received, analysed, the analysis transmitted, received and acted upon by buying or selling is very rapid, particularly in this era of cheap electronic data communication and processing.

Since there are large numbers of informed, highly motivated observers who are capable of quick action, we have good reason to believe that a sophisticated secondary capital market like the Stock Exchange could be efficient in its pricing of securities. The question now becomes, is it?

TESTS OF CAPITAL MARKET EFFICIENCY

Forms of efficiency

Attempts to assess efficiency have not so much addressed themselves to whether the capital markets are efficient or are not efficient but rather to what extent they are efficient. Roberts (1959) suggested that efficiency and tests of it should be dealt with under three headings:

(a) *Weak form.* If the market is efficient to this level, any information which might be contained in past price movements is already reflected in the securities' prices.

(b *Semi-strong form.* This form of efficiency implies that all relevant publicly available information is impounded in security prices.

(c) *Strong form.* If present this would mean that all relevant information, including that which is only available to those in privileged positions (e.g. managers) is fully reflected in security prices.

These are ascending levels of efficiency such that, if a market is strong-form efficient it must, therefore, also be semi-strong and weak-form efficient.

Approach taken by the tests

Propositions such as that relating to capital market efficiency are *not directly testable.* How can we test whether all available information is reflected in security prices? The researcher may not personally have all of the available information or even know that some of it exists. We can however test whether or not security price behaviour seems consistent with efficiency. All of the tests which have been carried out have tried to do this.

Most tests have sought to assess whether or not it seems possible to make *abnormal* returns by exploiting any possible inefficiency. Abnormal returns in this context means returns in excess of those which could be made over the same period in which the test was conducted, from securities of similar risk. Returns typically means capital gain plus dividend received over a period, expressed as a percentage of a security's price at the start of that period.

Tests of weak-form efficiency

It has long been popularly believed that security prices move in cycles which are predictable by those who study the matter closely enough. Many feel that past patterns of security price behaviour repeat themselves, so that spotting a repeat starting to occur can put the investor in a position to make abnormally large investment returns. Not surprisingly, adherents to this philosophy use graphs and charts of past security prices in order to facilitate recognition of the pattern early enough to benefit from it. These people are often referred to as *chartists.*

Others seek to develop trading rules which are perhaps easier to apply than those of the chartists. For example it is believed by some that the price of a particular security tends to hover around a particular value, rarely deviating from it by more than a small percentage. If the price starts to *break out* from the $\pm x\%$ band, they believe that this implies a large movement about to occur. This they feel can be taken advantage of by buying or selling according to the direction of the break-out. Such dealing rules are usually called *filter rules*. More generally, the practitioners of techniques like filter rules and charts, are known as *technical analysts*.

If the market is efficient this should mean that no gains could be made from technical analysis because there are so many observers at work that if any information were contained in past price movements it would be impounded in the current price as a result of buying and selling. Only new information would affect share prices. As new information is random, security prices would be expected to follow a random path or random walk. New information must be random or it would not be new information. That the sales of a Christmas card manufacturer were greater towards the end of some particular year than at other times during that year is not new information, because this pattern tends to occur each year and is predictable.

Let us suppose that the price of a particular security has followed the cyclical pattern shown in Fig. 9.1 over a number of years. There is obviously a regular pattern here. What should we do if we spotted this pattern at time t? Surely we should buy some of the securities and hold them until the next peak, sell them and rebuy at the following trough and so on until we became bored with making money! It seems too good to be true and of course it is. In real life we should not be the only ones to spot this repetition of peaks and troughs, in fact there would be a very large number of us who would notice it. As we try to sell at the peak, so would the others. Since few potential buyers would be interested at the peak price, the price would drop. Realising this, we should all try to sell earlier to try to beat the drop in price, which would simply cause it to occur still earlier. The logical conclusion of this is that the price would not in fact ever rise to the peak. Expecting the trough to be reached and eager not to miss it we should be buying earlier and earlier, thus keeping the price up and ensuring that the trough is never reached either.

The net result of all this is that if there are sufficient investors following past price patterns and seeking to exploit repetitions of them, those repetitions simply will not occur. In practice the more likely price profile of that security would approximate to the horizontal broken line shown in Fig. 9.1.

The first recorded discovery of randomness in a competitive market was by Bachelier when he observed it as a characteristic of commodity prices on the Paris Bourse as long ago as 1900. His discovery went somewhat unnoticed until interest in the topic was rekindled some years later.

Kendall (1953), accepting the popular view of the day that Stock Exchange security prices move in regular cycles, tried to identify the pattern, only to discover that there was none; prices seemed to move randomly.

Efficiency and randomness imply that there should be no systematic correlation between the price movement on one day and that on another. For example, it seems to be believed by some observers that if the price of a security rises today then it is more likely than not to rise again tomorrow, i.e. there are price trends. Similarly there are those who feel that the opposite is true and that a price rise today implies a fall tomorrow. These attitudes do not of course reflect any belief in efficiency.

Fig. 9.1
A graph of the daily share price against time for a hypothetical security

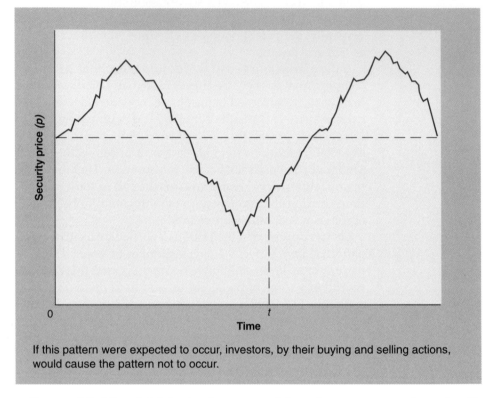

If this pattern were expected to occur, investors, by their buying and selling actions, would cause the pattern not to occur.

Figures 9.2, 9.3 and 9.4 depict the scatter of the price movement of one day (*t*) plotted against that of the following day (*t* + 1) for a particular security over a period. Figure 9.2 reflects a positive correlation, i.e. it suggests that an increase in the security price on one day will be followed by another increase on the following day. Figure 9.3 implies a negative correlation so that an increase in price on one day would mean a fall on the following day, and vice versa. Figure 9.4 shows what we should expect if the security were traded in a weak-form efficient market, i.e. there appears to be randomness between one day's price movement and that of the next. Sometimes an increase is followed by an increase, sometimes by a decrease, but with no patterns.

Many tests have sought to identify relationships between price movements on consecutive days, two or more days or weeks, and found no such relationships, either positive or negative, of significant size. This research shows that security price movements closely resemble the sort of pattern that would emerge from a random number generator. Probably the most highly regarded of these serial correlation tests was conducted by Fama (1965). Brealey (1970) and Cunningham (1973) conducted similar tests on security prices in the UK Stock Exchange and found evidence of weak-form efficiency.

Fig. 9.2
A graph of a security's price on one day (day *t*) against that of the following day (day *t* + 1) where the two movements are *positively* correlated

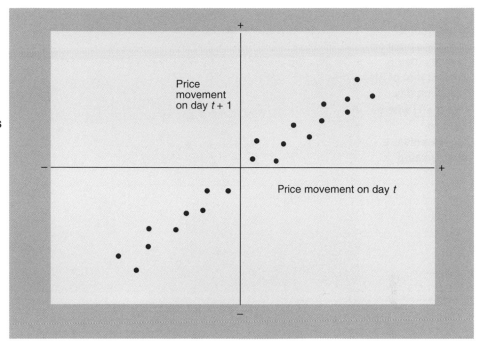

Fig. 9.3
A graph of a security's price on one day (day *t*) against that of the following day (day *t* + 1) where the two movements are *negatively* correlated

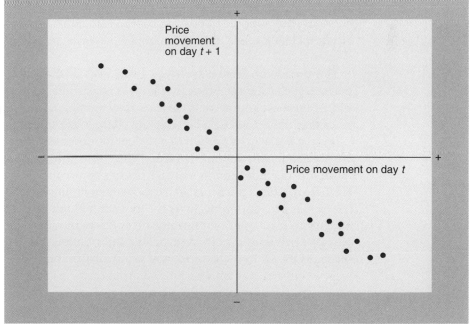

**Fig. 9.4
A graph of a
security's price on
one day (day *t*)
against that of the
following day
(day *t* + 1) where
the two
movements are
uncorrelated**

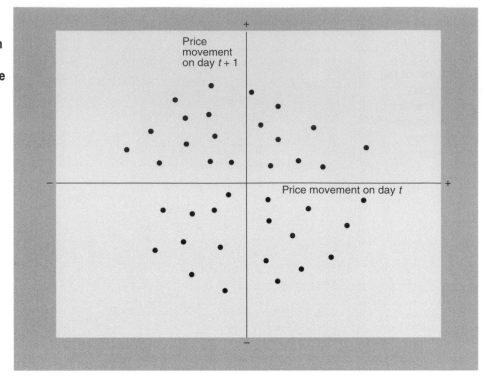

Most of the rules used by technical analysts have been tested. For example, Alexander (1961) used a filter rule and found that abnormal returns could be made, but as soon as dealing charges are considered the gains disappear. Dryden (1970), using filter tests on UK security prices, came to similar conclusions.

The broad conclusion on weak-form tests is that the evidence on capital markets including the Stock Exchange is consistent with weak-form efficiency. Whilst there are minor inefficiencies, they are not of any economic significance since they cease to exist when dealing charges are considered.

It is particularly important to note that randomness does *not* mean that prices are set irrationally. On the contrary, since new information becomes available randomly, its reflection in security prices should also be random if the market is efficient. After a particular price movement it may well be possible to explain, by reference to real events, why the movement took place. Randomness should not be confused with arbitrariness here. Prices moving in trends and repeating past patterns would point to available information not being fully reflected in those prices, i.e. to inefficiency and arbitrary pricing.

Tests of semi-strong-form efficiency

These have centred on questions of whether new information, which could reasonably be expected to affect a security's price, actually does so, in the expected direction and with the expected rapidity.

Tests of this type pose several methodological problems. Such is the number of factors acting simultaneously on the price of a particular security, that it is difficult to know to what extent prices are affected by the specific factor in which the researcher is interested and to what extent other factors are involved. For our present purposes let us accept what is believed by most qualified observers, that the major researchers in this area, some of whose work we shall consider, have sufficiently well overcome the practical problems for their results to be regarded as providing significant insights. Readers who are interested in looking at the methodological problems in detail should take up some of the references given during and at the end of this chapter.

A fertile area for testing to see whether security prices react rationally to new information is where some action of management might superficially seem to indicate something which on closer examination is not the case. If security prices seem to reflect the superficial view of the action and not the rational one it would imply that the market was not efficient (in the semi-strong form) due to the naïvety of investors. In other words, it would imply the managers would be able to fool the investors by window-dressing activities.

One example of this is *capitalisation* or *bonus share issues.* This is little more than a bookkeeping entry which gives existing equity shareholders an increase in their holding of shares, without increasing each individual's slice of the owner-ship of the firm. For example, an investor owning 100 ordinary shares in a firm whose total shares issued is 1 000 000 owns one ten-thousandth of the equity value of that firm. If the firm makes a bonus issue of one for two, our share-holder now has 150 shares but as the total number of shares at issue will now be 1 500 000 this still represents one ten-thousandth of the equity. As the total value of the equity has not changed as a result of the bonus issue, logically share prices should adjust so that three shares after the issue are worth as much as two were before. Naïve investors might feel that this was a real gain and see the post-issue price of two-thirds of the pre-issue one as a genuine bargain. This would cause them to come into the market as buyers forcing the price up. Research conducted on the Stock Exchange and on Wall Street by Firth (1977a), and by Fama, Fisher, Jensen and Roll (1969) respectively, found no such naïvety and that security prices reacted in the logical way.

Another example where the superficial interpretation of events could be the wrong one is where profits appear to improve as a result of a change in accounting procedures. Sunder (1973) looked at a number of US firms which had changed their method of stock-in-trade valuation so that they appeared to show higher profits than had the old method been adhered to. This would appear to be the perfect trap in which to catch the naïve investor, in that the economic consequences of the change would be adverse since the firms' tax charges (which are based on accounting profits) would increase. Rationally the change in accounting policy should cause a drop in equity share prices for those firms as the change would adversely affect the firms' cash flows (increased tax payments). Sunder found that reason appeared to have prevailed in that, for this group of firms, the change had an adverse effect on share prices. Sunder also took a group of firms which had altered their stock-in-trade valuation method in exactly the opposite way and found this had, as reason would demand, caused the opposite effect on share prices.

Using UK data Morris (1975) found that share prices had adjusted to take account of a reduction of earnings figures to adjust for inflation, even before the adjustment had been published.

Testing speed of reaction of security prices to new information presents great practical difficulties. It is hard to identify precisely when the new information becomes known and in some markets, including the Stock Exchange, difficult to know after the event precisely when the price movement occurred. On Wall Street records are available of all transactions and their timing, to the minute. Thus if a particular transaction is itself regarded as having possible informational content, researchers could know the timing of that transaction and the timing and price of subsequent transactions. Dann, Mayers and Raab (1977) conducted some research on the effect of trades of large blocks of shares of a particular firm, much larger than the number of shares traded in the typical stock market transaction. Amongst other things they noted that the *turbulence* caused by such trades, the period during which the market assessed the effect of the trade, lasted about 15 minutes at most. This is to say that an unexpected event, albeit an event occurring in the heart of the capital market (Wall Street in this particular case), had been assessed and was reflected in the new price within a quarter of an hour. Large block trades are felt to have possible informational content in that a purchase or a sale of a large quantity of the security might imply that the investor initiating the trade has some new information which has precipitated the action.

From the studies which we have reviewed here, the results of which are typical of the conclusions drawn from the research conducted on the world's secondary capital markets, the evidence seems consistent with the view that security prices adjust rationally and speedily to new information. Just as importantly, they seem to ignore bogus new information, i.e. data which appears to be relevant but which in fact is not. Thus the general conclusion is that the capital markets, including the Stock Exchange, are efficient in the semi-strong form.

Tests of strong-form efficiency

Strong-form efficiency would imply that there is no such thing as private information in the context of information relevant to the setting of security prices. As soon as information is available to any one person or group it is reflected in the price of the particular security or securities to which it relates.

Those who might have access to information which is not generally available include:

(a) *insiders* who have privileged positions with regard to such information (this might include managers, staff, auditors and other professional advisers); and

(b) *expert and professional investors.*

Intuition suggests that managers who are privy to information not yet publicly available could turn this knowledge into investment returns that are abnormally high compared with those of investors not possessing the information. Similarly we might expect that investment fund managers would be more successful, given their experience and research resources, than if they were to select investments with a pin.

In the UK insider dealing is much frowned upon by public opinion, by law and by ethical standards of professional bodies. Thus, if insider dealing goes on, it is done furtively and is therefore not readily observable by researchers. In the USA a different attitude used to be taken (until the 1960s) to insider dealing, though insiders were required to register their status when dealing. Tests on the success of insiders dealing on Wall Street have been conducted. Both Jaffe (1974) and Finnerty (1976) found that insiders could consistently earn abnormal returns as a result of their greater access to information.

As regards professional investors, much research has been conducted into the performance of unit and investment trusts. These are organisations which attract funds from the investing public which are then invested predominantly in marketable securities. These studies, including one conducted by Firth (1977b) on UK unit trust performance during the period 1965 to 1975, have found no superior performance. Some researchers have found that the results of investment by these experts are in fact less good than would be the outcome of an investment strategy based on selecting securities at random.

The advice of professional investment advisers has also been assessed and found not generally to lead to consistently abnormal returns.

The conclusion on strong-form efficiency would seem to be that insiders who have genuine new information can use it to advantage, revealing an inefficiency of the capital markets. However, those not having access to such information are not, on a continuing basis, able to achieve better than average returns irrespective of whether they are 'experts' or not.

We have reviewed by no means all of the research which has been conducted; however, other studies have reached similar conclusions to those which we have considered.

CONCLUSIONS AND IMPLICATIONS OF CAPITAL MARKET EFFICIENCY

The conclusions of tests on the efficiency of the Stock Exchange and of capital markets generally is that the evidence is consistent with efficiency in all forms, except that only publicly available information seems to be reflected in security prices. Information not yet publicly available is not necessarily reflected. Results of research, emerging from the USA particularly, are showing some minor capital market inefficiencies. This may indicate that the application of more modern and sophisticated statistical techniques is revealing inefficiencies which were not previously apparent. However, for most practical purposes we can probably say that the Stock Exchange efficiently prices securities which are traded there.

Implications for investors

Capital market efficiency implies that investors should not seek either by regard to historical information on security price movements or by analysis of new economic information to obtain abnormally high returns from investment. Only where an investor has access to as-yet unreleased information can better-than-average returns be made – except by sheer chance. Even putting trust in investment analysts or investing through one of the investing institutions will not, on a regular basis, be advantageous and it may well be costly.

Why, if the above statement is true, do so many investors indulge in precisely the activities which appear to be futile? There are several possible explanations for this apparently irrational behaviour.

(a) *Ignorance of the evidence on efficiency.* Many investors seem to be unfamiliar with the evidence on capital market efficiency so, naturally enough, they do not take account of it. Few people or organisations have a vested interest in publicising the evidence and many have the opposite interest. Newspapers and journals which deal partly or mainly in giving advice on which specific securities to buy or sell do not have an interest in pointing out that this advice is only going to prove valuable by sheer chance so that on average it will be of no value. Other investment advisers, stockbrokers, etc., are similarly placed.

(b) *Close examination of charts of past security price movements shows patterns repeating themselves.* This is undoubtedly true in some cases, but it is equally true that plotting random numbers will also sometimes do exactly the same. In other words, chance alone will sometimes cause a pattern to repeat itself; this does not imply that gains can be made by trying to spot repeats.

(c) *Proponents of certain technical rules have been shown to be successful.* Efficiency does not imply that investment cannot be successful, simply that being more than averagely successful is a matter of good luck. During some particular periods and generally throughout the twentieth century, investment in securities dealt on the Stock Exchange will have given positive returns. The value of securities generally has increased, not to mention the dividends or interest receipts from which the investor will also have benefited. It should not therefore surprise us that, despite efficiency, following most investment advice over a substantial period yields positive returns. Indeed, efficiency implies that it would be impossible to find investment advice to follow which would yield lower-than-average returns in the long run, for the level of risk involved, except by sheer chance.

(d) *We all know of cases of people who have been extremely successful in capital market investment.* Those who are particularly successful tend not to hide their light under a bushel; those who are disastrously unsuccessful tend to keep quiet about it. In both cases it seems to be sheer luck – good and bad, respectively. Those who are unsuccessful tend to acknowledge this fact; the successful ones – being human – may prefer to believe that skill in selection and timing of investment was the cause of their success.

Even in matters of sheer chance someone can still be successful, even staggeringly successful. Suppose that a coin-tossing championship of the UK were to be held and that all 60 million inhabitants entered. The rules are that we are all grouped into 30 million pairs; each of which tosses a coin. The member of each pair who calls correctly goes into the next round and the process is repeated until the winner emerges. We know that a winner must emerge, but would we really believe that skill was involved? We should more likely judge the winner to have had remarkably good fortune, in the face of a very small probability of success.

A notable paradox of capital market efficiency is that if large numbers of investors were not trying to earn abnormal returns by technical analysis and by the analysis of new information (fundamental analysis), efficiency would not exist. It is only because so many non-believers are actively seeking out inefficiencies to exploit to their own advantage that none exists which is, in practical terms, exploitable.

Implications for financial managers

These are vitally important and the main reason why we are discussing capital market efficiency at all in this book. Broadly the implications are:

(a) *It is difficult to 'pull the wool over the eyes' of investors.* Investors rationally interpret what the firm's management does, and embroidering matters will not cause security prices to rise.

(b) *The market rationally values the firm.* If the management want to issue new equity shares, then the existing equity price is the appropriate issue price. If the general level of prices is low on a historical basis, it would be illogical for the firm to wait for a recovery before issuing new equity. If security prices follow a random walk, there is no reason to believe that just because prices have been higher in the past they will return to previous levels.

(c) *Management should act in a way which maximises shareholder wealth.* As this is the generally accepted criterion for making investment decisions within the firm, if managers make decisions which logically should promote it, then provided that they release information on what they have done, security prices will reflect the managers' actions. In other words, if managers act in a way which promotes the interests of shareholders, this will in fact promote their interests through the share price.

(d) *Managers may have an interest in withholding unfavourable information.* The strong-form inefficiency revealed by research shows that not all information which exists is impounded in security prices. Thus management might have a vested interest in withholding such information. Whether this would in fact be valid in the long run is doubtful since most information sees the light of day sooner or later. Probably a widespread feeling among investors that managers are prepared to suppress unfavourable information would ultimately be detrimental to those managers.

(e) *The secondary capital markets rationally value assets which have risky returns.* In the same way that if we wish to value a second-hand car we might look at the price for similar cars in the second-hand car market, it is logical to try to assess the value of assets with particular risk and return expectations by looking at prices of similar assets in the secondary capital markets. This provides a major justification for the use of CAPM, in deriving an appropriate discount rate to apply to cash flows, in the assessment of real investment decisions made by firms.

The general position which efficiency engenders for management is that management and security holders are directly linked through security prices. Whilst this link may not be a rigid one where even relatively insignificant actions of management immediately reflect in security prices, nonetheless the evidence supports the view that security prices do react rapidly and rationally to new information. The implications of secondary capital market efficiency for managers will be referred to at various points throughout the remainder of this book.

SUMMARY

Capital markets have two functions: a primary finance raising one and a secondary security transfer function. The secondary function is vital to the interests of firms seeking to raise long-term finance as, without the facility to liquidate their investment, investors are reluctant to lay out funds. The Stock Exchange is, like most secondary markets round the world, closely regulated to promote fair treatment of all investors. Most capital markets, including the Stock Exchange, seem to be efficient in pricing the securities that are traded in them. Efficiency implies that prices at all times rationally reflect all available information which bears on the economic value of the security. Evidence suggests that the only manner in which capital markets show themselves to be inefficient is that they do not seem always fully to reflect information which is available only to insiders.

The implications of efficiency are important both to investors and to managers. Investors are wasting their time seeking out better-than-average investments; such investments are not recognisable until it is too late to benefit from their recognition. Managers should accept that the market at all times rationally values the firm and its securities. Efficiency also implies that managers' actions will be correctly interpreted by the market and reflected in security prices.

FURTHER READING The role and operation of the Stock Exchange is covered by a number of texts including Samuels, Wilkes and Brayshaw (1995). Facts and figures on the Stock Exchange are published annually in *The Stock Exchange Fact Book.*

Capital market efficiency is well reviewed in the literature. Iveson, Moss and Simpson (1986) refer to a number of tests carried out on UK data. Copeland and Weston (1988) discuss much of the more important capital market research and the methodological problems which the researchers encountered. Comment on all of the research reviewed in this chapter and more besides is made in these last two texts. Keane (1983) gives a most interesting coverage of the topic, including discussion of the tests and, particularly, of the implications.

For an impressive review of empirical studies of market efficiency, see Fama (1991).

REVIEW QUESTIONS

Suggested answers to review questions appear in Appendix 3.

9.1 What are the two roles of members of the International Stock Exchange (of the UK and the Republic of Ireland) (ISE) in respect of their secondary market activities?

9.2 When UK shareholders have shares which they wish to sell must the sale be made through the ISE?

9.3 What is 'price efficiency' in the context of stock markets?

9.4 Is a market which is 'strong-form efficient' necessarily 'semi-strong-form efficient'?

9.5 Without any knowledge of the evidence surrounding the efficiency of the ISE, would you expect it to be efficient? Explain your response.

9.6 Must all of the world's stock markets be price efficient? Explain your response.

PROBLEMS

Sample answers to problems marked with an asterisk appear in Appendix 4.

(Note that problem questions 9.1–9.5 are all basic level problems.)

9.1* 'The shares of XYZ plc are underpriced at the moment.'

How logical is this statement about some shares quoted on the International Stock Exchange (of the UK and the Republic of Ireland)?

9.2* 'Capital market efficiency in the semi-strong form implies that all investors are possessed of all of the knowledge which is publicly available and which bears on the value of all securities traded in the market.'

Comment on this statement.

9.3* 'In view of the fact that the market is efficient in the semi-strong form, there is no value to investors in companies publishing accounting reports, because the information contained in those reports is already impounded in share prices before that information is published.'

Comment on this statement.

9.4 'A graph of the daily price of a share looks similar to that which would be obtained by plotting a series of cumulative random numbers. This shows clearly that share prices move randomly at the whim of investors indicating that the market is not price efficient.'

Comment on this statement.

9.5 'A particular professionally managed UK equity investment fund produced better returns last year than any of its rivals. This means that it is likely to outperform its rivals again this year.'

Comment on this statement.

CHAPTER 10

Cost of capital estimations and the discount rate

INTRODUCTION

In Chapter 8 we took a brief look at typical sources of long-term finance of UK firms. Now we shall see how it is possible to make estimates of the cost to the firm of each of these individual sources.

Since logically the discount rate to be applied to the expected cash flows of real investment opportunities within the firm should be the opportunity cost of finance to support the investment, this discount rate should be related to the costs of individual sources in some way. In fact, using an average cost of the various sources of finance, weighted according to the importance of each source to the particular firm, seems to be regarded as a standard means of determining discount rates. Evidence (Petty & Scott 1981; Corr, 1983) suggests that this weighted average cost of capital (WACC) approach is widely used in practice.

The approach to estimation of the cost of specific sources of capital which we shall consider in this chapter is based on the logic that the rate is implied by the current value of the financial asset concerned, and by future expectations of cash flows from that specific asset. This is probably the approach which is adopted in practice.

In Chapter 7 we saw that by making several assumptions it is possible to derive a logical device for deciding on the appropriate discount rate to apply to expected cash flows from investment possibilities to be able to assess each possibility's effect on the value of the firm (and therefore on the wealth of the shareholders). This device, the capital asset pricing model (CAPM), deduces the cost of capital from capital market information. CAPM deals explicitly with risk via a risk premium based on expected excess returns determined by covariance of specific security returns with those from the generality of risky investments.

The traditional WACC approach is also capital market based (we use current security values in the calculation), but it deals much less formally with risk than does CAPM.

After having considered the traditional approach we shall try to reconcile it with the CAPM approach, and attempt to reach some conclusion on the theoretical appropriateness of each and of their relative practicality.

COST OF INDIVIDUAL CAPITAL ELEMENTS

An economic asset (which loan stocks, equities, etc., are to their owners) has the current value

$$v_0 = \sum C_n / (1+r)^n \tag{1}$$

where C is the cash flow associated with the asset, r the rate of return, and n the time of each cash flow. To a loan creditor or shareholder, the future cash flows, at any given moment, will usually be the future interest or dividend receipts (payable annually, biannually, or perhaps quarterly) and perhaps a repayment of the principal at some future specified date.

Logically, a rate of return to the investors represents a cost to the firm in which they invested. Therefore we make the general statement that

$$p_0 = \sum C_n / (1+k)^n \tag{2}$$

where k is the cost of capital to the firm and p_0 is the security's current market price.

Loan stocks

With quoted loan stocks we should know the current market value of the loan stock, the contracted interest payments and dates, and the contracted amount and date of the repayment of the principal. Thus in the valuation expression above we should know all of the factors except k. Solving for k will give us the cost of capital figure which we require.

EXAMPLE

A loan stock which was originally issued at par is currently quoted in the capital market at £93 per £100 nominal value, repayment of the nominal value in full is due in exactly five years' time, and interest at 10 per cent on the nominal value is due for payment at the end of each of the next five years. What is the cost of the loan stock?

Assume a 33 per cent rate of Corporation tax.

SOLUTION

Since we are seeking to deduce a rate which can be used to discount after-tax cash flows, we need an after-tax cost of capital. The loan stock interest would attract tax relief, but the capital repayment would not because it is not an expense.

The following statement holds true:

$$93 = \frac{10(1-0.33)}{(1+k_L)} + \frac{10(1-0.33)}{(1+k_L)^2} + \frac{10(1-0.33)}{(1+k_L)^3} + \frac{10(1-0.33)}{(1+k_L)^4} + \frac{10(1-0.33)}{(1+k_L)^5} + \frac{100}{(1+k_L)^5}$$

Solving this for k_L will give us the required cost of capital figure. We have met this situation before when deducing the internal rate of return of an investment opportunity. k_L is of course the IRR of the loan stock and, as such, the solution is only discoverable by trial and error. As annual returns of a net £6.70 are worth £93, a rate of less than 10 per cent is implied. Let us try 8 per cent.

	Cash flow	Discount factor	Present value
Year 0	(93.0)	1.000	(93.0)
1	6.7	0.926	6.2
2	6.7	0.857	5.7
3	6.7	0.794	5.3
4	6.7	0.735	4.9
5	106.7	0.681	72.7
			1.8

It seems that the cost of capital is above 8 per cent, let us try 9 per cent.

	Cash flow	Discount factor	Present value
Year 0	(93.0)	1.000	(93.0)
1	6.7	0.917	6.1
2	6.7	0.842	5.6
3	6.7	0.772	5.2
4	6.7	0.708	4.7
5	106.7	0.650	69.4
			(2.0)

Thus the cost lies very close to 8.5 per cent.

Some readers may be puzzled as to why, when the original amount borrowed was £100, the amount to be repaid is equally £100 and the coupon interest rate is 10 per cent, the cost of the loan stock is not 10 per cent, before tax or 6.7 per cent after tax.

We should remember that our purpose in calculating the cost of capital is to derive a discount rate to apply to investment projects. In previous chapters we have seen that the appropriate discount rate is the opportunity cost of capital. This means either the saving which would follow from repaying the capital source, or the cost of raising further finance from that source. At the present time this amount would be 8.5 per cent after tax. If the firm wishes to cancel the loan stock, it can do so by buying the stock in the capital market at £93 (per £100 nominal). This would save the annual interest payments of 6.7 per cent on the nominal value, and avoid the necessity to repay the capital after five years. If further finance is to be raised, presumably the same firm could raise £93 for a loan stock which pays £10 at the end of each of the next five years plus £100 at the end of the fifth year. So in either case, 8.5 per cent is the appropriate rate.

We might also ask why investors were at one time prepared to pay £100 (for £100 nominal value) for a loan stock which yields £10 per annum in interest (a 10 per cent return). The difference must arise either from interest rates having increased generally and/or from the capital market having changed its perceptions of the risk of default (by the firm) in payment of interest or principal. Thus a firm's cost of capital is not necessarily static over time. Assuming capital market efficiency, the cost of any element of a firm's capital is the market's best estimate of that cost for the future.

Perpetual loan stocks are occasionally issued by firms. These are loan stocks which have no repayment date and which will, in theory at least, continue paying interest for ever. Their cost of capital calculation is similar to, though simpler than, the calculation at which we have just looked.

Where each of the C_n values is identical and n goes on to infinity,

$$p_{L0} = \sum_{n=1}^{\infty} \frac{C_n(1-T)}{(1+k_L)^n}$$

Where T is the rate of Corporate tax, this can be rewritten as:

$$k_L = \frac{C_n(1-T)}{P_{L0}}$$

Thus in the above example, if there were to be no repayment of principal but the annual £10 interest payments were to continue indefinitely, then

$$k_L = \frac{10(1-0.33)}{93}$$

i.e.

$$k_L = 7.2\%$$

Term loans

With term loans and in fact with unquoted loan stocks, there is no readily accessible figure for p_0 which can be put into the valuation model (equation (2), p. 241) to deduce k. Logically p_0 should be the amount which the borrowing firm would need to pay immediately to induce the lender to cancel the loan contract. Alternatively it is the amount which could presently be borrowed by the firm given the future payments of interest and capital it is obliged to make under the terms of the loan in question. In theory these two should be alternative routes to the same value for p_0; in practice they may not be.

The real problem is that, equal or not, in practice p_0 is not readily observable, so some estimate of it needs to be made. In fact, unless the values of the loan are particularly large and/or there have been major changes in interest rates since the loan was negotiated, the contracted rate of interest would probably serve adequately as the present opportunity cost of the source. Alternatively an estimate, based on observation of current interest rates, could be made.

Financial leases

As we saw in Chapter 8, a financial lease is effectively a secured term loan with capital repayments at intervals during the period of the loan, rather than all at the end. Where it is not explicit in the lease contract, we can discover the interest rate fairly easily.

The value of the lease at the date of its being taken out is the cost of the asset which is the subject of the lease. Since this figure and the amount and timing of the future lease payments can be discovered, k can be discovered. To identify the present cost of a lease later in its life we should need to take a similar attitude to that which is necessary in respect of term loans and unquoted loan stocks. We could try to put some current value on the lease and solve for k in the valuation expression (equation (2) of p. 241). We could however assume that the current opportunity cost of the lease finance is more or less the same as it was when the lease was first taken out.

Trying to value the lease at some date after it has been in operation for a while would be likely to be a fairly difficult task, so we are probably left with making the assumption that the interest rate implied by the original contract is still appropriate. Alternatively some estimate of rates applying to current new leases could be used.

Preference shares

The calculation of the cost of preference shares is almost identical to that for loan stocks. The major differences between the two financing methods are:

(a) loans stocks attract Corporation Tax relief, preference dividends do not; and

(b) loan interest is paid under a contractual obligation, preference dividends are paid at the discretion of the firm's directors.

The first point simply means that tax may be ignored in the calculation of the cost of preference shares. The second implies that rather more uncertainty is involved with predicting preference dividends than with predicting loan interest payments, though this creates no difference in principle.

Ordinary shares

These too are similar to loan stocks in the basic calculation of the cost of capital. Ordinary shares have a value basically because they are expected to yield dividends. How, if at all, the pattern of dividends affects the value of equities we shall discuss in Chapter 12.

To say that equities should be valued on the basis of future dividends is not to assume any particular investor intends to hold a particular share for ever, though the proceeds of any future disposal of the share will itself depend on expectations, at the date of disposal, of future dividends.

If a firm is expected to pay a constant dividend d per share, at the end of each year indefinitely, the value of each ordinary share will be:

$$p_{E0} = \sum_{n=1}^{\infty} \frac{d_n}{(1+k_E)^n}$$

to the investor who intends to hold the shares for ever.

Suppose that the investor intends to sell the share at time t; its value at that time will be

$$\sum_{n=t+1}^{\infty} \frac{d_n}{(1+k_E)^n}$$

This would mean that the value to our shareholder would be:

$$p_{E0} = \sum_{n=1}^{t} \frac{d_n}{(1+k_E)^n} + \left(\sum_{n=t+1}^{\infty} \frac{d_n}{(1+k_E)^n} \times \frac{1}{(1+k_E)^t} \right)$$

i.e. the value depends on the dividends to be received until time t (suitably discounted) plus the market value at time t (suitably discounted at $1/(1+k_E)^t$).

This expression reduces to

$$p_{E0} = \sum_{n=1}^{\infty} \frac{d_n}{(1+k_F)^n}$$

so irrespective of whether disposal at some future date is envisaged or not, provided valuation always depends on dividends, the current value will be unaffected.

Unlike loan interest, which is usually fixed by the contract between borrower and lender, and preference dividends, which firms usually endeavour to pay (and for which there is a defined ceiling), ordinary share dividends are highly uncertain as to amount. This poses a major problem in the calculation of the cost of equities. The prediction of future dividends is a daunting task. Two simplifying approaches may be taken however:

(a) assume that dividends will remain as at present;
(b) assume some constant rate of growth in them.

If the first of these is adopted, the model similar to that for a perpetual loan stock is used, i.e.

$$p_{E0} = \sum_{n=1}^{\infty} \frac{d_n}{(1+k_E)^n} \tag{3}$$

which when all dividends are equal means

$$k_E = \frac{d_n}{p_{E0}} \tag{4}$$

If we assume a constant rate of growth g, then

$$p_{E0} = \frac{d_1}{1+k_E} + \frac{d_1(1+g)}{(1+k_E)^2} + \frac{d_1(1+g)^2}{(1+k_E)^3} + \sum_{n=4}^{\infty} \frac{d_1(1+g)^{n-1}}{(1+k_E)^n} \tag{5}$$

which reduces to

$$p_{E0} = \frac{d_1}{k_E - g} \tag{6}$$

so

$$k_E = \frac{d_1}{p_{E0}} + g \tag{7}$$

where d_1 is the expected dividend per share, payable next year.

This is known as the Gordon growth model, after the person who derived it.

EXAMPLE

A firm's ordinary shares are currently trading at £2.00 each in the capital market. Next year's dividend is expected to be £0.14 per share and subsequent dividends are expected to grow at an annual rate of 5 per cent of the previous year's dividend. What is the cost of the ordinary shares to the firm?

SOLUTION

$$k_E = \frac{d_1}{p_{E0}} + g$$

$$= \frac{0.14}{2.00} + 0.05$$

$$= 12\%$$

If a fixed proportion (b) of funds generated by trading each year is retained (as opposed to being paid as a dividend), and the funds are re-invested at a constant rate (r), then:

$$\text{rate of growth } (g) = b \times r$$

The simplifying assumptions made with the constant dividend and constant growth of dividend models clearly are unrealistic. In practice dividends tend to increase from time to time, and to remain steady at the new level for a period before the next increase.

Retained profit

As was made clear in Chapter 8, retained profit is not a free source of finance. It has an opportunity cost to shareholders because, if such profits were to be distributed, shareholders could use them to make revenue-generating investments. It would be incorrect, however, to deal with retained profit separately in deducing its cost. When we derive the cost of equity, we are deriving the cost of the share capital *and* of the retained profit. For example, the current market price of a share (p_{E0}) used in the dividend valuation model (above) would reflect the fact, if it is a fact, that there are retained profits attaching to the particular share. Thus, provided that the cost of equity is properly derived, the fact that the equity is part share capital and part retained profit will automatically be taken into account.

Convertible loan stocks

These may be viewed as redeemable loan stocks on which interest will be paid until a date in the future when they will be *redeemed* by their conversion into equities. Estimating the cost of convertibles is therefore a basically similar operation to valuing loan stocks, except that the redemption amount is unknown, to the extent that we do not know what the equity share price will be at the conversion date. As with estimating the cost of equities, we can make some assumptions – for example, that the equity dividends will remain constant or that they will grow at a steady rate.

EXAMPLE

A convertible loan stock of Tower plc currently trades in the capital market at £140 per £100 nominal. The stock pays annual interest of £11 per £100 nominal and may be converted in exactly five years' time at a rate of 50 ordinary shares in the firm per £100 nominal of loan stock. The present price of the ordinary shares is £2.20 which is expected to grow by 5 per cent per annum over the next five years. What is the cost of the convertible loan stock?

Note that Corporation tax is charged at 33 per cent.

SOLUTION

The price of the convertible p_{C0} is given by:

$$p_{C0} = \sum_{n-1}^{t} \frac{i}{(1+k_c)^n} + \frac{P_{E0}(1+g)^t R_C}{(1+k_c)^t}$$

where i is the interest payment in each year until conversion in year t, P_{E0} is the current market price of an equity share, g is the growth rate of the equity price, R_C the conversion rate, and k_C the cost of the convertible. In this example we have:

$$£140 = \frac{£11(1-0.33)}{1+k_c} + \frac{£11(1-0.33)}{(1+k_c)^2} + \frac{£11(1-0.33)}{(1+k_c)^3} + \frac{£11(1-0.33)}{(1+k_c)^4}$$

$$+ \frac{£11(1-0.33)}{(1+k_c)^5} + \frac{(1+0.05)^5 \times £2.20 \times 50}{(1+k_c)^5}$$

Solving for k_C (by trial and error) gives about 5 per cent as the cost of the convertible finance. Note that 5 per cent is an opportunity cost since:

(a) the firm should be able to issue some more convertibles with similar terms and expect to issue them at £140 per £100 nominal;

(b) if the firm were to buy back its own convertibles, for an investment of £140 it could gain £11 (less tax) each year for five years and issue the shares for cash in five years instead of using them to 'redeem' the loan stock.

This would represent an annual return of 5 per cent to Tower plc.

Warrants are valued similarly except that the returns from the warrant continue after the equity is taken up.

THE COST OF CAPITAL TO THE FIRM

We have seen how the cost of individual elements can be estimated from current capital market prices and predictions of future cash flows associated with the element concerned. Most firms use at least two of the financing methods which we have considered and each is likely to have a different cost. For example, to the capital market investor loan stock tends to be a much less risky prospect than do equities in the same firm. Expectations of returns from equities are therefore higher. Given this disparity in the cost of the various elements, which discount rate should be applied to discounting estimated cash flows of prospective investment projects?

Target gearing ratios

It has been suggested by some observers (e.g. Modigliani & Miller, 1963) that firms may have some target ratio, based on capital market values, of the various financing elements. In other words a particular firm seeks to keep equity finance as a relatively fixed proportion (by market value) of the total finance. Similarly, it seeks to keep loan-type finance as more or less a fixed proportion. Minor variations may occur from time to time, but firms are believed to take steps to get back to target as soon as it is practicable to do so.

It is believed that such target ratios exist because firms, taking account of such factors as levels of interest rates, tax advantages of loan interest relative to dividends, and the stability of the firm's operating cash flows, decide on an optimal mix of financing methods which they then try to establish and maintain. Such targets are not established for all time; changes in interest rates, tax rules, etc., may cause a change to a new target which may then rule for several years.

Targets will also vary from firm to firm, partly because of differences of opinion from one set of management to another. Such differences may also partly, perhaps mainly, arise from differences in the nature of the trade in which the particular firm is engaged. Marsh (1982) found that, in practice, most firms maintain a stable capital structure and appear to have a target gearing ratio.

The objective of trying to establish and maintain an optimal balance between various sources of finance, indeed raising finance from other than equities at all, is presumably to try to minimise the cost of capital. Whether such attempts actually work is a matter to which we shall return in Chapter 11. Meanwhile let us go back to the question of the choice of the discount rate.

Weighted average cost of capital

If we make three assumptions:

(1) There is a known target ratio for the financing elements which will continue for the duration of the investment project under consideration;

(2) the costs of the various elements will not alter in the future from the costs calculated; and

(3) the investment under consideration is of similar risk to the average of the other projects undertaken by the firm

then using the weighted average cost of capital (WACC) as the discount rate is logical.

Using opportunity cost implies looking at the savings in financing cost which would arise if finance were to be repaid instead of undertaking the investment project. Alternatively, it could be seen as the additional cost of raising the necessary finance to support the project. If there is a target, repayment of finance or additional financing would be carried out in accordance with the target. For example, suppose that a firm has a target debt/equity ratio of 50:50 (by market value). If the firm is to take on extra finance to support an investment project it will in principle do so in the same 50 : 50 proportion, otherwise it will disturb the existing position (presumably 50 : 50). Similarly, if the finance for the project is available but it could alternatively be repaid to suppliers, presumably 50 per cent would be used to cancel loan stocks and 50 per cent paid to ordinary shareholders, perhaps as a dividend.

The three assumptions stated at the start of this section are all concerned with the fact that in investment project appraisal, and in any other case where we may wish to assess the cost of capital, it is the future cost which we are interested in. The third assumption, relating to risk, perhaps needs a comment. We know from a combination of intuition, casual observation of real life and from a robust theoretical proposition (examined in Chapter 7) that the required rate of return/cost of capital depends partly on the level of risk surrounding the cash flows of the investment project concerned. It is not appropriate to use a WACC, based on a past involving investment projects of one risk class, as the discount rate for investments of an entirely different class.

EXAMPLE

Calculation of WACC

Hazelwood plc is financed by:

(a) 1 million ordinary shares (nominal value £1 each) which are expected to yield a dividend of £0.10 per share in one year's time; dividends are expected to grow by 10 per cent of the previous year's dividend each year; the current market price of the share is £1.80 each; and

(b) £800 000 (nominal) loan stock which pays interest at the end of each year of 11 per cent (of nominal) for three years, after which the loan stock will be redeemed at nominal value; currently the loan stock is quoted in the capital market at £95 (per £100 nominal).

The corporation tax rate is 33 per cent.
What is the firm's WACC?

SOLUTION

First we must find the cost of each of the individual elements.

(a) *Ordinary shares.* Here we can employ the standard dividend growth model (see equations (5)–(7), pp. 245–6)

$$\text{Cost of equity, } k_E = \frac{£0.10}{£1.80} + 10\%$$

$$= 15.6\%, \text{ say } 16\%$$

(b) *Loan stock.* We must use our IRR type trial and error here. We have the equivalent of an investment project where an investment of £95 now will bring in interest of £11 (less tax) i.e. £7.37 net, at the end of each of the next three years plus £100 at the end of the third year.

The discount rate which will give a zero NPV looks as if it is below 10 per cent. Try 8 per cent:

	Cash flow £	Discount factor	Present value £
Year 0	(95.00)	1.000	(95.0)
1	7.37	0.926	6.8
2	7.37	0.857	6.3
3	107.37	0.794	85.2
			3.3

The appropriate discount rate lies above 8 per cent. Try 9 per cent:

	Cash flow £	Discount factor	Present value £
Year 0	(95.00)	1.000	(95.0)
1	7.37	0.917	6.8
2	7.37	0.842	6.2
3	107.37	0.772	82.9
			(0.9)

Clearly the appropriate rate lies very close to 9 per cent; a closer approximation may be obtained by linear interpolation. It is very doubtful whether there is any point in seeking more accuracy than the nearest whole percentage (9 per cent) since:

(a) the cost of the other element in the financing (ordinary shares) has been calculated making some fairly sweeping assumptions about future dividends; *and*

(b) the cash flows which will be discounted by the resulting WACC cannot be predicted with any great accuracy.

We may say then that the cost of the loan stock, $k_L = 9\%$.
Next we need to value the two elements:

(a) Ordinary shares. The total value of the ordinary shares,

$$V_E = 1 \text{ million x } £1.80 = £1.80m$$

(b) Loan stock. The total value of the loan stock,

$$V_L = 800\ 000 \times \frac{95}{100} = \underline{\underline{£0.76\,m}}$$

$$\text{WACC} = \left(k_E \times \frac{V_E}{V_E + V_L} \right) + \left(k_L \times \frac{V_L}{V_E + V_L} \right)$$

$$= \left(16 \times \frac{1.80}{1.80 + 0.76} \right) + \left(9 \times \frac{0.76}{1.80 + 0.76} \right)$$

$$= 11.25 + 2.67$$

$$= 13.92\% \text{ say } \underline{\underline{14\%}}$$

Note that we used market values rather than the nominal values of the two elements as the weights. This simply reflects the fact that we are seeking the opportunity cost of capital. Market values reflect or indicate current opportunities, nominal values do not.

Realities of raising (and repaying) finance and the discount rate

Even if, as we have assumed, firms establish and maintain a target gearing ratio, the practical realities of raising and repaying finance are that it is not always economic to raise (or repay) each £1 of additional (or reduction in) finance strictly in the target proportions. This is because, as we have already seen in Chapter 8, there are fairly large fixed costs associated with share and loan stock issues. In practice firms seem to raise fairly substantial sums from each issue in order to take advantage of the economies of scale regarding the issue costs. This would tend to have the effect that the target is a factor around which the actual ratio hovers.

In the last example, the current ratio of loan stock to total finance for Hazelwood plc is 29.7 per cent (i.e. 0.76/(1.80 + 0.76)). Equity currently accounts for 70.3 per cent of the total. This suggests a target ratio of about 70:30. If the firm wished to raise £100 000, say, in order to undertake a new investment project, it is most unlikely that it would raise £70 000 in ordinary shares and £30 000 in loan stock. It is much more likely that it would raise the whole £100 000 from one source or the other. This would move its gearing ratio away from the 70 : 30 (approximately) which currently exists. The firm would get back nearer its target by raising the following increment of finance from the other source. The pattern would probably be something like that which is depicted in Fig. 10.1. Here the broken line represents the target ratio with the points A to E representing consecutive actual financing configurations. The firm here starts by raising some initial equity capital (0A) followed by an issue of loan stock of amount AB. It presumably chooses not to raise amount Ab as sufficient economies of scale as regards loan stock issue cost would not be available on such a small issue.

Fig. 10.1
A graph of the
capital structure of
a geared firm over
time

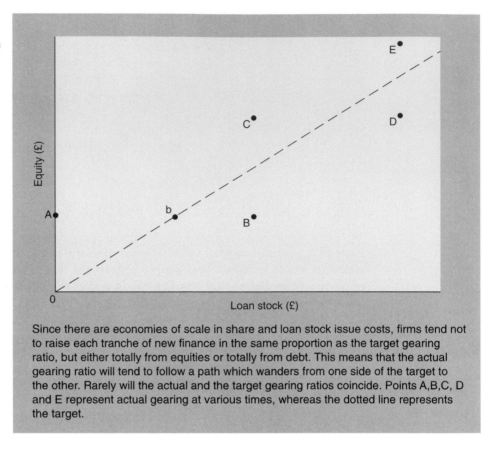

Since there are economies of scale in share and loan stock issue costs, firms tend not
to raise each tranche of new finance in the same proportion as the target gearing
ratio, but either totally from equities or totally from debt. This means that the actual
gearing ratio will tend to follow a path which wanders from one side of the target to
the other. Rarely will the actual and the target gearing ratios coincide. Points A,B,C, D
and E represent actual gearing at various times, whereas the dotted line represents
the target.

The next issue is of equities (amount BC) and so on until the present position
(E) is reached.

Specific cost or weighted average

The fact that a particular increment of finance is to be used in some particular
project should not lead the firm to use the specific cost of that finance as the
discount rate. Say, in the case of Hazelwood plc, that the £100 000 were to be
raised from an issue of loan stock at a cost of 9 per cent. It would clearly be
wrong to use 9 per cent as the discount rate in assessing the investment project
in the same way as 16 per cent would be inappropriate were the finance to be
raised by an ordinary share issue. To use 9 per cent would mean that a project
which might be acceptable if the firm were moving from point C to point D in
Fig. 10.1 might be rejected if it were moving from point D to point E, when a 16
per cent (cost of equity) rate would be used. This would clearly be illogical and
could lead to some bizarre investment decisions. It would be much more logical
to use WACC.

The target gearing ratio assumption

WACC weights the cost of each of the financing elements by its market value. When WACC is used as the discount rate to apply to real investment projects, there is the implicit assumption that the same weights will apply throughout the life of the project. This in turn assumes that firms have a target gearing ratio.

It seems logical that firms will take a fairly consistent view of the advantages (if any) of capital gearing and there is evidence that such targets actually exist in practice. Were they not to exist, the logic of using WACC as the discount rate must be called into question.

THE DISCOUNT RATE – CAPM VERSUS THE TRADITIONAL APPROACH

We have seen two means of deducing the cost of the individual elements of long-term finance:

- The CAPM approach explained in Chapter 7, which can be applied equally well to any element of financing, though we tended to concentrate on equity financing in that chapter; and
- The 'traditional' approach adopted in this chapter which bases the costs of the elements on the market price of the element, i.e. we created equations which contained the market price of the particular element (e.g. loan stock, equity, *etc.*), the cash returns which investors would expect to receive from the element and the cost of the element. Only the last of these was unknown and not estimated, so its value could be easily deduced.

Whichever of these two approaches is adopted, if the firm is not totally equity financed, the WACC must be used. Some people seem to believe that CAPM and WACC are alternative approaches. In fact, WACC is the correct approach even where CAPM is the means of estimating the cost of the individual elements.

Though both approaches must consider risk, CAPM probably has the advantage that it tends to focus more clearly on the risk of the specific project under consideration. There might be a tendency to make the implicit assumption that the risk of the project under consideration is similar to that of existing activities.

In Fig 10.2 the horizontal line represents the WACC for a particular firm. Logically the weighted average risk of the firm's existing projects must be β' as that is the risk level which, CAPM tells us, is consistent with the particular WACC. Only if projects under consideration are of exactly β' risk would WACC be the appropriate discount rate. If Project A (Fig. 10.2) were under consideration it should be accepted since it would have a positive NPV when discounted at r_A (the appropriate discount rate for its level of risk) even though if discounted at WACC its NPV would be negative. Similarly Project B, whose required rate of return is r_B, would have a positive NPV if discounted at WACC, yet a negative one if discounted at the more appropriate rate r_B. Thus use of WACC, irrespective of the risk attaching to the particular project under review, will cause some favourable projects (e.g. Project A in Fig. 10.2) to be rejected while others which would diminish the wealth of the shareholders (Project B) could be accepted.

**Fig. 10.2
A graph of the
expected return
against risk for
a firm**

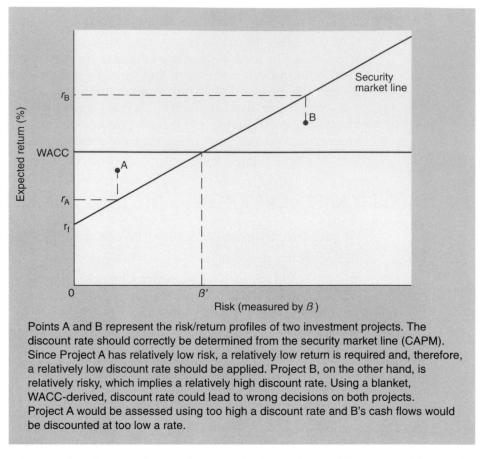

Points A and B represent the risk/return profiles of two investment projects. The
discount rate should correctly be determined from the security market line (CAPM).
Since Project A has relatively low risk, a relatively low return is required and, therefore,
a relatively low discount rate should be applied. Project B, on the other hand, is
relatively risky, which implies a relatively high discount rate. Using a blanket,
WACC-derived, discount rate could lead to wrong decisions on both projects.
Project A would be assessed using too high a discount rate and B's cash flows would
be discounted at too low a rate.

In practice firms tend to specialise in similar projects with, presumably, similar
risk, so that WACC might well be appropriate in most cases. Where a project
under consideration is not of similar risk level to that of the existing projects, it
might be possible to obtain the appropriate discount rate by looking at the
WACC of firms whose activities (and therefore presumably risk) are all similar
to the project under review. This is a similar approach to using the β of a firm
whose activities are all of the same type as the project under review where the
project is not typical of the existing projects of the investing firm, when deriving
the discount rate via CAPM.

Practicality of using the traditional approach as compared with using CAPM

Traditionalists seem to regard CAPM as a rather fanciful approach to deducing
discount rates, even though they may not disagree with CAPM in theory. The
objection seems to lie in their recognition of the difficulty of estimating the
parameters of CAPM (the risk-free rate, the expected market return and the β).
The traditionalists are right to be sceptical of our ability reliably to estimate these
(*see* Chapter 7). Where perhaps they are misguided is to believe that the
estimates necessary to arrive at the cost of capital via the 'traditional' route are
any less susceptible to error than are those for CAPM.

Typically it would seem that the traditional approach uses estimates either from expectations of future cash flows from the various elements of long-term finance, or from recent history of what the costs of each element have been. If based on future expectations, these estimates are not more reliable than those required when using CAPM. If WACC, to be used as a rate to discount future cash flows of a project, is derived from evidence of the recent past, this too seems pretty dubious. Merely to extrapolate unquestioningly from the past to the future is not always a good idea and seems a particularly poor one in this context.

Some further points on WACC

There are some other fine points which need to be made about using WACC as the discount rate. Since these require some understanding of the contents of Chapter 11, we shall leave it until the end of that chapter before we consider these few outstanding points.

SUMMARY

Traditionally the costs of individual sources of finance have been derived from models which, logically enough, relate the current market value of a security or of a loan contract to the discounted value of future expected cash flows from that source. The cost of a particular source of finance is the discount rate. With some sources, for example quoted loan stocks, where the future cash flows can be reliably estimated, this is a fairly reliable way of deducing the cost of capital. Where we are dealing with less predictable areas such as dividends from equities, the resultant cost figure will be much less reliable.

The correct rate at which to discount the predicted cash flows of potential investment opportunities is by finding the average of the costs of the firm's individual sources, weighted according to how much of each source is present in the firm's capital structure.

In principle the traditional approach is as good a way as CAPM of finding the opportunity cost of capital, to which extent the two methods are interchangeable. The traditional method does however have more potential for misuse since it tends to make assumptions about the level of risk of a potential project which may very well not be justified. This could cause incorrect decisions to be made.

Traditionalists seem inclined to regard CAPM as not too practical a means of deriving discount rates, yet it seems not to require more by way of assumptions about the future than does the traditional means.

FURTHER READING Most finance texts include fairly comprehensive treatment of the material discussed in this chapter. Samuels, Wilkes and Brayshaw (1995) give an interesting coverage of it; Levy and Sarnat (1988) and Copeland and Weston (1988) deal with it clearly. The last-mentioned goes into quite a lot of detail, particularly with regard to the costs of various types of finance.

REVIEW QUESTIONS

Suggested answers to review questions appear in Appendix 3.

10.1 What determines the value of an economic asset (as opposed to an asset which has value for reason of sentiment?)

10.2 If we know the projected cash flows from a loan stock and its current market value, what approach would we take to deducing the cost of the loan stock?

10.3 Why does it seem likely that firms have a 'target' gearing ratio?

10.4 What is wrong with using the cost of the specific capital used to finance a project as the discount rate in relation to that project?

10.5 When calculating the weighted average cost of capital (WACC), should we use market values or balance sheet values as the weights of debt and equity? Explain your response.

10.6 When deducing the cost of equity through a dividend model, must we assume either a constant level of future dividends or a constant level of growth of dividends? Explain your response.

PROBLEMS

Sample answers to problems marked with an asterisk appear in Appendix 4.

(Note that problem questions 10.1–10.4 are basic level problems, while questions 10.5 and 10.6 are more advanced and may contain some practical complications.)

10.1* Gregoris plc has some loan stock, currently quoted at £104 per £100 nominal value. This stock will pay interest at the rate of 8 per cent p.a. of the nominal value at the end of each of the next four years and repay £100 at the end of four years.

What is the cost of the loan stock? (Ignore taxation)

10.2 Shah plc has a cost of equity of 17 per cent p.a. The firm is expected to pay a dividend in one year's time of £0.27 per share. Dividends are expected to grow at a steady 5 per cent each year for the foreseeable future.

What is the current price of one share in Shah plc?

10.3* Fortunate plc's capital structure (taken from the firm's balance sheet) is as follows:

	£ million
Ordinary shares of £0.50 each	8
10% preference shares of £1.00	5
Reserves	6
12% debentures	10

The firm pays Corporation tax at the rate of 50 per cent and is expected to earn a consistent annual profit, before interest and tax, of £9 million.

The current market price of the firm's share is: preference shares   £0.65

ordinary shares   £0.80

The debentures are irredeemable and have a market value of £100 per £100 nominal value.

What is the firm's weighted average cost of capital, assuming that shareholders regard retained profit and dividends as equally valuable?

10.4 Doverdale plc has some convertible loan stock, with a current market value of £109 per £100 nominal value, on which the firm will pay interest at the rate of 12 per cent on their nominal value in one year's time and then annually until conversion. In four years' time the loan stock can be converted into ordinary shares in the firm at the rate of 25 shares per £100 nominal value of loan stock.

The cost of the loan stock is 15 per cent p.a.

What value does the market believe that the shares will have in four years' time, if it is assumed that conversion will take place at that time? (Ignore taxation throughout.)

10.5* Da Silva plc is a firm whose shares are not traded in any recognised market. The firm's sole activity is saloon car hire. The firm is financed by a combination of 2 million £0.50 ordinary shares and a £1.5 million bank loan. Very recently Mavis plc, a national car hire group, offered a total of £5.5 million to acquire the entire equity of Da Silva plc. The bid failed because the majority of shareholders rejected it because they wished to retain control of the firm, despite believing the offer to represent a fair price for the shares. The bank loan is at a floating rate of interest of 10 per cent p.a. and is secured on various of the firm's fixed assets. The value of the bank loan is considered to be very close to its nominal value.

Da Silva plc's current capital structure (by market value) represents what has been, and is intended to continue to be, its target capital structure.

Da Silva plc's management is in the process of assessing a major investment, to be financed from retained earnings, in some new depots, similar to the firm's existing ones. An appropriate cost of capital figure is required for this purpose. The dividend growth model (DGM) has been proposed as a suitable basis for the estimation of the cost of equity.

Recent annual dividends per share have been:

	£
19X0	0.0800
19X1	0.0900
19X2	0.1050
19X3	0.1125
19X4	0.1250
19X5	0.1350
19X6	0.1450
19X7	0.1550

The firm's rate of Corporation tax is expected to be 33 per cent, for the foreseeable future.

Estimate Da Silva plc's weighted average cost of capital (WACC). (Ignore inflation.)
What assumptions are being made in using the WACC figure which you have estimated as the basis for the discount rate?

10.6 Vocalise plc has recently assessed a new capital investment project which will expand the firm's activities. This project has an estimated expected net present value of £4 million. This will require finance of £15 million. At the same time the firm would like to buy and cancel £10 million of 15 per cent debentures which are due to be redeemed at par in four years' time. It is estimated that the firm will incur dealing costs of £0.3 million in buying the debentures.

There are plans to raise most of the necessary finance for the investment project and for buying the debentures, through a one-for-one rights issue of equity at an issue price of £0.50 per share. The remaining finance will come from the firm's existing cash resources. The issue will give rise to administrative costs of £0.4 million.

None of these plans has been announced to the 'market' which is believed to be semi-strong efficient.

The firm's capital structure is as follows:

	£m
Ordinary shares of £0.25 each	10
Reserves	14
	24
15% debentures	10
10% term loan	15
	£49m

10 per cent is the current and likely future rate of interest for loans to firm's like Vocalise plc. The firm's ordinary shares are currently quoted at £0.85 each.

Estimate the theoretical share price following the announcement of the firm's plans and the issue of the new shares, assuming that the only influences on the price are these plans. (Ignore taxation.)

Why might the theoretical price differ from the actual one?

CHAPTER 11

Gearing, the cost of capital and shareholders' wealth

In this chapter we shall deal with the following:

● the use of loan finance as part of firms' long-term financial needs

● the effect of capital gearing on WACC, the value of the firm and the shareholders' wealth

● the traditional view of this effect

● the Modigliani/Miller view

● the empirical evidence of the effects of gearing

● gearing and CAPM

● financial gearing and operating gearing

● a conjectural conclusion on gearing

INTRODUCTION

At several points in this book so far we have encountered the fact that many, probably most, firms raise part of their long-term financing requirements through borrowing, often by the issue of loan stocks or debentures. These give lenders contractual rights to receive interest, typically at a predetermined rate and on specified dates. Usually such loan stocks are redeemable; thus the contractual rights extend to the amount to be repaid and to the date of redemption. Loan finance could also be provided by a bank or similar institution, which would acquire similar contractual rights. The central point about loan finance, in the present context, lies in the fact that neither interest nor redemption payments are matters of the borrowing firm's discretion. Interest on such loans amounts to an annual charge on profits. This must be satisfied before the equity shareholders, who in the typical firm provide the larger part of the finance, may participate.

In Chapter 2 we found, subject to several assumptions, that financing through borrowing rather than equity does not seem to make any difference to the wealth of the shareholders. In this chapter we shall review the traditional view, that capital gearing does have an effect on shareholders' wealth, before we go on to develop the point raised in Chapter 2. After this we shall review the evidence and try to reach some conclusion on the matter.

IS LOAN FINANCE AS CHEAP AS IT SEEMS?

It is widely believed that the capital market prices securities so that expected returns from equities are higher than those from loan stocks. Historically this belief has been valid over all but fairly brief periods of time. Does the apparent cheapness of loan finance really mean that equity holders will benefit from the use of it in the firm's capital structure?

EXAMPLE

La Mer plc has one asset, a luxury yacht which is chartered to parties of jet-set holiday makers. Profits of the firm over the next few years are expected to be £140 000 p.a. La Mer is financed entirely by equity, namely 1 million ordinary shares whose current market value is £1 each. The firm is in the habit of paying all of the profit to shareholders by way of dividend. La Mer plc intends to buy an additional, similar vessel, also expected to generate annual profits of £140 000 p.a., at a cost of £1m. The finance for this is to be provided by the issue of £1m of 10 per cent loan stock. The loan is to be secured on the firm's two vessels.

Without the new yacht, the return per share is expected to be:

$$\frac{£140\ 000}{1\ 000\ 000} = £0.14 \text{ per share}$$

If the second yacht is acquired, the annual return per share will be:

Profit from chartering ($2 \times £140\ 000$)	£280 000
Less: Interest (£1m @ 10%)	100 000
	£180 000

i.e. $\dfrac{£180\ 000}{1\ 000\ 000} = £0.18$ per share

Thus the expected return (and presumably therefore the value of the ordinary shares) is increased by the use of loan stock. (Note that if the finance for the new yacht had been raised by issuing 1 000 000 ordinary shares of £1 each, the annual return per share, with the second yacht, would have remained at £0.14.)

Since the ordinary shares are priced at £1 each when returns are expected to be 14p per share we may infer that investors regard 14 per cent as the appropriate return for such an investment. If the expected returns increase to 18p per share, as acquisition of the second vessel engenders, this seems likely to push up the price of an ordinary share to £1 × 18p/14p = £1.286 (18p represents a 14 per cent return on £1.286). This implies that, were the second vessel to be financed by an issue of equity, the value of each ordinary share would be £1, whereas if the second vessel were to be financed by loan stock, the firm's ordinary shares would be worth £1.286 each. In short, the shareholders' wealth would be increased by borrowing instead of issuing equity.

Too good to be true? Probably yes, yet there is nothing in the example which seems too far-fetched. Expected returns on equities tend to be greater than those on loan stocks, so the 10 per cent interest rate is not necessarily unrealistic. Surely though, such alchemy cannot really work. It cannot be possible in a fairly rational world, suddenly to turn a 14 per cent return into an 18 per cent one, to increase a share's price from £1 to £1.286, quite so simply – or can it?

To try to get to the bottom of this enigma, let us look at the situation from the point of view of the suppliers of the loan finance. If there are 14 per cent returns to be made from investing in yacht chartering, why are they prepared to do so for a 10 per cent return? Why do they not buy ordinary shares in this firm? Are they so naïve that they do not notice the 14 per cent possibility? Perhaps they are, but this seems rather unlikely.

The difference between investing directly in yacht chartering, through the purchase of shares in La Mer, and lending money on a fixed rate of interest is the different level of risk. In the example, of the £140 000 p.a. expected profits from the second yacht, only £100 000 would be paid to the providers of the new finance. The other £40 000 goes to the equity holders, but with it goes all of the risk (or nearly all of it).

As with all real investment, returns are not certain. Suppose that there were to be a recession in the yacht charter business, so that the profits of La Mer plc fell to £70 000 p.a. from each vessel. This would mean:

Profit from chartering (2 × £70 000)	£140 000
Less : Interest (£1m @ 10%)	100 000
	£40 000

i.e. $\dfrac{£40\ 000}{1\ 000\ 000} = £0.04$ per share

(Note that had the second yacht been financed by equity the return per share would in the circumstances be £140 000/2 000 000 = £0.07, not quite such a disastrous outcome for equity holders.)

From this it seems clear that loan stocks provide an apparently cheap source of finance, but they have a hidden cost to equity shareholders.

BUSINESS RISK AND FINANCIAL RISK

Table 11.1 shows the annual dividend per share for La Mer (assuming the second vessel is acquired and that all available profit is paid as dividend) for each of the two financing schemes referred to above (all equity and 50 per cent loan financed) for various levels of chartering profits.

The inclusion of loan finance enhances returns on equity over those which could be earned in the all-equity structure, where annual profits are above £100 000 per vessel. Where annual profit per vessel falls below £100 000, however, the existence of loan finance weakens the ordinary shareholder's position. In fact, below a profit of £50 000 per vessel there would be insufficient profit to cover loan interest payments. Presuming that no other assets exist, the firm might have to dispose of one of the vessels to provide the finance to meet the interest payments.

At virtually all levels of profit, the loan stockholders could view the situation philosophically. After all, not only do they have the legal right to enforce payment of their interest and repayment of their capital, they even have the vessels as security. Only if major losses to the market value of the yachts were to occur, would the loan stockholders' position seriously be threatened.

Where gearing exists, the risk to which equity holders are exposed clearly is increased over that which they would bear in the all-equity firm. To business risk, the normal risk attached to investing in the real world, is added financial risk, the risk caused by being burdened with the obligation to meet fixed charges illustrated in Table 11.1.

Table 11.1 Returns per share in La Mer plc for various levels of profit under each of two different financial structures

(a) Annual profit per vessel	0	£50 000	£100 000	£150 000	£200 000
All equity					
(b) Profit [(a) × 2]	0	£100 000	£200 000	£300 000	£400 000
(c) Return per share [(b) ÷ 2 000 000]	0	£0.05	£0.10	£0.15	£0.20
50% loan finance					
(d) Profit [(a) × 2]	0	£100 000	£200 000	£300 000	£400 000
(e) *Less:* Interest (£1m @ 10%)	100 000	100 000	100 000	100 000	100 000
(f) Net profit	(£100 000)	0	£100 000	£200 000	£300 000
(g) Return per share [(f) ÷ 1 000 000]	(£0.10)	0	£0.10	£0.20	£0.30

Figure 11.1 depicts the relationship between business and financial risk where operating returns fluctuate. The amount of business risk depends on the area of activity in which the firm is invested; financial risk depends on how the firm is financed.

Intuition and modern portfolio theory both tell us that risk and return are related. Where investors perceive high risk they require high returns. Hence, referring back to the above example, while gearing will lift expected dividend per share to ordinary shareholders from 14p to 18p, this will not necessarily increase the share price (and therefore the wealth of the shareholder). Accompanying the increased expected dividend is a wider range of possible outcomes (*see* Table 11.1).

Not all of the new possibilities which gearing brings to the returns to equity holders are bad news. For example, for La Mer, Table 11.1 shows that for any chartering profit per vessel above £100 000 p.a., ordinary share dividends would be enhanced. Most investors, however, are risk-averse, which means that the possibility that profit per vessel could be below £100 000 tends to be more significant to them than the possibility that profits could be greater.

La Mer's ordinary shareholders will only be better off through the introduction of gearing if the capital market, when it reassesses the situation, following the loan stock issue and the purchase of the second yacht, prices the ordinary shares so that their expected yield is less than 18 per cent.

Before the firm's expansion these ordinary shares had an expected yield of

**Fig. 11.1
The return on
equity over time
for a financially
geared firm with
fluctuating profits**

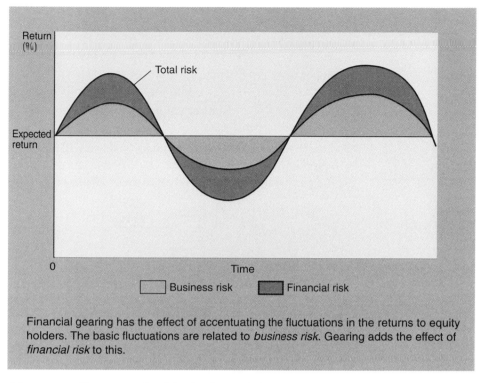

Financial gearing has the effect of accentuating the fluctuations in the returns to equity holders. The basic fluctuations are related to *business risk*. Gearing adds the effect of *financial risk* to this.

14 per cent. If, as a result of the higher risk level, after the expansion the market expected a return of, say, 16 per cent, the price per share would be

$$\sum_{n=1}^{\infty} \frac{£0.18}{(1+0.16)^n} = £1.125$$

i.e. an increase in value per share.

If on the other hand capital market requirements for the level of risk rose to 20 per cent, the price per share would become

$$\sum_{n=1}^{\infty} \frac{£0.18}{(1+0.20)^n} = £0.90$$

Put another way, will the introduction of gearing lower the weighted average cost of capital (WACC) and therefore make more valuable the investments in which the firm is involved, or not? Before the introduction of gearing in La Mer, WACC was 14 per cent (the return on the ordinary shares). If, after the issue of loan stock, the capital market required return on equity shares rose to 16 per cent, then

$$\text{WACC} = \left(\frac{£1m}{£2.125m} \times 10\% \right) + \left(\frac{£1.125m}{£2.125m} \times 16\% \right)$$

$$= 4.71 + 8.47$$

$$= 13.18\%, \text{ i.e. a lowering of WACC through gearing.}$$

(Remember that :

$$WACC = \left(\frac{\text{Market value of loan stock}}{\text{Market value of equity} + \text{Loan stock}} \times \text{Cost of loan stock} \right)$$

$$+ \left(\frac{\text{Market value of equity}}{\text{Market value of equity} + \text{Loan stock}} \times \text{Cost of equity} \right)$$

Also remember that the price per equity share will be £1.125 if required return is 16 per cent.)

If the capital market required a return of 20 per cent then

$$WACC = \left(\frac{£1m}{£1.9m} \times 10\% \right) + \left(\frac{£0.9m}{£1.9m} \times 20\% \right)$$

$$= 5.26\% + 9.47\%$$

$$= 14.73\%, \text{ i.e. an increase of WACC through gearing.}$$

Given the firm's overall objective of maximisation of shareholder wealth, how the capital market reacts, in terms of required returns, to the introduction of gearing is a very important matter. Gearing is presumably only undertaken with the objective of increasing equity shareholders' wealth.

THE TRADITIONAL VIEW

The traditional view seems to be that if the expected rate of return from equity investment in yacht chartering is 14 per cent, this will not be greatly affected by the introduction of capital gearing, not at least up to moderate levels. This view of the effect of gearing on capital market expectations of returns from equities, loan stocks and WACC is depicted in Fig. 11.2.

Figure 11.2 shows that, as gearing is increased, both equity investors and lenders perceive additional risk and require higher returns. At lower levels of gearing, however, neither group requires greatly increased returns to compensate for this risk, and WACC reduces. When gearing reaches higher levels, the risk issue becomes increasingly important to both groups, so required returns start to increase dramatically. Now WACC starts to rise steeply. Although the point at which each group's required return starts this steep rise is not necessarily the same, there is a point (or a range of points) where, according to traditionalists, WACC is at a minimum. This is the *optimal level of gearing* in Fig. 11.2. At this point the shareholders' wealth is maximised, i.e. the price per share would be at its peak. Note that a graph of share price against the level of gearing would resemble an inversion of the WACC (k_0) curve in Fig. 11.2.

The rationale for the traditional view seems to be that it is felt that lenders would recognise that at high levels of gearing their security is substantially lost

Fig. 11.2
The cost of capital for varying levels of gearing – the traditional view

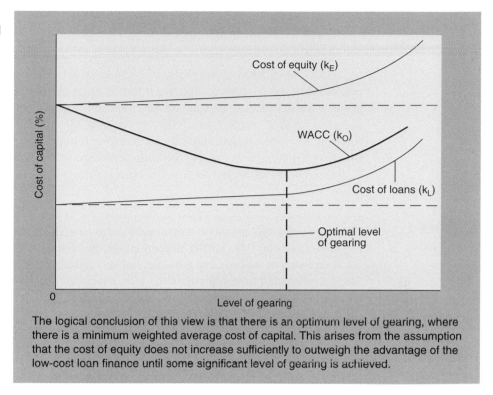

The logical conclusion of this view is that there is an optimum level of gearing, where there is a minimum weighted average cost of capital. This arises from the assumption that the cost of equity does not increase sufficiently to outweigh the advantage of the low-cost loan finance until some significant level of gearing is achieved.

and would begin to demand successively higher levels of interest to compensate them. It seems also to be believed that, up to a certain level of gearing, equity shareholders would not see the increased risk to their returns as too significant. After that point, however, they would start to demand major increases in returns for further increases in gearing.

A traditionalist would argue that, with La Mer at 50 per cent loan financing there is still plenty of security in the value of the vessels for the interest and the capital repayment, even if market prices of yachts dropped considerably. However, if the level of loan financing increased to, say, 90 per cent, a drop of more than 10 per cent in the market value of the yachts would erode the security of lenders. At the same time La Mer's equity holders would not see their position too badly threatened by the existence of moderate levels of loan finance and would not require returns great enough to negate the advantage of the apparently cheap loan finance.

Broadly, the traditional conclusion was that gearing is a good thing, in terms of shareholder wealth maximisation, at least up to a certain level past which it would start to have an adverse effect on WACC and therefore on shareholder wealth.

During the 1950s some observers started to question the value of gearing, finding it difficult to reconcile the 'something for nothing' aspect of the traditional view with the rapidly growing belief that securities are efficiently and rationally priced.

THE MILLER & MODIGLIANI VIEW OF GEARING

In 1958 Miller & Modigliani (MM) published an article, now almost legendary, questioning the traditional approach to the issue of gearing. MM argued that, given rational pricing in the capital markets, it is not possible for a firm to increase its total market value (lower its WACC) merely by doing what it is theoretically open to any of us to do, namely to borrow money. They asserted that if a particular firm is expected to generate some level of income, this should be valued without regard to how the firm is financed.

EXAMPLE

To see how the MM assertion would work in the case of La Mer, let us assume that the firm raised the £1m for the second vessel by issuing a 10 per cent debenture (i.e. borrowing at 10 per cent p.a.). Let us also assume that there is another firm, Sea plc, identical in every respect to La Mer, but completely financed by 2m ordinary shares of £1 each.

Franco, a holder of 1 per cent of the equity of La Mer (i.e. 10 000 shares) would expect a return on them of £1800 p.a. since, as we have seen, each one is expected to yield 18p p.a. Franco could equally well obtain the same expected income by borrowing the equivalent of 1 per cent of La Mer's borrowings (i.e. £10 000) at the rate of 10 per cent p.a. and using this to help finance the purchase of 1 per cent of the ordinary shares in Sea (20 000 shares). The Sea shares would be expected to yield 14p each and so £2800 in total which, after paying interest on the borrowing, would leave £1800 p.a. of expected income of equal risk (business and financial) as that of the expected income from La Mer. Franco's situation may be restated and summarised as follows:

	Investment	Income
Present position		
10 000 shares in La Mer		
(i.e. 1% of total shares)	£10 000	£1800
Alternative position		
Borrow £10 000	(£10 000)	(£1000)
Buy 20 000 shares in Sea		
(i.e. 1% of total shares)	20 000	2800
	£10 000	£1800

Since securities (indeed, any economic assets) are valued by reference only to their expected return and risk, each of the above positions must be equally valuable to Franco, or to any other investor. Both positions offer identical risk/return expectations.

If in the above circumstances Sea's shares fell in price below that of La Mer's shares, Franco could make the switch from the original to the alternative position, have the same expected return and risk, but make a profit on the switch. Since the sale of the La Mer shares and purchase of the Sea shares could be achieved simultaneously (an action known as *arbitraging*), a risk-free gain would be available. The actions of Franco, and others spotting this opportunity, would increase both the demand for Sea's shares and the supply of those of La Mer. As a result, the price of the shares would equalise.

MM's central point is that if Franco wants to be involved with gearing, but wishes to hold shares in Sea, Franco can undertake the gearing personally, i.e. *homemade* gearing.

Similarly, another individual, Merton, who owns shares in Sea, but wishes to invest in La Mer though not to be involved with gearing, can easily *ungear* an investment in La Mer. Merton can do this by lending the same proportion of the money to be invested, as La Mer borrows of its total financing.

	Investment	Income
Present position		
20 000 shares in Sea	£20 000	£2800
Alternative position		
Lend £10 000	£10 000	£1000
Buy 10 000 shares in La Mer	10 000	1800
	£20 000	£2800

Once again, a switch from the present to the alternative position would result in the same expected return with the same risk.

It would seem illogical for firms to be able to increase the wealth of their shareholders merely by *packaging* the firm's income in a particular way.

This is made especially illogical by the fact that individual shareholders can adjust the packaging to their own convenience, merely by borrowing and/or lending. Income of similar risk and expected return should be similarly priced in a rational market, irrespective of the packaging.

It seems clear from these examples that:

$$\frac{\text{Total value of the equity of Sea}}{100}$$

$$- \frac{\text{Total value of the equity of La Mer}}{100}$$

$$+ \frac{\text{Total value of the borrowings of La Mer}}{100}$$

Rearranging this gives:

Total value of the equity of Sea = Total value of the equity and
borrowings of La Mer

and more generally,

$$V_U = V_G$$

where V_U and V_G are the total value of the ungeared and geared firms respectively.

The implication of the MM proposition is that the value of the firm is not affected by the financing method (i.e. $V_U = V_G$), therefore the cost of capital is not reduced (or affected at all) by the introduction of gearing. The only matters on which the value of the firm and its WACC depend are:

(a) the cash flows which the firm's investments are expected to generate, and
(b) their risk (i.e. their business risk).

This is another phenomenon following the same pattern as Fisher separation (*see* Chapter 2). MM were in effect saying that management should concentrate all its efforts on finding and managing investment opportunities, leaving the financing arrangements for individual shareholders to decide for themselves.

The effect suggested by MM is shown graphically in Fig. 11.3. Here we can see that the potential which increasing amounts of *cheap* loan finance have for reducing WACC is exactly offset by the increasing cost of equity. Thus WACC is impervious to the level of gearing.

Fig. 11.3
The cost of capital for varying levels of gearing – the MM (pre-tax) view

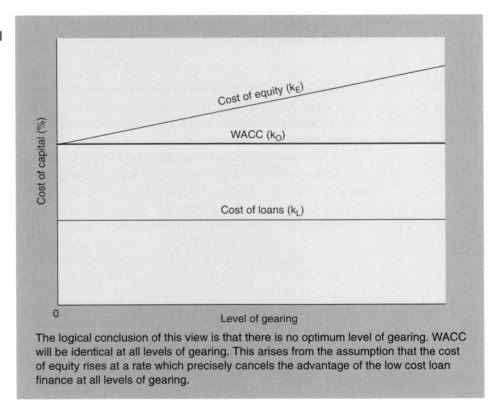

The logical conclusion of this view is that there is no optimum level of gearing. WACC will be identical at all levels of gearing. This arises from the assumption that the cost of equity rises at a rate which precisely cancels the advantage of the low cost loan finance at all levels of gearing.

We see from Fig. 11.3 that shareholders in geared firms expect a return equal to the expected return from the identical ungeared firm, plus a premium which is directly proportional to the level of gearing. Thus, whilst gearing increases earnings per share, it also increases capital market expectations of the share's returns because of higher risk. The net effect of these factors on the value of each share will be zero, i.e. the effects will be equal and opposite (according to MM).

According to MM the relationship between the return expected by the capital market and the level of gearing is:

$$E(r_{EG}) = E(r_{EE}) + (E(r_{EE}) - r_L)\frac{L_G}{S_G}$$

where $E(r_{EG})$ and $E(r_{EE})$ are respectively the expected returns from shares in the geared and all-equity firm; L_G and S_G are respectively the total market value of the loan stock and shares of the geared firm.

Thus the introduction of 50 per cent gearing into the capital structure of La Mer would push the capital market's expected return on the firm's equities up to 18 per cent, ($E(r_{EG}) = 14 + (14 - 10)$ (£1m/£1m) = 18%). The expected earnings per share of 18p (*see* p. 260) would still only be worth £1.

MM's disagreement with the traditionalists was that MM saw the capital market's return expectations increasing as soon as gearing is introduced, and increasing in proportion to the amount of gearing. The traditionalists felt that this would not occur at lower levels of gearing.

The formal proof of the MM proposition is developed in Appendix I of this chapter.

The MM assumptions

(a) Shares can be bought and sold without dealing costs

This is obviously unrealistic: brokers' commissions and other costs are involved with trading in shares. It is doubtful, however, whether the weakness of this assumption seriously undermines the proposition. It might mean that investors would be unable to make a profit by exploiting minor instances of mispricing of shares of geared firms, relative to those of ungeared firms. The larger ones could be exploited despite the existence of dealing charges.

(b) Capital markets are efficient

The evidence seems to show that they are efficient, for practical purposes, in the weak- and semi-strong form (*see* Chapter 9). This implies that investors would see through the financial packaging and realise that income of a particular risk class is equally valuable irrespective of how it is wrapped. It seems that this assumption is reasonable.

(c) Interest rates are equal between borrowing and lending, firms and individuals

Clearly this is invalid. In particular, there is usually a difference between the rates at which individuals and firms can borrow. Large firms, in particular, can often offer good security, can borrow large amounts, and can exploit borrowing opportunities not open to most individuals, e.g. borrowing overseas. The importance of this assumption lies in the question of homemade gearing, where the investor borrows on his or her own account and buys shares in the ungeared firm.

There is no reason, however, why the investor who exploits any mispricing of shares need be an individual; it could be a large firm, e.g. a large unit or investment trust. After all, most investment in securities, in the UK at least, is undertaken by the institutions rather than by individuals. Nor is it necessary that every investor in the economy seeks to exploit any mispricing in order to correct it. The action of a couple of investors, well placed to exploit the situation, would be sufficient. Probably the weakness of this assumption is not sufficient to call the MM proposition too seriously into question.

MM also made the implicit assumption that the corporate cost of borrowing does not increase with the level of gearing. This seems less plausible, a point to which we shall return later in the chapter.

(d) There are no bankruptcy costs

This assumption suggests that if a firm were to be liquidated the shareholders would receive, in exchange for their shares, the equivalent of their market value immediately before the liquidation. This assumption envisages a situation where, as a result of a firm defaulting on interest and/or capital repayment, it is liquidated at the instigation of loan stock holders. This sort of action would obviously be more likely with very highly geared firms.

The assumption is invalid since dealing costs would be involved in the disposal of the firm's assets, legal costs would arise in formally bringing about the demise of the firm and, perhaps most importantly, the market for real assets is not generally efficient in the same way that capital markets seem to be. This last point implies that a machine worth £1000 to firm A does not necessarily have that same value to firm B, because firm B, for some reason, may not be able to use it as effectively as firm A. Before the liquidation, firm A's equity value may have been based partially on a £1000 value for the machine, but when the machine comes to be sold it may only fetch £500. Furthermore, there are costs of administering a potentially bankrupt firm, even if it is saved.

This assumption's lack of validity undermines the MM proposition in its broad form. It is doubtful, however, whether the assumption is a very important one where gearing levels are moderate, which appears typically to be the case in practice. On the other hand the existence of bankruptcy costs may well be the reason for the modest gearing levels which we tend to see in real life.

(e) Two firms identical in income (cash flow) and risk exist, one all-equity, the other geared

This assumption is most unlikely strictly to be true. It seems not to be an important impediment to the validity of MM's proposition. CAPM, and modern portfolio theory in general, suggest that business risk can explicitly be dealt with so that it is possible to relate two firms of different risk. That is, there is an established mechanism for pricing risk which enables returns for one firm's shares to be reconciled with those of another firm. But even if CAPM, etc., is questioned, MM were really referring to one firm and making the point that if there were two firms identical except only for their financing method they would be equally valued. Stiglitz (1974) showed that it is not necessary for two such firms actually to exist in order for the proposition to be valid.

(f) There is no taxation

This is clearly invalid. MM were much criticised for this fact and were forced to reconsider their proposition because of it.

The revised *after-tax* version asserts that market forces must cause

$$V_G = V_U + T\,L_G$$

where L_G is the value of the firm's borrowings and T is the relevant Corporation Tax rate, at which loan stock interest will be relieved. The derivation of the above is shown in Appendix II to this chapter. The term 'TL$_G$' is often referred to as the *tax shield* of debt.

The after-tax proposition implies that the value of the geared firm is greater than the value of the all-equity one; also that the greater the level of gearing, the greater the value of the firm. The inevitable conclusion is that the value of the firm is highest and WACC lowest, when gearing is at 100 per cent, i.e. all finance is provided by loan stock holders.

Figure 11.4 shows the MM after-tax view of capital gearing. There is a contrast with the pre-tax position depicted in Fig. 11.3. In the after-tax case the cost of debt is low enough (due to higher tax relief on loan interest) for increasing amounts of loan finance to reduce WACC at a greater rate than the increasing demands of equity holders are raising it. Thus the WACC line slopes downward.

It is doubtful if this 100 per cent loan finance conclusion is tenable in practical terms, however. At very high levels of gearing the loan stock holders would recognise that their security had been substantially eroded and that while they might be lenders in name, as risk takers they are equity holders in reality. They would therefore seek a level of return which would compensate them for this risk, a level of return similar to that which the equity holders seek. This would mean that at very high levels of gearing, both in the pre-tax and in the more important post-tax propositions, the cost of loans would rise significantly.

Fig. 11.4
The cost of capital for varying levels of gearing – the MM (post-tax) view

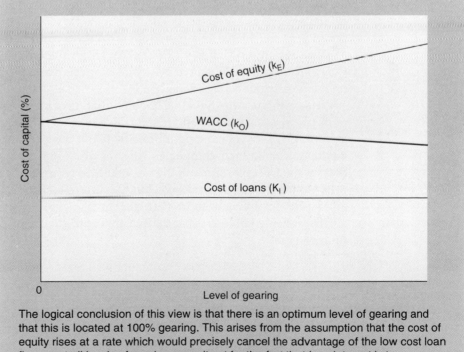

The logical conclusion of this view is that there is an optimum level of gearing and that this is located at 100% gearing. This arises from the assumption that the cost of equity rises at a rate which would precisely cancel the advantage of the low cost loan finance at all levels of gearing, were it not for the fact that loan interest is tax deductible. The fact that interest is deductible means that the greater the amount of loan finance the greater the tax benefit to the firm.

In order for MM conclusions to hold, this requires that the rate of increase in the cost of equity starts to fall. In Fig. 11.4, if the cost of loans line is going to start turning upwards at some high level of gearing, the WACC line can only continue its downward path if the cost of equity line becomes less steep. (Remember that the WACC line is the average of the other two.)

The idea of the rate of increase in the cost of equity, as gearing is increased, suddenly starting to reduce at high gearing levels seems to defy logic. Why should investors start to behave contrary to all the theories and evidence of investor reaction to increasing risk? This suggests a weakness in the MM analysis which perhaps means that their conclusion in the after-tax case is not all that logical.

OTHER THOUGHTS ON THE TAX ADVANTAGE OF LOAN FINANCING

Miller (1977), showed that the tax benefits of gearing for a particular firm will depend on the personal tax positions of both the loan stock holders and the shareholders. Thus firms will tend to attract investors (both lenders and shareholders) who are suited to the firm's capital structure. This is known as a 'clientele' effect, where particular policies attract particular types of investor. If Miller is right about this, the implication is that firms should probably try to avoid altering their capital structure because this would lead to investors selling their loan stocks or shares and investing their money in a firm which matches their preferences. This is because the dealing costs involved with selling and buying securities would have an adverse effect on the wealth of the investors.

More recently, Dempsey (1991) showed, in the context of the UK tax and financial environment, that in theory gearing has a relatively small *adverse* effect on the wealth of shareholders.

We saw in the Appendix to Chapter 8 that, provided that the firm pays most of its profit as a dividend and that it is in a normal tax-paying situation, the tax advantage of loan financing in the UK is not too profound. In fact, for firms paying tax at the small companies' rate, the difference does not exist. This means that, in the UK environment, the original MM assumption of no taxes is not an unreasonable one. Taxes do exist, but the difference between their effect on loan and equity financing is not that great.

It is probably fair to say that the question of the tax benefits of gearing remains unanswered.

CAPITAL/FINANCIAL GEARING AND OPERATING GEARING

We saw earlier in this chapter that the existence of debt finance in the capital structure accentuates the effect of variations in operating (i.e. pre-interest) profits on returns to shareholders. This is because, at any significant level of gearing, the interest payment represents a large fixed commitment which must be met irrespective of the level of operating profit.

There is also a gearing aspect to firms' operating activities. That is to say, it is not just capital gearing which causes returns to shareholders to vary. Virtually all firms' trading operations have costs which are fixed, irrespective of the level of sales (fixed costs), and costs which vary with the level of sales (variable costs). The relative proportions of each of these types of cost in terms of the total costs vary from firm to firm, depending on the nature of the firm's activities. This phenomenon is known as *operating* gearing. A form is said to be highly operationally geared when a large proportion of its total costs are fixed costs.

EXAMPLE

Consider two firms High plc and Low plc. Their cost structures are as follows:

	Fixed costs per annum	*Variable costs per £ of sales*
High plc	£100 000	£0.20
Low plc	£50 000	£0.50

For a range of sales figures operating results would be as shown in Table 11.2.

Table 11.2 Operating results for High plc and Low plc for various levels of sales

	£	£	£	£
Sales	0	200 000	300 000	400 000
High plc				
Fixed costs	100 000	100 000	100 000	100 000
Variable costs	0	40 000	60 000	80 000
Total costs	100 000	140 000	160 000	180 000
Operating profit	(100 000)	60 000	140 000	220 000
Low plc				
Fixed costs	50 000	50 000	50 000	50 000
Variable costs	0	100 000	150 000	200 000
Total costs	50 000	150 000	200 000	250 000
Operating profit	(50 000)	50 000	100 000	150 000

The table shows that the more highly operationally geared, High plc, shows much greater fluctuations with alterations in the level of sales than does Low plc. You will remember that we saw a similar effect with capital gearing in Table 11.1 (p. 262).

If a firm is simultaneously highly geared both in operating and capital terms, relatively small fluctuations in the level of sales can have a dramatic effect on returns to shareholders. This means that the risk of bankruptcy is greater with firms which are highly geared in both senses, particularly where their sales are susceptible to fluctuations from year to year. It is expected that firms whose cost structure is such as to make them relatively highly geared on the operations side tend not to indulge in too much capital gearing.

EVIDENCE ON GEARING

Some casual observations

Before going on to some of the sophisticated studies relating to gearing, it is well worth noting some important points which arise from casual observation. These are:

(a) A very large proportion of firms, perhaps even a large majority of them, go in for some level of capital gearing. Few firms raise all of their financial requirements from equity shareholders. Assuming that managements are pursuing a shareholder wealth maximisation objective, they are presumably using gearing to promote that objective. Rightly or wrongly, therefore, managements seem to believe that gearing lowers WACC.

(b) Very high levels of gearing are rarely seen. Managements seem not to believe that the value of the firm is maximised (WACC minimised) by very high gearing levels.

Some formal evidence

The questions to which the answers are of real interest are:

(a) Does WACC change with gearing as MM (post-tax) suggested and

(b) Does it move to a minimum at some level of gearing of less than 100 per cent and then increase as gearing is further increased?

The publication of the MM articles on capital structure was followed thick and fast by a number of studies bearing on the above questions.

Miller & Modigliani (1958) themselves took the lead with a study using data concerning a number of oil firms and of electrical utility firms and came to the conclusion that WACC is not dependent on the level of gearing (supporting their pre-tax proposition).

Weston (1963) criticised the MM results on the basis that they had made too many simplifying assumptions. Weston himself used data on electrical utility firms to show that the MM post-tax proposition was valid in that WACC seemed to decrease with increased gearing.

Miller & Modigliani (1966) returned to the scene and, again using the electrical utilities found evidence to support the after-tax propositions.

Hamada (1972), using CAPM to deal with risk differences, found that the cost of equity increases with the level of gearing.

Masulis (1980) found that announcements of a firm's intention to increase the level of gearing tend to be associated with increases in the price of the firms' equity, and that announcements of intentions to reduce gearing tend to have an adverse effect on the equity values. This clearly supports the MM post-tax proposition. It also implies that, if there *is* an optimal level of gearing, investors tend to believe that firms are operating below it.

DeAngelo and Masulis (1980) found an increase in the value of the firm, as gearing increases up to a certain point, and a reduction as more debt is added. This was ascribed to the fact that the tax advantages can become decreasingly valuable with higher gearing since the firm may not have sufficient taxable operating profits against which to set the interest expense, i.e. the tax deductibility of interest becomes irrelevant.

Homaifar, Zeitz and Benkato (1994) found evidence based on US data that the level of gearing tends to be higher with firms exposed to higher corporate tax rates, i.e. the greater the value of the tax shield, the higher the level of debt. They also found that larger firms tend to be more highly geared than smaller ones, perhaps reflecting the greater ease with which larger firms are able to raise external finance.

The formal evidence seems to answer question (a); WACC decreases with increased gearing. It does not really deal with question (b) and so we do not know from the formal evidence whether or not WACC bottoms out at some point below 100 per cent gearing, after which it starts to increase.

Kester (1986) found dramatic differences between industrial sectors as regards levels of gearing. The highest average level of gearing was found in steel manufacturers (where debt was 1.665 times the market value of equity). The lowest occurred in pharmaceutical manufacturers (where the ratio of debt to the market value of equity was 0.079 : 1). It is not clear why there should be such differences, in general, nor why these two industries should occupy the positions indicated. One theory concerns the potential costs of bankruptcy. Some industries can liquidate their assets more easily than can others, with less difference between the value of the assets sold on a 'going concern' basis and on a bankruptcy sale basis.

GEARING AND THE COST OF CAPITAL – CONCLUSION

The central question on gearing is whether in reality it is the traditionalists or MM who best explain the effect of gearing.

The traditional view, that somehow equity shareholders do not pay much attention to the increased risk which rising amounts of gearing engender until it reaches high levels, seems naïve. It appears to conflict with most of the evidence on the efficiency of the capital market. Tests of capital market efficiency indicate that little of significance goes unnoticed. It is difficult to believe that increased levels of gearing are insignificant to equity shareholders, since gearing increases the range of possible returns. As most investors seem to be risk-averse, increasing the range of possible outcomes will be unattractive to them.

The formal evidence on the effects of gearing cited above also cuts across the traditional view since it appears that gearing levels broadly affect equity returns and WACC in the manner suggested by MM (post-tax).

On the other hand, casual observation shows that firms' managements do not seem to believe in very high levels of gearing, which rather supports the traditional view.

There is a conflict here, though perhaps it is possible to reconcile these two factors.

The MM (post-tax) analysis relies on a number of assumptions, most of which seem not to be so far-fetched as seriously to weaken their conclusions. Two of them, however, call their proposition into question.

(a) There are no bankruptcy costs

The importance of this assumption lies in the fact that the existence of high levels of loan finance exposes the firm to the risk that it will not be able to meet its payment obligations to lenders, not at least out of its operating cash flows, if the firm should experience a particularly adverse period of trading. Whilst it is equally true that the all-equity firm might have difficulty paying dividends in similar economic circumstances, there is an important difference.

Lenders have a contractual right to receive interest and capital repayment on the due dates. If they do not receive these, they have the legal power to enforce payment. The exercise of such power can in practice lead to the liquidation of all of the firm's assets and its winding up. For the reasons we have already discussed (principally through an apparently inefficient market in real assets), this will usually disadvantage the ordinary shareholder to a significant extent.

By contrast, neither in a geared, nor in an ungeared, firm do ordinary shareholders have any rights to enforce the declaration and payment of a dividend.

This bankruptcy risk is probably insignificant at low levels of gearing, if only because any shortage of cash for interest payments could be borrowed from some other source – a possibility probably not so readily available to highly geared firms in distress.

(b) The interest rate demanded by lenders remains the same at all levels of gearing

At very low levels of gearing the position of lenders is one of great security, with the value of their loan probably covered many times by the value of the firm's assets. As gearing increases, this position erodes until at very high levels lenders, because they provide most of the finance, bear most of the risk.

Going back to the La Mer example, suppose that the unexpanded firm (i.e. just one yacht worth £1m) were financed 90 per cent by equity shares and 10 per cent by loan stock. Here the value of the yacht would have to fall by 90 per cent before the security of the lenders would be threatened. Even if the equity/loan ratio moved to 80 : 20, the lenders' security, whilst in theory slightly weakened, is not less in practical terms than had they only supplied 10 per cent of the finance. If however the ratio moved to 10 : 90, only a small drop (10 per cent) in the value of the yacht would leave the lenders bearing all the risk. Naturally enough, lenders would demand high returns to induce them to buy loan stocks in such a highly geared firm, presumably something like the returns expected by equity shareholders.

Logically, the loan stock holders would not see risk (and required return) increasing significantly with increases in gearing at the lower end. After all, unless the asset on which security rests is extremely volatile in its value, an asset value/loan ratio of 5: 1 is probably as good as 10 : 1; the lenders only need to be paid once. If this ratio increases to nearer 1 : 1, lenders would no doubt start to see things differently.

It is notable that neither of these two 'weak' assumptions of MM significantly affect the position at lower levels of gearing. At higher levels, however, they start to loom very large. In the light of this and taking account of the evidence which we briefly discussed, we may perhaps draw a tentative conclusion.

Up to moderate levels of gearing the tax advantages of loan finance will cause the WACC to decrease as more gearing is introduced. Beyond moderate levels, bankruptcy risk (to equity shareholders) and the introduction of real risk to lenders will push up the returns required by each group, making WACC a very high figure at high gearing levels.

Figure 11.5 depicts this conclusion with k_E, k_0, and k_L all following the same pattern as shown in Fig. 11.4 (MM post-tax) up to a moderate level of gearing and then all starting to take off to very high levels as further gearing is introduced.

**Fig. 11.5
The cost of capital for varying levels of gearing – a possible reconciliation of the traditional view, the MM (post-tax) view and what appears to happen in practice**

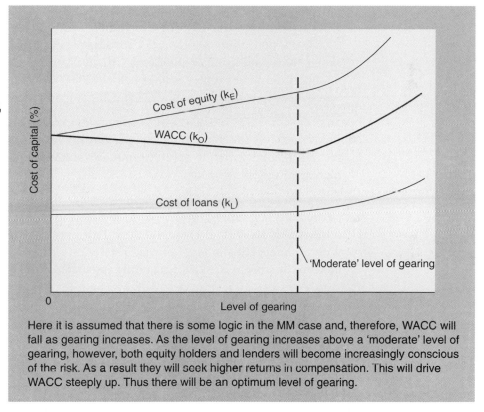

Here it is assumed that there is some logic in the MM case and, therefore, WACC will fall as gearing increases. As the level of gearing increases above a 'moderate' level of gearing, however, both equity holders and lenders will become increasingly conscious of the risk. As a result they will seek higher returns in compensation. This will drive WACC steeply up. Thus there will be an optimum level of gearing.

It is more likely that, in real life, *moderate* is not a fixed point for any particular firm; it is rather a range below which MM's proposition holds, but above which it clearly does not. Of course the vital question is what does 'moderate' mean? The problem is that it is likely to be difficult to define and, as such, a matter of judgement of financial management. It must be the point at which the balance is struck between the tax advantage on the one hand and bankruptcy cost and rising cost of borrowing on the other. This will vary from industry to industry and will to some extent depend upon the business risk (perhaps measured by β) of the investments in which the particular firm is engaged.

More formally the relationship between the value of the geared and ungeared firms can be expressed as:

$$V_G = V_U + TL_G - \text{Present value of the expected cost of bankruptcy}$$

As gearing increases, the value of the tax shield (TL_G) increases but so does the expected cost of bankruptcy. At some point the latter will outweigh the former.

LIKELY DETERMINANTS OF CAPITAL GEARING

Having reviewed the theory and evidence on gearing, we can probably summarise the factors which will influence a firm's decision on capital gearing. These are:

● *The rate of tax.* In the UK, for companies with taxable profits much over £300 000 a year, there are clear tax advantages in paying £1 of loan interest rather than paying £1 of dividend. This will, in general, encourage debt finance. Companies with earnings below £300 000 a year will not really find interest cheaper than dividends, so such companies will not really see the same tax advantage.

● *Tax capacity.* A tax deductible expense has no value unless there is taxable income against which to set it. Companies with low earnings tend to find high gearing less attractive.

● *Fluctuating sales and/or high operating gearing.* Either of these factors, and particularly a combination of them, can lead to severe fluctuations in the returns paid to ordinary shareholders. This may confront the shareholders with an unacceptable level of risk in relation to their returns. It may also increase the risk of bankruptcy and its associated costs to the shareholders.

● *Nature of the firm's assets.* Firms with assets whose value is much greater on a 'going concern' than on a bankruptcy sale basis, i.e. those with potentially high bankruptcy costs, are likely to avoid high levels of gearing.

● *Costs of raising the capital.* Most equity finance comes from retaining profits. Issue costs are zero whereas issues of shares, even rights issues, are relatively expensive. Loan finance tends to be cheap to raise. Inevitably, these facts will affect most decisions on capital gearing.

● *Costs of servicing the capital.* The prevailing rates of interest will also be a relevant factor.

MM, MPT AND CAPM

Before leaving the subject of capital gearing and its effect on WACC, perhaps we should consider how these matters relate to modern portfolio theory in general, and the capital asset pricing model in particular.

Earlier in this chapter we saw that the introduction of capital gearing exposes the ordinary shareholder to two types of risk, namely business risk and financial risk. The question now arises as to how these two relate to specific risk and systematic risk.

We should recall from Chapter 7 that business risk has two components, the specific or diversifiable part and the systematic part which the investor must bear. Figure 11.1 (p. 263) depicts the relationship between business risk and financial risk; it shows that financial risk simply augments or accentuates business risk. It seems logical therefore that, if business risk is part specific and part systematic, this must also be true for financial risk. This means that, as with business risk, part of financial risk can be diversified away; it also means that part of it cannot be eliminated by diversification.

The logical conclusion of this is that equity shares in geared firms have higher βs than those in all-equity firms. Indeed, this is the case. We know that βs are additive. That is, the β for a portfolio is the average (weighted by market value) of the βs of the constituents of the portfolio. Therefore (ignoring tax):

$$\beta_{EE} = \beta_{EG}\frac{S_G}{S_G + L_G} + \beta_{LG}\frac{L_G}{S_G + L_G}$$

where

β_{EE} is the beta of the equities of the all-equity firm;
β_{EG} is the beta of the equities of the geared firm;
β_{LG} is the beta of the loan stock of the geared firm.

This assumes that the two firms are identical in all respects except their financing method.

If we take account of the 'tax shield' of debt, the relationship between the βs is:

$$\beta_{EE} = \beta_{EG}\frac{S_G}{S_G + L_G(1-T)} + \beta_{LG}\frac{L_G(1-T)}{S_G + L_G(1-T)}$$

where T is the Corporation tax rate.

If we assume that the loan stock is without risk ($\beta_{LG} = 0$), then

$$\beta_{EE} = \beta_{EG}\frac{S_G}{S_G + L_G}$$

Rearranging gives

$$\beta_{EG} = \beta_{EE}\left(1 + \frac{L_G}{S_G}\right)$$

$$\beta_{EG} = \beta_{EE} + \beta_{EE}\frac{L_G}{S_G}$$

or

$$\beta_{EG} = \beta_{EE} + \beta_{EE}\frac{L_G(1-T)}{S_G}$$

if we take account of Corporation tax.

In other words, the risk attaching to the equities in a geared firm is equal to the risk to equities in the equivalent all-equity firm plus a financial risk premium which depends on the basic all-equity risk and on the level of gearing.

This is simply another way of saying:

Total systematic risk (of equities in a geared firm)
= Systematic business risk + Systematic financial risk

Business risk can, as we know, be measured by β and financial risk is simply an accentuation of that same risk. This is entirely consistent with MM's assertions.

WEIGHTED AVERAGE COST OF CAPITAL REVISITED

Towards the end of Chapter 10 it was said that there is a couple of points about using WACC which would be better to consider now.

The cost of capital of elements of financing at different levels of gearing

We have seen in this chapter that the cost of the various elements of long-term finance is partially dependent on the level of capital gearing. It is a basic tenet of both the MM and the traditional models that as gearing increases so does the cost of equity. Whether we deduce costs of capital using the 'traditional' approach (based on market prices) or using CAPM, the figures which we calculate will be based on a particular level of gearing and, therefore, the deduced costs will be affected by that level of gearing. If that level of gearing is not the level which will be relevant to the investment under consideration, the WACC must reflect this difference in the gearing level.

For example, a firm's equity may have been calculated to have a cost of 20 per cent p.a. This, however, assumes a particular level of gearing. Say that in this case we are talking about an all-equity firm, i.e. zero gearing. Suppose that the firm is to take on some loan finance, this means that, all other things being equal, the cost of equity will increase. If we now want to calculate a WACC, at which to discount the estimated cash flows of an investment project under consideration, we must adjust the cost of equity from 20% to reflect the level of gearing before we do the weighted averaging.

Adjusted net present value

Linked to the previous point is the fact that we have a problem in that undertaking a positive NPV project changes the level of gearing (unless the firm is all-equity financed) and, therefore, the WACC. The value of a positive NPV project entirely accrues to the shareholders and increases the value of the equity. This alters the WACC. This means that the WACC which was used to deduce the NPV was the wrong one. The problem is that until we have deduced the NPV we do not know what the gearing ratio and, therefore, the correct WACC is. Without knowing what the correct WACC is, we cannot calculate the correct NPV.

The most practical way to deal with this problem is to deduce the NPV in two stages. First we calculate the NPV assuming that the investment is all equity financed, then when we know the NPV on this basis we adjust it for the tax effect of the debt finance.

This is very similar (for good reason) to the relationship between the value of the geared and ungeared firm which appears on p. 270.

For the firm as a whole

$$V_G = V_U + TL_G$$

For the investment project

$$NPV_G = NPV_U + TL_P$$

where NPV_G = NPV if the project is undertaken by the geared firm
NPV_U = NPV if the project is undertaken by the all-equity firm
T = the Corporation tax rate
L_P = the value of the loan finance used to finance the project.

SUMMARY

Firms typically raise part of their finance from apparently cheap borrowings. The inclusion of a fixed commitment of interest payments and an obligation to repay the principal of the loan increases the risk to, and hence the return required by, ordinary shareholders.

Traditionalists argue that the net effect of gearing, at least up to a certain level, is to lower WACC and so increase the value of the equities. Modigliani and Miller, developing their argument with blinding logic (given certain assumptions), showed that, in the absence of all taxes, gearing made no difference. If the tax advantage of gearing is considered, MM showed that the introduction of a higher proportion of loan finance will always benefit ordinary shareholders, though subsequently Miller argued that the tax advantage of gearing does not exist.

Most of the assumptions made by MM seem reasonable, but those concerning bankruptcy cost and constant cost of loan finance seem highly questionable. The evidence, both formal and casual, of real life suggests that MM are correct up to a point. Beyond that point the unrealistic assumptions manifest their lack of reality.

It seems that increasing gearing does lower WACC but that it reaches its low point some time before 100 per cent gearing is reached and then starts to rise again.

FURTHER READING The subject of capital gearing is well written up in the literature. There is good coverage of it by Lumby (1994), Levy and Sarnat (1994) and Davis and Pointon (1994). The empirical evidence on the effects of gearing is well covered by Copeland and Weston (1988). It is worth reading the original MM articles which are reprinted in Archer and D'Ambrosio (1967).

REVIEW QUESTIONS

Suggested answers
to review questions
appear in Appendix 3.

11.1 Why is loan finance usually cheaper than equity finance in the same firm?

11.2 According to Modigliani and Miller (MM) (ignoring taxation), what happens to the cost of equity as gearing increases?

11.3 According to MM (taking account of taxation), what happens to the cost of equity as gearing increases?

11.4 One of the MM assumptions is 'no bankruptcy costs'. What costs does this phrase represent?

11.5 How do we know that the managements of most firms believe in the benefits of gearing?

11.6 What is the difference between the value of an ungeared and a geared firm according to MM (taking account of taxation)?

PROBLEMS

Sample answers to
problems marked with
an asterisk appear in
Appendix 4.

(Note that problem questions 11.1 and 11.2 are basic level problems, while questions 11.3–11.6 are more advanced, and may contain some practical complications.)

11.1* Shiraz plc is financed by 10 million shares, whose current market value is £2.40 a share, and 10 per cent debentures with a nominal and market value of £14 million. The return on the ordinary shares is 20 per cent.

Making Modigliani and Miller's original assumptions (including that of no taxes), what would be the equity rate of return and the share price of an identical firm which was all-equity financed?

11.2 Merlot plc is financed by 10 million shares, whose current market value is £2.40 a share, and 10 per cent debentures with a nominal and market value of £14 million. The firm plans to issue additional shares to raise £14 million and to use the cash generated to pay off the debentures. The firm's Corporation tax rate is 33 per cent.

Making Modigliani and Miller's assumptions (in a world with taxes), how would the restructuring described affect the value of the firm?

If the shareholders gain, who would lose, OR if the shareholders lose, who will gain?

11.3* Particulate plc is an all-equity financed firm with a market value of £35 million and a cost of capital (after tax) of 20 per cent p.a.

The firm intends to purchase and cancel £8 million of equity finance using the cash raised from issuing a 10 per cent irredeemable loan stock. The firm's rate of Corporation tax is 33 per cent.

Assuming that the assumptions of Modigliani and Miller (in a world with taxes) are correct, how will the capital restructuring affect:

(a) the market value of Particulate plc;

(b) the firm's cost of equity; and

(c) the firm's weighted average cost of capital?

11.4 Mile Long Merchants Limited (MLM) runs a couple of small supermarkets. The firm's equity is owned by members of the Long family.

The directors are keen to open an additional supermarket. The cost of doing this would be significant, perhaps equal to 30 per cent of the estimated current value of the firm.

The firm generates profit at a level which leads to it paying the 'small companies' rate of Corporation tax. This is likely to continue even with the additional supermarket.

The firm has limited cash available because most of the surpluses of the past few years have been distributed to the shareholders.

As Finance Director, you have been asked to prepare a paper to brief the other directors on the key issues before the board meeting. The agenda for the meeting states that the decision is between either asking the firm's bankers to grant a term loan to cover the projected expenditure or seeking the necessary funds from shareholders, through a rights issue.

Outline the main issues which you would include in your briefing paper.

11.5* Ali plc is a Stock Exchange listed firm. It is all-equity financed by 40 million 25 pence ordinary shares which are currently quoted at £1.60 each. In the recent past, annual profit has been an average of £12.8 million. The average rate of return on capital employed, is expected to continue for the future. All of the profit is paid as a dividend each year. The firm intends to raise some finance for expansion, either through a one for four rights issue, at a price of £1.20 per share or through the issue of 10 per cent unsecured loan stock to raise the same amount of cash.

Lee is an individual who owns 10 000 of the firm's shares.

Making the same assumptions as were made by Modigliani and Miller in their original proposition on capital gearing (including a world without taxes), calculate and compare the effect on Lee's income of:

(a) personally borrowing the cash necessary to take up the rights; and

(b) the firm deciding to make the loan stock issue instead of the rights issue.

What general conclusion do you draw from this comparison?

11.6 Cavendish plc is a listed firm whose main activity is producing a low value material used in large quantities in the building/construction industries. Production is such that a large proportion of its costs are fixed relative to the level of output.

The firm is financed by a combination of ordinary shares and loan stocks. At present the capital gearing ratio is a little below the average for companies in the building materials industry.

Cavendish plc has identified a possible investment opportunity in taking over the operation of a smaller firm, Darley Ltd which is involved in producing another more recently developed building material, which is increasingly being used as a substitute for a more traditional material. The decision has been taken to make the acquisition, and a price has been negotiated with the owners of Darley Ltd. The owners will only accept cash as the consideration for the acquisition. The acquisition will expand Cavendish plc's total funds invested by around 20 per cent.

Cavendish plc does not have sufficient cash to be able to finance the acquisition without making some form of capital issue. For various reasons, including potential loss of the economies of scale in respect of issue costs, the directors have decided either to make a rights issue of equities OR a loan stock issue, rather than a combination of the two.

A board meeting has been scheduled to make a decision as to the means of financing the acquisition.

In advance of the meeting, individual directors of Cavendish plc have made the following comments:

Director A: 'We don't want to make a rights issue of equities at present. With this depression in the construction industry dragging our share price down, we are going to have to issue a lot of shares to get the amount needed.'

Director B: 'The trouble with a loan stock issue is that it will push our gearing level above the sector average and that won't help our share price.'

Director C: 'My daughter is taking a business finance course as part of her degree, and she has told me that there's a theory that it doesn't make any difference to the existing shareholders whether new finance is raised from a share issue or by borrowing.'

Prepare some notes which will brief the directors, in advance of the meeting, on the likely key issues which they will need to consider, including the points which have already been made to you.

APPENDIX I –
PROOF OF THE MM COST OF CAPITAL PROPOSITION (PRE-TAX)

The following symbols will be used.

$V_U = S_U$ = market value of the ungeared (all equity) firm
S_G = market value of the equity of the geared firm
L_G = market value of the loan capital of the geared firm
$V_G = S_G + L_G$ = market value of the geared firm
i = interest rate
X = net operating income of both firms
α = the proportion of either firm's securities owned by an individual

Suppose that an individual owns proportion α of the shares of the ungeared firm. This is an investment valued at αV_U (or αS_U) which will produce income of αX.

The same income could be obtained (with, according to our assumption, the same risk) by buying proportion α of both the equity and loan stock of the geared firm:

	Investment required	*Income produced*
Buy proportion α of geared firm's equity	$\alpha S_G = \alpha(V_G - L_G)$	$\alpha(X - iL_G)$
Buy proportion α of geared firm's loan stock	αL_G	$\alpha i L_G$
Total	$\overline{\alpha V_G}$	$\overline{\alpha X}$

If $V_U > V_G$, the investor would sell the equity shares in the ungeared firm and buy equity shares and loan stock. Thus the investor would end up with the same income and make a profit on the difference between the price at which the equity shares of the ungeared firm could be sold and what would have to be paid to buy the equity shares and loan stock of the geared firm.

Such action by our investor (and by others similarly placed) will have the effect of reducing the value of the ungeared firm's equity and increasing that of the geared firm's securities. This would occur until the value of the two firms was equal. Efficient capital market research suggests that such a process would not take long.

The commodity which is being traded here (as far as our individual is concerned) is annual income of amount αX. MM argued that it would be irrational for this to be priced differently merely because it is not packaged in the same way. They contended that the packaging of the income is irrelevant since the individual investor can repackage it personally without (according to MM's assumption on frictionless capital markets) any personal cost.

MM also tackled the proof from the other starting point.

Suppose that an individual owns proportion α of the equity shares of α geared firm. This would have a market value of αS_G (or $\alpha(V_G - L_G)$, since $V_G = S_G + L_G$) and produce annual income $\alpha(X - iL_G)$.

In order to get the same income the individual could buy proportion α of the ungeared firm's equity and finance it partly by personal borrowing:

	Investment required	Income produced
Buy proportion α of ungeared firm's shares	$\alpha S_U = \alpha V_U$	αX
Borrow (personally) an amount equal to αL_G	$- \alpha L_G$	$- \alpha i L_G$
Total	$\overline{\alpha(V_U - L_G)}$	$\overline{\alpha(X - iL_G)}$

Thus by investing $\alpha(V_U - L_G)$ the investor can get the same income as had been obtained from an investment valued at $\alpha(V_G - L_G)$. If the market value of the geared firm (V_G) is greater than that of the ungeared one (V_U) it will benefit our investor to sell the equity stake in the geared firm and then go in for some 'personal' gearing.

Once again the action of investors in selling the geared firm's equity and buying that of the ungeared firm would, by the laws of supply and demand, quickly drive the two market values $(V_U$ and $V_G)$ back into equality.

The assumptions on which the above analysis is based are stated and discussed in the chapter.

APPENDIX II–
PROOF OF THE MM COST OF CAPITAL PROPOSITION (POST-TAX)

It is proved below that

$$V_G = V_U + TL_G{}^*$$

Suppose that an individual owns proportion α of the shares of an ungeared firm. This would be an investment valued at $\alpha(V_U)$ (or αS_U) which will produce income $\alpha X(1 - T)$, i.e. proportion α of the after-tax income of the firm.

*Note that $\displaystyle\sum_{n=0}^{\infty} \frac{iTL_G}{(1 + i)^n} = TL_G$

i.e. the present value of the tax saving on loan interest (iTL_G) is TL_G.

The same income could be obtained by buying proportion α of the equity and proportion $\alpha(1 - T)$ of the loan stock of the geared firm:

	Investment required	Income produced
Buy proportion α of geared firm's equity	$\alpha S_G = \alpha(V_G - L_G)$	$\alpha(X - iL_G)(1 - T)$
Buy proportion $\alpha(1 - T)$ of the geared firm's loan stock	$\alpha L_G(1 - T)$	$\alpha i L_G(1 - T)$
Total	$\overline{\alpha(V_G - TL_G)}$	$\overline{\alpha X(1 - T)}$

If $\alpha(V_G - TL_G) < \alpha V_U$, i.e. if $V_G < V_U + TL_G$, it means that the investor could retain the same income ($\alpha X(1 - T)$) by selling the ungeared equities and replacing them with the cheaper geared firm's shares and loan stocks. The action of investors making this switch will tend to cause $V_G = V_U + TL_G$.

Tackling the proof from the other starting point, suppose that an investor holds proportion α in the equity of a geared firm. This would give an income of $\alpha(X - iL_G)(1 - T)$. (This is because the loan interest (iL_G) is tax deductible.) The investor could obtain the same income from selling these shares and buying proportion α of the shares of the ungeared firm and by borrowing amount $\alpha(1 - T)L_G$ to help finance the purchase of the shares.

	Investment required	Income produced
Buy proportion α of the ungeared firm's shares	$\alpha S_U = \alpha V_U$	$\alpha X(1 - T)$
Borrow (personally) $\alpha(1 - T)L_G$	$-\alpha(1 - T)L_G$	$-\alpha(1 - T)iL_G$
Total	$\overline{\alpha[V_U - (1 - T)L_G]}$	$\overline{\alpha(X - iL_G)(1 - T)}$

If $\alpha[V_U - (1 - T)L_G] < \alpha S_G$, then $V_U < S_G + L_G(1 - T)$, which would encourage holders of the geared firm's equity to switch to the ungeared firm's equity (with personal borrowing) since they could continue with the same income but make capital gains on the switch. Such switching would cause:

$$V_U = S_G + L_G(1 - T)$$

Therefore this equality must hold.

CHAPTER 12

The dividend decision

In this chapter we shall deal with the following:

- the nature of dividends
- the theoretical position of dividends as residuals
- the Miller/Modigliani view that the pattern of dividends is irrelevant to the value of shares (and WACC)
- the traditional view of dividends
- the evidence on dividends

INTRODUCTION

Dividends are payments made by firms to their shareholders. They tend to be viewed both by the firm's management and by the recipient shareholders as the equivalent of an interest payment to a loan creditor, a compensation for the shareholders' delaying consumption, etc. Dividends are also seen as a distribution of the firm's recent profits to its owners, the shareholders.

A share, like any other economic asset (i.e. an asset whose value is not wholly or partly derived from sentiment or emotion), is valued on the basis of future cash flows expected to arise from it. Unless a takeover, liquidation or share repurchase is seen as a possibility, the only possible cash flows likely to arise from a share are dividends. So it would seem that anticipated dividends are usually the only determinant of share prices and hence of the cost of equity capital.

It would appear then that management would best promote the shareholders' welfare by paying as large a dividend as the law will allow in any particular circumstances.

This attitude begs several questions, however. What if the firm sees advantageous investment opportunities; would it be beneficial to shareholders for the firm to fail to pay a dividend in order to keep sufficient finance available with which to make the investment? Alternatively, should the firm pay a dividend and raise the necessary finance for the investment opportunity by issuing additional shares to the investing public, perhaps including any of the existing shareholders who wish to be involved?

Even where the firm's management cannot see any particularly advantageous investment opportunities, should it err on the side of caution and pay less than the full amount of dividend which the law allows?

Just what should the firm's dividend policy be, and does it really matter anyway? We shall consider these questions during this chapter.

MILLER AND MODIGLIANI ON DIVIDENDS

In 1961 MM published another important article, this time dealing with dividends and their effect on shareholders' wealth. Their theme further developed the principle, Fisher separation, which we discussed in Chapter 2. In that chapter we looked at a very simple example, which suggested that firms' managers need not concern themselves with the payment of dividends. Provided that the firm takes on all available investment projects which have positive NPVs, when discounted at the borrowing/lending rate, shareholders' wealth will be maximised. Individual shareholders can, by borrowing or lending, achieve the pattern of receipts which maximises their personal utility of wealth.

MM took this slightly further by asserting that the value of a share in a firm will be unaffected by the pattern of dividends expected from it. If shareholders want dividends they can create them by selling part of their shareholding. If dividends are paid to shareholders who would rather leave the funds in the firm, they can cancel these dividends by using the cash received to buy additional shares in the firm, in the capital market.

Let us use an example to illustrate the MM proposition.

EXAMPLE

White plc has net assets whose net present value is £5.0m. This includes cash of £1.0m which the firm has identified could be invested in a project whose anticipated inflows have a present value of £2.0m. Assuming that the firm is financed by 1m ordinary shares (no gearing) and that the investment is undertaken and no dividend paid, the value of each share should be £(5 + 2 − 1)m/1m = £6. If instead of making the investment the £1.0m cash were used to pay a dividend, each share would be worth £(5 − 1)m/1m = £4 and the holder of one share would have £1 (the dividend) in cash.

Clearly it would be to the shareholder's advantage for the firm to make the investment and so it should be made. If White plc wants both to pay the dividend (using up all available cash) and to make the investment, it would need to raise new finance. Assuming that it wished to retain its all-equity status it would need to issue new shares to the value of the dividend. Since the value of the firm after paying the dividend and making the investment would be £5m, this engenders an issue price of the new shares of £5 each (200 000 of them to make up the £1m required).

It also means that the original shareholders would gain £1 per share by way of dividend and lose £1 per share as each share would have a value of £5 instead of the £6 which would apply if no dividend were paid. In other words, the dividend would make no difference to the wealth of the shareholders.

Note that, provided the new investment is undertaken, the worth of the original shares would be £6 each. This value is in some combination of share price and dividend. Irrespective of the amount of dividend paid by the firm, the individual shareholder can choose how much dividend to take. Suppose that no dividend is paid on the White plc shares, but a particular shareholder owning 100 of the shares wants cash of, say, £60? The shareholder can create a 'homemade' dividend by selling 10 shares (at £6 each, their current value).

Conversely, assuming that the firm pays a dividend of £1 per share (and creates an additional 200 000 shares to finance it), shareholders who do not want a dividend but prefer to keep their investment intact could negate the effect of the dividend payment by using the whole of the dividend receipt in buying new shares. Let us again consider the holder of 100 shares who receives £100 by way of dividend. This cash could be used to buy 20 new shares (at £5 each) increasing the investment to 120 shares in total. These will be worth £600, the same as the 100 shares would have been worth had no dividend been paid. Using the whole of the dividend to buy new shares will ensure that our shareholder retains the same proportion of the ownership (120 of the 1.2m) as was held before the dividend and the new issue (100 of the 1.0m shares).

This example illustrates MM's central point, which is that the primary decision is the investment one. Any funds remaining, once all investments which yield a positive NPV when discounted at the shareholders' opportunity cost of capital, should be paid to the shareholders, enabling them to pursue other opportunities. Thus dividends are a *residual*. MM contended that it would be illogical for the capital market to value two, otherwise identical, firms differently just because of their dividend policy. If the firm wants to pay a dividend it can do so and raise any necessary finance by issuing new equity. Also individual shareholders who do not like the firm's dividend policy can alter it to suit their taste through 'homemade' creation or negation of dividends.

MM's assertion does of course rely on several assumptions of dubious validity in the real world. We shall consider the limitations of these assumptions later in the chapter.

A formal derivation of the MM proposition is contained in the Appendix to this chapter.

What MM really said

Before we go on to assess what MM said about dividends against the traditional view and against the evidence of what actually seems to happen in real life, it might be worth clarifying exactly what they really said.

What they did *not* say is that it does not matter whether dividends are paid or not as far as the value of the firm is concerned. If shareholders are never to receive a dividend or any other cash payment in respect of their shares, the value of those shares must be zero. What MM did say is that the pattern of dividends is irrelevant to valuation. Provided that the firm invests in real assets up to the point where all projects have a positive NPV when discounted at the firm's cost of capital, and provided that eventually all of the fruits of the investment are paid in cash to shareholders, it does not matter when payment is made. 'Eventually' may be a very long time, but this in principle does not matter. Even if no cash is expected to be forthcoming until the firm is liquidated this should not of itself cause the shares to be less valuable than were there to be a regular dividend until that time. Thus MM do not cast doubt on the validity of the dividend model for valuing equities, which we discussed in Chapter 10 (p. 245).

In principle, the timing of a particular dividend does not matter to the shareholder, provided that the later dividend is $(1+r)^n$ times the earlier alternative, where r is the shareholder's expected return and n is the time lapse between the earlier and later dividends.

Suppose that a firm could pay a dividend now of amount D. Alternatively the firm could invest the amount D now in a project which will produce one cash inflow after n years which will be paid as a dividend at that time. The shareholders would be indifferent as to whether the dividend is paid now or in n years, provided that the later dividend is $D(1+r)^n$. This is because $D(1+r)^n$ has the present value D (i.e. $D(1+r)^n/(1+r)^n$). Thus dividend D now, or $D(1+r)^n$ in n years, should have equal effect on the value of the shares.

If the firm were able to invest in a project which yields an inflow of amount greater than $D(1+r)^n$ (i.e. a project with a positive NPV), this would enhance the value of the shares.

Of course, as MM pointed out, it is always open to individual shareholders to create dividends by selling part of their shareholding if the delay in the dividend does not suit their personal spending plans.

THE TRADITIONAL VIEW ON DIVIDENDS

Before MM made their assertion and presented a plausible proof of it, the view had been taken not only that dividends are the paramount determinant of share values but that £1 in cash is worth more than £1 of investment.

Going back to the example of White plc (p. 288), the traditionalists would value the shares differently dependent on whether a dividend were to be paid or not. Greater value would be placed on the situation where a dividend was to be paid (and a share issue undertaken) than where this was not the case. This is a view based on a 'bird in hand is worth two in the bush' approach, i.e. the notion that a certain receipt enhances the value of the asset from which it derives. So in the White plc example, if the shares are priced at £6 before a £1 per share dividend, the price of the share will not fall to £5 ex-dividend, but perhaps to £5.50. Thus the wealth of a shareholder will be enhanced by £0.50 per share as a result of the dividend.

The traditional view implies that the payment of dividends reduces the capital market's perceptions of the level of risk attaching to future dividends. This means that the discount rate to be applied to expected future dividends will be lower and the market price will be enhanced.

ARE MM RIGHT ABOUT DIVIDENDS?

The traditional view on dividends seems to suffer from a fundamental lack of logic. The only circumstances where shareholders should logically value £1 in cash more highly than £1 in investment, is where they feel that the firm is using retained cash to make disadvantageous investments (i.e. those which have negative NPVs when discounted at a rate which takes account of the level of risk attaching to the particular project). Since ultimately the shareholders must receive all of the fruits of the firm's investments, provided firms only invest in projects with positive NPVs then investment is to be preferred to present dividends.

MM seem to have logic on their side, yet firms appear to behave as if the pattern of dividends does matter. Financial managers seem to devote quite a lot of thought to fixing the levels of dividends. Most firms seem to maintain pretty stable levels of dividends, implying that they set aside a similar amount for dividends each year. Yet it would be a remarkable coincidence if each year there were a similar amount of cash for which profitable investment opportunities could not be found.

MM's assertion that the pattern of dividends does not matter is based, as we have seen, on several assumptions. The extent to which these weaken their analysis might explain why the logic of the MM proposition does not seem to be accepted in practice. We shall now review these assumptions.

(a) *There are frictionless capital markets, which implies that there are neither transactions costs nor any other impediments to investors behaving in practice as they might be expected to do in theory.* Obviously this is invalid and probably sufficiently so to call the MM view into question. MM rely on the ability of individual shareholders to sell their shares to create dividends or to buy shares to eliminate dividends. The fact that dealing in the capital market involves real and significant cost (agents' fees, etc.) means, for example, that receiving a dividend and liquidating part of an investment in a particular share are not perfect substitutes for one another.

(b) *Securities are efficiently priced in the capital market.* The evidence (as reviewed in Chapter 9) tends to support the validity of this assumption. The assumption is necessary, otherwise (in the above example) White plc undertaking the investment will not necessarily increase the share price by £1, nor the payment of the dividend necessarily reduce the share price by £1.

(c) *Shares may be issued by firms without any legal or administrative costs being incurred.* This assumption is not valid, and this is probably significant in the present context. MM see paying no dividend on the one hand, and paying a dividend and raising an equal amount by share issue on the other hand, as equivalent. This will not be true in practice; issuing new shares tends to involve the firm in fairly large legal and administrative costs (*see* Chapter 8). It seems likely that this is an important factor in making decisions on dividend payment levels.

(d) *Taxes, corporate and personal, do not exist.* Certainly this is untrue, but is it important? From the firm's point of view, its Corporation tax liability is not dependent on the level of dividends, provided that dividends are met from current taxable profit, which will usually be the case. There is a tax cash flow timing disadvantage to paying dividends due to the incidence of ACT (*see* Chapter 8) but this is probably not very significant.

On the personal tax front the main question is whether it is more *tax efficient* to receive dividends or to make capital gains. The answer depends on the individual's level of income and capital gains for the year concerned. If both of these are modest then neither dividend nor capital gains will attract tax, at least no more than will already have been paid by the firm. For shareholders whose income and capital gains are less modest, personal Income Tax and Capital Gains Tax become significant. To the extent that it is possible to generalise, it is probably true to say that for individuals with high levels of dividends and capital gains, further dividends are probably taxed at the same rate as capital gains.

A feature of the UK investment scene is the increasing tendency for equities to be owned by the investing institutions. Many of these, for example pension funds and life assurance funds, are exempt from taxes both on income and on capital gains. As a result they are able to reclaim some of the Corporation tax paid by the firm whose dividends they receive. For such investors, dividends are more tax efficient than are capital gains. The situation is complicated still further by the fact that the firm's Corporation tax liability will, to a large extent, depend on what it does with any funds which it retains. From the firm's point of view, some investments in real assets are more tax efficient than are others, e.g. an investment in a factory attracts tax relief, an investment in an office block does not.

MM's 'no tax' assumption is perhaps not significant provided that firms show some consistency in their dividend policy, a point to which we shall shortly return.

The deficiencies of the individual assumptions do not seem sufficiently profound to destroy the MM case. Clearly the existence of non-trivial dealing and share issue costs must weaken it, but there seems no reason why MM's analysis should not reasonably represent the true position – not, at least, as far as their analysis goes.

OTHER FACTORS

There are some other factors which might bear on the position and explain why firms do seem to regard the dividend decision as an important one.

Informational content of dividends

The view is held by some that the level of dividends, perhaps more particularly changes in the level of dividends paid by a firm, conveys new information to the world. For example, an increased level of dividend might be (and seems often to be interpreted as) a signal that the firm's management views the future with confidence.*

Assuming this view to be correct, whether such a signal is meant as one or is inadvertent probably varies from case to case. Certainly a typical tactic of an unwilling target firm's management in a merger battle is to increase its dividend level; perhaps this is a deliberate signal to inspire the shareholders' confidence in the firm's future.

If dividend increases are meant to act as signals, it seems reasonable to ask why management does not simply issue a statement. Surely a statement would be much less ambiguous than an increased dividend. Perhaps managements feel that actions speak louder than words.

Incidentally if the signalling view of dividends is correct, it would be expected that an increased dividend would have a favourable effect on the share price in the capital market. Such a phenomenon would represent a further piece of evidence that the capital market is not efficient in the strong form (*see* Chapter 9), because it implies that information available to firms' managers may not be impounded in the share price.

Clientele effect

It is widely believed that investors have a *preferred habitat*, i.e. a type of investment which they feel best suits them. In the context of dividends, their preference might well be dictated by their personal tax position. A person with a high marginal Income Tax rate might well be attracted to shares of firms where dividend payouts are low. On the other hand an investor such as a pension fund which is tax exempt, but which needs regular cash receipts in order to be able to meet payments to pensioners, might go for shares in firms whose dividend payments are relatively high. Such an investor could, of course, generate cash by selling shares, but this would involve brokers' fees etc. which obviously are best avoided.

If there really is a clientele effect it means that at least a proportion of any firm's shareholders acquired that firm's shares, because they are suited by the firm's dividend policy. If the firm is inconsistent in its policy on dividends, many investors would be put off the shares as they would not know whether the levels of dividends would suit their preferences or not. The lack of popularity of the shares would have an adverse effect on the share price and therefore on the cost of capital. Even if a particular firm were to be fairly consistent in its dividend policy but then undertook a major change, those of its investors who particularly liked the previous dividend policy (perhaps this might be all of the shareholders) would probably seek to move to the shares of a firm with a dividend policy more acceptable to them. While it might well be the case that

*This contrasts strikingly with the conclusion that might be reached by following MM's analysis. Paying any dividend, let alone one which showed an increase over the previous year, might well indicate that the firm's management cannot find sufficient investment opportunities to use all the finance available to it, so it is returning some to shareholders. This would not suggest too much confidence in the future on the part of management.

a new *clientele* would find the dividend policy attractive, the friction caused by one set of investors selling to a new set of investors would have a net adverse effect on the shareholders. Not only this, but the uncertainty in the minds of investors which the change may precipitate, as to how consistent the firm was likely to be in future, could also have a dampening effect on the share price.

Liquidity

It has been suggested that the level of dividends paid by a particular firm, at a particular time, is largely dictated by the amount of cash available. Certainly this is what MM suggest should be the case. On the other hand, if failure to pay a dividend is interpreted adversely by the capital market, the best interests of shareholders' wealth might be advanced by making sure that cash is available, perhaps by borrowing or even, by passing up otherwise beneficial investment opportunities.

'Pecking order' theory

It has been suggested that firms act in a way which suggests that they link dividend policy and capital gearing. Of course they *are* linked to the extent that paying any dividend reduces the size of the shareholders' funds retained in the firm, which affects the level of gearing.

The pecking order theory is really concerned with the cost of raising, and availability of funds for investment. It may be summarised as follows:

- Retained profit costs nothing to raise, i.e. there are no issue costs.
- External finance is expensive to raise.
- Debt is relatively cheap to raise, particularly if it is in the form of a term loan from a bank or similar institution.
- Equity has relatively high issue costs, particularly where it involves an issue to the general investing public, but even rights issues are relatively expensive.

These factors imply that, where the firm has funds built up from profitable trading which it can dip into for investment purposes, it will tend to do so. If there are insufficient investment funds available from retained profit, debt financing will be favoured next, while equity financing through a new issue of shares will come last in the list of preferences. This might encourage the firm to have lower levels of gearing than the arguments put forward in Chapter 11 would suggest. It will also have the general effect of lowering dividends because cash being used to finance investments cannot be used to pay dividends.

This is not to say that the 'pecking order' is rigidly followed. It will be tempered by other factors. It normally would not mean that no dividends will be paid, but generally they will tend to be paid at lower levels than might otherwise be the case. Other factors, e.g. the tax benefits of capital gearing, will affect the gearing decision.

DIVIDENDS: THE EVIDENCE

Stability of dividend policy

The evidence of casual observation is that financial managers treat the dividend decision as an important one. It also seems that firms try to maintain dividends at previous levels, reductions in dividends seem relatively rare occurrences.

These impressions are supported by some findings of Lintner (1956) arising from interviews with financial managers of 28 selected firms. He found evidence that firms are reluctant to change dividend levels, particularly to reduce them or to increase them to a level which cannot be sustained in the longer term.

Fama and Babiak (1968) analysed relevant data from 201 firms over a 19-year span and came to conclusions which broadly supported Lintner's findings.

Effect of dividends on share price

Friend and Puckett (1964) tested the relationship between share prices and dividend policy. Whilst they experienced some methodological problems they found no close correlation between dividends and share prices.

Black and Scholes (1974) undertook a similar study to that of Friend and Puckett but overcame some of the problems encountered. They too found no evidence that higher or lower dividend levels lead to higher or lower returns either before or after taxes.

A number of subsequent tests, conducted both on UK and US data, has failed to show a clear relationship between dividends and share prices.

Informational content of dividends

Pettit (1972) found clear support for the proposition that the capital market takes account of dividend announcements as information for assessing share prices.

This finding has fairly consistently been supported by subsequent studies, for example, Aharoney and Swary (1980). The evidence on the informational effect of dividends seems fairly conclusive.

Clientele effect

Elton and Gruber (1970) conducted a rather interesting study to test for the *clientele effect*. By looking at the fall in share price when a dividend is paid, they were able to infer an average marginal Income Tax rate for any particular firm's shareholders. They found that lower Income Tax rates were associated with high dividend shares and higher Income Tax rates with low dividend shares, i.e. they found a clientele effect.

Pettit (1977) gained access to information on the security portfolios of a large number of clients of a large US stockbroker. He found that low levels of dividends seemed to be preferred by investors with relatively high marginal

295

Income Tax rates, by younger investors and by those who were less than averagely risk-averse (high β share owners).

However Lewellen, Stanley, Lease and Schlarmbaum (1978), using the same data but a different approach to that taken by Pettit reached the dissimilar conclusion that there is only a very weak clientele effect. Litzenburger and Ramaswamy (1982) undertook a study which produced results which seemed to support the clientele effect. Crossland, Dempsey and Moizer (1991), using UK data, also found clear evidence of a significant clientele effect. The various studies on the clientele effect broadly seem to support its existence.

'Pecking order' theory

This is reasonably well supported by the evidence, for example Griner and Gordon (1995), who assessed the relationship between operating cash flows from existing investments and levels of new investment by a range of large US firms, and found a positive relationship.

CONCLUSIONS ON DIVIDENDS

As with capital gearing, we do not know whether the traditionalists or MM are correct in their assertions. We do, however, have a certain amount of empirical evidence on the subject and so we might be able to reconcile the two views.

MM's assertion that patterns of dividends are irrelevant has some credibility. The assumptions are not entirely convincing but they do not seem sufficiently wide of the mark totally to invalidate the irrelevancy assertion. Importantly the evidence seems to support the MM view in that valuation seems not to be closely related to levels of dividends.

From the evidence there does seem to be a clientele effect in that the dividend policy associated with particular shares appears to attract an identifiable group of investors. Recognition of the clientele effect by managers could well explain their reluctance to alter dividend payment levels.

Perhaps we can conclude that MM are broadly correct that dividends do not affect values provided that investors know the dividend policy of the firm. Probably the most effective way of informing investors of the firm's policy is to establish a fairly constant pattern and to stick to it. Failure to show consistency is likely to lead to uncertainty for investors and to the necessity for shareholders to leave one *habitat* in favour of another, more preferred one. In either case the effect of changes in dividend policy seems likely to lead to lower share prices and higher costs of capital. This implies that liquidity may not be a particularly important factor in the dividend decision, that firms will make sure that sufficient cash is available for the dividend, one way or another.

SUMMARY

Dividends are payments made by firms to their shareholders. They are often portrayed as rewards to shareholders in terms of distributions of the previous or current year's profit and as a vital determinant of share prices. First principles suggest that this view is illogical as failure to pay dividends simply means that the wealth of individual shareholders will be more in the value of their shares and less in cash.

MM, depending on several simplifying assumptions, showed that the pattern of dividends is irrelevant to shareholders' wealth. Since it is open to firms to pay very large proportions of their profits as dividends and then to raise such finance as they need for investment purposes from new share issues, it would be illogical if managements could manipulate things and as a result increase the wealth of the shareholders.

The evidence on dividends tends to suggest that MM are broadly right. There does however appear to be a clientele effect which means that investors with particular dividend preferences are attracted to shares whose dividend record matches those preferences. Firms can probably best serve their shareholders by establishing a dividend policy and sticking to it as closely as possible.

FURTHER READING Most business finance texts deal with the question of dividends and dividend policy. Brealey and Myers (1991) and Puxty and Dodds (1991) each contain interesting sections on it.

Copeland and Weston (1988) discuss this topic, particularly the empirical evidence giving more detail of some of the particular studies mentioned in this chapter.

REVIEW QUESTIONS

Suggested answers to review questions appear in Appendix 3.

12.1 According to MM, what is the difference between the value of a dividend received now and one received in the future, if the shareholders are indifferent as to whether they receive the dividend now or in the future?

12.2 According to MM, what rule should a firm follow in paying dividends to its shareholders?

12.3 What are 'homemade dividends' in the context of MM? Why might a shareholder want such a dividend?

12.4 What, in outline, is the traditional view on the payment of dividends?

12.5 Why is the MM position on dividends partly dependent on their assumption of no taxes?

12.6 Why should we find that firms attract a 'clientele' of shareholders as a result of their dividend policy?

PROBLEMS

Sample answers to problems marked with an asterisk appear in Appendix 4.

(Note that problem questions 12.1–12.4 are basic level problems, while questions 12.5 and 12.6 are more advanced, and may contain some practical complications.)

12.1* The shareholders of Distributors plc have an opportunity cost of capital of 20 per cent. The firm makes a steady profit of £25 million each year which is all paid out as a dividend. The opportunity has arisen to invest the dividend which is about to be paid (£25 million). This investment will give rise to a single payoff in three years' time. The normal £25 million dividend will be paid next year and subsequently, in the normal way.

What dividend needs to be paid in three years' time so that the shareholders will be equally content to wait the three years, adopting the Modigliani and Miller assumptions on dividends?

12.2 'According to Modigliani and Miller, shareholders are indifferent between a dividend and a capital gain.'

Comment on this statement which you have overheard.

12.3* HLM plc, an all-equity financed firm, has just paid a dividend totalling £1.5 million. This amount has been paid on a regular basis for many years, and the market expects this to continue. The firm has 10 million ordinary shares currently quoted at £1 each. The directors have identified the opportunity to invest £1 million in one year's time, and a similar amount in two years' time, in a project which will generate an annual cash flow of £0.4 million for ever, starting in three years' time.

The only possible way of financing this investment is by paying a reduced dividend for the next two years.

If the directors were to announce their intention to make this investment and to publish full details of it and the financing method, what would happen to the firm's share price? Ignore taxation.

12.4 Durodorso plc is a Stock Exchange listed firm which has built up a cash mountain equal in size to about 25 per cent of the firm's market capitalisation as a result of the continuation of restricted dividend policy and a consistent failure to identify investment opportunities. Since the directors continue to see no investment opportunities, a decision has been made to use the cash pay a 'special' dividend.

When the directors met to discuss the 'special' dividend, the Finance Director told the other directors, 'We've always been modest dividend payers in the past so our shareholders would probably welcome a large dividend'.

What would you advise the directors to do regarding the 'special' dividend?

12.5* Images plc is an all-equity financed, Stock Exchange listed firm. The firm has been a steady profit and cash flow generator over recent years, and it has distributed all of its after tax profit as dividends.

More recently, the firm has been actively seeking new investment opportunities. In the financial year which has just ended, the firm reported profits of £5 million, a figure similar to that of recent years.

Four potential investment projects have been identified, all of which could commence immediately. The estimated cash flows and timings of these projects are as follows:

Project	I	II	III	IV
	£ million	£ million	£ million	£ million
Year 0	(2.0)	(2.0)	(3.0)	(1.0)
1	0.75	0.65	0.80	0.50
2	0.75	0.65	0.80	0.50
3	0.75	0.65	0.80	0.50
4		0.65	0.80	
5		0.65	0.80	

Each of these projects falls within the same risk class as the firm's existing projects.

It has been estimated that the firm's cost of equity is 15 per cent p.a.

The directors would be very reluctant to raise outside finance to help finance any of the above projects.

What advice would you give the directors as to the level of dividend which the firm should pay this year?

12.6 The directors of Bellini plc, a Stock Exchange listed firm, are contemplating purchasing some of the firm's shares in the market, and cancelling them, as an alternative to paying a dividend. Some of the directors believe that this would be preferred by certain shareholders.

What considerations should the directors particularly take into account when making this decision.

APPENDIX – PROOF OF THE MM DIVIDEND IRRELEVANCY PROPOSITION

In the proof of their assertion MM considered firm j during a time period which starts at time t and ends at $t + 1$.

They used the following symbols:

D_{jt} is the total dividend paid during the period starting at time t.

d_{jt} is the dividend per share paid during that period.

P_{jt} is the price per share at time t.

r_t is the return per share during the period starting at time t.

n_t is the number of shares of the firm at time t.

m_t is the number of new shares issued during the period starting at time t.

V_{jt} is the value of the firm at time t (i.e. $V_{jt} = n_t \times P_{jt}$)

$$r_t = \frac{d_{jt} + P_{j(t+1)} - P_{jt}}{P_{jt}} \qquad (1)$$

the return per share during the period is the dividend paid during it *plus* the increase in price per share ($P_{j(t+1)} - P_{jt}$) expressed as a fraction of the price at the start of the period.

$$P_{jt} = \frac{d_{jt} + P_{j(t+1)}}{1 + r_t} \qquad (2)$$

Rearranging (1) gives:

i.e. the price per share is the discounted value of the dividend for the period plus the price per share at the end of the period.

Market forces will tend to ensure that equations (1) and (2) hold to the extent that the current price P_{jt} will be such to cause r_t to be similar to that of other shares of similar risk to those of firm j.

$$n_{(t+1)} - n_t = m_{(t+1)} \qquad (3)$$

i.e. the difference between the number of shares at the start and end of the period is accounted for by those issued (or withdrawn) during the period

$$V_{jt} = \frac{D_{jt} + n_t P_{j(t+1)}}{1+r_t} \tag{4}$$

From equation (2), the value of the whole firm is the discounted value of the total dividend payable during the period plus the value of the firm at the end of the period.

Expressed alternatively:

$$V_{jt} = \frac{D_{jt} + V_{(t+1)} - m_t P_{(t+1)}}{1+r_t} \tag{5}$$

i.e. the value of the firm at the start of the period is the discounted value of the dividend for the period plus the value of the firm at the end of the period less the value of any share capital raised during the period. This is because:

$$V_{(t+1)} = n_t P_{(t+1)} + m_t P_{(t+1)} \tag{6}$$

From equation (5) we can see that the value of the firm at time t is dependent upon anticipated dividends, the value of the firm at the end of the period and the value of any new shares issued. However, the quantity of new shares which it is necessary to issue is, in turn, dependent on the size of dividends paid.

$$m_t P_{(t+1)} = I_t - (X_t - D_t) \tag{7}$$

where I_t is the real investment and X_t the operating cash flow surplus during the period.

That is to say that the value of the finance which must be raised from new share issues is the excess of the funds invested over the operating cash flow surplus after dividends have been paid. In other words the value of the new issues depends on the extent to which new investment exceeds retained profit.

Substituting equation (7) into equation (5) for $m_t P_{(t+1)}$ gives:

$$V_t = \frac{D_t + V_{(t+1)} - I_t + X_t - D_t}{1+r_t}$$

The D_t terms cancel each other out to give:

$$V_t = \frac{V_{(t+1)} - I_t + X_t}{1+r_t}$$

Thus V_t is independent of the amount of dividend paid during the forthcoming period, but depends on the anticipated value of the firm at the end of the period, the anticipated level of investment and cash flow surplus.

Dividends can be at any level. Any cash deficiency caused by dividends being paid in excess of operating cash flows can be made up through capital issues of new equity.

The assumptions made and their validity are discussed in the chapter.

PART 4

Mixed decisions

There are some areas of business finance which do not fall distinctly into either investment or financing decisions, but involve some combination of both. These areas are discussed in this part of the book. Working capital, the subject of Chapter 13, is such an area. Working capital consists of the firm's short-term assets and liabilities. Since these are in a constant state of change, as the firm carries out its normal activities, decisions on investment and finance are frequent and, for the most part, routine. Progressive firms in an open economy should be constantly seeking ways of reorganising themselves, so as best to be able to relate to their environment and to achieve their objectives. Such reorganisation, the subject of Chapter 14, typically involves altering some aspect, often a fundamental aspect, of their investment or financing strategy. Small firms are increasingly seen as a major part of the future of business. Chapter 15 considers to what extent, if at all, small firms should be treated differently from large ones, when making financial decisions.

CHAPTER 13

Management of working capital

OBJECTIVES

In this chapter we shall deal with the following:

- the nature of working capital and the working capital cycle
- its importance as a source and use of short-term finance
- liquidity of firms and working capital
- the management of the individual elements of working capital
  - stocks
  - trade debtors
  - cash (and bank overdrafts)
  - trade creditors
- the necessity for establishing policies on each element of working capital in order to provide a framework for its practical management

INTRODUCTION

When firms make investment decisions they must not only consider the financial outlay involved with acquiring the new machine or the new building, etc., they must also take account of the additional current assets which are usually involved with any expansion of activity. Increased production tends to engender a need to hold additional stocks of raw materials and work-in-progress. Increased sales usually means that the level of debtors will increase. A general increase in the firm's scale of operations tends to imply a need for greater levels of cash.

The current assets (stock-in-trade, debtors and cash) tend not to be financed entirely from the firm's long-term sources of finance. Most firms also have access to two major short-term sources of finance. The first of these is trade credit, arising from the fact that purchases of goods and services are usually on credit, i.e. the buying firm does not have to pay immediately on delivery but may be allowed to delay payment for a period, say 30 days. The second is a source with which many of us are all too familiar in our private lives, the bank overdraft.

Since the relationship between these short-term sources of finance (or current liabilities) and the current assets tends to be very close, it seems logical to deal with both of them in the same chapter.

It could be argued that it is wrong to separate discussion of current assets from that of the investment decision generally, and similarly to discuss short-term finance separately from long-term finance. The reason for taking the present approach is simply that there are features of the management of current assets and of current liabilities which particularly commend dealing with them together, yet separate from the longer-term investment and financing decisions. These features include the systematic nature of the management of the working capital elements and the frequency with which decisions have to be taken in respect of most of them.

Perhaps another reason for discussing current assets and current liabilities together is that care needs to be taken by financial managers to ensure a reasonable balance between the relative levels, so it is important not to lose sight of their interrelationship. In fact, so closely related are these two, that they are frequently netted against one another and considered as a single factor, namely working capital (current assets *less* current liabilities).

The working capital cycle

The upper portion of Fig. 13.1 depicts, in a highly simplified form, the chain of events in a manufacturing firm as regards working capital. The chain starts with the firm buying raw materials on credit. In due course this stock will be used in production, work will be carried out on the stock and it will become part of the firm's work-in-progress (WIP). Work will continue on the WIP until it eventually emerges as the finished product. As production progresses, labour costs and overheads will need to be met. Of course at some stage trade creditors will need to be paid. When the finished goods are sold on credit, debtors are increased. They will eventually pay, so that cash will be injected into the firm.

Each of the areas – stocks (raw materials, work-in-progress and finished goods), trade debtors, cash (positive or negative) and trade creditors – can be viewed as tanks into and from which funds flow. Most of this chapter will be devoted to questions of why any of these 'tanks' need exist at all and, if they are necessary, what attitude managers should take on the amounts which should be held in each tank at any given time.

Working capital is clearly not the only aspect of the firm which impacts on cash. The firm will have to make payments to government, both central and local, for taxation. Fixed assets will be purchased and sold. Lessors of fixed assets will be paid their rent (lease payment). Shareholders (existing or new) may provide new funds in the form of cash, some shares may be redeemed for cash and dividends will normally be paid. Similarly long-term loan creditors (existing or new) may provide loan finance, loans will need to be repaid from time to time and interest obligations will have to be met by the firm. Unlike movements in the working capital items, most of these 'non-working capital' cash transactions are not everyday events. Some of them are annual events (e.g. tax payments, lease payments, dividends, interest and, probably, fixed asset purchases and sales). Others (e.g. new equity and loan finance and redemption of old equity and loan finance) would typically be rarer events. A factor which most of these non-working capital transactions have in

**Fig. 13.1
The working
capital cycle for
a manufacturing
firm**

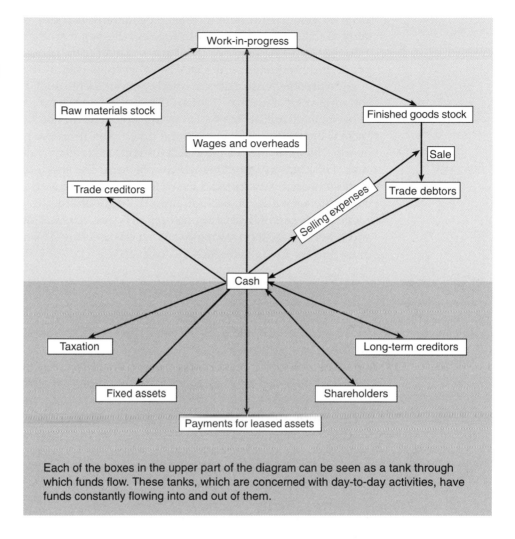

Each of the boxes in the upper part of the diagram can be seen as a tank through which funds flow. These tanks, which are concerned with day-to-day activities, have funds constantly flowing into and out of them.

common is their size; they are likely individually to involve large amounts of cash.

It is obvious that the management of working capital, particularly of cash, is very closely linked to financing decisions and to decisions involving investment in fixed assets. This linkage involves both quantities of cash and the timing of cash flows. For example, if a particular long-term debt is to be redeemed under a contractual obligation, thought must be given to the question of the source of that cash. If cash has not been generated through the working capital cycle, some other source (e.g. new equity or loan finance) will need to be considered. These themes will be further developed later in this chapter.

Measuring the operating cycle and cash cycle

The working capital cycle, represented descriptively in the top part of Fig. 13.1, can also be represented in a more quantitative manner, as shown in Fig. 13.2.

Here the length of time which each element of working capital, except cash, takes in the cycle is shown. Both figures refer to a manufacturing firm.

In Fig. 13.2, raw material (RM) stock is held for a period of time before it is taken into production, the stock now becomes part of the work-in-progress, along with other costs (labour, overheads, etc.) until such time as it completed and forms part of finished goods (FG) stock. Finished stock is held until it is sold to become a trade debtor which in due course is met by the customer and the cycle is completed. The sum of the time taken from the purchase of the raw material stock to the receipt of cash from the customer is known as the *operating cycle*. This cycle must be financed by the firm. The shorter the operating cycle, the less finance is required. One of the objectives of working capital management is to keep this cycle to a minimum length of time.

Of course, part of this operating cycle is financed by suppliers of raw materials and other inputs, who normally sell on credit terms. This means that the firm must find the funds to finance the 'cash cycle'.

**Fig. 13.2
The operating and cash cycles for a manufacturing firm**

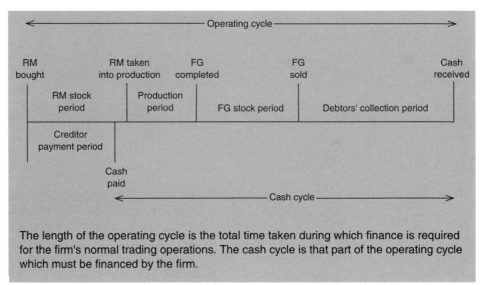

The length of the operating cycle is the total time taken during which finance is required for the firm's normal trading operations. The cash cycle is that part of the operating cycle which must be financed by the firm.

EXAMPLE

The following information relates to Jittery plc for last year:

	£ million
Purchases of raw materials	67
Usage of raw materials	65
Sales of finished goods (all on credit)	250
Cost of sales of finished goods	180
Average creditors	14
Average of raw materials stock	12
Average work-in-progress	10
Average of finished goods stock	21
Average debtors	47

What are the lengths of the operating and cash cycles?

SOLUTION

days

RM stock period	$\dfrac{\text{RM stock}}{\text{RM usage}} \times 365$	$= \dfrac{12}{65} \times 365$	$= \quad 67$
Production period	$\dfrac{\text{WIP}}{\text{cost of sales}} \times 365$	$= \dfrac{10}{180} \times 365$	$= \quad 20$
FG stock period	$\dfrac{\text{FG stock}}{\text{cost of sales}} \times 365$	$= \dfrac{21}{180} \times 365$	$= \quad 43$
Debtors' collection period	$\dfrac{\text{debtors}}{\text{sales}} \times 365$	$= \dfrac{47}{250} \times 365$	$= \quad 69$
Operating cycle (days)			$= \quad \overline{199}$
Creditors' payment period	$\dfrac{\text{creditors}}{\text{RM purchases}} \times 365$	$= \dfrac{14}{67} \times 365$	$= \quad (76)$
Cash cycle (days)			$\underline{\overline{123}}$

Notes to the solution

It should be noted that days in the above solution are not of equal importance in economic terms. For example, reducing the debtors collection period by one day will save funding of £684 000 (i.e. £250m/365). Increasing the creditors payment period by one day will save funding to the extent of only £184 000 (i.e. £67m/365).

The scale of working capital

It is tempting to believe that with working capital we are dealing with trivial matters. Such a view is very wide of the mark for the typical UK firm; the amounts involved tend to be vast. For the typical commercial firm, the investment in stocks, debtors and cash is of the same order as the investment in fixed assets (land, plant, etc.). This large investment in current assets is, of course, partly offset by the fact that it is financed substantially by 'free' trade credit.

The relative vastness of the typical firm's investment in working capital has led to the subject of management of working capital increasingly being treated as fundamental to the welfare of the firm and to its ability to survive.

The nature of decisions on working capital

The difference between working capital decisions and those involving fixed assets and long-term finance does not apparently lie in the amount of finance involved; to the extent that there is such a difference it lies in the tendency for working capital decisions to be short-term, reversible at relatively short notice, and made more frequently.

While they may be made more frequently, many working capital decisions are easy since they tend to be repetitive. There will (or should be) a policy which creates a set of rules to be followed. For example, each time a customer seeks to buy goods from the firm on credit, a decision will be needed as to whether to grant credit at all and, if so, how much. Most firms will have decided on some formula which can be applied to help them to reach a decision. The existence of such formulae has the advantage that many decisions can be made by employees quite low in the management hierarchy and therefore they can be made fairly cheaply.

In establishing these formulae or sets of rules for the day-to-day management of working capital, great care should be taken to assess which approach will most advance the firm's objectives. Once a set of rules has been established it should be regarded as the framework within which all operating decisions must be made.

It is unlikely that rules established at one time will continue to represent the most beneficial approach over long periods of time. Circumstances, including the firm's competitive position, interest rates and the economic environment generally, alter over time. Policies must therefore be reviewed and, if necessary, revised periodically.

The use of budgets

Probably few areas of financial management can benefit as much as the control of working capital from the use of detailed plans in the form of budgets. The ability to assess in advance the calls which will be made on the various elements of working capital enables managers to ensure that the 'tanks' are always adequately full.

Few firms have steady and regular working capital requirements from week to week throughout the year; this is due, amongst other things, to seasonal factors. Prior knowledge of what the demands are likely to be at various times is of enormous value.

General attitude to working capital

Broadly, firms should seek to minimise the level of each type of current asset which they hold and to maximise the benefits of cheap short-term finance. This is, of course, subject to the costs involved with doing so to the extreme. For example, granting credit to customers is expensive (in lost interest on the funds, if nothing else), so ideally credit should not be given. However, failing to give credit is very likely to mean that the firm will be unable to make sales (perhaps because competitors do offer credit). Clearly the firm's credit policy must seek to strike a balance between the costs of taking one extreme view and those of taking the other extreme view.

Since working capital elements tend to be of high financial value, getting the balance between the extremes wrong tends to be an expensive matter. Indeed, as we shall shortly see, it can even be a fatal one.

WORKING CAPITAL AND LIQUIDITY

Not only do firms need to seek to strike a reasonable balance between the extremes in respect of individual working capital elements: a balance should also be sought between exploiting 'cheap' sources of short-term finance (current liabilities) to the fullest possible extent, and the risks and possible costs involved with being heavily reliant on suppliers of finance who can demand repayment at very short notice. That is to say, firms need to maintain sufficient current assets to enable them to be able to meet short-term claims as they become due. They need to be able to do this since failure to meet them would entitle the short-term claimants (the current liabilities) to take steps to put the firm into liquidation. This would normally involve the forced sale of some or all of the firm's assets, including its fixed assets.

If bankruptcy costs were not significant and if the market for real assets were efficient, from a shareholder wealth maximisation perspective the liquidation threat would be unimportant. This is because shareholders could expect, on the liquidation of the firm, to receive for their shares an amount equal to the capital market price of the shares immediately before the liquidation. In other words, liquidation would not affect a shareholder's wealth. In reality, of course, since bankruptcy costs are likely to be significant and markets for real assets do not seem to be efficient, liquidation would usually be expected to have a severely adverse effect on shareholders' wealth.

One way to avoid the risk of liquidation is to maintain a large amount of cash on short-term interest-bearing deposit. In this way, should a need for cash to meet current liabilities suddenly arise, cash could be made available quickly to meet the demand. Obviously there would be no point in taking such an approach unless the funds used to establish the short-term deposit were provided from long-term sources. Otherwise the ploy would have the effect of solving the original problem by creating another group of short-term claimants who could create the same problem.

The approach of using long-term finance to create a short-term fund would offer the perfect solution to the liquidity problem but for imperfections in the capital market. These tend to mean, amongst other things, that firms usually cannot lend at as high a rate of interest as that which they have to pay to borrow. Also long-term interest rates are usually higher than short-term ones. So, for the average firm, borrowing long term and lending short term in order to maintain good liquidity and avoid the risk of liquidation is likely to be an expensive solution to the problem.

In practice firms seem to try to strike a balance between the levels of their current assets and current liabilities, i.e. a balance between exploiting cheap sources of short-term finance and the risk inherent in doing so.

It is probably fair to say that, irrespective of the root problem (e.g. lack of profitability), most business failures result from a deficiency in working capital.

Financing working capital

The amount of funds tied up in working capital would not typically be a constant figure throughout the year, only in the most unusual of firms would there be a constant need for working capital funding. For most firms there would be weekly fluctuations. Many firms operate in industries which are, to a significant extent, seasonal in demand pattern. This means that sales, stocks debtors, etc. would be at higher levels at some fixed parts of the year than at others.

In principle, the working capital need can be separated into two parts; a fixed part and a fluctuating part. The fixed part is probably defined in amount as the minimum working capital requirement for the year.

It is widely advocated that the firm should be funded in the way depicted in Fig. 13.3. The more permanent needs (fixed assets and the fixed element of working capital) should be financed from fairly permanent sources (e.g. equity and loan stocks), the fluctuating element should be financed from a short-term source (e.g. a bank overdraft) which can be drawn on and repaid easily and at short notice.

Fig. 13.3
Financing the firm

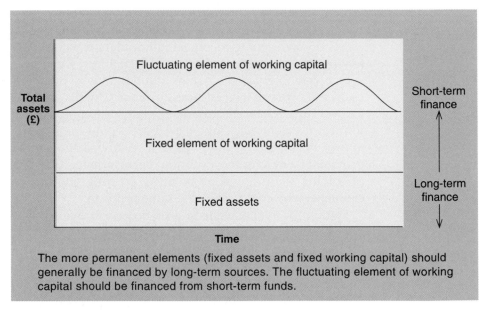

The more permanent elements (fixed assets and fixed working capital) should generally be financed by long-term sources. The fluctuating element of working capital should be financed from short-term funds.

Figure 13.3 assumes no basic alterations in the levels of any of the assets, except the fluctuating working capital. In practice, expansion, contraction or structural alteration of the firm's operations would alter the pattern of finance required.

The use of accounting ratios in the management of working capital

Accounting ratios are widely used in the management of working capital. The following are some of the ratios used to assist in the management of working capital. You may care to look back at Chapter 3 for more details of these ratios.

(a) The current ratio (current assets/current liabilities).
(b) Acid test ratio (liquid assets/current liabilities).
(c) No-credit period (liquid assets/average daily cash running costs).

Probably managers can best use these ratios by employing them to monitor their firm's actual liquidity position and to compare it constantly with some standard or target figure, taking steps to correct any significant deviations. The standard might be one which emerges from within the firm, or an industry average, or perhaps some combination of the two. One way or another, firms should actively seek to maintain liquidity and the confidence of short-term creditors that they will be paid.

OVERTRADING

A particular firm in particular circumstances will have particular working capital requirements, though what these are is a matter of managerial judgement. For example, the management of a retailing firm with a particular level of demand for its merchandise will decide on a level of stock requirement. If demand were to alter, a different level of stock holding would normally be required. A doubling of the level of demand would not necessarily imply a need to double stock levels, but it would normally imply a need for a significant increase in the amount of stock available to customers. The same point is broadly true for firms in any line of business in respect of all working capital aspects. It is obviously necessary, not only that management decides on the level of working capital which will be required, but that it also ensures that finance is available to provide for the investment in that amount of working capital. Not to be able to provide the level of working capital required to sustain a particular level of trading is known as *overtrading*.

Problems do arise in practice for firms who experience an expansion of trading activity due to an upturn in demand, particularly when the increase in demand is rapid and unexpected. The temptation for a firm to exploit profitable new trading opportunities is frequently overwhelming. Yet increased activity without increased working capital to sustain it can lead to serious overtrading problems, possibly culminating in complete financial failure of the firm. At first sight the problem seems capable of solving itself, since the increased profits from the additional business will provide the finance necessary to expand the working capital. This view is usually misleading, however, since the working capital requirement (additional stocks, additional cash for labour and other costs) generally precedes any additional cash flows from the increased business. This arises from the fact that the typical firm, irrespective of its line of business, has to pay cash to meet most of the costs of making a particular sale before cash is forthcoming from the customer. The extent of this problem varies from one type of business to another. Clearly it is a greater problem for a manufacturer (relatively large stock and debtor levels) selling on credit than it is for a firm providing services for immediate cash settlement, e.g. a hairdressing business. In fact, for a hairdressing firm rapid expansion of trading may pose no problems at all. Put another way, manufacturers tend to have long cash cycles whereas hairdressers do not.

STOCK-IN-TRADE (INVENTORIES)

As we saw in Fig. 13.1, manufacturing firms typically hold stocks at various stages of completion, from raw materials to finished goods. Trading firms (wholesalers, retailers, etc.) by the nature of their business hold stock in only one condition. Broadly speaking, the level of investment in stocks by manufacturers tends to be relatively large compared with that of traders.

Even with traders there may be vast differences. A jeweller would normally hold much more stock (in value terms) than would a greengrocer with the same level of annual turnover. The perishable nature of the latter's wares would partly account for this, as would the high value of the individual items in the stock of the former. Another factor might be that when we buy jewellery we usually demand a choice, which is less likely to be the case when we buy potatoes.

With some firms the requirement for stocks varies with the time of year. Firework manufacturers in the UK who experience high sales in the period leading up to 5 November may well find it necessary to hold very large stocks during each summer as they *stockpile* Catherine wheels, etc., for the forthcoming period of high demand.

Irrespective of the nature of the trade, firms should seek to balance the costs of holding stock with those of holding no or low levels of stock. While the costs of holding stocks tend to be fairly certain, if difficult to identify, those of failing to hold stocks may or may not occur, i.e. there is a risk. Thus such costs are in the nature of *expected values*, where costs are combined with their probability of occurrence.

The costs of holding stocks

These include:

(a) Lost interest This could be earned on the finance tied up in the stocks. This cost is partly mitigated by a certain amount of free credit granted by suppliers of the stock which would only be available if stock is bought. The existence of this aspect is very important to some types of business. High street supermarkets, because their stock turnover is rapid, typically have their entire stocks financed by suppliers of these stocks. For other types of business where this is not the case, the opportunity cost of interest should be based on the returns from an investment of risk similar to that of investing in stocks.

(b) Storage costs These include rent of space occupied by the stock and the cost of employing people to guard and manage the stock. With some types of stock it might include the cost of keeping it in some particular environment necessary for its preservation. This is likely to be particularly true for perishables such as food.

(c) Insurance costs Holding valuable stocks exposes firms to risk of fire, theft, etc., against which they will usually insure, at a cost.

(d) Obsolescence Stocks can become obsolete, for example because they go out of fashion or lose their value due to changes in the design of the product in whose manufacture they were intended to be used. Thus apparently perfectly good stock can become little more than scrap. The firm holding no stock is clearly not exposed to the risk of this cost.

The costs of holding low (or no) stocks

These include:

(a) Loss of customer goodwill Failure to be able to supply a customer due to having insufficient stock may mean the loss not only of that particular order, but of further orders as well. The extent to which this is important depends to a large degree on the nature of the trade and on the relative market power of supplier and customer.

(b) Production dislocation Running out of raw materials when other production facilities (factory, machinery, labour, etc.) are available can be very costly. How costly depends on how flexible the firm can be in response to a *stock-out*, which in turn probably depends on the nature of the stock concerned. For example, a motor car manufacturer running out of a major body section probably has no choice but to stop production. If the firm runs out of interior mirrors, it is probably quite feasible for these to be added at the end of the production cycle rather than at the scheduled stage, without too much costly dislocation.

(c) Loss of flexibility Firms which hold little or no stock inevitably lead a 'hand to mouth' existence where purchasing and manufacture must be very closely geared to sales. This may preclude maximising the efficiency of production runs or of buying materials in batches of economically optimum sizes. Such an existence also means that, unless things go precisely to plan, costly problems are likely to occur. For example, if there is even a slight increase in sales demand it will be unable to be met.

Stock holding creates a 'margin of safety' whereby mishaps of various descriptions can occur without major and costly repercussions.

(d) Re-order costs Any firm existing on little or no stock will, among other things, be forced to place a large number of small orders with short intervals of time between each one. Each order gives rise to costs including the physical placing of the order (buyer's time, telephone, postage, etc.) and the receipt of the goods (storemen's time, costs of processing the invoice and making payment).

Stock management models

Models have been developed to aid managers in their task of balancing costs. Each of these models seems to have its strengths and its limitations.

**Fig. 13.4
A graph of the
stock level against
time for some item
of stock**

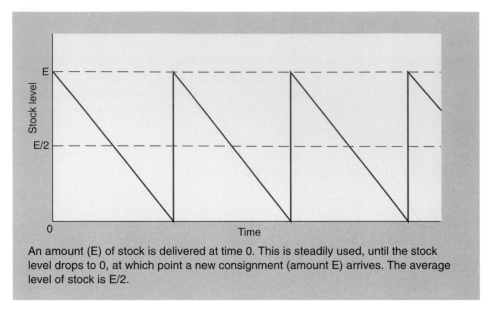

An amount (E) of stock is delivered at time 0. This is steadily used, until the stock
level drops to 0, at which point a new consignment (amount E) arrives. The average
level of stock is E/2.

One such model can be used to identify the optimum size of order to be placed
for the purchase of new raw materials, given a particular rate of usage of stock
and other relevant factors. The model is based on the assumption that the level
of each stock item will be as shown in Fig. 13.4. This shows the stock level falling
evenly over time until just as the stock completely runs out it is replaced by
quantity E. Since the stock level falls evenly from E to zero, the average stock
holding level is $E/2$. The model seeks to balance stock holding costs with the
cost of placing orders.

If C is the cost of placing each order, A the annual demand for (i.e. usage of)
the stock item, and H the cost of holding one unit of the stock item for one
year, then the annual cost of placing orders will be ($A/E \times C$) and the cost of
holding the stock will be ($E/2 \times H$). The total costs associated with placing
orders and holding stock is the sum of these two. (Note that we are not interested in the purchase price of the stock itself as this is defined by the annual
usage and the price per unit and is independent, except for the question of
possible discounts for bulk orders, of the size of each order and the average
stock level.)

Figure 13.5 shows the behaviour of the costs with various levels of stock. As
stock levels and, following our assumptions depicted in the graph in Fig. 13.4,
order size increase, the annual costs of placing orders decrease but holding
costs increase. Total cost drops as stock level increases until at point M it
reaches a minimum and starts to increase. What we want to know is the
size of order quantity E which will minimise the total cost, i.e. identify
point M.

The total cost, and therefore the expression plotted as such in Fig. 13.5, is

$$\frac{AC}{E} + \frac{HE}{2}$$

**Fig. 13.5
A graph of the
stock holding
costs and stock
order costs
against the average
stock level for
some item of
stock**

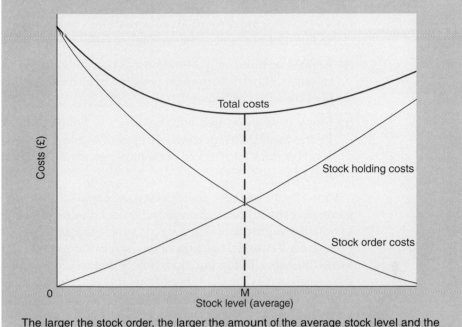

The larger the stock order, the larger the amount of the average stock level and the
higher the stock holding costs. On the other hand, large stock orders mean relatively
infrequent orders and, therefore, relatively low total order costs. There seems likely to
be an optimum stock order size, which will balance the two types of cost.

This will be a minimum where the differential of the expression (with respect
to E) is equated to zero (the point of zero slope, M in Fig. 13.5, i.e. where

$$\frac{-AC}{E^2} + \frac{H}{2} = 0$$

so

$$E = \sqrt{\frac{2AC}{H}}$$

EXAMPLE

A firm uses 1000 units of a particular stock item each year. The costs of holding one
unit of it for a year are £3 and the cost of placing each order is £30. What is the most
economical size for each order?

SOLUTION

$$E = \sqrt{\frac{2AC}{H}}$$

$$= \sqrt{\left(\frac{2 \times 1000 \times 30}{3}\right)}$$

$$= 141.4, \text{ say 141 units}$$

Thus each order will be placed for 141 units (or perhaps a round figure like 140 or
150), necessitating about seven orders being placed each year.

We should note the weaknesses of this model, the most striking of which are:

(a) Demand for stock items may fluctuate on a seasonal basis, i.e. the diagonals in Fig. 13.4 may not all be parallel, or even straight.

(b) Annual demand may be (almost certainly is) impossible to predict with certainty, though it may be possible to ascribe statistical probabilities to possible levels of demand.

(c) Many costs associated with holding and failing to hold stocks are ignored by the model. This particularly applies to some of the costs of holding low levels of stock such as loss of customer goodwill, production dislocation and loss of flexibility.

Virtually all of these deficiencies are capable of being accommodated by increasing the sophistication of the model. For example, the loss of customer goodwill and production dislocation problems can to some extent be dealt with by revising the model to incorporate a safety margin reflecting a pattern of stock levels over time, following more closely that which is depicted in Fig. 13.6 than the one shown in Fig. 13.4. How large this margin of safety should be must be a matter of managerial judgement. Some estimate of the costs of holding the additional stock, the costs of a 'stock-out' and the probability of its occurrence, must give some guidance in the exercise of the judgement.

Fig. 13.6
Graph of the stock level against time for some item of stock, assuming a safety margin

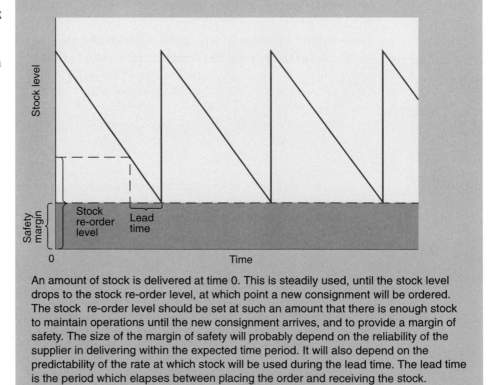

An amount of stock is delivered at time 0. This is steadily used, until the stock level drops to the stock re-order level, at which point a new consignment will be ordered. The stock re-order level should be set at such an amount that there is enough stock to maintain operations until the new consignment arrives, and to provide a margin of safety. The size of the margin of safety will probably depend on the reliability of the supplier in delivering within the expected time period. It will also depend on the predictability of the rate at which stock will be used during the lead time. The lead time is the period which elapses between placing the order and receiving the stock.

Note that incorporating a safety stock means that the average stock holding level is no longer $E/2$ and so the basic model is not strictly valid; however, the model can quite easily be adjusted to cope with this.

Let us be clear that the model which we derived is a highly simplified, even simplistic, attempt to balance the two types of cost. However, the model can be extended to deal with most factors which the simpler version glosses over. Several of the references at the end of this chapter go into some of the sophistications which can be incorporated. The model may also be used with a little adaptation for WIP and finished stocks as well as for bought-in raw materials.

Some practical points on management of stocks

Optimum order quantities

These should be established for each item of stock, using either the model which we derived (above) or some more sophisticated version. These quantities should be periodically revised, but between revisions should be regarded as the size of order which should be placed, except in most unusual circumstances.

Stock re-order levels

The level of stock at which the next order must be placed should also be established and adhered to. The actual level for a particular stock item largely depends upon the lead time, i.e. how long it takes between placing the order and the stock actually arriving at the factory, and the rate of usage of stock. One way or another, the order should be placed early enough for the stock to arrive just as the safety level is expected to be reached. This is depicted in Fig. 13.6.

To illustrate this, let us assume that in the economic order quantity example (above) the lead time is three weeks. As the weekly usage is about 20 units (i.e. 1000/52), if the order is placed when the stock level drops to about 60 units and all goes according to plan the new stock will arrive just as existing stocks are running out. This, of course, leaves no safety margin, but as we have already seen such devices can easily be incorporated.

Most computer packages dealing with stock records have a facility for incorporating re-order levels for each stock item so that the computer's output will draw attention to the need to place the next order.

Budgeting and planning

Much of successful stock management is concerned with knowing what to expect in terms of levels of demand for and costs associated with stocks. The importance of forward planning and budgeting probably cannot be overestimated.

Reliable stock records

Unless firms know what they have in stock, stock management becomes very difficult. It is rarely possible in practice to gain sufficient information on stocks from physical observation.

Ratios

These can be useful in managing stocks, particularly the *stock holding period* ratio (average stock × 365/annual stock usage), which indicates the average period, in days, for which stock is held. The inputs for calculating the ratio may be stated either in terms of physical units of stock or in money terms. It is important that both inputs are stated in similar terms; usually cost is used.

The ratio may be calculated for a firm's entire stock (in which case the inputs would need to be expressed in money terms), for a section of the stock (e.g. stocks of tyres of a motor car manufacturer) or for specific items (e.g. stock of a particular size and quality of tyre). Such figures may be used as a check that policies laid down are in fact being followed.

Security and authorisation

Routine systems should be established to ensure that stock may only be ordered (or manufactured) and used on the authority of some fairly senior employee. This involves specifying the employees who are empowered to authorise the placing of orders and ensuring that stock is kept in some enclosed area, only to be issued on the authority of other specified employees. Clearly management needs to use some common sense here so as not to make the purchase and issuing of stock a major obstacle to the firm's activities. However, a system where anyone can order stock and where it can be used without authority is likely to lead to chaos.

To summarise, these practical points are really concerned with establishing routines to be applied systematically. Stock management should not be (though, perhaps inevitably, sometimes it is) a haphazard operation.

'JUST IN TIME' STOCKHOLDING

There is a tendency, which seems to have originated in the USA but to have been developed in Japan, for manufacturing firms to operate a system where there is a fairly continuous flow of raw material stock into the factory, of work-in-progress through the factory and of finished stocks to the customer. In such a system, large amounts of stock (raw materials, work-in-progress and finished stock) would never build up. Finished goods stocks would be produced just as they are needed to supply to customers, inputs of internally manufactured components and sub-assemblies would pass to the next stage of production just as they are needed to be used and raw material deliveries would arrive from suppliers just as they are needed in production. In essence the just in time (JIT) approach means that production and purchasing are linked closely to sales demand on a week-to-week basis, obviating the necessity to hold 'buffer' stocks to see the firm through unexpected demand peaks.

Though at first sight JIT is a technique of stock and production control, its effective implementation requires the acceptance of a particular philosophy and culture. An effective JIT system requires a flexible attitude on the part both of suppliers and of the internal workforce to expand and contract output at short notice. It also requires a concentration on quality of outputs at each stage, both by suppliers and by the internal workforce. If raw material stocks are to arrive just in time to go straight into production, those stocks must be of guaranteed quality which need not be tested or checked before being taken into production. The same general point about quality follows through each stage of production and into sales.

The JIT system can only be reliably established where there are very close relationships between users and suppliers. This requires that the user is prepared to guarantee only to buy from the one supplier in respect of a particular stock item and to give the supplier access to the user's production/sales plans. This enables the supplier to match its production to the needs of the user in much the same way as would a department of the user firm supplying components or sub-assemblies to another internal department. To work well, the system probably requires that supplier and user are geographically fairly close to one another so that deliveries can be made frequently and, when necessary, at short notice.

Achievement of low stock levels of internally produced components and sub-assemblies, and of finished stocks, normally requires short production runs, i.e. each production batch of a particular product or component is fairly small. To be economical this normally means that the costs of setting up each production run are fairly low. High-technology production methods (robots and computer-controlled manufacturing) typically have low set-up costs and considerable flexibility. This makes the achievement of an effective JIT system something which was not really achievable in the past.

An effective system of JIT also requires a workforce willing to increase and decrease its working hours from one period to another. This can pose serious problems for implementing a JIT system, particularly in a UK or US environment where regular weekly working hours are an established feature of industrial employment. The existence of a pool of labour willing to come in at short notice to supplement the 'core' workforce during production peaks may provide a solution in some cases.

Clearly a JIT policy will tend to lead to lower stock levels from the user's point of view and therefore to stock holding cost savings. The concentration on quality control and assurance is also likely to lead to net financial benefits. On the other hand, there may be additional opportunity costs arising from the fact that the user cannot, in the short term at least, buy from different suppliers according to price. Also, it may be fairly expensive to maintain a flexible workforce. However, the increasing popularity of the JIT approach implies that many firms regard the policy as having net benefits for them.

TRADE DEBTORS (ACCOUNTS RECEIVABLE)

With the exception of the retail trade, where immediate cash settlement predominates, most commercial sales are made on credit. When the goods or service pass to the customer firm it becomes a trade debtor of the supplying firm until such time that it settles its debt by paying cash.

It appears that attitudes to the granting of credit vary from trade to trade, with time-honoured credit policies being perpetuated by virtue of the fact that individual firms find it hard to break patterns with which their competitors intend to continue.

In determining credit policy the financial manager must try to strike the balance between the costs of granting credit and those associated with denying or restricting credit.

The costs of granting credit

These include:

(a) Lost interest

Granting credit is tantamount to making interest free loans. Since trade debtors are not usually secured they tend to be fairly risky loans, thus the interest lost is at a fairly high rate.

(b) Loss of purchasing power

Where price inflation is present, which in the UK has been much of the twentieth century including every single year since the Second World War, value transfers from lender to borrower. This is because the borrower (trade debtor in this context) pays the debt in £s of lower value than those which were borrowed. To some extent this point is covered in (a) but fairly recent experience of very high inflation rates showed that at such times interest rates do not necessarily increase fully to compensate lenders for the erosion of their money's purchasing power. Those granting trade credit should be aware that they are likely to be forgoing more than just interest in times of inflation.

(c) Assessing the potential customer's creditworthiness

It is usual before granting credit to a new customer or perhaps when increasing the credit limit of an existing customer to assess creditworthiness. This would usually be done by some combination of references from the customer's bank and other traders who have already granted credit to that customer. It might also include examination of the customer's published accounts for clues as to liquidity and financial rectitude and paying a credit rating agency for a report on the customer.

Carrying out these procedures costs money, though to a large extent the cost, once incurred, is unlikely to need to be repeated. Typically firms, once having granted credit to a particular customer, reassess that customer on the basis of their own experience of the customer's 'track record' of payment.

(d) Administration and record keeping costs

Most firms which grant credit find it necessary to employ people to act in the role of credit controllers, i.e. to devote themselves to the administration and collection of trade debts. The granting of credit usually involves a greatly increased volume of accounting transactions.

(e) Bad debts

Unless the firm is adopting an extremely cautious credit granting policy it is almost inevitable that some trade debts will never be paid, due for example to the defaulting customer's financial collapse. This risk can be insured against though typically it is borne by the supplier, either way there is a cost.

(f) Discounts

It is quite common for firms to offer their credit customers a discount if they settle their debts quickly. For example, a $2\frac{1}{2}$ per cent discount may be offered if customers pay within 30 days of receipt of the goods or service. What the effective cost of such a ploy would be of course depends upon how long the customers who pay quickly and claim the discount would take to pay were no discount available. If, say, in the above example they would on average take 40 days but the discount causes them to pay exactly on day 30, the effective cost of the discount is $2\frac{1}{2}$ per cent per 10 days or about 100 per cent per annum (compounded). Obviously giving discounts for prompt payment can represent a significant cost so its use should be treated with caution. We should bear in mind however that discount-induced prompt payment may well reduce some of the costs which we have already discussed, particularly those associated with bad debts and administration of debtors.

The costs of denying credit

These include:

(a) Loss of customer goodwill
If its competitors grant credit it will be very difficult for a firm to deny credit, not at least without offering some special inducement (e.g. discounted prices) which itself may be as expensive as granting credit. Where the supplier is in a monopolistic or near-monopolistic position it may be able to sell as much of its wares as it wishes without offering credit. In a competitive market, however, credit may be used as a basis of competition, so that it may be necessary to offer unusually extended credit in order to attract large and recurring orders.

(b) Inconvenience and loss of security of collecting cash
Administratively supplying goods or services on credit can be very convenient. Cash is not usually paid until the customer is satisfied that the goods are as ordered, etc., which avoids the necessity for refunds in respect of defective goods. Cash is collected centrally, usually by cheques received by post, or by direct bank credit. It is unnecessary for delivery drivers to collect cash, thus the delay and potential administrative and security problems likely to arise from such decentralised cash collection may be avoided. The existence of trade credit tends to allow specialisation and segregation of duties; delivery drivers deliver the goods and credit controllers collect the cash.

Some practical points in management of trade debts

(a) Establish a credit policy
The firm should consider whether it judges it appropriate to offer trade credit at all, and if so how much, to whom and under what circumstances. A firm might, for example, decide generally that trade credit is not a good idea, but nonetheless identify specific circumstances where it is prepared to offer it. For example, a retailer may be prepared to offer credit only for orders above, say, £100.

One way or another firms should establish a policy, not merely accept that credit is inevitable.

(b) Assess customers' creditworthiness
Even though in principle the firm may have decided that it is in its best interests to offer credit, it should not offer unlimited credit to any potential customer who seeks it. Those seeking credit are in effect asking for a loan, and supplying firms should see matters in those terms.

The firm should establish a policy for investigating creditworthiness and should not be prepared to grant credit before satisfying itself that the risk of doing so in respect of each customer is an acceptable one. It is not just a question of either granting credit or not. Credit limits should be established and these will almost certainly vary from customer to customer depending on the supplying firm's confidence in each customer's individual creditworthiness. Once established, each customer's credit limit should be rigorously observed until such time as there is some fundamental review by a fairly senior employee.

The supplying firm should try to establish some 'ear to the ground' routines so that signs that any particular established credit customer is experiencing liquidity problems can be picked up quickly and some action taken. Such routines might include regularly monitoring the customers' financial accounts. Another approach which could also be used is to look out for customers who are taking longer than they usually do to pay their debts; this may indicate a weakening liquidity position.

(c) Establish effective administration of debtors

Systems should be established to ensure:

(i) that no goods are dispatched until it has been confirmed that the present order will not take the customer above the predetermined credit limit for that customer;

(ii) that invoices for goods supplied on credit go off to the customer as soon as possible after the goods, thus encouraging the customer to initiate payment routines sooner rather than later; and

(iii) that existing debtors are systematically reviewed and that slow payers are sent reminders.

Most computer packages for dealing with trade debtors can produce a list of debtors with each customer's debt analysed by length of time for which the debt has been outstanding. This (known as an ageing summary) and similar devices can usefully be employed by credit controllers in the pursuit of trade debts.

(d) Establish a policy on bad debts

At some stage it will often become more costly to pursue reluctant payers than their debt is worth. The firm should decide what its policy on writing off bad debts should be. Once having been established, the policy should be followed except in unusual circumstances.

It is important that writing off a bad debt only occurs when all the steps identified in the policy have been followed. It is also important that writing off bad debts can only be authorised by a fairly senior employee.

(e) Consider offering discounts for prompt payment

The costs and advantages of allowing discounts should be assessed. If the firm establishes a particular policy of allowing discounts, care should be taken to ensure that customers are allowed to deduct discounts only when they have in fact paid within the specified period.

(f) Consider factoring debts

It is possible to enter into an arrangement with a firm of debt factors (many are subsidiaries of commercial banks). Here the factor collects the debts on behalf of the supplier firm. The precise arrangements can vary considerably but, fairly typically, payment (at a discount) is made immediately after the sale by the factor, who then goes on to collect the debt and to manage all accounting and administrative matters concerned with it. This relieves the supplier firm of the administrative and financial burden of granting trade credit, but at a cost.

(g) Manage exchange rate risk

Where the firm is involved with credit sales in a foreign currency there is the danger that an adverse shift in the exchange rate during the period from the credit sale to its settlement will reduce the value of the debt. One way to avoid this is to make it a condition of the sale that settlement must be in sterling. This may not be commercially acceptable to some overseas customers, however. An alternative is to use 'derivatives' of the foreign exchange market to 'insure' against an adverse shift in exchange rates.

For example, it is possible to negotiate an option to sell a particular currency on a specified future date at a specified rate of exchange. Entering into an appropriate option contract has a cost. It is not certain that the option will need to be exercised by the firm. However, this is in the nature of 'insurance', in that we pay a fee to indemnify ourselves against the effects of an uncertain, adverse occurrence.

(h) Ratios

These can be useful in debtor management. Probably the most widely used is *debtor collection period* (average debtors × 365/annual credit sales) which indicates the average time taken between a sale being made and the cash being received. It gives an overall impression of what is actually happening with debtors, which can be compared with the firm's policy on debtor collection to provide a control device. Where collection periods are in fact exceeding those specified in the firm's policy, steps can be taken to try to correct matters.

In summary, the firm's management of trade debtors should be thought through in advance and conducted in a systematic manner. Incidences, by accident or by design, of departure from the firm's credit policy should be highly exceptional.

CASH (INCLUDING OVERDRAFTS AND SHORT-TERM DEPOSITS)

If we glance back at Fig. 13.1 on p. 305, we see that cash is sooner or later involved in everything that the typical firm does. Some firms may not hold stock (perhaps because they sell services rather than goods), others may have no trade debtors or creditors (because they neither give nor receive credit), but all of them have cash. Admittedly some firms have negative cash balances (overdrafts) but a business with no cash balance at any given moment would be rare.

Cash tends to be held for three reasons:

(a) to meet planned needs to pay suppliers, labour, etc.;
(b) as a fund to meet unexpected obligations, e.g. a short-term creditor demanding payment earlier than expected; and
(c) to enable unexpected opportunities to be taken, e.g. to place a larger than planned order for stock to exploit some temporary price advantage.

As we saw in our discussion of Fig. 13.1 earlier in the chapter, cash is much more than just one of the elements of working capital. As the medium of exchange and store of value it provides the linkage between all financial aspects of the firm. More specifically it links short- and long-term financing decisions with one another and with decisions involving investment both in fixed assets and working capital.

Clearly, cash management is one of the key roles in any organisation of any size or description. Treasury management, as this role is increasingly being called, requires a specialism of skills, knowledge and experience. This has led to a tendency for treasury managers in larger organisations to be specialists whose career path lies exclusively in that functional area. Not surprisingly, in smaller organisations the role of treasury manager is likely to be filled by the accountant.

We shall first have a look at the costs involved with holding cash/not holding cash, before we go on to the closely related topic of the use of bank overdrafts to overcome temporary cash shortages.

The costs of holding cash

These include:

(a) Loss of interest

If cash is held in its most liquid form (notes and coins), it will yield no interest at all. Even if it is in a current account with a bank it will not yield income at a very high rate. It may be possible for a firm to have some, perhaps most, of its cash on some very short-term deposit from which it can be withdrawn at short notice should the need arise. Even where this is done there is still a cost, since short-term interest rates tend to be lower than longer-term ones.

(b) Loss of purchasing power

As with trade debts, during a period of inflation there is an erosion in the value of money. This is not necessarily compensated for by interest rates. Holding cash in one currency can lead to a loss of purchasing power in another one, where there is a movement in the exchange rate between the two currencies.

The costs of holding little or no cash

These include:

(a) Loss of supplier goodwill

'Supplier' here is used in its widest sense to include employees as suppliers of labour. Failure to meet financial obligations on time due to cash shortages may mean the loss of further supplies from injured parties. This could be extremely damaging, especially where the particular commodity is one which is vital to the firm's continuing operations, e.g. labour. Failure to meet a financial obligation to a creditor puts that creditor into a position where it could take steps to instigate the defaulting firm's liquidation. Given the bankruptcy costs and an inefficient market for real assets, such an outcome must be a matter of great concern to shareholders seeking to increase or at least to maintain their wealth.

(b) Loss of opportunities

Cash shortages will tend to mean that it may be impossible to react quickly to an opportunity. For example, if a firm is offered a contract which must be fulfilled at short notice by overtime working, it may have to be refused if cash is not available to meet the additional labour costs.

(c) Inability to claim discounts

Discounts for prompt payment are very advantageous, in percentage terms, to the purchasing firm. Cash shortages may preclude the claiming of such discounts.

(d) Cost of borrowing

Shortages of cash may force the firm to borrow short-term to be able to meet unexpected obligations. Interest costs for such borrowings can be expensive, particularly where the money has to be raised at very short notice and under pressure.

As ever, optimally balancing these two types of cost is the aim of the financial (treasury) manager. There are some models which can be helpful in this task.

Cash management models

A number of cash management models has been developed. The simplest one is substantially the same as the economic stock order quantity model which we derived on p. 315. This cash model assumes that the firm keeps all of its cash on an interest-yielding deposit from which it can make withdrawals as it needs. It also assumes that all of the firm's receipts (from debtors, etc.) are put straight into the deposit and that cash usage is linear over time, following exactly the same pattern as Fig. 13.4 (p. 314) does for stocks. The model derives the amount of money to withdraw from the deposit so that the costs of withdrawal are optimally balanced with those of interest, etc., forgone by holding cash. The model can be stated as:

$$C = \sqrt{\frac{2WP}{H}}$$

where C = the optimum amount of cash to be withdrawn each time;
W = the cost of making each withdrawal (a cost independent of the size of the withdrawal);
P = the planned payments for the forthcoming time period;
H = the interest forgone on the cash withdrawn (i.e. the interest rate of the deposit).

EXAMPLE

A firm plans to use £20 000 of cash during the forthcoming year. It holds most of its cash in a deposit account from which it costs £30 to make each withdrawal and pays interest at 10 per cent p.a. What is the optimal size for each withdrawal?

SOLUTION

$$C = £\sqrt{\left(\frac{2 \times 30 \times 2000}{0.10}\right)}$$

$$= £3464$$

So the firm should withdraw about £3464 from the deposit; when all that is spent, it should withdraw a similar amount, and so on.

As with its close relation, the economic order quantity, this model takes a very simple view of the world, though it is probably better than nothing.

Sophistications to the basic model have been proposed by Miller and Orr (1966), and another approach has been suggested by Beranek (1963).

Bank overdrafts

These are facilities allowed by commercial banks for firms to have negative balances on their current accounts. The bank overdraft is obviously therefore a form of borrowing for which the bank will charge interest, typically at 1 or 2 per cent above the relevant base lending rate. Banks usually make a fixed charge for establishing the facility as well.

Once the facility is established, the firm may continue to conduct its bank account as normal except that it can now incur a negative balance up to a specified limit. This tends to be a cheap form of finance, as the firm is only required to pay for the funds used for as long as they are being used. In fact, overdrafts are essentially short-term loans with fluctuating interest rates; the actual rate charged is likely to be relatively low compared with those associated with longer-term loans.

As was discussed on p. 310, firms seem to use overdrafts particularly to overcome temporary cash shortages, caused perhaps by seasonal fluctuations. For example, a firm whose main trading period is during the summer holiday season, will tend to stock up during the late spring. This will put a temporary strain on its cash resources which will gradually be relieved as the summer progresses. The alternative to overdraft finance may only be some long-term source. If the firm made a debenture issue, it would then be saddled with interest payments throughout the year on funds which it only needs for a month or two. The firm could, of course, put the spare cash on deposit for the other 10 or 11 months, but imperfections in the market for finance will tend to mean that interest received will not match interest paid on those funds.

Bank overdrafts have a major disadvantage compared with long-term loans: they are usually repayable at call (i.e. immediately) as a condition of the facility being granted. Where overdrafts are being used, as in our example, to overcome temporary shortages of cash, this is probably not a problem since, whatever 'at call' means in theory, in practice it probably means at a couple of months' notice. To the firm seeking to use a bank overdraft as a more permanent source of finance this can be a serious problem, however.

Some practical points in the management of cash and overdrafts

(a) Establish a policy

The firm should, with the aid of models and taking into account matters not covered by the models, establish a policy for cash. This policy should be adhered to, except in the most unusual circumstances, until such a time as the policy is reviewed.

(b) Plan cash flows

Forward planning is vitally important in this area; failure to balance cash inflows with cash outflows can be fatal.

The formal statement of financial plans, i.e. the budget, can probably best be explained through an example.

EXAMPLE

A firm has the following plans for the next few months:

1 *Sales:*

	£
September	60 000
October	60 000
November	70 000
December	90 000

All sales will be made on credit. Half of the debtors are expected to pay within the month of sale and to claim a 2 per cent cash discount. The remainder are expected to pay in the following month.

2 *Raw material purchases:*

	£
September	20 000
October	40 000
November	40 000
December	30 000

The firm plans to pay its creditors (in full) in the month following that of the purchase.

3 *Wages and salaries:*

	£
September	12 000
October	15 000
November	17 000
December	13 000

All employees are paid in full in the month in which the wage or salary is earned.

4 Rent of £10 000 each quarter is payable in March, June, September and December.

5 Other cash overheads of £2000 per month are payable.

6 Some new plant due for delivery in September will be paid for in November at a cost of £25 000.

7 On 1 October the firm plans to have £10 000 in the bank.

A cash budget for the months of October to December (inclusive) is to be prepared.

SOLUTION

Cash budget for the three months ending 31 December:

	October £	November £	December £
Cash inflows:			
Debtors: Current month	29 400	34 300	44 100
Previous month	30 000	30 000	35 000
Total cash inflows (A)	59 400	64 300	79 100
Cash outflows:			
Creditors	20 000	40 000	40 000
Wages and salaries	15 000	17 000	13 000
Rent	–	–	10 000
Overheads	2 000	2 000	2 000
Plant acquired	–	25 000	–
Total cash outflows (B)	37 000	84 000	65 000
Cash surplus/(deficit) for the month (A–B)	22 400	(19 700)	14 100
Cumulative cash balance	32 400	12 700	26 800

Notes to the solution

1. The above statement reflects the timing and the amount of cash payments and receipts and the resultant balance. It is not, and is not intended to be, a profit and loss account. The profit or loss for these months will almost certainly be different from the cash surplus or deficit.

2. Knowledge of the projected cumulative cash balance enables plans to be made to use the surplus to effect; even if the most effective prospect is putting it on short-term deposit, it is better than nothing.

(c) Make judicious use of bank overdraft and deposit accounts

Bank overdrafts should be avoided if possible, by scheduling payments and receipts with a view to staying in credit. Use temporary cash excesses by putting the money on deposit, even for very short periods. Where the cash surplus looks more permanent, thought should be given to whether it should be used in real investment or repaid to suppliers of long-term funds, thus saving the cost of servicing it.

(d) Bank frequently

Do not allow cheques received to gather dust in the accounts department when they could be in the bank saving overdraft interest or on deposit earning interest. Firms with large receipts of notes and coin (e.g. retailers) should consider banking several times each day, if only for security reasons.

(e) Time transactions to the best cash flow effect

There are several areas, particularly relating to tax payments, where with a little forethought a payment can legitimately be delayed or a receipt hastened. For example, Corporation tax is based on the individual firm's accounting year and the timing of capital allowances is dependent on the date of acquisition of fixed assets. If a new piece of plant is purchased at the end of a firm's accounting period, the tax relief will first manifest itself in cash flow terms a year earlier than if the acquisition is delayed the short period until the start of the new accounting year.

TRADE CREDITORS (ACCOUNTS PAYABLE)

This is money owed for goods and services purchased on credit by the firm. It is the other side of the coin from trade debtors; one firm's trade debts are another firm's trade credit. Within an economy it will be true that:

$$\Sigma \text{ Trade debts} = \Sigma \text{ Trade credits}$$

Trade credit is a very important source of 'free' finance which firms should take very seriously. That trade credit is strictly free is doubtful, since firms will build the cost of granting credit into the pricing policy. However, unless suppliers are willing to discriminate in their pricing between those who settle their bills immediately and those who do not, there is no obvious differential cost of taking credit. There may be less obvious costs involved so, as ever, the balance must be sought between that cost and the cost of not taking trade credit.

The costs of taking credit

These include:

(a) Price Some suppliers might offer cheaper prices for immediate settlement – in effect a discount for prompt payment. Cash-and-carry wholesalers in the grocery trade are examples of traders who are prepared to offer lower prices because they do not offer credit (or delivery). The small retail grocer has the choice of dealing with wholesalers who do offer credit but usually charge higher prices.

(b) Possible loss of supplier goodwill If credit is overstepped, suppliers may discriminate against delinquent customers if supplies become short. As with the effect of any loss of goodwill, it depends very much on the relative market strengths of the parties involved.

(c) Administration and accounting Taking credit almost certainly engenders administrative and accounting costs which would not otherwise be incurred.

(d) Restrictions Many suppliers insist that in order to be granted credit, orders must be of some minimum size or even regularity.

The costs of not taking credit

These include:

(a) Interest cost Trade credit is, in effect, an interest-free loan, so failure to exploit it has an interest cost. It may well be worth incurring some of the costs of taking credit in order to get it, particularly when interest rates are high.

(b) Inflation In periods of inflation, borrowers are favoured over lenders with the levels of interest rates not seeming totally to redress the balance.

(c) Inconvenience   It may be inconvenient, for the reasons discussed in the context of trade debtors, to pay on delivery of the goods or performance of the service. It will probably also inconvenience the supplier. Indeed, insistence on paying on the nail may even be a cause of loss of supplier goodwill. If the supplier's systems are geared to deferred payment, a customer who insists on immediate settlement may not be welcome.

Some practical points in the management of trade credit

(a) Establish a policy   After weighing the two types of cost a policy should be established and followed. It may well be that suppliers are treated differently according to:

(i)   the discounts offered for prompt payment;
(ii) the attitude to credit taken by individual suppliers;
(iii) the weight of any possible repercussions arising from loss of supplier goodwill.

(b) Exploit trade credit as far as is reasonable   It is unlikely that, for the typical firm, the costs of claiming credit outweigh the considerable advantage of doing so.

(c) Manage exchange rate risk   Where the firm is involved with purchases on credit in a foreign currency, there is the danger that an adverse shift in the exchange rate during the period from the purchase to its settlement will increase the amount actually to be settled. This is the other side of the coin from the similar problem related to trade debtors which we discussed in that context earlier in the chapter.

As with the trade debtor problem, one way to avoid this is to make it a condition of the purchase that settlement must be in sterling. Another possibility is to buy the required foreign currency immediately, thus fixing the exchange rate and removing the risk. This solution may be less than perfect, however, since it involves an immediate outflow of cash, but the cash could be put on interest bearing deposit until payment to the creditor is due. Use of the foreign exchange market to purchase an option to buy a particular currency on a specified future date at a specified rate of exchange provides another possibility, but there is the cost of the options contracted to be considered.

(d) Ratios   The most useful ratio in the monitoring of trade credit is the *creditor payment period* (average trade creditors × 365/annual credit purchases). This gives a view of how long, on average, the firm is taking to pay its creditors, which can be compared with the planned period.

SUMMARY

The management of working capital is important to the firm. Very large amounts of resources tend to be involved in working capital, and its mismanagement can lead to dire effects on the firm. Poor liquidity tends to be seen as evidence of a firm in financial difficulties; thus poor management of working capital can cause pressure to be applied to the firm by those with whom it deals.

It is important that firms establish policies for the day-to-day management of each element of working capital and strive to follow those policies. The policies should not be regarded as immutable, but until some fundamental review takes place they should be adhered to. Broadly, firms should seek to establish and follow policies which seem best to balance the costs of having each of the working capital elements with the costs of not having them or having too little of them. The object of striking the balance is to maximise the shareholders' wealth.

FURTHER READING Drury (1996) gives a full, yet clear, review of the various aspects of the management of working capital. Samuels, Wilkes and Brayshaw (1995), and Weston and Copeland (1988) each has one or more chapters covering the topics of this chapter and deal with them in a UK context. An interesting article by Moyes (1988) discusses the features and problems of JIT.

REVIEW QUESTIONS

Suggested answers to review questions appear in Appendix 3.

13.1 Why is working capital a particularly important area of concern for financial managers?

13.2 What is meant by 'overtrading', and how does it arise?

13.3 How is 'obsolescence' a cost of holding stock?

13.4 In what ways is the basic stock reorder model   deficient in representing reality?

13.5 What credit checks would most prudent firms take before despatching goods in respect of a credit sale?

13.6 What is 'exchange rate risk' in the context of trade debtors, and how can it be managed?

PROBLEMS

Sample answers to problems marked with an asterisk appear in Appendix 4.

(*Note that all the problem questions appearing in this chapter are basic level problems.*)

13.1* Dixon plc uses a component, which it buys in, in its manufacturing process. The estimated annual usage is 23 000 and these are used fairly steadily throughout the year. It is estimated that the various stockholding costs amount to £1.50 per unit per year. Investigation indicates that it costs about £50 to process each order for the component. Experience shows that delivery always occurs within one week of placing an order.

(a) What is the economic order quantity for the component?
(b) At what stock level should the order be placed to be confident that delivery will occur before the existing stock of the components is all used?

13.2 Pithead Products Ltd plans to sell its single product for £35 a unit.

Credit plans for the next six months are as follows:

– 70 per cent of sales are made on credit and 30 per cent for cash.

Of the credit sales:

– 40 per cent will be paid during the month of sale (with the customers claiming a cash discount of 2 per cent of their debt);
– 40 per cent will be paid during the month following the month of sale;
– 18 per cent will be paid during the second month after the sale; and
– the remaining 2 per cent will prove to be bad debts and are expected never to be paid.

Sales for the next few months are budgeted as follows:

	Units
July	5100
August	5500
September	5200
October	5000
November	4800
December	4700

How much cash will be budgeted to be received from sales during October?

13.3* Arcadia Ltd has only one product, a garden gnome, for which it plans to increase production and sales during the first half of next year. The plans for the next eight months are as follows:

Month	Production (gnomes)	Sales (gnomes)
November	700	700
December	800	800
January	1000	800
February	1200	1000
March	1200	1200
April	1400	1300
May	1500	1400
June	1500	1600

The selling price for each gnome will be £10. The raw materials will cost £4 per gnome, wages and other variable costs are expected to be £3 per gnome.

Salaries and other fixed overheads are expected to amount to £1400 per month during November and December, to rise to £1600 per month from January to April (inclusive) and to increase to £2000 per month for May and June.

Sales of 60 per cent are made on a cash basis (paid on delivery). The remainder are sold on credit, debtors being expected to pay in full in the second month after the sale.

Payment is planned to be made for raw material purchases one month after delivery and materials are expected to be held in stock for one month before they are used in production.

Wages and other variable costs are expected to be paid during the month of production. Salaries and other fixed overheads are planned to be paid 80 per cent in the month in which they are incurred and 20 per cent in the following month.

In order to promote the expanded sales, an advertising campaign is to be undertaken. This will engender payments to the advertising agency of £1000 in January and £1500 in April.

A new machine, to help cope with the increased production, has been ordered and it should be delivered in February. The agreement is to pay the £6000 for the machine in three equal instalments of £2000 each in March, April and May.

The firm intends to pay a dividend of £600 to its shareholders in April.

The firm expects to have a bank current account balance (in funds) of £7500 on 1 January.

Produce a cash budget for the firm for the first six months of next year, showing the net cash position at the end of each month.

13.4 Anithesis Ltd sells its service on credit at the rate of £6 million a year. Customers take varying lengths of time to pay, but the average is 65 days. The firm does not experience any significant level of bad debts because it spends £50 000 a year on debt collection procedures.

The firm is considering a proposal to introduce a cash discount of two per cent of the amount paid if customers pay within 30 days after the sale. It is estimated that 60 per cent of customers would pay on the thirtieth day and claim the discount. The remaining customers would be the slower payers, and they would be expected to take an average 75 days to pay. The cost of debt collection procedures would be expected to fall to £20 000 a year. The cost of funds to finance the debtors is 12 per cent p.a.

In terms of effect on net profit (after interest, before tax), should the proposed debtor policy be introduced?

13.5* North Anglia Engineering Ltd (NAE), a manufacturing firm, has recently obtained the accounts of some of its industry rivals and has discovered that it holds, on average, twice the level of stock for its output, compared to its rivals.

How should NAE set about trying to judge what levels of stock to hold?
What approach would you take to investigating NAE's relatively high stock level?

13.6 Supertraders Ltd is experiencing severe liquidity problems which you, as a business consultant, were asked to investigate. You have identified the problem as being caused principally by a very poor trade credit system, with no member of staff responsible for managing trade credit.

Your major recommendation is that the firm appoints a credit manager.

(a) Outline the job description of the person to be appointed as credit manager.

(b) Set out the main headings which you would advise the new credit manager to consider, in respect of each of the following:

   – assessing a particular customer's creditworthiness;
   – major sources of information that can be used to assess a customer's creditworthiness; and
   – addressing a proposal to alter the firm's credit policy.

CHAPTER 14

Corporate restructuring (including takeovers and divestments)

OBJECTIVES

In this chapter we shall deal with the following:

- the nature of corporate restructuring
- the background to mergers
- the technicalities of mergers
- the regulation of mergers in the UK
- the economic success of mergers
- a review of a recently contested merger
- divestments and the various means of achieving them
- the means of financing divestments
- other corporate restructuring devices

INTRODUCTION

A striking feature of the post-war business scene, throughout the world but particularly in the UK, is the extent of the use of various corporate restructuring devices. This feature has become more evident over time, perhaps promoted by the emergence of increasingly sophisticated techniques for achieving corporate restructures.

Changes in the economic environment and in the objectives being pursued by a particular firm may be seen by its management as necessitating significant changes in the firm's structure. Such changes may be concerned with the assets employed by the firm; or with the manner in which those assets are financed, or by some combination of both of these. Whatever the precise nature of a particular corporate restructuring, logically it should be undertaken to work towards the achievement of the firm's objectives. On the assumption that the firm's major financial objective is the maximisation of the shareholders' wealth, it is against that objective that the effectiveness of any particular restructuring should be assessed. Corporate restructuring is clearly a necessary and desirable feature of any dynamic and flexible economic environment. Despite the bad publicity which has attached to some aspects of certain corporate restructures, for example aspects of the Guinness takeover of Distillers in 1985–6, corporate restructuring should not be seen as anything but a means for firms to pursue their legitimate objectives.

We shall start our consideration of the major restructuring devices which are found at present in the UK by concentrating in a little detail on two of the more important areas, namely takeovers (mergers) and divestments. Following that we shall take a look at some other corporate restructuring devices found in the UK today.

TAKEOVERS AND MERGERS

In recent years, buying existing businesses in their entirety has become a very popular way of investing. Not all firms do this, nor do those firms which have done so necessarily do it habitually, yet scarcely a week seems to pass without the city pages of the national newspapers telling us of an attempt on the ownership of some firm or another, often with quite large ones as targets.

In practice this type of investment is typically effected by one firm (the *bidder*) buying sufficient ordinary voting shares in the other firm (the *target*) to be able to exercise control or even to have complete ownership.

Whether we refer to a particular situation as a *takeover* or as a *merger* is a matter of semantics. Where the two firms are of similar size and/or there is agreement between the two sets of management as to the desirability of the outcome then it tends to be referred to as a 'merger'; otherwise the expression 'takeover' tends to be used. In this chapter, for convenience, we shall use the word merger irrespective of the circumstances.

Despite certain apparent differences, from the bidder's viewpoint, between a merger and the more traditional investment opportunity, the same basic principles should be applied to its appraisal. That is to say, a merger which would represent a net increase in the current worth of the bidder (a positive net present value) should be pursued, if the firm's financial objective is to be achieved.

REASONS FOR MERGERS

Theoretically a firm will become a bidder when it sees an opportunity to make an investment with a positive incremental net present value. It is likely to perceive such an opportunity, either

(a) where it considers that the incremental cash flows from the investment, when discounted at a rate consistent with the level of risk associated with those cash flows, are positive; or

(b) where the reduction in the level of risk associated with the bidder's existing cash flows causes the appropriate rate for discounting those cash flows to fall, thus increasing the NPV of the existing cash flows of the bidder.

Frequently a particular merger is attractive to the bidding firm for both of these reasons.

EXAMPLE

Bidder plc has an existing business which is expected to generate net positive cash flows of £1m for each of the next five years. The level of risk associated with these cash flows is perceived by the capital market as justifying a rate of return of 15 per cent p.a. Thus the net present value of Bidder is: £1m × 3.352 = £3.352m (where 3.352 is the annuity factor relating to 15 per cent p.a. for five years).

Bidder sees an opportunity to acquire the entire equity of Target plc. Forecasts indicate that the annual net positive cash flows of the merged firm would be £1.5m for each of the next five years and that the required rate of return would be 12 per cent p.a. The net present value of Bidder after the merger, should it take place, would become: £1.5m x 3.605 = £5.408m (where 3.605 is the annuity factor relating to 12 per cent p.a. for five years).

This would imply that it would be worth Bidder paying any amount up to £2.056m (i.e. £5.408m–£3.352m) for Target. Note that part of this amount arises from the existing cash flows of Bidder being discounted at a lower rate than previously. This factor would only arise where the merger had the effect of reducing risk.

It is quite feasible that £2.056m exceeds the current market value of Target. The reasons why this could be the case include:

(a) the target's expected cash flows being less than £0.5m p.a., i.e. the merged business might be able to generate more expected cash flows than the sum of the expected cash flows of the separate firms;

(b) the possibility of the risk attaching to the combined firm being less than applies to the overall level of risk of the separate parts.

Over the years a number of observers has sought to identify the factors which make mergers attractive, particularly to the bidder. Let us now consider some of these factors and discuss each of them in the context of the overall risk reduction and cash flow expansion mentioned above.

(a) Elimination or reduction of competition

Where the bidder and target are in competition for the market for their output, a merger could lead to a monopoly or at least a larger market share for the merged unit. This strength in the market place might enable prices to be raised without loss of turnover – hence an increase in cash flows. (As we shall see later in this chapter, in the UK such a merger may well fall foul of the Monopolies and Mergers Commission.)

(b) Safeguarding sources of supply or sales outlets

A bidder may be attracted to a merger where the target is a supplier of some vital raw material which is in short supply or which the target could stop supplying, beyond the control of the bidder. Similarly, where the target represents a major sales outlet for the bidder, the target could cause problems for the bidder if it started to promote sales of the product of one of the bidder's competitors. Here a merger may not increase annual cash flows but it may well lower the perceived risk because the cash flows of both parts of the combined business would become more certain.

(c) Access to the economies of scale that a larger business could yield

Such economies may be in a wide variety of areas: for example, a larger buying power may lead to lower prices being paid for raw materials, larger production runs may become possible leading to savings in set up costs and other overheads; combining administration and accounting activities may lead to savings in the associated costs. The effect of these would tend to decrease total cash outflows.

(d) Access to some aspect of the target which the bidder considers under-utilised

These might include:

(i) particular tangible assets, including land, plant and cash, which are not fully exploited; and

(ii) particular intangible assets such as its standing in some market, perhaps an export market or a particular contract; or technological expertise, which could be better exploited.

Under-utilisation of assets suggests poor management and bidders will sometimes be attracted to such targets where they have an abundance of management skills themselves. Firms must seek ways of promoting rising management talent, and expansion through merger with mismanaged firms provides an excellent means of creating promotional opportunities. Under-utilisation of assets implies the possibility of acquiring assets at a discount on their potential economic value.

The overall effect of such mergers would be expected to be an increase in positive cash flows, though stronger management skills being brought to bear on the target's assets may also decrease uncertainty about the cash flows, i.e. reduce risk.

(e) Risk spreading and reduction through diversification

Merging two firms with different activities will reduce risk since the returns from the different activities are unlikely to be perfectly positively correlated with one another.

Though this fact is frequently put forward as the justification for such mergers, in the context of maximisation of shareholders' wealth, it is invalid in itself. This is because, as we saw in Chapter 7, such diversification could be, and probably is, undertaken by individual shareholders at little or no cost. Their wealth will not be increased by having this done for them, because security market prices seem to assume that such diversification will already have taken place.

As we saw in Chapter 2, this provides us with an example of possible conflict of interests between shareholders and managers. Shareholders are unlikely to be benefited by the merger because they will typically have undertaken such risk-reducing diversification on a 'homemade' basis.

The managers, on the other hand, do not hold portfolios of employments, so the only way that they can achieve this risk reduction is through diversification at the firm level. A popular, though by no means the only, way to diversify is through merger.

Legislation to protect the public interest from monopolies has meant that mergers within the same industry have sometimes been impossible to achieve. This could leave firms which are ambitious to expand with diversification as their only possibility. It should be noted that, irrespective of the benefits of diversification, the other reasons for merger could still apply to a particular merger between firms in different industries. Even economies of scale, particularly in the administration of the merged firm, could apply.

Synergy

We can see then that, in theory, mergers can bring real benefits to shareholders due to genuine increases in positive cash flows and/or risk reduction. These benefits are often referred to as arising from *synergy*, a 'two plus two equals five' syndrome with the whole being greater than the sum of the parts.

We should note that these synergy benefits should accrue to the shareholders of the target as well as to those of the bidder. Merger can only take place where target shareholders are prepared to sell their shares. They will only do this where they are offered something in excess of what they perceive to be the current value (usually the Stock Exchange quotation) of those shares. Unless the shareholders of the target and the management of the bidder are basing their valuations on different information from one another, this excess can only exist due to the synergy benefits perceived by the bidder's management.

Going back to our example, the excess of £2.056m over the current market value of the equity of Target is a measure of the value of the synergy benefits. If the current market value of Target's equity is as high as £2.056m then there will be no synergy benefits of merger and, from a financial viewpoint, it should not take place. If the market value of Target's equity immediately before the merger is below £2.056m but Bidder has to pay as much as this in order to persuade the shareholders to sell, then all of the benefits from synergy would accrue to Target's shareholders, and none of it to those of Bidder. It is therefore unlikely that Bidder would offer as much as the £2.056m.

FINANCING OF MERGERS

It is important to realise that mergers are basically open market transactions with one party buying assets belonging to another party. How much the bidder firm offers and how it proposes to pay are matters of judgement which must be decided by the management. In practice, often such decisions are only made after taking advice from experts, usually merchant bankers.

As regards financing, the bidder must seek a method which is both attractive to the target's shareholders and acceptable to itself.

The following are commonly-encountered merger financing approaches.

(a) Cash

Cash has its attractions to the recipients as it gives something which they can use immediately, either for consumption or reinvestment, without having to incur any cost. Target company shareholders receiving shares or loan stock which they do not wish to keep, must incur cost and effort to turn them into cash. The receipt of cash will, however, in most cases be treated as a disposal for Capital Gains Tax purposes and many shareholders would not welcome the possibility of a charge arising from this.

From the bidder's point of view, cash may not be available and can only be obtained by making a public issue of shares or loan stock for cash, or borrowing in some form – a course of action which, for various reasons including cost, the bidder may not wish to follow.

(b) Ordinary shares in the bidder firm

Ordinary shares may be attractive to the recipients, who would simply cease being shareholders in the target and become shareholders in the bidder. After all, before the merger they hold shares in one firm (the target) so are obviously not hostile to equity investment *per se*. This is not to say that they wish to hold shares in the bidder, in which case the problems of disposal, mentioned above, will come into play. From the bidder's viewpoint, issuing shares to exchange for those of the target, has its attractions. Cash will not need to be raised and the firm will not be taking on the contractual commitments to pay interest or to repay capital as would be the case with loan stock issues.

We should not feel that share issues cost the bidder's original shareholders nothing, however. Issuing shares as the consideration in a merger represents an opportunity cost to the bidder, since presumably the issue could alternatively be made for cash.

(c) Loan stocks of the bidder firm

Loan stocks have their part to play but have serious disadvantages from both viewpoints. As we have seen, they create binding contractual obligations on the bidder both as regards interest and capital repayment. To the equity holder of the target they represent a distinct change of investment, a change to a risk/return profile which they may find unacceptable. Switching back to equities will involve them in inconvenience and cost, possibly including a Capital Gains Tax liability. The advantages of loan stocks in the merger context would seem to be twofold. To the bidder they would not have the effect of diluting control as a result of extending its share ownership (loan stock holders do not usually have votes at the annual general meeting). To the recipient they may have the attraction that, as they will have fixed interest payments and usually have a fixed capital repayment date, their market value is supported. Where target shareholders are sceptical about the future success of the merged firm, they may prefer an investment in it whose returns are surer than are those from the equity capital.

As well as the specific factors referred to in respect of each financing method, the bidder will need to have regard to its desired level of gearing. Perceptions as to what this should be may well change with the merger. The bidder's management may feel that, due to perceived changes in risk caused by the merger, the merged firm's gearing potential is different from that of the bidder alone.

Table 14.1 Recent takeovers and mergers by industrial and commercial companies within the UK

Year	Total number	Mean Value £m	Cash %	Ordinary shares %	Preference shares and loan stocks %
1987	1528	10.8	35	60	5
1988	1499	15.2	70	22	8
1989	1337	20.4	82	13	5
1990	779	10.7	77	18	5
1991	506	20.6	70	29	1
1992	432	13.8	63	36	1
1993	526	13.4	81	16	3
1994	674	12.3	64	34	2
1995	482	66.6	79	20	1

Source: Office for National Statistics.

Table 14.1 shows how recent UK mergers have been financed. Though the mix varies from merger to merger and over time, it is clear that cash and ordinary shares of the bidder company are very much more important than preference shares and loan stock. The decline in merger activity over recent years, which appears to have been continued to 1993, is almost certainly partly caused by the economic recession of the early 1990s.

Other possible reasons for the reduction in the number of takeovers since the late 1980s will be discussed later in this chapter when we are assessing the evidence on the success of mergers.

However, 1995 saw a number of very large mergers including Glaxo and Wellcome (pharmaceuticals) and TSB and Lloyds (banks).

APPRAISAL OF THE MERGER

By the bidder

A merger is simply an investment and should be appraised as one. The expected cash flows from the merged firm must be estimated and discounted according to a cost of capital factor which incorporates consideration of market perceptions of the risk of the merged firm, i.e. the systematic risk. The cash flows which must be assessed will include all of the normal operating cash flows of the new undertaking. In addition any cash flows arising from disposing of any unwanted divisions of the target (or of the bidder) arising from the merger, including any cost of making employees redundant, must be taken into account. We must also include the amount paid to acquire the target's equity. Where payment is not all in cash, the amount should include the opportunity cost of the equity and/or loan stock issue, i.e. it should include the amount of cash that would have been received for the share/loan stock issue had it been made for cash, assuming that all other factors would have been the same.

If the net present value calculated from the above is positive, then logically the investment should be made.

There will usually be non-financial factors to consider such as the acceptability of declaring employees redundant in order to gain potential economies of scale. These will have to be balanced with the strictly financial aspects when reaching a decision.

By the target's shareholders

Appraisal of the offer by this group is just as much a capital investment decision as it is for the bidder. Each shareholder must assess whether future cash benefits from accepting the offer, suitably discounted, will exceed the discounted cash flow benefits of retaining the shares of the target.

What level of expertise and sophistication will be applied to this appraisal and whether it will be done at all, on the basis suggested above, depends on the individual shareholder. The large investing institutions will, it is presumed, reach their decisions on the basis of reason and logic. This may be less the case with the individual private investor.

HOSTILE AND FRIENDLY MERGERS

Many merger attempts are resisted by the directors of the target firm, i.e. they are 'hostile' mergers. This may be for a variety of reasons including:

- a belief that there is a lack of commercial logic in the merger;
- a feeling that the price being offered to the target shareholders for their shares is too low; and
- an understandable desire by the target firm's directors to protect their personal futures. The immediate outcome of many mergers is the departure of some or all of the target's directors.

Hostile mergers often capture the headlines. We shall shortly be reviewing a recent hostile merger involving Granada and Forte.

An increasing number of mergers are 'friendly' rather than hostile. Here the directors of both firms negotiate the terms and conditions which will be offered to the target firm's shareholders. When the formal bid is made, it is recommended, by the target's directors, that it should be accepted. The weight of such a recommendation tends to be sufficient to sway the shareholders to accept. An example of a friendly merger occurred when two major banks (Lloyds and TSB), joined forces in 1995.

REGULATION OF MERGERS IN THE UK

In the UK mergers are regulated in two ways, each by a different agency. The way in which this is done provides an interesting example of statutory regulation and 'self'-regulation working hand in hand.

The Monopolies and Mergers Commission

This is a statutory body which derives its power from the Fair Trading Act 1973. It is concerned with the outcome of the merger, rather than the conduct of the merger operation itself.

The Monopolies and Mergers Commission is empowered by statute to delay and to investigate any merger referred to it by the Secretary of State for Industry. The Secretary of State will refer mergers to the Commission on the advice of the Director General of Fair Trading, where it is considered that it may be against the public interest for them to proceed. The Secretary of State will not usually refer a particular merger to the Commission unless a monopoly is likely to result. The Commission publishes its findings in reports that are sometimes long and detailed.

In fact, relatively few of the many mergers which have taken place since the Commission was established have been referred to it. Of those which have been investigated, few have resulted in the Commission exercising its statutory power of veto in respect of them.

It seems that the Commission has not had great effect in restricting merger activity, nor was it intended to. The general philosophy of the legislation and of the Commission is that it is up to firms and shareholders to decide on the economic desirability of particular mergers, with the state stepping in only when it fears that the public interest is threatened by the outcome of a merger.

The City Panel on Takeovers and Mergers

The Panel is a self-regulatory body which includes in its membership representatives of most of the leading financial institutions of the City of London. These include the Stock Exchange and the Committee of London Clearing Banks. The Panel and the Code which it administers were established in 1968, following a number of merger battles in the 1960s, which many observers saw as involving tactics which did not reflect well on big business and the financial institutions. Many of the less savoury encounters involved firms which are (or were) household names, thus attracting a high level of press and broadcasting attention.

The main fears were that actions of the bidders' and of the targets' managements, particularly in cases where the bid was opposed by the target's management, were having adverse effects on shareholders, more particularly small shareholders, of the target. Specifically it seemed that there were differences in the treatment of different shareholders as regards the quality and quantity of information each received pertaining to the merger.

The Code, which is constantly under review, comprises a set of rules defining the steps to be followed by both bidder and target in the course of the merger negotiations. The Code does not really address itself to wider questions of the desirability of the merger *per se*, it deals only with the conduct of the merger operation. The Panel has no statutory powers to enforce the Code, but it is able to apply moral pressures on offenders. Ultimately it can request that one of its members – the Stock Exchange – excludes the offending firm from quotation.

Whether the Panel and the Code have achieved their objectives is a question open to debate, though most observers appear to feel that much of the more extravagant behaviour evident in the 1960s is not obvious today.

PRACTICAL STEPS TOWARDS THE MERGER

Most mergers are effected by the bidder buying from the target's shareholders sufficient ordinary shares to give control or even total ownership of the equity. This is usually done in two stages:

(a) by the bidder buying shares, for cash, in the capital market; and then
(b) by its making a formal offer to remaining shareholders by direct mailing and therefore outside the established capital market.

It is not common for bidders to acquire a large proportion of the required shares by buying them in the capital market. Once investors realise that there is a large buyer in the market, the share price will tend to rise in anticipation of a formal offer, making it uneconomic for the bidder to proceed further in this way. The formal offer to each shareholder probably becomes cheaper at the point where the capital market quotation reaches the proposed formal offer price. Of course all capital market purchases have to be paid for in cash, which may be a disincentive to a bidder who wishes to finance the merger in some other way. The formal offer document, which is usually communicated to shareholders by post, contains the precise terms of the offer and a statement explaining why, in the view of the bidder's management, it should be accepted. The offer document must be submitted for the approval of the Director General of Fair Trading and of the City Panel.

Usually offers are made on condition that they are accepted by the owners of a specified percentage of the shares concerned. In this way the bidder can ensure that, in the event of insufficient acceptance being forthcoming, it will not end up being forced to buy shares which it may not want. If, for example, the bidder wishes to obtain a minimum of 60 per cent of the shares of the target, it would probably prefer not to be forced to buy, say, 25 per cent if the owners of the other 75 per cent decide not to accept the offer. The proportion of 90 per cent is often stated on offer documents because UK company law gives any firm, which owns that percentage of the equity of another firm, the right to acquire the remaining 10 per cent, with or without the consent of their owners, on the same terms as those on which the others were acquired.

A question which the target shareholders must consider on receiving the offer is whether to accept this particular offer or to hope for an improved one. Whilst the failure of an offer can cause the bidder to withdraw, frequently the bidder's reaction is to make an increased offer. This can be a difficult question for the shareholder because withdrawal by the bidder will probably result in the quoted share price of the target dropping back, from the high figure which it will probably have reached in the light of the offer, to the pre-offer price. On the other hand, rejection of the first offer is quite likely to result in a better one. Perhaps, though, this is no worse than the dilemma which all shareholders experience when they see their shares quoted at a high price; should they sell and take advantage of it or should they wait, in the hope that the price will go even higher?

The management of the target is most unlikely to react passively to advances made by a bidder to the target shareholders. Quite often the bidder will seek the support of the target management in advance of its formal offer. If the management supports the offer, because for example it feels that there is commercial logic in such a merger, it is likely that the offer document will include a statement by the target's management to that effect.

Frequently, however, the target's management will be hostile to the offer and will oppose it with some vigour. Typical tactics employed by hostile target management include:

(a) issuing statements countering the claims of the bidder and putting forward the arguments for remaining independent;

(b) revaluing the target firm's assets in an attempt to show that the bidder's offer undervalues them; and

(c) releasing other information relevant to the target's future as an independent firm.

The object of these tactics is probably to increase the share price of the target to a point where the bidder's offer looks low and will be rejected.

Quite often these battles are long and bitter with claims of one side being met with counter-claims from the other, and offers being increased, until eventually an offer is accepted or the bidder withdraws. The battles can be damaging; they are expensive and, if the merger finally takes place, much bitterness can be carried into the management of the merged firm.

The results of the battle are not necessarily all bad: much new information about both parties tends to be forthcoming in statements and this enables the market to value the firms better.

ARE MERGERS SUCCESSFUL?

Having looked at why and how mergers occur, it seems appropriate to ask whether or not they appear to be successful. A number of studies has considered this question. These have fallen into three types:

(a) those which have asked managers of merged firms whether they consider the merger to have been successful or not;

(b) those which have tried to measure the success of mergers in terms of accounting profits; and

(c) those which have looked at the returns available to the shareholders of merged firms to see if these were better than they were likely to have been had the merger not taken place. Returns in this context are capital gains, plus dividends for the period as a percentage of the share's market value at the start of the period.

Of the first type, the general conclusion of managers seems to be that the mergers had not been beneficial. Coopers and Lybrand (1993) undertook a study during 1992 which comprised in-depth interviews with senior managers of 50 large UK firms which had been involved in a merger. The conclusion was that 54 per cent of mergers were not financially successful. This was remarkably consistent with the result which Coopers and Lybrand found when they conducted a similar study in 1973 and with that which Newbould (1970) found. The 1993 study identified several major causes of failure. These are set out in Table 14.2.

Table 14.2 Causes of failure of UK mergers

Cause of failure	% of interviewees who mentioned the factor as a cause of failure
Management attitudes	85
Lack of post-acquisition integration planning	80
Lack of knowledge by the bidder of the target and its industry	45
Poor management and management practices in the target	45
Little or no experience of the bidder management in acquiring other firms	30

Source: Coopers and Lybrand

Typical of the results of the second type were those shown by Meeks (1977). This study, again using UK data, found that average profitability prior to the merger exceeds that for the post-merger period, to a significant extent.

Generally the results from the third type of study are in conflict. Franks, Broyles & Hecht (1977) found significant gains to the target shareholders, particularly in the period leading up to the merger. They also found no detriment to the bidder's shareholders, either before or after the merger; in fact small gains were made by this group.

Franks and Harris (1989), using a large sample of UK mergers, found positive gains for both sets of shareholders during the pre-merger and immediate post-merger periods. They also found, however, post-merger losses by the bidder's shareholders. Limmack (1991) came to a similar conclusion to that of Franks and Harris.

Broadly, the results of these three types of study are in agreement. Generally mergers seem not to be successful. This fact may well explain why the number of mergers seems to have reduced fairly dramatically since the late 1980s (*see* Table 14.1). Other possible reasons include:

● a greater professionalism among corporate management leading to fewer cheap targets;
● relatively depressed share prices of 1980s being increased, again leading to fewer cheaper targets;

● a change in the perceptions of corporate managers of the desirability of large, diversified units. This point is raised again, in the context of divestment, later in this chapter.

CASE STUDY: GRANADA AND FORTE

To give some impression of the way in which many mergers are conducted, it might be useful to consider a recent case. It is important to recognise that there is nothing unusual or peculiar about this particular example; it is fairly typical of such merger battles.

On 22 November 1995 Granada formally offered either four Granada shares and £23.25 for every fifteen Forte shares or an all-cash alternative of £3.2167 per Forte share. The directors of the latter firm recommended that the shareholders refuse the bid.

The bidder and target firms

Granada Group plc: The bidder firm was first formed in 1934 as Granada Theatres Ltd, a firm operating a chain of cinemas. Since then it had expanded massively into television (35 per cent of its turnover), leisure and services (34 per cent) and rental and computer services (31 per cent). Profits had risen strongly year by year over recent years. Its pre-tax profit for the last full year before the Forte takeover was £351m. Granada is a well regarded firm which had successfully moved from a large 'family' firm dominated by the Bernstein family to one where by 1991, senior management was in the hands of professionals. Gerry Robinson was appointed Chief Executive at that time.

Forte plc: The target was another family firm, also first formed in 1934 when Charles Forte, the son of an Italian immigrant family, started a 'milk bar' (a cafe/restaurant). Since then the firm had expanded into a major restaurant and hotel business. Charles (now Lord) Forte had handed over the Chief Executive role to his son Rocco (now Sir Rocco) in 1982, and the chairmanship was also handed over in 1992. Many commentators believe that the firm had not really shaken off its 'family' nature in the way that Granada had. Certainly Forte's recent profit record had been uninspiring, with every subsequent year's profit lower than the figure for 1991.

Events before the formal offer

At the date of the offer, Granada owned few, if any, shares in Forte. It would appear that it had made no real attempt to buy shares through the Stock Exchange in advance of the formal offer.

The offer

A formal offer document, was sent to each Forte shareholder, explaining the offer and requiring that acceptances were to be received by 23 January 1996. It was understood that the motivation for the bid was Granada's belief that the 'clear strategic focus, strong financial disciplines and management skills', which its management could supply, would release the potential of Forte's assets to generate higher levels of profitability.

Forte's reaction to the offer

Forte's directors advised rejection of the bid at the outset. In their defence document, sent to shareholders, Sir Rocco Forte claimed that the bid had 'no commercial logic'. He also claimed that a new management team, which had been installed since he became Chairman in 1992, was having a beneficial effect on profits. These were forecast to be 46 per cent up on the previous year's figure for the year to end on 31 January 1996. Sir Rocco had already announced the firm's intention to spin-off the firm's restaurant business by the middle of 1996. (Spin-offs are explained a little later in this chapter.) During the course of the battle, Forte sold one of its assets, Lillywhites sports shop at Piccadilly Circus, London, for £28.5m. This was seen as a demonstration that the firm's assets were worth much more than the Granada bid or the market recognised. With the same objective in mind, Forte had its hotels professionally revalued. It also negotiated a cash deal to sell its restaurant and 'Travelodge' business to Whitbread, the brewery firm. Forte promised its shareholders a special dividend when the Whitbread deal had been completed.

On 2 January 1996, Forte announced its intention to buy back some of its shares, assuming that the Granada bid failed. This was an attempt to avoid the collapse in the share price which usually accompanies the failure of a merger bid. This might have provided an antidote to the tendency for target firm shareholders to accept the offer rather than let it fail and suffer the attendant fall in the share price.

Third party reaction to the offer

A considerable amount of Press comment supported the point made in the Forte defence document that the bid lacked commercial logic. The Press broadly seemed to believe that the price was quite a good one from the point of view of a Forte shareholder. The immediate post-offer share price was £3.48, compared with £2.75 immediately before the offer. The fact that the price settled well above the offer price of £3.22 clearly implied that the market expected to see an increased offer. As the battle progressed, however, this expectation seemed to weaken, and the price dropped back closer to the offer price.

A revised offer

On 9 January 1996, Granada raised its offer to £3.62 per share in cash, and the equivalent in shares and cash. The shares and cash deal included a special dividend to be paid to the former Forte shareholders after the bid had succeeded. Shortly before the revised offer Forte's share price stood at £3.25, only slightly above the original offer price. However, press comment tended to suggest that Forte's defence had been well handled and that the bid was likely to fail.

On 16 January 1996, Granada sought to increase its chances of success by buying 9.2 per cent of the Forte shares as normal transactions through the Stock Exchange. The following day it used the same means to increase its holding to 9.98 per cent. The Takeover Code limits the shares which can be acquired in this manner to less than 10 per cent.

Forte's reaction to the revised offer

Sir Rocco Forte continued to advise rejection of the bid on the grounds that the offer was misguided, and undervalued Forte. Under pressure from shareholders, Sir Rocco agreed to split his roles as Chairman and Chief Executive by making the current Deputy Chairman a new non-executive Chairman. Investors, perhaps institutional investors, in particular, do not seem to like the narrow senior management structures often found in the family-type firm. On 19 January 1996, following Granada's acquisition of the Forte shares through the Stock Exchange, Sir Rocco bought 0.4 per cent of the Forte shares by the same means, in an attempt to control more shares.

Third party reaction to the revised offer

The Press view appeared to be that the offer was a reasonable one, yet the general view seemed to be that the success of the bid hung in the balance. The share price settled just above the new offer price. By the closing date of 23 January, enough acceptances had been received for Granada to have won the battle.

Some comments on the battles

In most ways the events, which we have just reviewed, are typical of the majority of merger battles and of the tactics employed by target and bidder firms. Three particular issues seem to emerge from this case.

(a) At commencement of the merger move, did Granada have a ceiling price in mind or was it carried along by events into making a large final offer? In the end Granada paid more than 12 per cent above its original offer.

Obviously bidders in free markets do not always open the bidding at their ceiling price, but it could be the case that once Granada had set its sights on Forte, it was unwilling to accept defeat and to be seen to do so.

(b) Would the Forte group have given information about itself and its future had the bid not existed? It is unusual for firms to issue a profit forecast, yet Forte did so. It also announced divestment and future dividend plans; again unusual announcements.

Clearly these announcements were made in an attempt to enhance the Forte share price and to defeat the bid. If shareholder wealth maximisation is the objective pursued by firms, and if this can be achieved by the release of such information, why are firms so reluctant to release information about themselves under more normal circumstances? If releasing such information were to be seen as a means of defeating a takeover bid, logically it could also be used as a means of preventing one. If disclosure of information has the effect of increasing share prices, it could also have the effect of making the shares too expensive for a potential bidder to contemplate. Forte might have been able to avoid a costly and, ultimately, unsuccessful defence against the bid in this manner.

(c) Would the enhanced dividends, announced by Forte, really have enhanced the share price? Presumably this was the reason for the increases in dividends, but the theories and evidence, which we examined in Chapter 12, do not support this view at all. Could this imply that corporate managers are either not aware of, or do not believe, the theories and evidence on dividends and share prices.

INTERNATIONAL MERGERS

The increasing internationalisation of commerce has led to mergers between firms in different countries. The European Union's single market, which started in 1993, seems to have led to UK firms being particularly active in mergers with firms in other EU countries. It appears that, in 1993, UK firms were the most active merger participants in the EU, both as bidders and as targets (Hollinger 1993). A recent example of a UK firm taking over an overseas one outside the EU, was ICI paying $390 million for Bunge, a South American paint manufacturer, in March 1996. Compagnie Lyonnaise des Eaux paying £823m for the utility Northumbrian Water in November 1995, provides an example of an overseas firm taking over a UK one.

DIVESTMENTS

In some circumstances a firm may wish to sell off some part of its business, perhaps a division or subsidiary company. The reasons for this could include:

(a) A desire to concentrate on its core activities

A firm operating in a range of areas of business, either as a result of organic growth or following mergers, may decide that it would prefer to concentrate on its main area of expertise. Such rationalisations have become quite common recently and possibly reflect a view, which we shall discuss in Chapter 15, that the future lies with smaller, more focused businesses.

An example of a recent sell-off, where the reason given was a desire to concentrate on core activities, was provided by Pilkington, the glass-making firm, when it sold its contact lens business to a US specialist contact lens firm for £51 million, in July 1996.

(b) A wish to get rid of some part of its business which is causing problems

For example, a lack of profitability. This, together with reason (a), perhaps provides an example of the opposite of synergy, i.e. a 'five plus one equals four' syndrome, where the sum of the parts is greater than the whole.

(c) A need to raise cash

The need to raise cash may arise from a desire to make investments in other parts of the business, perhaps including a merger. The reason given for many recent sell-offs has been the desire to raise cash to enable a reduction in the level of capital gearing. An example of the latter was when, in March 1993, United Biscuit, the UK confectionery manu-facturer, sold Terry's, its chocolate division, to the US food and tobacco group Philip Morris for £220 million. United Biscuit also gave a desire to concentrate on its core activities, of biscuit and savoury snack manufacture, as part of the reason for the sale. Some sell-offs, particularly those involving smaller firms, might be caused by a need to raise cash to avoid being forced into liquidation (bankruptcy) as a result of an inability to meet financial obligations.

In effect, divestments are the opposite of mergers. Indeed, many of the divestments which have occurred recently were of subsidiaries acquired by rash mergers during the 1970s and 1980s.

When assessing the effectiveness of a divestment, the corporate objectives of both seller and buyer should be the touchstone. Assuming that shareholder wealth is the major financial criterion, an NPV analysis of the financial benefits and costs should be undertaken by both parties.

There are various means which are used to effect divestments, the more important of which we shall briefly consider.

Management buy-outs

Here the management of the particular part of the business which is to be disposed of buy it from the firm. These, according to KPMG Corporate Finance, have grown enormously in number over recent years in the UK. In 1980 there were about 100, but during 1995 there were about 560. The average value has also dramatically increased from a mean value per buy-out of £0.4 million in 1980 to £12.0 million per buy-out in 1995.

Some management buy-outs have proved to be very successful and have led to successful stock market flotations of the bought-out undertakings. Some of these have made millionaires of the managers concerned. When Allied Carpets was floated in 1996 managers who had invested in the buyout saw the value of their investment yield 25 times what they had paid for it in 1991; a floated value of £189m. These returns should be set against the risk which the managers took in investing in a carpet retailer in the depths of a recession both in consumer spending and of the housing market.

Since the managers are unlikely to be able to raise all of the cash necessary to make the buy-out, some fairly complicated financing arrangements have been developed. Loans have accounted for much of the finance, hence the label 'leveraged buy-out'. The high level of gearing required has engendered relatively high risk, high coupon rate lending, known in the US as 'junk bonds'. 'Mezzanine' finance has also been a feature of a number of management buy-outs. This is basically a high coupon rate loan with equity possibilities. Usually there is some right to convert the loan finance into equity, but only if the firm through which the buy-out is effected becomes quoted on the Stock Exchange. The evidence on the success of management buy-outs is thin and inconclusive; however, it appears that managers taking over the business which they run is likely to continue to occur.

Buy-ins

Here a group of individuals puts together an offer for part, or possibly all, of the business of a firm with which they have previously had no particular connection. Like management buy-outs, buy-ins have become increasingly popular in the 1980s and 1990s. According to the Centre for Management

Buyout Research at Nottingham University, there was just one UK buy-in, worth £0.5m, during 1979. In 1995, however, there were 163 buy-ins. Most of the features of management buy-outs are present with buy-ins, including the means of financing such deals. Many buy-ins involve very large sums of money.

In March 1996, Sears sold the Millets chain of outdoor and camping shops for £17m to a buy-in team. Sears said that the objective of the sale was to focus on fewer retail formats.

Buy-ins seem to occur quite often where the majority shareholder of a small family-type company wishes to retire. An example of this occurred in 1996, when a buy-in team bought a family bakery based in Aberdare, Wales (Ferrari's Bakery) from the Ferrari family.

Sell-offs

Sell-offs involve one established firm selling part of its business to another established firm, normally for cash. Some sell-offs have occurred under threat of takeover. Forte made some disposals of this type during the merger battle with Granada.

OTHER CORPORATE RESTRUCTURING ARRANGEMENTS

Spin-offs

Part of a firm's business is floated (spun-off) as a separate (probably quoted) firm and the existing shareholders receive the appropriate number of shares in the new firm. There is no change in ownership, except that the shareholders directly own the spun-off part, instead of owning it through the intermediary of the original firm. The reasons for doing this might include:

(a) *A desire to give the spun-off firm its own distinct corporate identity.*

(b) *Avoidance of a takeover attempt on the whole firm.* The value of the spun-off portion may not have been noticed in the original firm, except perhaps by a potential predator. By spinning-off a particularly valuable part of the business, the market will have the opportunity to assess that part as a separate unit. This may make it unattractive to predators. This point does imply a lack of belief in the efficiency of the capital market.

In 1996 Thorn EMI de-merged its record and rental interests from the rest of its operations. The Thorn EMI Chairman said of this spin-off that both businesses would be 'better focused' and 'more motivated' as separate firms. Hanson, the major conglomerate, also spun-off three new firms in 1996 again in an attempt to focus activities more clearly.

Share repurchase

The Companies Act 1981 gave firms the right, provided that certain conditions were complied with, to purchase some of their shares from existing shareholders, should those shareholders wish to sell. The reasons for this include:

(a) *The possibility that it will increase the share prices.* This is because the number of shares will be reduced, which reduces the potential supply. Repurchase could also increase earnings per share where the cash which has been used for the repurchase was previously not very effectively used.

(b) *The provision of a means for a particular shareholder in a firm not quoted, or not actively traded, to liquidate an equity investment.* It could therefore provide an 'escape route' for a financier who only wished to have a limited-term equity investment with the firm.

SUMMARY

Corporate restructuring is an increasingly significant aspect of the means by which firms seek to pursue their corporate objectives. All forms of restructuring should, in the context of a shareholder wealth maximisation goal, seek either to increase the firm's cash flows or to reduce the level of the riskiness of those cash flows. Any restructuring scheme should therefore be assessed by all parties on an NPV basis.

An important type of restructuring is the takeover or merger. Mergers are financed in a variety of ways, typically in a combination of some of these ways. Merger activity in the UK is regulated by the Monopolies and Mergers Commission and by the City Panel. Usually the bidder buys shares in the target firm through the Stock Exchange, before making the formal offer. Despite doubts about the commercial success of mergers, evidence suggests that on the whole they prove not to be beneficial to shareholders. The Granada/Forte merger 'battle' was typical of such battles in most respects. The behaviour of the managements of those firms raises several issues relating to business finance.

Divestments, of various types, are another increasingly important form of corporate restructuring. Means of achieving divestment include management buy-outs, buy-ins and sell-offs. The reasons for divestment are varied but include a desire on the part of many firms to rationalise their operations and to concentrate on their core activity.

Other types of corporate restructuring include spin-offs and share repurchasing.

FURTHER READING Samuels, Wilkes and Brayshaw (1995) and Weston and Copeland (1988) both give good coverage of most aspects of corporate restructuring, in a UK context. Wright, Thompson and Robbie (1996) give an interesting discussion of management buy-outs. Rybczynski (1989) provides a very useful review of corporate restructuring generally, but also making comparisons between practice in the UK and in other countries, particularly the USA, Germany and Japan.

REVIEW QUESTIONS

Suggested answers
to review questions
appear in Appendix 3.

14.1 Is corporate restructuring a good thing for firms which are pursuing a shareholder wealth maximisation objective? Explain your response.

14.2 How should shareholders in a 'target' firm logically assess an offer for their shares (on a share-for-share exchange basis) from the bidder firm?

14.3 What is the general stance of UK monopolies regulation with regard to mergers and takeovers?

14.4 What is the difference between a management 'buy-in' and a management 'buy-out'?

14.5 What is the difference between a 'sell-off' and a 'spin-off'?

14.6 Generally, have mergers in the UK been successful?

PROBLEMS

Sample answers to
problems marked with
an asterisk appear in
Appendix 4.

(*Note that problem questions 14.1 and 14.2 are basic level problems, while questions 4.3 and 4.4 are more advanced, and may contain some practical complications.*)

14.1* ABB plc has a cost of capital of 20 per cent p.a. and it is expected to generate annual end of year cash inflows of £12 million a year forever.

The firm's capital projects department has identified a smaller firm, CDD Ltd, which it is believed would be a suitable takeover target for ABB plc. It is estimated that the combined operation would have a perpetual end of year cash inflow of £14 million.

ABB plc's capital projects department analysts estimate that it would be worth the firm paying up to £27.5 million to acquire the entire equity of CDD Ltd.

What cost of capital must the analysts have estimated for the combined operation? (Ignore taxation.)

14.2 Taking the same circumstances as in Problem 14.1, without the takeover CDD had expected annual end-of-year cash inflows of £1.5 million forever, and an estimated cost of capital of 18 per cent p.a.

What is the minimum which the shareholders of CDD Ltd should logically accept for their shares in the takeover?
Logically, what should be the finally agreed total price for CDD Ltd's equity?

14.3* Thruster plc is a dynamic, expanding firm. Relaxation plc is a solid, but unambitious firm operating in the same industry. Thruster plc has recently launched a takeover bid for Relaxation plc. The offer is that Thruster plc will give one of its shares to a shareholder in Relaxation plc for every three shares in the latter firm.

After-tax cost savings are estimated to be £8 million p.a. as a result of administrative efficiencies, compared with the total costs historically incurred by the two firms.

Summarised accounting statements for the two firms for the year just ended are as follows:

Profit and loss account

	Thruster plc £m	Relaxation plc £m
Turnover	650	200
Profit before tax	72	17
Taxation	24	6
Profit after tax	48	11
Dividends	7	5
Retained profit for the year	41	6

Balance sheet as at the end of the year just ended

	Thruster plc £m	Relaxation plc £m
Fixed assets	350	200
Working capital	110	50
	460	250
Less: long-term liabilities	180	60
	280	190
Capital and reserves		
Ordinary shares of £0.50 each	170	90
Reserves	110	100
	280	190
Pre-bid price earnings ratio (PE)	18	14

Observers believe that, following the takeover, the PE ratio of Thruster plc will be 16.

Assuming that the market value of their shareholdings is the only factor of concern, would the shareholders of each firm welcome a successful takeover?

14.4 Expansion plc is a firm which has consistently expanded its activities over the past decade, partly through takeover and partly through retention of much of its operating profits. Consolidation plc is a firm operating in a mature, stable industry. Expansion plc is about to launch a takeover bid for the entire equity of Consolidation plc. The offer will be that Expansion plc will give one of its shares for every ten shares in Consolidation plc.

Analysts at Expansion plc believe that there are potential savings in total after-tax administrative costs of the merged operation, relative to the existing total administrative cost of the two firms totalling £10 million.

Summarised accounting statements for the two firms for the year just ended are as follows:

Profit and loss account

	Expansion plc £m	Consolidation plc £m
Turnover	940	730
Profit before tax	156	75
Taxation	52	25
Profit after tax	104	50
Dividends	20	40
Retained profit for the year	84	10

Balance sheet as at the end of the year just ended

	Expansion plc £m	Consolidation plc £m
Net assets	1750	2400
Less: long-term liabilities	870	1150
	880	1250
Capital and reserves		
Ordinary shares of £0.50 each	400	1000
Reserves	480	250
	880	1250
Pre-bid price earnings ratio (PE)	25	10

Observers believe that, following the takeover, the PE ratio of Expansion plc will be 20. It seems likely that Expansion plc will continue to distribute the same proportion of its after-tax profits as in the most recent year.

Assuming that both sets of shareholders are concerned both with the level of dividends and with the market price of their shares, how would the shareholders of each firm be likely to react to the takeover offer?

CHAPTER 15

Small firms

OBJECTIVES

In this chapter we shall deal with the following:

- the importance of the small firm's sector of the economy and a definition of small
- the objectives of small firms
- the likely legal form of the small firm
- taxation and the small firm
- risk and the discount rate to apply in appraising real investment opportunities for the small firm
- problems experienced by small firms with raising external long-term finance
- valuing the shares of small firms
- gearing in the small firm
- dividends and small firms

INTRODUCTION

What people mean by *small* in the present context seems to vary widely: number of employees, total funds invested, and sales turnover are often used in the definition. For our present purposes a strict definition probably does not matter. The sorts of firms which we shall be discussing are those displaying the following features.

(a) They are more substantial than the very small businesses that act as the medium for the self-employment of their owners.

(b) The firm's securities are not quoted in any established capital market, i.e. they are not traded in an efficient market.

(c) The ownership of the firm's equity and hence its control lie in the hands of a small close-knit group, i.e. it is a *family-type* firm.

Small firms, as we have defined them, are an important part of the UK private sector. They probably account for over one-fifth of the private sector's output and over two-fifths of its employment opportunities. In the opinion of many, including the UK Government, it is a part of the UK economy which is likely to grow.

There are good reasons to believe that small firms will become increasingly important in the UK. The industrial restructuring which occurred in the 1980s shifted the balance still further away from the manufacturing, mineral extracting and power generation industries towards the service industries. Service industries, perhaps because they do not depend so much on the economies of scale, tend to operate in smaller units. Even in manufacturing, the new computer-based technologies have tended to make smaller firms more viable. This is because the flexibility of such technologies has meant that the economies of scale, in manufacturing, are much less profound than was the case with more traditional industrial methods. As we saw in Chapter 13 in the context of 'just-in-time' systems, flexibility is increasingly important in manufacturing industries. Small firms have probably shown themselves to be more flexible. There seems to be an increasing trend towards a future where firms of all sizes will increasingly subcontract or buy-in services and components, as they need them, from firms specialising in such work, rather than seeking to do virtually everything 'in house' (this is known as *outsourcing*). This will promote a need for many small firms, each one specialising in the provision of some product or service. Already there is an increasing number of examples of firms 'outsourcing' such functions as personnel and IT. Not only will it promote the need for the output of the small firms, this tendency will also have the effect of providing labour to staff the small firms. This is because larger firms will shed labour with skills other than in what those firms see as their 'core' activity. The restructuring, including management buy-outs, which we discussed in Chapter 14, may be seen as the start of a trend towards smaller units and a concentration on core activities.

Small firms are also seen as being particularly important in that they provide an environment in which innovation tends to flourish. Claims are made that a very high proportion, perhaps a majority, of new ideas emerge and are first tried in the small firm sector.

There are few areas of business finance where the broad principles which apply to large firms do not equally well apply to small ones, but there are certainly some areas where the emphasis is different and where small firms tend to have their own particular problems. In this chapter we shall consider some of these areas.

Failure of small firms

A sad fact about small firms is the *failure rate*. Ryan (1995) points out that of all the firms which have been started since 1945, only one per cent remains in business today. Of all new firms started, less than 16 per cent remain in business after five years. Thus failure is very much the normal, though far from inevitable, fate of a new firm. Not all new firms are small firms, but it is very likely that most of them will be.

CORPORATE OBJECTIVES

In the context of larger firms we reached the conclusion that maximisation of shareholder wealth is a reasonable statement of the goal which most financial managers are likely to pursue. How different is this likely to be for smaller firms?

Management goals versus shareholder goals

With larger firms where the managers are probably not very substantial shareholders, conflict can arise between the objectives of each group.

In the case of the small firm the managers and the shareholders are likely to be substantially the same people or at least closely connected with one another. This might lead us to the conclusion that decisions are less likely to be made with a shareholder wealth maximisation goal as the major determinant, it being more likely that managers' welfare may be more important. On the other hand, it could equally well be argued that as managers are likely to be substantial shareholders they would make decisions following a pure wealth maximising goal more determinedly than would be the case with the typical large firm's management.

What we can probably say with conviction is that, whereas the vast majority of investors who buy shares in large firms do so with only an economic motive, those who involve themselves in smaller firms may well have other motives. These motives might include a desire to experience the satisfaction of building up a business, a desire to lead a particular way of life, or a desire to keep some (perhaps family) tradition alive. Since it is possible for managers to know the personal objectives of the shareholders of the smaller firm, decisions can probably be made with these in mind.

Irrespective of what other goals may be pursued by a small firm, decisions cannot be taken which consistently ignore the question of wealth. A firm which makes a series of decisions, each causing wealth to diminish, will sooner or later fail.

We may probably come to the conclusion that the wealth maximisation goal is very important to small firms and that, even where it is not necessarily the only objective, it cannot be ignored. This implies that the NPV investment appraisal technique is as relevant to small firms as it should be to large ones. In fact the evidence which we discussed in Chapter 4 suggests that NPV is not widely used by smaller firms.

ORGANISATION OF SMALL FIRMS

Typically the small firms which we are considering here will be organised as private limited companies. In essence these are identical to their public counterparts. The main differences are:

(a) Private companies need be of no minimum size; public companies must issue at least £50 000 of nominal share capital of which at least 25 per cent must be paid up. There is no upper limit on the size of a private company.

(b) Private companies are entitled to restrict the transfer of their shares, i.e. it is possible for the company's Articles of Association to contain a clause giving the directors the power to refuse to register a transfer, at their discretion.

(c) Whilst private companies must publish annual accounts, the volume of detail is rather less than that which the law requires of public companies.

(d) Private companies must generally include the word 'limited' or its abbreviation 'Ltd' in their names; public limited companies must include 'plc' in theirs.

Probably in practice the only one of these distinctions which is of any great significance is the second, concerning the restriction on transfer of shares. To the small firm the effect of the right of restriction can be something of a two-edged sword.

(a) It enables the majority of the shareholders to stop the minority, be it one or more shareholders, from transferring their shares to a third party unacceptable to the majority. In this way control, and even just influence through voting power, may be kept in the hands of those acceptable to the majority. In a family-type firm it may be important to the shareholders that ownership remains in the same hands, not necessarily for financial reasons.

(b) Potential equity investors would be reluctant to buy shares in a firm which effectively had the power to stop them selling the shares when they wished to. Not unnaturally most established secondary capital markets, certainly the International Stock Exchange, will not allow dealings in shares where there is a restriction on transfer. For small firms eager to expand, being a private limited company may be an impediment to growth.

It is not necessarily true that all small firms will be private limited companies, but given the attractions of the lesser requirement to account publicly and the ability to control their membership through share transfer restrictions, many of them are.

TAXATION OF SMALL FIRMS

As far as tax on corporate profits is concerned the only likely difference between large and small firms is the Corporation tax rate. For firms whose profits are less than £300 000 p.a. the rate is 23 per cent, for firms with annual profits of £1 500 000 or more the rate is 33 per cent.

Note that 'large' and 'small' for tax purposes are defined entirely in terms of profit and that firms can and do move from being large to being small from one year to the next.

Tax avoidance

Perhaps where the distinction between small and large firms is likely to be most profound, in the context of taxation, is in the extent to which firms take actions purely for tax reasons.

Since small firms typically can know the personal circumstances of the shareholders, actions can be taken which will maximise the net (after-tax) wealth of their shareholders. For example, where all shareholders pay Income Tax at a high marginal rate it might be to their net advantage for profits to be retained by the firm instead of being distributed. This would possibly lead, in the long term, to a Capital Gains Tax liability on disposal of the shares, but this may be more tax efficient.

RISK AND THE DISCOUNT RATE

In the context of large firms it seems that discounting expected cash flows using a discount rate derived from CAPM is a reasonable way for considerations of risk to be incorporated into investment decision making. With small firms this would probably be invalid. It is thought to be true that investors in a large firm typically hold a relatively small proportion of that firm's total equity, as a relatively small proportion of a reasonably well diversified portfolio of equities.* For this reason investors would be exposed to relatively little specific risk, so a CAPM derived discount rate, i.e. one which deals only with systematic risk, is logical. Typically shareholders of small firms will not be well diversified. They may hold shares in many different firms but it is likely that their holding in the small firm will represent a large proportion (by value) of their total investment in equities. If the small firm were to fail, most of their wealth might be lost.

Since shares of small firms will tend not to be held in efficient portfolios, the discount rate which should be applied to the small firm's investment opportunities should take account of specific as well as systematic risk.

This means that there is no direct way of arriving at an appropriate discount rate, though CAPM can be used to discover a figure below which it should not lie. Probably the impressionistic devices such as sensitivity analysis and attempts to assess the worst possible outcome, best estimate and the best possible outcome could be used to gauge the level of risk.

Risk diversification within the firm

In our previous discussion of diversification and risk reduction the point emerged that, with large firms, the shareholders would probably not be advantaged by attempts by management to diversify its operations within the firm. This is because shareholders can and do diversify their security portfolios to achieve the same effect. For the reason mentioned above, shareholders in small firms may not be able to do this for themselves so there may be some point in the firm's management doing it for them, with the objective of reducing specific risk. Of course, because the firm is small, the practicality of internal diversification may be much less than would be the case with a larger firm.

* Casual observation shows this broadly to be true. The majority of equities (about 80 per cent) quoted on the International Stock Exchange are owned by the investing institutions which tend to hold large, well diversified portfolios.

SOURCES OF FINANCE

In modern times there have been four UK Government-sponsored inquiries which have dealt at least partly with the financing of small firms. These were:

(a) The MacMillan Committee on finance and industry (1931);
(b) The Radcliffe Committee on the working of the monetary system (1959);
(c) The Bolton Committee of inquiry on small firms (1971); and
(d) The Wilson Committee to review the functioning of financial institutions (1980).

Each of these discovered, to a greater or lesser extent, that small firms find it more difficult and more expensive to raise external finance than do larger firms. For this reason they are forced to rely on internally generated funds (retained profits) to a great extent.

It seems that large firms also rely heavily on retained profits as a major source of finance, with capital issues averaging about 25 per cent of total new finance over recent years. Perhaps if a problem does exist it applies almost equally well to large firms.

No doubt small firms do experience some problems in raising external finance and, triggered off by the publication of the first three (particularly the first two) of the above committee reports, a number of schemes and agencies was established to make it easier for them. The Industrial and Commercial Financing Corporation (ICFC) is an example of one of the agencies.

The last two committee reports suggested not so much the absence of sources available to small firms, as an ignorance on the part of their management of the existence of those sources. Efforts to plug the *information gap* are manifest in the modern UK, with press and television advertising the Small Firms' Information Centres set up by the Department of Trade and Industry. These centres offer advice on and contacts with potential providers of finance.

Recently the Government has called the Income Tax system to the aid of small firms, offering potential investors relief from tax for making equity investments in small firms.

No doubt it remains more difficult and expensive for small firms to raise external finance, but at least their managers and shareholders may take comfort from the fact that just about everyone with any influence in the matter, most particularly the UK Government, seems eager to improve the situation.

Exit routes

A particular problem faced by small firms in their quest for equity capital is the lack of an 'exit route'. Generally investors require that there is some way of liquidating their investment before they are prepared to commit funds to it. With firms listed on the Stock Exchange, or a similar market, this normally poses no great problem. However, small firms find this a significant problem.

The possibilities facing the potential equity investors are that:

- The firm will be able to buy back the shares from the shareholder, but this requires that the firm has generated sufficient cash, and that it does not need that cash for further investment. This is not a very attractive option for the firm. One of the key advantages of equity is the absence of the need to liquidate it.

- The firm will obtain a listing on the Stock Exchange. This may be a possibility, particularly in view of the recently established Alternative Investment Market (*see* below), but it is still only firms towards the larger end of the small firm sector which will be able to follow this route.

- The firm is sold to another firm or to a management buy-out or buy-in team.

Since none of these can be regarded as likely possibilities, particularly for very small firms, finding equity backing is a real problem for small firms. In the end, for most of them, the personal savings of their founders and ploughed back profits are the only significant sources of equity finance.

Venture capital

Venture capital is the name given to equity finance provided to support new, expanding and entrepreneurial firms. Venture capitalists usually prefer to take a close interest in the firm which is the subject of their investment. This could involve taking part in decisions made by the firm. Much venture capital comes from funds contributed to by a number of smaller investors, in many cases taking advantage of the tax incentives available to providers of equity finance through such funds.

Alternative Investment Market (AIM)

AIM was established in June 1995, by the Stock Exchange (of the UK and the Republic of Ireland) for small, young and growing firms. Many of these are family-type firms and/or firms established as a result of management buy-outs and buy-ins. AIM has proved to be a very successful means for firms to establish a market in which new equity finance could be raised and its shares could be traded. Firms listed on AIM tend to be in the range £1m to £300m, though most fall within the £3m to £30m range.

AIM is cheap to enter compared to the costs of obtaining a full Stock Exchange listing. Nevertheless, an AIM listing is not without its cost. Obtaining a listing and raising funds costs about £100 000 plus three per cent of the amount of funds raised.

EVIDENCE ON SMALL FIRM FINANCING

A useful source of information on UK small firm financing is contained in a report on an annual survey conducted by Deloitte and Touche (Chartered Accountants). The survey is of about 230 owner-managed firms with an annual turnover of between £5 million and £150 million each. The survey results are analysed (by annual sales turnover) as follows:

- £5 million to £10 million;
- £10 million to £20 million;
- £20 million to £50 million;
- £50 million to £150 million.

The results which are now discussed were contained in the report published in 1996 which dealt with the position in 1995.

For all firms in the survey, the proportion of debt finance in relation to all long-term finance (debt plus equity) was about 27 per cent, with only 17 per cent of the firms surveyed having a ratio as large as 50 per cent. Some 63 per cent of the firms had gearing ratios below 25 per cent. A large proportion of the debt finance (about 50 per cent for all firms) comes from overdrafts and other short-term debt. The very smallest firms seem much less reliant on overdrafts (about 30 per cent of their debt finance). Long- and medium-term debt accounted for about 60 per cent of debt for the £5 to £10 million turnover firms. This contrasts with the largest firms in the survey where overdrafts and short-term finance accounted for about 55 per cent of total debt, and medium- and long-term debt accounted for about 30 per cent.

This might be rather surprising since it is generally believed that the very smallest firms are the most heavily dependent on overdrafts and that the larger firms tend to have their finances on a more secure footing.

VALUATION OF SMALL FIRMS

The existence of an apparently efficient market for the securities of large firms implies that unless we have access to 'inside information' there is no reason to believe that the current market price is not the best estimate of the security's value available to us. With small firms, as we have defined them, this will not be true since there is no current market price. Nonetheless it is sometimes necessary to value the ordinary shares of small firms, either to fix a price for a transfer for value (a sale) or where the transfer has been partly or fully gratuitous and a value is needed for Capital Gains or Inheritance Tax purposes.

There are basically four approaches which can be taken to such a valuation. We should bear in mind that we are seeking by each approach to value the equity of a firm. Since each one has the same objective, in theory they should if used correctly give the same result. This they will not usually do, possibly reflecting inefficiencies or imperfections in the market for real assets. We shall now look at each approach in turn.

Dividend yield

This approach is based on the notion that the ordinary shares of two different firms should have a similar dividend yield provided that the firms are roughly similar in size, activity, capital gearing and proportion of profit paid as dividend (dividend cover). If the shares of one of these firms are quoted and valued by an efficient market (i.e. listed on the Stock Exchange), this enables us to value the other one.

EXAMPLE

A plc and B Ltd are two firms similar in size, activity, gearing and dividend cover. A plc is a Stock Exchange listed firm, B Ltd is not. The dividend yield (gross) for A is 10 per cent and B has recently paid annual dividends of £0.15 per share. What is the value of each B Ltd share?

SOLUTION

Bearing in mind that

$$\text{Dividend yield} = \frac{\text{Dividend paid (grossed up)}}{\text{Current market price per share}}$$

Then,

$$10\% = \frac{0.15 \times 100/80}{P_B}$$

(assuming an Income Tax rate of 20 per cent) and

$$P_B = £1.88 \text{ per share}$$

The following points should be noted on using the dividend yield approach in practice:

(a) The difficulty of finding a listed firm sufficiently like the unlisted one in the ways mentioned for the comparison to be valid.

(b) The doubts as to whether it is valid to assume that current dividend levels are the sole determinant of share values.

(c) The fact that prices are more likely to relate to future dividends; past dividends will tend only to be useful as a guide to the future.

(d) The lack of marketability of unquoted shares: this will tend to make them less valuable than apparently identical quoted ones.

This approach tends to be used where a minority holding is being valued. This is because the minority shareholder has little control over events and simply receives a dividend.

Price/earnings

This approach is similar to the dividend yield approach but concentrates on earnings rather than dividends and takes the view that the shares of two similar firms will have equal PE ratios.

EXAMPLE

C plc and D Ltd are two firms similar in size, activity and gearing. C plc is listed, D Ltd is not. The PE ratio for C is 12, the post-tax earnings per share for D have been £0.30 p.a. over recent years. What is the value of each D Ltd share?

SOLUTION

Bearing in mind that:

$$PE = \frac{\text{Current market price per share}}{\text{Post-tax earnings per share}}$$

Then,

$$12 = \frac{P_D}{0.30}$$

Clearly most of the points which apply to the dividend yield approach also apply to this approach. The PE approach does overcome the question of dividend policy, which MM assert is irrelevant in any case.

This approach tends to be used to value a majority holding where the shareholder has some control over the firm.

Net assets

Here the approach is to value the firm by reference to the individual values of its assets.

EXAMPLE

The balance sheet of E Ltd is as shown below. What is the value of each E Ltd share?

Balance sheet of E Ltd at 31 December

Sources of finance (claims)	£m	Uses of finance (investments)	£m
Ordinary shares of £1 each	8	Fixed assets	11
Retained profit	7	Working capital	10
Total equity	15		
Long-term loans	6		
	21		21

SOLUTION

$$P_E = \frac{11+10-6}{8}$$

$$= £1.875$$

The above calculation is based on the book values of the assets and liabilities. It need not be done on this basis. Some current market value would be more logical, including a value for the firm's goodwill, if any. Since the assets concerned here are presumably purely economic ones, their value should be based on their ability to generate future benefits. For this reason there is no reason why the net assets basis should give us a different value than would the price/earnings approach.

Economic value (based on 'free' cash flows)

This approach is the most logical of them. It bases the valuation on the discounted (present) value of the estimated future net cash flows of the firm. Logical it may be, but it is problematical. Cash flows will be difficult to estimate, certainly beyond the first year or two. A discount rate will need to be identified which poses another problem. This might be able to be solved by using CAPM, with the average β for the industry in which the firm is engaged.

In practice, there tend to be differences between the values obtained from each approach. The dividend yield basis tends to be used to value minority shareholdings where the potential shareholder will not own sufficient shares to exercise any power nor perhaps any influence over dividend policy. Controlling shareholdings tend to be valued on the net assets or price/earnings bases.

Perhaps we should conclude this section by saying that valuing the shares of unquoted firms is a highly inexact science – value is in the eye of the beholder. In practice, the price at which a transfer occurs, or (for tax purposes) is deemed to have occurred, is likely to be the result of negotiation and compromise between the concerned parties.

GEARING

Once again the small firm is not in a fundamentally different position from that of the larger one on the issue of gearing. As we saw in Chapter 11, financial risk to which capital gearing gives rise, tends to emphasise business risk which will be present with or without gearing. Business risk is part specific and part systematic. Since small firms' shareholders may not be able to diversify sufficiently to eliminate most of the specific risk, they are likely to be more exposed to financial risk than would their typical large firm counterparts.

The relatively low Corporation tax rates which apply to small firms mean that the effective relief for interest payments on borrowings and dividends are similar. This means that the greater tax efficiency of debt financing does not really apply to small firms.

In Chapter 11 we suggested that there might be some optimal level of gearing which balances the increased risk to equity investors which gearing engenders, against the tax advantages. For the reasons which we have just reviewed this optimal level might be much lower for a small firm than for a larger one.

DIVIDENDS

Much of what is true concerning dividends in the context of large firms also applies to small ones, though there are differences. Perhaps most importantly it is feasible for the directors of small firms to know their shareholders' preferences as regards dividend policy and to make efforts to accommodate those preferences. This really is necessary; since typically it is not very practical for shareholders to sell their shares and replace them with those of another firm whose dividend policy appeals rather more.

SUMMARY

Small firms are an important sector of the UK economy and tend to have their own peculiarities as regards business finance while having most other features in common with large firms.

Corporate objectives are more likely to relate to aspirations of individual shareholders than is likely to be the case with large firms. Shareholder wealth maximisation is probably a fairly important objective for most small firms.

Many small firms are private limited companies, a status which gives them the benefits of corporate existence yet enables their directors to a great extent to control into whose hands the shares fall. It also limits the level of public accountability required of the small firm.

Small firms are taxed on their profits at a lower rate than are larger ones. They are also more likely than are large ones to take the personal tax position of their shareholders into account when making their decisions.

It is probably the case that shareholders in small firms do not hold efficient portfolios. CAPM as a device for deriving the discount rate for use in investment appraisal in the firm is therefore less appropriate than it would be for a larger firm. Perhaps the more impressionistic devices for assessing risk are particularly valid for small firms.

Observers have consistently noted the difficulty of small firms in raising external long-term finance. Past action to put them on equal terms with large firms has not been completely successful due, it would seem, to a lack of information on the part of small firms. Attempts to fill this information gap are being made.

For various reasons the shares of unquoted firms sometimes need to be valued and there are several approaches which can be taken to this. Ultimately the final agreed value is likely to be the outcome of a certain amount of 'horse trading' between the interested parties.

The optimum level of gearing should logically be lower for small firms than for large ones because the risk to equity holders caused by gearing is higher and the tax saving is lower. The dividend policy of a small firm is much more likely to reflect individual preferences of shareholders than will (or can) be the case with a large one.

FURTHER READING Samuels, Wilkes and Brayshaw (1995) and Weston and Copeland (1988) provide quite good coverage of small firms generally. The references given at the end of previous chapters generally provide coverage of particular topics in the context of both large and small firms. The report of the Wilson Committee (1980) gives some relatively up-to-date information on financing problems of small firms.

REVIEW QUESTIONS

Suggested answers to review questions appear in Appendix 3.

15.1 What recent business trend is tending to promote the establishment and expansion of small, specialist firms?

15.2 Why would it normally be appropriate for a small firm to discount project pre-tax cash flows at a higher rate than might be applied to a similar prospective project under consideration by a larger firm?

15.3 When valuing unquoted shares, what problems arise when basing the valuation on the price earnings ratio and/or dividend yield of a similar quoted firm?

15.4 What is wrong with using the balance sheet values of assets and claims when deducing the value of the shares of a small firm?

15.5 What particular problem will face potential equity investors in small firms, which may make the investors hesitant to buy shares and/or to seek higher expected returns than they would normally seek from a larger, stock market listed one?

15.6 Why would dividend policy tend to be easier to decide for the typical small firm, than for the typical larger one?

PROBLEMS

Sample answers to problems marked with an asterisk appear in Appendix 4.

(*Note that problem questions 15.1 and 15.2 are basic level problems, while questions 15.3 and 15.4 are more advanced, and may contain some practical complications.*)

15.1* Tiny Tim Ltd (a private company) is a firm quite like Mega plc (a public, Stock Exchange-listed firm) in terms of activities and gearing. Tiny Tim Ltd has steady after-tax profits of £350 000 a year. Mega plc's published price earnings ratio is 16.

Estimate the total value of the shares in Tiny Tim Ltd, bearing in mind its private company status.

15.2 XYZ Ltd (a private company) is a firm quite like ABC plc (a public, Stock Exchange-listed firm) in term of activities, gearing and dividend policy. XYZ Ltd recently paid a dividend for the year of £0.20 per share. The effective Income Tax rate is 24 per cent. ABC plc's gross dividend yield is 12 per cent.

Estimate the value of a share in XYZ Ltd, bearing in mind its private company status.

15.3* PR Industries plc, a major conglomerate, is considering acquiring an interest in Howard Pope Ltd, a private company which has been trading for about 40 years as a manufacturer of domestic appliances.

The latest available summarised accounts of Howard Pope Ltd are as follows:

Profit and loss account for the year ended 31 December 1996

	£m
Profit on ordinary activities after tax	15.30
Dividends	5.00
Profit retained	10.30

Balance sheet as at 31 December 1996

	£m
Fixed assets	50.67
Net current assets	92.75
	143.42
Issued share capital (ordinary shares of 5p)	2.00
Share premium account	6.00
Revenue reserves	105.42
Floating rate term loan	30.00
	143.42

In recent years the directors of Howard Pope Ltd have adopted a policy of increasing dividends by approximately 10 per cent each year.

The cost of equity of listed companies in the same industry as Howard Pope Ltd, which are similarly capital geared, is estimated at 13 per cent. The average price earnings ratio of such companies is 15.0.

The directors of PR Industries plc have not yet decided what proportion of the share capital of Howard Pope Ltd they wish their company to acquire and you have been asked to consider the possibility of acquiring either a minority or a majority stake.

Estimate the value of a share in Howard Pope Ltd. Would your view be different according to whether PR Industries plc is acquiring a controlling or a minority interest?

15.4 Alcantage Ltd owns a chain of dry-cleaning shops in South Wales. A UK-wide dry-cleaning firm is considering making an offer to the shareholders of Alcantage Ltd with the idea of obtaining all the ordinary shares.

The draft accounts of Alcantage Ltd, for the year which has just ended, can be summarised as follows:

Profit and loss account for last year

	£m
Turnover	24.7
Profit before interest and tax	8.4
Interest	0.5
Profit before taxation	7.9
Corporation tax	2.6
Profit after taxation	5.3
Dividend	1.5
Retained profit	3.8

Balance sheet as at the end of last year

	£m	£m
Fixed assets		
Freehold land and buildings at cost	5.9	
Less: depreciation	1.0	4.9
Plant at cost	12.7	
Less: depreciation	5.1	7.6
		12.5
Current assets		
Stock	4.3	
Debtors	0.7	
Cash at bank	4.1	
	9.1	
Less: creditors, amounts falling due in less than one year		
Creditors	6.1	
Dividends	1.5	
Taxation	2.6	
	10.2	
Working capital		(1.1)
		11.4
Less: creditors, amounts falling due in more than one year		
Debenture loan		4.7
		6.7
Share capital and reserves		
Ordinary shares of £1 each		3.2
Retained profits		3.5
		6.7

Analysts estimate that the net cash flows of Alcantage Ltd, after taking account of tax and the need to replace fixed and current assets, will be:

	£m
Next year	6.7
Year 2	7.1
Year 3	7.5
Year 4	8.2
Year 5 and thereafter	8.5

The cost of equity of firms in the industry, taking account of the level of capital gearing, is 12 per cent.

Professional valuers have recently assessed some of Alcantage Ltd's assets to have market values as follows:

	£m
Freehold land and buildings	12.3
Plant	6.2
Stock	4.8

The average of listed firms in the industry for dividend yield is 7 per cent and for the price earnings ratio it is 14. The effective basic rate of Income Tax is 20 per cent.

Estimate the value of a share in Alcantage Ltd on the basis of as many methods as you can from the information provided.

If you were a shareholder in Alcantage Ltd how, in general terms, would you assess whatever offer you may receive from the national firm?

References

Alexander, S. (1961). Price movements in speculative markets, trends or random walks. *Industrial Management Review* (May).

Archer, S. H. and D'Ambrosio, C. A. (eds) (1983). *The Theory of Business Finance: A Book of Readings*, 3rd edn (Collier-Macmillan).

Atrill, P. F. and McLaney, E. J. (1996). *Financial Accounting for Non-Specialists* (Prentice-Hall).

Beaver, W. H. (1989). *Financial Reporting: An Accounting Revolution*, 2nd edn (Prentice-Hall).

Beranek, W. (1963). *Analysis for Financial Decisions* (Irwin).

Bierman, H. and Smidt, S. (1988). *The Capital Budgeting Decision*, 7th edn (Collier-Macmillan).

Black, F. and Scholes, M. (1974). The effect of dividend policy on common stock prices and returns. *Journal of Financial Economics* (May).

Boardman, C. M., Reinhart, W. J. and Celec, S. E. (1982). The role of the payback method in the theory and application of duration to capital budgeting. *Journal of Business Finance and Accounting* (Winter).

Bowman, C. and Asch, D. (1987). *Strategic Management* (Macmillan).

Brealey, R. A. (1970). The distribution and independence of successive rates of return from the British equity market. *Journal of Business Finance*.

Brealey, R. A. and Myers, S. (1991). *The Principles of Corporate Finance*, 4th edn (McGraw-Hill International).

Carsberg, B. and Hope, A. (1976). *Business Investment Decisions Under Inflation* (Institute of Chartered Accountants in England and Wales).

Chen, S. and Clark, R. L. (1994). Management compensation and payback period method in capital budgeting: a path analysis. *Journal of Accounting and Business Research* (Spring).

Cole, W., Shears, P. and Tiley, J. (1990). *Law in a Business Context* (Chapman & Hall).

Coopers and Lybrand (1993). *A review of the acquisitions experience of major UK companies.* (Coopers and Lybrand).

Copeland, T. E. and Weston, J. F. (1988). *Financial Theory and Corporate Policy*, 3rd edn (Addison-Wesley).

Corr, A. V. (1983). *The Capital Expenditure Decision.* (National Association of Accountants and the Society of Management Accountants of Canada).

Crossland, M., Dempsey, M. and Moizer, P. (1991). The effect of cum- to ex-dividend charges on UK share prices. *Accounting and Business Research*, vol. 22, no. 85.

Cunningham, S. W. (1973). The predictability of British stock market prices. *Applied Statistics*, vol. 22.

Cyert, R. M. and March, J. G. (1964). *A Behavioural Theory of the Firm* (Prentice-Hall).

Dann, L., Mayers, D. and Raab, R. (1977). Trading rules, large blocks and the speed of adjustment. *Journal of Financial Economics* (Jan.).

Davis, E. and Pointon, J. (1994). *Finance and the Firm*, 2nd edn (Oxford University Press).

DeAngelo, H. and Masulis, R. (1980). Optimal capital structure under corporate and personal taxation. *Journal of Financial Economics* (Mar.).

Deloitte and Touche. (1996). *Finance for Owner Managed Businesses.* Available free of charge from Deloitte and Touche (Chartered Accountants) Stonecutter Court, 1 Stonecutter Street, London EC4A 4TR.

Dempsey, M. J. (1991). Modigliani & Miller again revisited: the cost of capital with unequal borrowing and lending rates. *Accounting and Business Research* (Summer).

Dimson, E. (1996). Assessing the rate of return. *Mastering Management Part 1* (Financial Times).

Drury, C. (1996). *Management and Cost Accounting,* 4th edn (Chapman & Hall).

Drury, C. and Braund, S. (1990). The leasing decision: a comparison of theory and practice. *Accounting and Business Research,* vol. 20, no. 79 (Summer).

Drury, C., Braund, S., Osborne, P. and Tayles M. (1993). *A survey of management accounting practices in UK manufacturing industries.* (The Chartered Association of Certified Accountants).

Dryden, M. M. (1970). A statistical study of UK share prices. *Scottish Journal of Political Economy* (Nov.).

Elton, E. J. and Gruber, M. J. (1970). Marginal stockholders' tax rates and the clientele effect. *Review of Economics and Statistics* (Feb.).

Evans, J. and Archer S. H. (1968). Diversification and the reduction of dispersion: an empirical analysis. *Journal of Finance* (Dec.).

Fama, E. F. (1965). The behaviour of stock market prices. *Journal of Business* (Jan.).

Fama, E. F. (1977). *Foundations of Finance* (Basil Blackwell).

Fama, E. F. (1991). Efficient capital markets II. *Journal of Finance* (Dec.).

Fama, E. F. and Babiak, H. (1968). Dividend policy: an economic analysis. *Journal of the American Statistical Association* (Dec.).

Fama, E. F. and French, K. R. (1992). The cross-section of expected stock returns. *Journal of Finance* (June).

Fama, E. F., Fisher, L., Jensen, M. and Roll, R. (1969). The adjustment of stock prices to new information. *International Economic Review* (Feb.).

Finnerty, J. (1976). Insiders and market efficiency. *Journal of Finance* (Sept.).

Firth, M. (1977a). An empirical investigation of the impact of the announcement of capitalisation issues on share prices. *Journal of Business Finance and Accounting.*

Firth, M. (1977b). *The Valuation of Shares and the Efficient Markets Theory* (Macmillan).

Franks, J. R., Broyles, J. E. and Hecht, M. (1977). An industry study of mergers in the UK. *Journal of Finance* (Dec.).

Franks, J. R. and Harris, P. (1989). Shareholder wealth effects of corporate takeovers: the UK experience (1955–1985). *Journal of Financial Economics,* 23.

Friend, I. and Puckett, M. (1964). Dividends and stock prices. *American Economic Review* (Sept.).

Gregory-Allen, R., Impson, C. M. and Katafiath, I. (1994). An empirical study of beta stability. *Journal of Business Finance and Accounting* (Sept.).

Griner, E. H. and Gordon, L. A. (1995). Internal cash flow, insider ownership and capital expenditures. *Journal of Business Finance and Accounting* (Mar.).

Hamada, R. S. (1972). The effect of the firm's financial structure on the systematic risk of common stocks. *Journal of Finance* (May).

Harper, W. M. (1982). *Operational Research,* 2nd edn (Macdonald & Evans).

Harper, W. M. (1991). *Statistics,* 6th edn (Pitman Publishing).

Hirshleifer, J. (1958). On the theory of optimal investment decisions. *Journal of Political Economy*, reprinted in Archer and D'Ambrosio (1983).

Ho, S. S. M. and Pike, R. H. (1991). Risk analysis in capital budgeting contexts: simple or sophisticated. *Accounting and Business Research*, vol. 21, no. 83.

Holinger, P. (1993). UK leads in European cross-border takeovers. *The Financial Times* (19 October).

Homaifar, G., Zeitz, J. and Benkato, O. (1994). An empirical model of capital structure; some new evidence. *Journal of Business Finance and Accounting* (Jan.).

Ibbotson, R. C. and Sinquefield, R. (1979). *Stocks, Bonds and Inflation* (Financial Analysts Research Foundation).

Iveson, S., Moss, C. and Simpson, M. (1986). *British Readings in Financial Management* (Harper and Row).

Jaffe, J. (1974). Special information and insider trading. *Journal of Business* (July).

Jenkinson, T. J. (1990). New equity issues in the United Kingdom. *Bank of England Quarterly Bulletin* (May).

Keane, S. M. (1983). *Stock Market Efficiency* (Philip Allan).

Keenan, D. (1997). *Advanced Business Law,* 10th edn (Pitman Publishing).

Kendall, M. G. (1953). The analysis of economic time series. *Journal of the Royal Statistical Society*, vol. 96, part 1.

Kester, W. C. (1986). Capital and ownership structure. *Financial Management* (Spring).

Levy, H. and Sarnat, M. (1988). *Principles of Financial Management* (Prentice-Hall).

Levy, H, and Sarnat, M. (1994). *Capital Investment and Financial Decisions*, 5th edn (Prentice-Hall International).

Lewellen, W. G., Stanley, K. L., Lease, R. C. and Schlarbaum, G. G. (1978). Some direct evidence of the dividend clientele phenomenon. *Journal of Finance* (Dec.).

Limmack, R. J. (1991). Corporate mergers and shareholder wealth effects: (1977–1986). *Accounting and Business Research*, vol. 21, no. 83.

Lintner, J. (1956). Distribution of incomes of corporations among dividends, retained earnings and taxes. *American Economic Review* (May).

Litzenberger, R. and Ramaswamy, K. (1982). The effects of dividends on common stock prices: tax effects or information effects? *Journal of Finance* (May).

Lumby, S. (1994). *Investment Appraisal and Financing Decisions*, 5th edn (Chapman & Hall).

McIntyre, A. D. and Coulthurst, N. J. (1985). Theory and practice in capital budgeting. *British Accounting Review* (Autumn).

Marsh, P. (1982) The choice between equity and debt: an empirical study. *Journal of Finance* (Mar.).

Masulis, R. (1980). The effect of capital structure changes on security prices. *Journal of Financial Economics* (June).

Meeks, G. (1977). *Disappointing Marriage: A Study of Gains from Merger* (Cambridge University Press).

Merrett, A. J. and Sykes, A. (1966). Return on equities and fixed interest securities 1919–1966. *District Bank Review* (June).

Miller, M. H. (1977). Debt and taxes. *Journal of Finance*, vol. 32, no. 2 (May).

Miller, M. H. and Modigliani, F. (1961). Dividend policy, growth and the valuation of shares. *Journal of Business* (Oct.).

Miller, M. H. and Modigliani, F. (1966). Some estimates of the cost of capital to the electrical utility industry 1954–57. *American Economic Review* (June).

Miller, M. H. and Orr, D. (1966). A model of the demand for money by firms. *Quarterly Journal of Economics* (Aug.).

Mills, R. W. (1988). Capital budgeting techniques used in the UK and USA. *Management Accounting* (Jan.).

Modigliani, F. and Miller, M. H. (1958). The cost of capital, corporate finance and the theory of investment. *American Economic Review*, reprinted in Archer and D'Ambrosio (1983).

Modigliani, F. and Miller, M. H. (1963). Corporate income taxes and the cost of capital. *American Economic Review* (June).

Moore, J. S. and Reichert, A. K. (1983). An analysis of the financial management techniques currently employed by large US corporations. *Journal of Business Finance and Accounting*, vol. 10, no. 4.

Morris, R. (1975). Evidence of the impact of inflation accounting on share prices. *Accounting and Business Research* (Spring).

Moyes, J. (1988). The dangers of JIT. *Management Accounting* (Feb.).

Newbould, A. (1970). *Management and Merger Activity* (Guthstead Press).

Pettit, R. R. (1972). Dividend announcements, security performance and capital market efficiency. *Journal of Finance* (Dec.).

Pettit, R. R. (1977). Taxes, transactions costs and clientele effects of dividends. *Journal of Financial Economics* (Dec.).

Petty, J. W. and Scott, D. F. (1981). Capital budgeting practices in large US firms. Reprinted in *Readings in Strategy for Corporate Investment*, ed. Derkinderin, F. G. J. and Crum, R. L. (1982) (Pitman Publishing).

Pike, R. H. (1982). *Capital Budgeting in the 1980s* (Institute of Cost and Management Accountants).

Pike, R. H. (1985). Owner–manager conflict and the role of the payback method. *Accounting and Business Research* (Winter).

Pike, R. H. (1992). Capital budgeting survey: an update. Bradford University Discussion Paper, cited in Pike, R. H. and Neale, C. W. (1993). *Corporate Finance and Investment* (Prentice-Hall International).

Pike, R. H. and Ooi, T. S. (1988). The impact of corporate investment objectives and constraints on capital budgeting practices. *British Accounting Review* (Aug.).

Pike, R. H. and Wolfe, M. (1988). *Capital Budgeting in the 1990s* (Chartered Institute of Management Accountants).

Puxty, A. G. and Dodds, J. C. (1991). *Financial Management; method and meaning*, 2nd edn (Chapman & Hall).

Roberts, H. (1957). Stock market patterns and financial analysis. *Journal of Finance* (Mar.).

Ross, S. A. (1976). The arbitrage theory and capital asset pricing. *Journal of Economic Theory* (Dec.).

Ross, S. A., Westerfield, R. W. and Jaffe, J. F. (1996). *Corporate Finance*, 4th edn (Irwin).

Rutterford, J. and Carter, D. (eds) (1993). *Handbook of UK Corporate Finance*, 2nd edn (Butterworth).

Ryan, R. (1995). *Strategic Accounting for Management* (The Dryden Press).

Rybczynski, T. (1989). Corporate restructuring. *National Westminster Bank Quarterly Review* (Aug.).

Samuels, J. M., Wilkes, F. and Brayshaw, R. E. (1995). *Management of Company Finance*, 6th edn (Chapman & Hall).

Scapens, R. W., Sale, J. T. and Tikkas, P. A. (1987). *Financial control of divisional capital investment* (Chartered Institute of Management Accountants).

Sharpe, W. (1963). A simplified model for portfolio analysis. *Management Science* (Jan.).

Sharpe, W. (1995). *Investments*, 5th edn (Prentice-Hall).

Sizer, J. & Coulthurst, N. (1984). *A Casebook of British Management Accounting* (Institute of Chartered Accountants in England and Wales).

Stiglitz, J. E. (1974). On the irrelevance of corporate financial policy. *American Economic Review*, vol. 64, no. 6 (Dec.).

Stock Exchange Fact Book (annually) (The International Stock Exchange, London).

Sunder, S. (1973). Relationship between accounting changes and stock prices: problems of measurement and some empirical evidence. *Journal of Accounting Research* (supplement).

Taffler, R. (1995). *The Use of the Z-Score Approach in Practice*. Available from the City University Business School, Barbican Centre, Frobisher Crescent, London EC2Y 8HB.

Watts, R. (1973). The information content of dividends. *Journal of Business* (Apr.).

Weston, J. F. (1963). A test of capital propositions. *Southern Economic Journal* (Oct.).

Weston, J. F. and Copeland, T. E. (1988). *Managerial Finance*, 2nd UK edn (Cassell).

Wilson Committee (1980). *Committee to Review the Functioning of Financial Institutions* (HMSO, London).

Wright, M., Thompson, S. and Robbie, K. (1996). The IBO is here, the MBO is back. *Accountancy* (Mar.).

APPENDIX 1

Present value table

Present value of £1 in n years at discount rate r.

Discount rate (r)

Periods (n)	1%	2%	3%	4%	5%	6%	7%	8%	9%	10%	
1	0.990	0.980	0.971	0.962	0.952	0.943	0.935	0.926	0.917	0.909	1
2	0.980	0.961	0.943	0.925	0.907	0.890	0.873	0.857	0.842	0.826	2
3	0.971	0.942	0.915	0.889	0.864	0.840	0.816	0.794	0.772	0.751	3
4	0.961	0.924	0.888	0.855	0.823	0.792	0.763	0.735	0.708	0.683	4
5	0.951	0.906	0.863	0.822	0.784	0.747	0.713	0.681	0.650	0.621	5
6	0.942	0.888	0.837	0.790	0.746	0.705	0.666	0.630	0.596	0.564	6
7	0.933	0.871	0.813	0.760	0.711	0.665	0.623	0.583	0.547	0.513	7
8	0.923	0.853	0.789	0.731	0.677	0.627	0.582	0.540	0.502	0.467	8
9	0.914	0.837	0.766	0.703	0.645	0.592	0.544	0.500	0.460	0.424	9
10	0.905	0.820	0.744	0.676	0.614	0.558	0.508	0.463	0.422	0.386	10
11	0.896	0.804	0.722	0.650	0.585	0.527	0.475	0.429	0.388	0.350	11
12	0.887	0.788	0.701	0.625	0.557	0.497	0.444	0.397	0.356	0.319	12
13	0.879	0.773	0.681	0.601	0.530	0.469	0.415	0.368	0.326	0.290	13
14	0.870	0.758	0.661	0.577	0.505	0.442	0.388	0.340	0.299	0.263	14
15	0.861	0.743	0.642	0.555	0.481	0.417	0.362	0.315	0.275	0.239	15

	11%	12%	13%	14%	15%	16%	17%	18%	19%	20%	
1	0.901	0.893	0.885	0.877	0.870	0.862	0.855	0.847	0.840	0.833	1
2	0.812	0.797	0.783	0.769	0.756	0.743	0.731	0.718	0.706	0.694	2
3	0.731	0.712	0.693	0.675	0.658	0.641	0.624	0.609	0.593	0.579	3
4	0.659	0.636	0.613	0.592	0.572	0.552	0.534	0.516	0.499	0.482	4
5	0.593	0.567	0.543	0.519	0.497	0.476	0.456	0.437	0.419	0.402	5
6	0.535	0.507	0.480	0.456	0.432	0.410	0.390	0.370	0.352	0.335	6
7	0.482	0.452	0.425	0.400	0.376	0.354	0.333	0.314	0.296	0.279	7
8	0.434	0.404	0.376	0.351	0.327	0.305	0.285	0.266	0.249	0.233	8
9	0.391	0.361	0.333	0.308	0.284	0.263	0.243	0.225	0.209	0.194	9
10	0.352	0.322	0.295	0.270	0.247	0.227	0.208	0.191	0.176	0.162	10
11	0.317	0.287	0.261	0.237	0.215	0.195	0.178	0.162	0.148	0.135	11
12	0.286	0.257	0.231	0.208	0.187	0.168	0.152	0.137	0.124	0.112	12
13	0.258	0.229	0.204	0.182	0.163	0.145	0.130	0.116	0.104	0.093	13
14	0.232	0.205	0.181	0.160	0.141	0.125	0.111	0.099	0.088	0.078	14
15	0.209	0.183	0.160	0.140	0.123	0.108	0.095	0.084	0.074	0.065	15

APPENDIX 2

Annuity table

Present value of £1 receivable at the end of each year for *n* years at discount rate r.

Discount rate (r)

Years (n)	1%	2%	3%	4%	5%	6%	7%	8%	9%	10%	
1	0.990	0.980	0.971	0.962	0.952	0.943	0.935	0.926	0.917	0.909	1
2	1.970	1.942	1.913	1.886	1.859	1.833	1.808	1.783	1.759	1.736	2
3	2.941	2.884	2.829	2.775	2.723	2.673	2.624	2.577	2.531	2.487	3
4	3.902	3.808	3.717	3.630	3.546	3.465	3.387	3.312	3.240	3.170	4
5	4.853	4.713	4.580	4.452	4.329	4.212	4.100	3.993	3.890	3.791	5
6	5.795	5.601	5.417	5.242	5.076	4.917	4.767	4.623	4.486	4.355	6
7	6.728	6.472	6.230	6.002	5.786	5.582	5.389	5.206	5.033	4.868	7
8	7.652	7.325	7.020	6.733	6.463	6.210	5.971	5.747	5.535	5.335	8
9	8.566	8.162	7.786	7.435	7.108	6.802	6.515	6.247	5.995	5.759	9
10	9.471	8.983	8.530	8.111	7.722	7.360	7.024	6.710	6.418	6.145	10
11	10.37	9.787	9.253	8.760	8.306	7.887	7.499	7.139	6.805	6.495	11
12	11.26	10.58	9.954	9.385	8.863	8.384	7.943	7.536	7.161	6.814	12
13	12.13	11.35	10.63	9.986	9.394	8.853	8.358	7.904	7.487	7.103	13
14	13.00	12.11	11.30	10.56	9.899	9.295	8.745	8.244	7.786	7.367	14
15	13.87	12.85	11.94	11.12	10.38	9.712	9.108	8.559	8.061	7.606	15

	11%	12%	13%	14%	15%	16%	17%	18%	19%	20%	
1	0.901	0.893	0.885	0.877	0.870	0.862	0.855	0.847	0.840	0.833	1
2	1.713	1.690	1.668	1.647	1.626	1.605	1.585	1.566	1.547	1.528	2
3	2.444	2.402	2.361	2.322	2.283	2.246	2.210	2.174	2.140	2.106	3
4	3.102	3.037	2.974	2.914	2.855	2.798	2.743	2.690	2.639	2.589	4
5	3.696	3.605	3.517	3.433	3.352	3.274	3.199	3.127	3.058	2.991	5
6	4.231	4.111	3.998	3.889	3.784	3.685	3.589	3.498	3.410	3.326	6
7	4.712	4.564	4.423	4.288	4.160	4.039	3.922	3.812	3.706	3.605	7
8	5.146	4.968	4.799	4.639	4.487	4.344	4.207	4.078	3.954	3.837	8
9	5.537	5.328	5.132	4.946	4.772	4.607	4.451	4.303	4.163	4.031	9
10	5.889	5.650	5.426	5.216	5.019	4.833	4.659	4.494	4.339	4.192	10
11	6.207	5.938	5.687	5.453	5.234	5.029	4.836	4.656	4.486	4.327	11
12	6.492	6.194	5.918	5.660	5.421	5.197	4.988	4.793	4.611	4.439	12
13	6.750	6.424	6.122	5.842	5.583	5.342	5.118	4.910	4.715	4.533	13
14	6.982	6.628	6.302	6.002	5.724	5.468	5.229	5.008	4.802	4.611	14
15	7.191	6.811	6.462	6.142	5.847	5.575	5.324	5.092	4.876	4.675	15

APPENDIX 3

Suggested answers to review questions

1.1 Reasons for the popularity of the limited company include the following:

- *Number of participators.* The partnership, which is the only feasible alternative, is restricted from having more than 20 participators in most cases. This limits the firm which wishes to involve large numbers of participators providing equity finance, to operating as a limited company.

- *Limited liability.* Potential equity investors are more likely to be prepared to invest where the liability for losses is limited. Thus limited companies are able to attract equity finance more easily than partnerships.

- *Perpetuity.* Limited companies continue to exist despite changes in their ownership. Thus if a shareholder transfers his or her shares, the company is strictly unaffected. When a partner leaves a partnership, the partnership comes to an end.

- *Transferability.* Linked to the previous point is the fact that shares can easily be transferred from one person to another. This means that one shareholder can sell shares to another, perhaps through the Stock Exchange.

- *Credibility.* Since most substantial firms operate as limited companies, not to do so may imply some lack of substance or permanence about the firm. This is not to say that operating as a limited company guarantees reliability, but this may, to some extent, accord with public perceptions.

1.2 In essence there is no difference between the position of a limited company and a human person, in respect of its financial obligations to others. Both are fully liable to the extent to which they have assets to meet the obligation. In both cases, under normal circumstances, the assets of third parties cannot be required to meet any shortfall between the obligation and the assets. Thus shareholders in limited companies cannot normally be asked to contribute assets to meet unsatisfied financial obligations of the company in which they own shares.

1.3 The position of the shareholders is that, so long as they have provided any funds which they have pledged to pay into the company, they cannot normally be required to make payments to cover any failure of the company to meet its financial obligations.

The owner of a sole proprietorship business (a sole trader) can be required to meet all of the debts of the business using what may be regarded as personal assets (e.g. the sole trader's house) if necessary.

Thus owners/part owners of different types of business find themselves in very different positions regarding the extent to which they risk their 'personal' assets as a result of their participation in the business.

1.4 Preference shares are part of the equity or ownership of the business, usually entitling their owners to the first portion of any dividend paid by the company, but there is no obligation for the company to pay a dividend, nor usually to redeem the preference shares.

Loan stocks represent loans made by people or investing institutions under a contract with the company concerned. The contract would normally specify the rate of interest to be paid, the date of payment of the interest and the amount and date of repayment of the principal of the loan.

Preference shares and loan stock have a superficial resemblance in that they both tend to attract a fixed annual payment and are redeemed at some point. The essential difference is that such payments are contractual and can be enforced in the case of loan stocks, but not in the case of preference shares.

1.5   Many financing and investment decisions are vitally important to the firm because they involve very significant amounts of finance over long periods of time. Thus misjudgements can have very far reaching, possibly disastrous, effects.

Of course, not all such decisions are so significant, but many tend to be.

1.6   Both theory and practice indicate that investors seek higher returns to compensate them for bearing higher risk. The required return would be a risk-free rate, plus a risk premium. The risk-free rate would normally be equal to the rate that is available for very safe investments, like short-term deposits with very safe borrowers, such as a stable government. The risk premium would relate to the perceived level of risk.

2.1   The two criteria are:

- The information must relate to the *objective(s) which is being pursued* by the decision maker. Thus if a decision needs to be made on whether to travel to a particular destination by car or by train, and the only objective being pursued is to spend the least possible time on the journey, only the time taken is relevant. The cost, level of comfort, and convenience would all be irrelevant, given the sole objective of least journey time.

- The information must be *different* between the two courses of action. Thus if the time taken is identical between car and train, the length of time is irrelevant, given the least journey time objective.

2.2   It is considered incomplete because it lacks a timescale. If the objective were to maximise accounting profit for next year, this might easily be able to be achieved by taking short-term actions which could have adverse long-term effects. For example, all research and development could be abandoned with resulting cost savings. This would be likely to have disastrous long-term effects since new products and methods would not be developed, making the firm vulnerable to losing markets to rival firms which had continued to innovate.

2.3   On the face of it, the higher the price which can be charged the better for the shareholders. However, in the medium- and long-term, such behaviour may be very adverse to the interests of the shareholders. This may manifest itself in the following ways:

- The attentions of a regulatory body concerned with monopolies, like the UK Monopolies and Mergers Commission, may be attracted. This could lead to an order to reduce prices.

- Large profits could attract other suppliers to enter the market. Not only would this lead to price competition and lower prices, but the bad public sentiment of the market towards the exploiter could well cause the market to favour the newcomers, even where the price and quality were similar.

Thus there is nothing inconsistent between reasonable treatment of customers and the best interests of the shareholders.

2.4 The separation theorem says that the investment should be undertaken if it generates a higher rate of return than the rate which the firm has to pay for its finance. Doing this will make the shareholders more wealthy.

How the investment is financed is a separate matter and, under the assumptions made by the separation theorem, unimportant. Either the dividend could be paid and money borrowed (or raised from a share issue) to make the investment, or the dividend not paid and the existing cash used to make the investment.

2.5 According to the assumptions made by the separation theorem, any dividends paid to a shareholder can be invested at the prevailing rate of interest. If the firm has to pay that same rate to borrow cash to finance an investment, the shareholder gains an amount from lending which is equal to the shareholders' share of the interest paid on cash borrowed to make the investment.

2.6 The most obvious reasons for this are:

● The firm, because it is better established in the financial market and because it would be borrowing a relatively large amount, may well be able to borrow at lower rates than could an individual shareholder borrowing a small amount.

● In the context of the UK tax system, the interest payable would be tax deductible to the firm but not to an individual shareholder.

3.1 A balance sheet is a list of assets and financial obligations of an organisation at a specified point in time. The assets are typically shown at how much they cost when they were acquired by the organisation (historic cost). Depreciating fixed assets are normally shown at cost, less some proportion of that cost depending on the anticipated useful life of the asset, and how much of that life has already expired.

Since assets are valued on the basis of their cost, the balance sheet does not provide any reliable indication as to how much the organisation is worth, in market value terms. Some assets may be overstated in the balance sheet, relative to their current economic value, some may be understated, and some assets (e.g. goodwill), which have a current economic value may not appear in the balance sheet at all because they have no cost.

3.2 The profit is the net increase in assets arising from trading activities. Net cash inflow from trading activities is the increase in cash. The difference between them arises from two broad factors:

● *Depreciation of fixed assets*, which is an expense deducted from profit, but which has no effect on cash flow.

● *Increases and decreases in stocks, debtors and creditors* which each have the effect of absorbing or releasing cash. Thus, for example, if stocks increase over the period under consideration, this additional investment means that the amount of increase in cash will be reduced.

3.3 A strong balance sheet normally means that the business is in a healthy position as regards the balance of assets and financial obligations. This usually refers to two areas:

● *Working capital.* Here the relationship between current assets, particularly the more liquid of them, and current liabilities is the issue. Thus ratios such as the current ratio and the quick assets (acid test) ratio would be fairly large in a strong balance sheet.

● *Long-term finance.* The relationship between equity capital and fixed return capital is the issue. A strong balance sheet would have a fairly modest capital gearing ratio and, probably, available assets to offer as security for further borrowings.

3.4 The matching convention says that expenses should be matched to the revenues which they helped to generate, within the same period as those revenues were realised (recognised).

3.5 This is presumably because Taffler found that it added little or nothing to the reliability of the model. This is not to say that the ratio has no value, or even that it has little or no value in trying to identify problem firms. It is probably the case that other ratios which are included in the model, and which are substantially correlated with the acid test ratio, perform better in the context of the model.

3.6 A careful reading of the accounts is certainly extremely valuable in drawing helpful conclusions about a firm. It can provide insights which ratio analysis cannot provide. Ratio analysis can, however, by formally relating one figure to another, provide insights which a normal reading of the accounts cannot provide. A major reason for this is that ratios can correct for size differences between the firms or time periods which are to be compared. Thus comparing the profit of Firm A with that of Firm B will not usually be very helpful, but comparing the profit per £1 of capital employed by Firm A with that of Firm B will usually be informative.

4.1 Discounting is intended to take account of the effective cost of using the funds in the investment project under consideration. This cost is made up of three elements:

● A 'pure' rate of interest.
● An allowance for risk.
● An allowance for inflation.

Inflation is a factor, but it is not the only reason for discounting. Discounting would need to be undertaken even where no inflation was expected over the lifetime of the project under consideration.

4.2 Opportunity cost of finance is the rate at which the firm (or, more strictly, its shareholders) could invest the funds if they were not to be used in the investment project under review. Where relevant, this would take account of the risk involved with the project.

4.3 It is the fact that NPV is unique among the four methods which are found in practice, in relating directly to the presumed objective of private sector firms to maximise the wealth of shareholders. Reliance on the other three methods will only, by coincidence, cause decisions to be taken which will work towards a wealth maximisation objective.

4.4 There seem to be two basic possibilities:

● Some users do not realise that it is flawed.

● Some users realise that it is flawed but feel that, nevertheless, it gives helpful information. Since it is easy to calculate, it is not expensive to produce, certainly not where the cash flows are to be estimated for use with, say, NPV.

4.5 IRR is flawed because it does not address the generally accepted objective of shareholder wealth maximisation. Following IRR would promote those projects which maximise the return on investment from being undertaken. Since this coincides, in most cases, with those projects which will maximise shareholder wealth, using IRR will tend to give the right signals, however.

IRR also has some anomalies, like giving more than one IRR or no IRR, but these tend not to occur with typical projects.

4.6 Possibilities include:

- Using only one method per decision, but using different methods for each type of decision, e.g. using NPV for projects involving an investment of more than £100 000, but using payback period for smaller decisions.

- Using more than one method for each decision so that a fuller picture of the decision data can be obtained.

5.1 No, it is not illogical. Profit and NPV have two entirely different objectives. Profit is concerned with assessing trading effectiveness for a period of time which is shorter than the typical investment project's life. If some allowance for the cost of using fixed assets during that accounting period is to be made, depreciation must be calculated and charged. NPV has another objective, which is to look at the effectiveness of an asset (or set of assets) over its full life. In a sense, NPV assessments do take account of depreciation since the project is charged (cash outflow) with the capital cost of the asset, normally at the beginning of the project, and given credit (cash inflow) for any disposal proceeds, normally at the end of the project.

5.2 This is not logical as discounting takes account of the financing cost of the project.

5.3 It is slightly more complicated than this. The relationship is:

1 + 'money' rate = (1 + 'real' rate) × (1 + inflation rate)

5.4 The two approaches are:

- Identify the '*money*' cash flow and discount this at the 'money' cost of capital.

- Identify the '*real*' cash flow and discount this at the 'real' cost of capital.

These two approaches are both equally valid and will give precisely the same NPV. In practice, the former tends to involve a more straightforward calculation, particularly where such complications as tax and working capital are involved.

5.5 'Hard' capital rationing arises where it is simply impossible to raise the funds to support all of the available projects. It can be argued that, in practice, funds can always be raised provided that a high enough rate of return is offered to the providers of the finance. This rate may well be too high to enable the project to be viable (i.e. it leads to a negative NPV), but this simply means that the project should not be undertaken, not that capital rationing exists.

5.6 The profitability index is a measure of a project's NPV per £1 of initial investment required. It can be useful for solving single period capital rationing problems.

It is not normally a helpful approach to dealing with multi-period capital rationing problems. This is because the profitability index may suggest one project as being the most beneficial in the context of one year's capital shortage, but a different one in the context of that of another year.

6.1 The two main limitations are:

- It assumes that only one of the variables will differ from its predicted value, i.e. it is too static. In reality they will probably all differ from prediction to some extent.

- It is difficult to interpret the results. This would be equally true even if the first limitation were overcome by using a 'scenario building' approach.

6.2 Approach 1 has the advantage in that all possible outcomes, and their probability of occurrence, can be identified. This will give you a 'feel' for the distributions of possible outcomes, or it will enable you to calculate the standard deviation.

The number of possible outcomes could, in real life, be absolutely vast which would make such an approach untenable.

Approach 2 is much more practical because it will be relatively easy to carry out the calculations. Since averages are used throughout, it is not possible to gain any 'feel' or deduce statistics about the spread of possible outcomes and, therefore, of the risk involved.

6.3 *Specific risk* is peculiar to the project, but not necessarily to other projects. Combining projects in a 'portfolio' will enable this risk to be eliminated.

Systematic risk is present in all projects, to some extent or another, and so cannot be diversified away by portfolio investment. This type of risk tends to be caused by macro-economic factors.

It is helpful to distinguish between these two types of risk because the decision maker will be able to judge the extent to which total risk can be eliminated by investing in a portfolio of projects.

6.4 Utility is a measure of the degree of satisfaction which will be derived by an individual as a result of having a particular amount of something desirable, such as wealth.

6.5 In non-technical terms, a risk-averse person will only accept risk where this is rewarded. Because such people derive a decreasing utility from each additional £1 of wealth, they require an increased reward for each additional increment of risk undertaken.

It is fairly obvious that most human beings are risk averse, certainly where more than trivial amounts are involved.

6.6 The additional risks are of two types:

- *Political risk*. This includes the risk that the foreign government may take actions which are unfavourable to the project; that law and order may collapse; that funds generated by the project may not be able to be remitted to the home country.

- *Exchange rate risk*. For example, the risk that sales projected to be made when the home currency has a particular exchange rate with the foreign currency, are in fact made at a time when a less favourable rate applies.

7.1 It needs to be assumed that returns are 'normally' distributed around the expected value, and that investors are risk-averse.

Evidence tends to suggest that investment returns from quoted securities are close to showing a 'normal' distribution. Observation also tends to show that most people are risk-averse.

7.2 The first statement is correct. The second one is not. The relationship is very much more complicated and depends, among other things, on the coefficient of correlation between the securities in the portfolio.

7.3 There is no other portfolio which will give a higher expected return for that portfolio's level of risk, and there is no other portfolio which will offer a lower level of risk for that portfolio's level of return.

7.4 It means that all rational, risk-averse investors will choose to invest their wealth in one of two ways – the market portfolio of risky investments on risk-free deposit (at the risk-free rate). The risk-free investment might be twice a negative one, i.e. borrowing, for the less risk-averse investors.

7.5 The statement is not true. The β only relates to the risk premium. Thus the risk premium of the former security will be expected to be twice that of the latter. In either case, the total return is the risk-free rate plus the risk premium.

7.6 This is justified on two grounds:

- The stock market is a free, efficient and observable market where risky investments are bought and sold. It thus provides us with the basis of price for risky investments not actually traded in that market.
- The returns from real investments made within firms feed through to the investment returns of those firms' shareholders. Thus there is a clear link between real investment returns and stock market returns.

8.1 Loan finance is risky to the borrowing firm because the firm must meet contractual obligations (normally) to pay interest and repay the principal of the borrowing on the due date. Failure to meet these obligations could cause the firm to be put into liquidation, with resulting losses to shareholders. By contrast, equity finance does not create these obligations.

8.2 If profits are paid out to shareholders as a dividend, the cash can be invested by the shareholders. If profits are retained, there is an opportunity cost to shareholders for which they will require compensation from the firm, equal to the value of that lost income.

8.3 The cost of 'raising' retained profits is zero. Unlike other forms of raising equity, no administrative or legal costs have to be paid. This makes it very cheap to raise finance by retaining profit. Also, provided that profits have been made, retained profits represent a pretty sure means of raising finance. Other ways of raising equity depend on decisions made by those to whom new shares are issued. Although the risk that investors will not buy new shares can be insured against through underwriters, the fees involved tend to be rather costly.

8.4 Except where the loan stock has just been issued, it would be unusual for the coupon rate to equal the pre-tax cost of the loan to the firm. Interest rates prevailing in the economy vary over relatively short periods of time. To cause the return from the loan stock (which is fixed as the coupon rate) to represent the market level of return, the market price of the loan stock will move away from its issue price. Also, some loan stocks are issued at a discount or redeemed at a premium on the value at which the coupon rate is calculated. In this case the 10 per cent does not represent the complete return from the loan stock.

8.5 A convertible loan stock is one which shows all of the characteristics of a pure loan stock until some pre-determined date at which loan stock holders will be offered a number of ordinary shares in the firm in exchange for their loan stock.

Factors which affect the value of loan stock include:

- The prevailing interest rates.
- The perceived riskiness of the loan stock.
- The rate of conversion (i.e. how many shares per £100 of loan stock).
- The anticipated value of the shares at the date of conversion.
- Volatility of the share price.

8.6 A firm which wishes to buy a particular fixed asset, and use borrowed funds to do so, can borrow the cash from a bank, by issuing a loan stock etc. and buy the asset. It then pays interest on the loan and at the end of the loan period repays the loan. It may be the case that the loan will be repaid piecemeal.

In the case of leasing, the firm arranges for a financier (e.g. a bank) to buy the asset outright. The firm then leases the asset from the financier for the duration of that asset's useful life. Each year the firm pays the financier an equal leasing fee. From the financier's point of view, this fee must be sufficient to compensate for the cash tied up in the asset and repay the loan. Thus a lease of this type closely resembles a loan which is repaid piecemeal over the period of the loan. If the latter is a source of finance, which undoubtedly it is, then the former must also be a source of finance.

9.1 Members of the ISE, and most other of the world's stock markets, act as:

- agents for their clients who wish to buy securities through the ISE.
- *market makers* who buy and sell securities of particular types much as any other trader does.

9.2 No. Shareholders can sell the shares as they wish. If a potential buyer can be identified, the shares can be transacted privately between the parties. The problem lies in finding a buyer. Since the ISE is the location where buyers and sellers, including ISE members in their market-making role, congregate (electronically, if not physically), this is a convenient place to sell the shares.

9.3 Price efficiency means that security prices always rationally reflect all information relevant to their value.

9.4 Yes. If the market reflects all information (public and private), it clearly reflects all public information.

9.5 Yes. Given the amount of research which is undertaken into individual firms and their economic environment, by intelligent and skilled analysts, and that the results of the research feed into decisions to buy and sell securities, we should expect that, through the pressures of buyers and sellers, prices would rationally reflect all known, relevant information. The financial rewards to investors for getting the price right are such that the pressure and incentive to do so are enormous.

9.6 Not necessarily, but wherever there is a significant amount of valid research into the securities, and there is an orderly and fair market, we should expect price efficiency to exist, at least to some extent.

10.1 The discounted value of all future cash flows which will be generated by the asset.

10.2 The approach (unless the loan stock would only generate returns for the next one or two years) would have to be to deduce the 'internal rate of return' of the loan stock by trial and error.

10.3 The level of capital gearing is such an important factor for firms that it seems likely that the benefits (tax relief) and costs (potential bankruptcy, etc.) would be carefully weighed and no target established. Even if this is not really true for smaller firms, it seems likely that larger firms will pay attention to establishing a target.

10.4 The reason is that the appropriate discount rate is the opportunity cost of capital for that particular project, which takes account of the risk involved in the project, etc. There is no reason why the cost of the particular finance just raised, bears any resemblance to the rate at which the project's cash flows need to be discounted. The suppliers of the finance will not see that they are specifically financing the project. They will see themselves as providing part of the finance for the firm as a whole.

10.5 Market values should be used because WACC is meant to represent the opportunity cost of finance. Market values reflect the cost of any new capital which the firm might raise, or the cost saving achieved by returning some finance to its providers.

10.6 No. These are both simplifying assumptions, one of which it is often expedient to make. Other assumptions could be made. Future dividends are difficult to predict, so a simple assumption is usually favoured.

11.1 There are two main reasons:
- Because loan capital is the subject of a clear contractual relationship, regarding interest payments and repayment of capital, between the lender and the firm, the risk borne by the loan stock holder is much less than the equity holder. Consequently loan stock holders do not expect such high returns.

- Loan stock interest is deductible for Corporation tax purposes, returns to shareholders are not.

11.2 It increases, to reflect the higher level of risk associated with higher gearing.

11.3 It increases, to reflect the higher level of risk associated with higher gearing. Taxes do not really make any difference.

11.4 These include costs such as:
- Any legal costs which might be involved with winding up the firm.
- Any losses arising from selling off assets at a lower value than they were worth to the firm as a going concern.
- Any loss of profits involved in trying to keep a wounded firm afloat.

11.5 We know because, in practice, nearly all firms raise part, and in many cases a substantial part, of their total finance from borrowing.

11.6 The geared firm is worth the same as the ungeared firm *plus* $(T \times D)$, where T is the firm's rate of corporation tax and D is the market value of the borrowings.

12.1 The future dividend must be equal to:

$$D_0(1 + k)^n$$

where D_0 is the present dividend, k is the shareholders opportunity cost of finance, and n is the number of years into the future that the dividend will be received.

12.2 All investments which yield a positive NPV, when discounted at the shareholders' opportunity cost of capital should be made. If any funds remain in the firm they should be paid out by way of a dividend.

12.3 A homemade dividend is a cash flow which arises from a shareholder selling a part of his/her holding as a substitute for receiving a dividend from the firm itself. A shareholder might create such a dividend where his/her individual preference for dividends did not match the firm's dividend policy.

12.4 The traditional view of dividends seems to be that dividend levels are the key determinant of share prices, and that the payment of a steady dividend enhances the market value of shares, even if good investment opportunities must be foregone to pay dividends.

12.5 The tax position of many shareholders, and to some extent of the firm itself, is affected by a decision as to whether to pay a dividend or to invest the funds. The MM 'dividend irrelevance' argument starts to weaken when taxes are taken into account.

12.6 Since creating or negating dividends by 'homemade' methods (i.e. selling or buying the firm's shares) has costs, it is often better for shareholders to hold shares in firms whose dividend policy suits their needs. The costs include dealing charges for buying and selling shares and, possibly, the tax effects of doing so.

13.1 The large amounts of investment in stocks and debtors, the funds held in cash and the amount of finance provided by trade creditors makes working capital a very important area for the average firm.

13.2 *Overtrading* is the name given to a state of affairs where the amount of finance devoted to investment in working capital is insufficient to sustain the level of activity at which the firm is operating. It can arise under any set of circumstances where this state of affairs exists, but it is often associated with a sudden and significant increase in activity.

13.3 Items of stock may lose value simply because they became less desirable. A simple case is fashion clothing which can rapidly lose appeal as fashion changes. Another example is a bought-in component which was acquired for incorporation into a product which the firm has decided not to make in the future. Note that, in both of these examples, there is no suggestion that the stock has physically deteriorated in any way.

13.4 Deficiencies include the following:
- A failure to allow for a safety level of stock, i.e. it is assumed that stock will run down to zero just as the next delivery arrives.
- The assumption is made that stock is used on a constant rate per time period.

13.5 These would include:

- Establishing the creditworthiness of the potential credit customer. If this is not a new customer, this should already have been established and reviewed.

- Ensure that the current sale will not take the customer's outstanding debt over the credit limit which has been established for that particular customer.

13.6 *Exchange rate risk* relates to the loss which can take place as a result of an adverse movement in the exchange rate between the home currency and the currency in which the sale was made. If, between the date of the sale and the date that the proceeds are converted into the home currency, the home currency gains value relative to the foreign currency, there will be a loss.

One way to manage this risk is to sell the foreign currency immediately, for delivery on the date that the debtor will pay. Another possibility is to borrow foreign currency equal in amount to the debt and immediately convert it into the home currency. When the debtor pays, the amount can immediately be used to pay off the borrowing.

14.1 *Corporate restructuring* means firms reorganising themselves in some way or another, in an attempt to meet their objectives more effectively. Thus, in principle, it is a good thing. Whether it is such a good thing in practice, is another matter.

14.2 Like any other investment, the shareholders should assess the present value of future cash flows from the existing shares with the equivalent for the shares in the 'bidder' firm. These cash flows may be difficult to predict, but this is true of all future events, to some extent or another.

14.3 The general approach is that it is up to the private sector to organise itself as it sees fit, unless the public interest is threatened. This threat may arise where a particular merger creates an effective monopoly.

14.4 In the former case, the managers who are doing the buying are not existing managers in the firm which is selling part of its operation. In the latter case, the managers work for the firm, usually in the part which is the subject of the sale.

14.5 A *sell-off* involves selling part of a firm's business, perhaps to another firm, perhaps to the managers. A *spin-off* involves dividing the existing firm's operations into two (or, possibly, more) parts by creating a new firm (or firms) to take responsibility for the spun-off part. Shareholders are given shares in this new firm (or firms) in proportion to the shares which they already own in the original firm. Thus the shareholders own the same assets, but through two (or more) separate shareholdings.

14.6 The evidence about takeovers suggests that they are not necessarily successful.

15.1 There is apparently an increasing trend towards larger firms concentrating on their *core* activities and buying in ancillary services and products from outside. This tends to create opportunities for smaller firms to establish and thrive.

15.2 Most larger firms could assume that their shareholders hold efficient (well-diversified) portfolios of shares. Thus when such firms assess projects, they can assume that shareholders do not need to be rewarded for bearing systematic risk. The shareholders of smaller firms are much less likely to hold efficient portfolios.

15.3 The real problem is finding the equivalent firm. Differences are likely to lie in differences between the two firms in the following areas:

- Activities
- Size
- Capital gearing levels
- Dividend policy (particularly relevant to the dividend yield basis of valuation).

15.4 The balance sheet provides a very unreliable basis for valuing shares. The reason is that, rightly or wrongly, the balance sheet is not intended to represent market values, either of individual assets or of the firm as a whole. The balance sheet comprises a list of where funds came from (claims) and how those funds were deployed (assets). Current asset balance sheet values tend to bear some relation to current market values, albeit with a strong bias towards understatement relative to market values. With fixed assets, there is normally little resemblance between market and balance sheet values.

15.5 The principal problem is the lack of a reliable 'exit route' available to such investors when they wish to withdraw their funds. If there is no ready market for the shares (they are not capable of being sold through the stock market) it is often a question of selling the shares to an existing shareholder or to an outsider acceptable to the other shareholders. This means that it is unlikely that the would-be departing shareholder can obtain a fair value for the shares.

15.6 Ideally, dividend policy should be based partly on the particular position of the shareholders regarding matters such as needs for a regular cash income and personal tax position. It is not practical to know the personal circumstances of all of the shareholders in the typical larger firm. With smaller firms it *is* possible to know which dividend policy most shareholders would prefer, and, therefore, to tailor dividend policy to meet their needs.

Suggested answers to selected problem questions

(Answers to the remaining problem questions are to be found in the Lecturer's Guide which accompanies this text.)

CHAPTER 3

3.1   **Counterpoint plc**

There has been a marked downturn in performance as measured both by RONA and by ROE. The proportional reduction is rather greater for ROE than it is for RONA. This difference between the reduction in RONA and ROE could be consistent with the increase in gearing in that, all other things being equal, higher gearing implies higher interest costs.

The downturn in gross margin must have been caused by an increase in the cost of sales relative to sales. (Note that this does not mean that cost of sales has increased, it may, for example have reduced but if so, sales have reduced even more.)

The fact that net margin has declined by exactly the same percentage (10 per cent) as gross margin implies that the decline in the net margin was entirely due to the decline in gross profit.

The increase in debtors' collection period is something which needs investigating. It may be a deliberate strategy to encourage trade. It is often the result of a lack of control, however. The increase in the creditors' payment period is good, because the firm is gaining more free credit than was the case last year. However, this may be at the cost of discounts for prompt payment and/or supplier goodwill.

The current ratio has declined although not necessarily to an alarming extent, given the nature of the business which probably has a fairly fast stock turnover. The quick assets ratio has also declined. This may be of concern since it could indicate weakness to potential suppliers of credit.

By general standards the debt to equity ratio looks uncomfortably large and should probably be investigated.

Some comparison with other companies in the industry would probably be very helpful. 'Internal' time series analysis is very limited in this context.

3.3   **Persona Ltd**

Table of ratios

	Last year	This year
Return on capital employed (net assets) $$\frac{\text{Net profit before long-term interest and tax}}{\text{Total assets less creditors falling due within one year}} \times 100\%$$ $$\frac{37}{185} \times 100\%$$ $$\frac{31}{190} \times 100\%$$	20.0%	16.3%
Return on equity (shareholders' funds) $$\frac{\text{Net profit after long-term interest and tax}}{\text{Share capital and reserves}} \times 100\%$$ $$\frac{16}{130} \times 100\%$$ $$\frac{6}{130} \times 100\%$$	12.3%	4.6%
Gross profit margin $$\frac{\text{Gross profit}}{\text{Sales}} \times 100\%$$ $$\frac{164}{499} \times 100\%$$ $$\frac{179}{602} \times 100\%$$	32.9%	29.7%
Net profit margin $$\frac{\text{Net profit before long-term interest and tax}}{\text{Sales}} \times 100\%$$ $$\frac{37}{499} \times 100\%$$ $$\frac{31}{602} \times 100\%$$	7.4%	5.1%
Current ratio $$\frac{\text{Current assets}}{\text{Current liabilities}}$$ $$\frac{154}{79}$$ $$\frac{181}{116}$$	1.95:1	1.56:1

	Last year	This year
Quick assets (liquid or acid test) ratio $$\frac{\text{Liquid assets}}{\text{Creditors falling due within one year}}$$ $$\frac{154-68}{79}$$ $$\frac{181-83}{116}$$	1.09:1	0.84:1
Stock holding period $$\frac{\text{Stock held}}{\text{Stock used}} \times 365$$ $$\frac{68}{335} \times 365$$ $$\frac{83}{423} \times 365$$	74 days	72 days

3.5 **Prospect plc**

Table of ratios

	Last year	This year
Return on capital employed (net assets) $$\frac{\text{Net profit before long-term interest and tax}}{\text{Total assets less creditors falling due within one year}} \times 100\%$$ $$\frac{2\,100}{10\,474} \times 100\%$$ $$\frac{4\,618}{16\,600} \times 100\%$$	20.0%	27.8%
Return on equity (shareholders' funds) $$\frac{\text{Net profit after long-term interest and tax}}{\text{Share capital and reserves}} \times 100\%$$ $$\frac{1\,248}{6\,874} \times 100\%$$ $$\frac{2\,926}{9\,000} \times 100\%$$	18.2%	32.5%

	Last year	This year
Gross profit margin $$\frac{\text{Gross profit}}{\text{Sales}} \times 100\%$$ $$\frac{6\,510}{14\,006} \times 100\%$$ $$\frac{10\,792}{22\,410} \times 100\%$$	46.5%	48.2%
Net profit margin $$\frac{\text{Net profit before long-term interest and tax}}{\text{Sales}} \times 100\%$$ $$\frac{2\,100}{14\,006} \times 100\%$$ $$\frac{4\,618}{22\,410} \times 100\%$$	15.0%	20.6%
Stockholding period $$\frac{\text{Stock held}}{\text{Stock used}} \times 365 \text{ days}$$ $$\frac{2\,418}{7\,496} \times 365$$ $$\frac{4\,820}{11\,618} \times 365$$	118 days	151 days
Debtor collection period (Days debtors) $$\frac{\text{Trade debtors}}{\text{Credit sales}} \times 365 \text{ days}$$ $$\frac{1\,614}{14\,006} \times 365$$ $$\frac{2\,744}{22\,410} \times 365$$	42 days	45 days
Current ratio $$\frac{\text{Current assets}}{\text{Current liabilities}}$$ $$\frac{4\,356}{2\,482}$$ $$\frac{7\,974}{7\,844}$$	1.76:1	1.02:1

	Last year	This year
Quick assets (liquid or acid test) ratio		
$\dfrac{\text{Liquid assets}}{\text{Creditors falling due within one year}}$		
$\dfrac{4\,356 - 2\,418}{2\,482}$	0.78:1	
$\dfrac{7\,974 - 4\,820}{7\,844}$		0.40:1
Debt to equity ratio		
$\dfrac{\text{Borrowings (long and short-term)}}{\text{Total equity}} \times 100\%$		
$\dfrac{3\,600}{6\,874} \times 100$	52.4%	
$\dfrac{7\,600 + 3\,250}{9\,000} \times 100$		120.6%

General comments

This firm has experienced a major expansion in activities over the two years. This has led to an increase in the ROCE ratio, but a ROCE in excess of the interest rate caused a greater increase in ROE, an effective use of gearing. Despite the benefits of gearing, its level is now very high, and much of it is short-term and represents a distinct risk to the firm.

The gross profit ratio increased significantly. This was accompanied by an increase in the net profit margin.

The liquidity position has weakened considerably from a healthy position to one which looks distinctly unhealthy. Stock is now turning over rather slowly compared to last year. Attention needs to be paid to liquidity and gearing, which are linked since part of the gearing comes from the overdraft.

An equity investor's perspective

This person will probably be pleased with the expansion in sales and profit; also with the effective use of gearing. The high level of gearing and the significant deterioration in liquidity are major causes of concern.

The bank's perspective

The bank will be concerned at the very weak liquidity position and the security for the overdraft. The latter should not pose a problem; there seem to be plenty of assets, though we do not know what quality they are as security, in terms of marketability.

CHAPTER 4

4.1   **Barclay plc**

	Cash flow £m	Factor	Present value £m
Year 0	(10)	$1/(1+0.15)^0$	(10.00)
1	5	$1/(1+0.15)^1$	4.35
2	4	$1/(1+0.15)^2$	3.02
3	3	$1/(1+0.15)^3$	1.97
4	2	$1/(1+0.15)^4$	1.14
		Net present value	0.48

On the basis of NPV the project should be accepted since it is positive. On the basis of discounted PBP it should be rejected because it does not pay back until year 4. For a wealth maximising firm, the latter is not important.

4.3   **Turners Ltd**

(a) NPV

	Discount factor	Machine A Cash flows £000	PV £000	Machine B Cash flows £000	PV £000
Year 0	1.000	(120)	(120.00)	(120)	(120.00)
1	0.909	40	36.36	20	18.18
2	0.826	40	33.04	30	24.78
3	0.751	40	30.04	50	37.55
4	0.683	20	13.66	70	47.81
5	0.621	40	24.84	50	31.05
	net present value		17.94		39.37

Machine B shows itself to be significantly more desirable from an economic viewpoint than does Machine A. Since both machines have a positive NPV either would be worth buying.

(b) IRR

Clearly the IRR of both machines lies well above 10 per cent (the NPV at 10 per cent is fairly large relative to the initial outlay).

For our second trial, 10 per cent (above) being the first, let us try 20 per cent.

	Discount factor	Machine A Cash flows £000	PV £000	Machine B Cash flows £000	PV £000
Year 0	1.000	(120)	(120.00)	(120)	(120.00)
1	0.833	40	33.32	20	16.66
2	0.694	40	27.76	30	20.82
3	0.579	40	23.16	50	28.95
4	0.482	20	9.64	70	33.74
5	0.402	40	16.08	50	20.10
			(10.04)		0.27

The IRR of Machine A lies below 20 per cent, but above 10 per cent. That of Machine B is just above 20 per cent. Further trials using other discount rates could be undertaken. Alternatively, a short-cut can be made to a reasonable approximation, i.e. linear interpolation.

(c) APR

	Machine A £000	Machine B £000
Outlay	120	120
Total return over years 1–5	180	220
Surplus for 5 years	60	100
ARR = Surplus /5=	12	20
ARR = (as a % of outlay)	10%	16.7%

Machine B would be selected, as the ARR (accounting rate of return) is higher.

(d) PBP

	Machine A £000	Machine B £000
Outlay	120	120
Payback period	3 years	3 years, 104 days

Machine A would be selected, as the initial outlay is repaid in a shorter period.

4.5			Cantelevellers plc			
	19X3 £000	19X4 £000	19X5 £000	19X6 £000	19X7 £000	19X8 £000
Capital cost and proceeds	(5 000)					1 000
Sales revenue		3 000	3 000	3 000	3 000	3 000
Material cost (see workings)		(510)	(620)	(570)	(570)	(570)
Lease payments	(450)	(450)	(450)	(450)	(450)	
Redundancy payments	250					(300)
Staff costs		(200)	(200)	(200)	(200)	(200)
Overheads		(200)	(200)	(200)	(200)	(200)
	(5 200)	1 640	1 530	1 580	1 580	2 730
Discount factor	1.000	0.870	0.756	0.658	0.572	0.497
Present values	(5 200)	1 426.8	1 156.7	1 039.6	903.8	1 356.8
Net present value	£683.70					

On the basis of the project's NPV, the project should be undertaken.

Workings

1 Annual material cash flows

19X4

First 500 units	
£380 – 120 = £260/unit	
500 × £260 =	£130 000
Other 1000 units	
1000 × £380 =	380 000
	£510 000

19X5

Opportunity cost of C15s	
500 × £100 =	£50 000
Purchase of components	
1500 × £380 =	570 000
	£620 000

19X6
    1500 × £380 =   £570 000

19X7
    1500 × £380 =   £570 000

19X8
    1500 × £380 =   £570 000

CHAPTER 5

5.1   **Dodd Ltd**

	19X1 £000	19X2 £000	19X3 £000	19X4 £000	19X5 £000
Investment and residual value*	(250)			58	
Annual cash flows*		168	176	116	
Tax on annual cash flows (25%)			(42)	(44)	(29)
	(250)	168	134	130	(29)
Discounted at 15.5% (see below)	(250)	146	100	84	(16)
NPV	64				

* Subject to inflation.

Discount rate

$$(1 + r_m) = (1 + r_r)(1 + i)$$

Where r_m = the 'money' discount rate
        r_r = the 'real' discount rate
        i = the rate of inflation

$$r_m = (1 + 0.05)(1 + 0.10) - 1$$
$$r_m = 0.155 \text{ or } 15.5\%$$

5.4   **Livelong Ltd**

Calculation of present cost of operating the machine for its expected life.

	Machine Alpha £	Machine Beta £
Initial cost	50 000	90 000
Salvage value 5000 × 0.683	(3 415)	
7000 × 0.513		(3 591)
Annual running costs		
10 000 × 3.170	31 700	
8 000 × 4.868		38 944
Present cost (a)	78 285	125 353
Annuity factor (b)	3.170	4.868
Equivalent annual value (a)/(b)	£24 696	£25 750

Where the equivalent annual cost of A the same as B, then the present cost of operating A for four years would be £81 628 (i.e. £25 750 × 3.170). Thus the initial cost would be £53 343 (i.e. £81 628 – 31 700 + 3415), so the increase would be £3343.

5.5   **Mega Builders plc**

(a) 'Money' cost of salaries, wages and materials

'Real' cost (p.a.) = £1.3m + 2.5 + 0.25 = £4.05m

19X6	£4.05m × 1.03 = £4.172m
19X7	£4.05m × 1.03 × 1.04 = £4.338m

Plant

	£000	*Tax effect (and date)*
Cost (19X4)	6 000	
199X WDA (25%)	1 500	
	4 500	
199X proceeds	2 500	
Balancing allowance	2 000	@ 33% = £660 000 (31 Dec. 19X6)
	OR	
WDV at 31 Dec. 19X5	4 500	
Additions	100	
	4 600	
19X5 WDA (25%)	1 150	@ 33% = £379 500 (31 Dec. 19X6)
	3 450	
19X6 WDA (25%)	862.5	@ 33% = £284 625 (31 Dec. 19X7)
	2 587.5	
19X6 proceeds	zero	
Balancing allowance	2 587.5	@ 33% = £853 875 (31 Dec. 19X8)

Tax on incremental cash flows

Total incremental cost (excluding depreciation) = £4.172m + 4.338 = £8.510m
$\frac{1}{3}$ thereof = £2.837m
Tax charge (£4.500m − 2.837) @ 33% = £0.549m

'Money' discount rate

19X6 = 1/(1.00 + 0.10) × (1.00 + 0.03) = 0.8826
19X7 = 0.8826 × 1/(1.00 + 0.10) × (1.00 + 0.04) = 0.7715
19X8 = 0.7715 × 1/(1.00 + 0.10) × (1.00 + 0.05) = 0.6680
19X9 = 0.6680 × 1/(1.00 + 0.10) × (1.00 + 0.05) = 0.5783

Schedule of 'MONEY' cash flows

31 December	19X5 £m	19X6 £m	19X7 £m	19X8 £m	19X9 £m
Contract price	—	4.500	4.500	4.500	—
Incremental costs	—	(4.172)	(4.338)	—	—
Plant and capital allowances	(2.500)	(0.660)	0.285	0.854	—
	(0.100)	0.380			
Tax			(0.549)	(0.549)	(0.549)
	(2.600)	(0.048)	(0.102)	4.805	(0.549)
PV	(2.600)	0.042	(0.079)	3.210	(0.317)
NPV	0.256				

Thus the contract would be financially advantageous to BC at £13.5m.

If the contract price were £12m, the differential 'money' cash flows would be as follows:

31 December	19X6 £m	19X7 £m	19X8 £m	19X9 £m
Lower contract receipts	(0.500)	(0.500)	(0.500)	—
Lower tax charge		0.165	0.165	0.165
	(0.500)	(0.335)	(0.335)	0.165
PV	(0.441)	(0.258)	(0.224)	0.095
NPV	(0.828)			

NPV at a contract price of £12.0m = 0.256 − 0.828 = (0.572)

'Break-even' contract price = £13.5m − ((13.5m − 12.0m) × (0.572/(0.256 + 0.828)) = £12.463m or 3 instalments of £4.154m each.

Possible 'other factors' include:

- The small margin of safety means that the success of the contract will be sensitive to the accuracy of the input data.
- Civil engineering tends to be a fairly risky activity since outcomes are difficult to predict.
- In the long run, the contract price must bear head office costs.
- Precedent for future contracts.
- Level of competition in the market.
- The contract size, relative to the size of the firm.

CHAPTER 6

6.1   Easton Ltd

Different cash flows of Machine A

		2000 demand £	3000 demand £	5000 demand £
Year 0		(15 000)	(15 000)	(15 000)
1	(£4–£1)/unit	6 000	9 000	15 000
2		6 000	9 000	15 000
3		6 000	9 000	15 000
Discounted: Factor		£	£	£
Year 0	(1.00)	(15 000)	(15 000)	(15 000)
1	(0.94)	5 640	8 460	14 100
2	(0.89)	5 340	8 010	13 350
3	(0.84)	5 040	7 560	12 600
		1020	9 030	25 050

Expected value = (0.2 × 1020) + (0.6 × 9030) + (0.2 × 25 050)
= £10 632

Differential cash flows of Machine B

		2000 demand £	3000 demand £	5000 demand £
Year 0		(20 000)	(20 000)	(20 000)
1	(£4–£0.5)/unit	7 000	10 500	17 500
2		7 000	10 500	17 500
3		7 000	10 500	17 500
Discounted: Factor		£	£	£
Year 0	(1.00)	(20 000)	(20 000)	(20 000)
1	(0.94)	6 580	9 870	16 450
2	(0.89)	6 230	9 345	15 575
3	(0.84)	5 880	8 820	14 700
		(1 310)	8 035	26 725

Expected value = $(0.2 \times (1310)) + (0.6 \times 8035) + (0.2 \times 26\,725)$
        = £9 904

A more direct route to expected values would be to take the 'expected' demand [$(0.2 \times 2000) + (0.6 \times 3000) + (0.2 \times 5000) = 3200$] and then find the NPV assuming that level of demand.

6.2   Easton Ltd

(a) The expression for the NPV may be put as follows:

$$\text{NPV} = D(S - V)A_n^r - I$$

Where D is annual demand (in units)
     S is the selling price per unit
     V is the variable cost per unit
     A_n^r is the annuity factor at rate r over n years
and I is the initial investment

Thus NPV = $(2000(4 - 1)2.673) - 15\,000$
        = £1038

Since the NPV is a significant positive figure the machine should be acquired.

(b) Sensitivity analysis

(i) *Annual demand*
This requires setting NPV at zero, putting in all inputs except annual demand and solving for annual demand

i.e. $(D(4 - 1)2.673) - 15\,000 = 0$

$$D = \frac{15\,000}{3 \times 2.673} = 1871 \text{ units}$$

(ii) *Selling price per unit*

$2000(S - 1)2.673 = 15\,000$

$$S = \frac{15\,000}{2000 \times 2.673} + 1 = £3.806$$

(iii) *Variable cost per unit*

$2000(4 - v)2.673 = 15\ 000$

$$v\frac{-15\ 000}{2000 \times 2.673} + 4 = \underline{\underline{£1.194}}$$

(iv) *Discount rate*

$2000(4 - 1)A_3^r = 15\ 000$

$$A_3^r = \frac{15\,000}{6000} = \underline{\underline{2.500}}$$

Looking at the annuity table for the 3 years row, 2.5 lies between 9 per cent and 10 per cent, nearer to 10 per cent, so say $\underline{\text{10 per cent}}$.

(v) *Years of the project*

$A_n^6 = 2.500$ (from (iv) above)

Looking down the 6 per cent column in the annuity table, 2.5 lies between 2 and 3 years, nearer to 3 years, so say 3 years.

(vi) *Initial investment*

$I = 2000(4 - 1)2.673$

$= \underline{\underline{£16\ 038}}$

Table of Sensitivities

Factor	Original estimate	Breakeven point	Difference	Difference as % original
D	2000 units	1871 units	129 units	6%
S	£4	£3.806	£0.194	5%
V	£1	£1.194	£0.194	19%
r	6%	10%	4%	67%
n	3 years	3 years	0 years	0%
I	£15 000	£16 038	£1038	7%

Note that *r* and *n* could be found with considerably more accuracy (if this were thought to be useful) by linear interpolation.

6.5 **High Fido plc**

(a) *Cash flows*

	1996 £000	1997 £000	1998 £000	1999 £000	2000 £000
Plant	(1000)				
Tracker sales		2160	2208	1104	
Materials cost		(756)	(773)	(386)	
Additional labour		(97)	(99)	(50)	
Lost Repro contributions		(432)	(442)	(221)	
Management	120	(48)	(48)	(188)	
Working capital	(243)	(5)	124	124	
Taxation		43	(211)	(233)	54
	(1123)	865	759	150	54
Discounted at 8%	(1123)	801	651	119	40

NPV = $\underline{\underline{488}}$ (positive)

On the basis of this analysis, the project should go ahead.

Expected sales

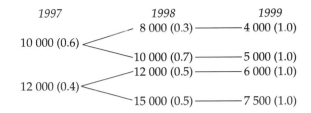

	1997	1998	1999

1997

$(10\ 000 \times 0.6) + (12\ 000 \times 0.4) = 10\ 800\ (\times £200) = \underline{\underline{£2\ 160\ 000}})$

1998

$(8000 \times 0.6 \times 0.3) + (10\ 000 \times 0.6 \times 0.7) + (12\ 000 \times 0.4 \times 0.5) + (15\ 000 \times 0.4 \times 0.5)$
$= 11\ 040\ (\times £200) = \underline{\underline{£2\ 208\ 000}})$

1999

$11\ 040 \times 0.5\ (\times £200) = \underline{\underline{£1\ 104\ 000}})$

Additional labour
Hours required per pair of Trackers = 3
Hours released per pair of Repros = 4
Additional hours required per pair of Repros = 3 – (4/2) = 1, paid at £6 × 150% = £9

Effective loss of contribution per Repro sale
For each unit lost = £100 – 20 = £80.

Capital allowances

1996	£000
Cost	1000
WDA (25%)	250

1997	
Brought down	750
WDA (25%)	188

1998	
Brought down	562
WDA (25%)	140

1999	
Brought down	422
Disposal proceeds	zero*
Balancing allowance	422

* This assumes that the project is abandoned after three years.

Taxation

	1996 £000	1997 £000	1998 £000	1999 £000
Tracker sales		2160	2208	1104
Materials		(756)	(773)	(386)
Additional labour		(97)	(99)	(50)
Lost Repro sales		(432)	(442)	(221)
Management	120	(48)	(48)	(188)
Capital allowances	(250)	(188)	(140)	(422)
	(130)	639	706	(163)
Tax at 33%	(43)*	211	233	(54)

* This assumes that there are sufficient taxable profits elsewhere in the company to set the negative figure in 1996.

Working capital

	1997 £000	1998 £000	1999 £000
Tracker sales revenues	2160	2208	1104
Lost Repro sales	(540)	(552)	(276)
Net increase in sales	1620	1656	828
15% thereof	243	248	124

CHAPTER 7

7.1

Specific risk factors might include:

- The possible loss of business arising from the opening of the channel tunnel.
- Decline in trade between the UK and Western Europe.
- A loss of interest in UK residents taking holidays in Western Europe.
- Bad publicity arising from an accident involving one of the company's vessels.

Systematic risk factors might include:

- Levels of interest rates.
- Fuel prices.
- Levels of demand in the economy.

7.4 Court plc

(a)

		r_m	$r_m - \bar{r}_m$	$(r_m - \bar{r}_m)^2$	r_i	$r_i - \bar{r}_i$	$(r_i - \bar{r}_m)(r_i - \bar{r}_i)$
Year	1	.13	.07	.0049	.19	.12	.0096
	2	(.07)	(.13)	.0169	(.08)	(.15)	.0195
	3	(.13)	(.19)	.0361	(.12)	(.19)	.0361
	4	.04	(.02)	.0004	.03	(.04)	.0008
	5	.08	.02	.0004	.08	.01	.0002
	6	.10	.04	.0016	.17	.10	.0040
	7	.15	.09	.0081	.14	.07	.0063
	8	.16	.10	.0100	.14	.07	.0070
	9	.16	.10	.0100	.14	.07	.0070
	10	(.02)	(.08)	.0064	.01	(.06)	.0048

$$\sum r_m = .60 \qquad \sum (r_m = \bar{r}_m) \ \ .0948 \qquad .70 = \qquad \sum r_i \qquad .0953 =$$

$$\bar{r}_m = \frac{.60}{.10} \qquad\qquad \bar{r} = \frac{.70}{.10} \qquad \sum (r_m = \bar{r}_m)(r_i = \bar{r}_i)$$

$$= \ .06 \qquad\qquad\qquad = \ .07$$

$$\text{Var}(r_m) = \frac{.0948}{10 - 1} = 0.0105$$

$$\text{Cov}(r_i r_m) = \sum \frac{(r_m - \bar{r}_m)\ (r_i - \bar{r}_i)}{10 - 1} = \frac{0.953}{9} = \underline{\underline{0.0106}}$$

$$\beta = \frac{\text{Cov}(r_i r_m)}{\text{Var}(r_m)} = \frac{0.0106}{0.0105} = \underline{\underline{1.0}}$$

(b) Since Court's β is 1.0, irrespective of the risk-free rate, if the expected return from equities generally is 12 per cent, then the expected return from Court will also be 12 per cent.

CHAPTER 8

8.1

The reasons for the relative popularity of convertible loan stocks include the following factors:

- They might be easier to issue than equity, in terms of acceptability to potential investors, because they are a loan stock as long as the stockholder wishes them to be, yet they can be converted to equity if it is beneficial to the stockholder to do so. Thus their value is underpinned by their value as a pure loan stock, yet they have 'upside' potential because, in effect, they bestow the right to buy equity at a pre-determined price.
- The firm may prefer to issue loan stocks to gain advantage from the tax relief on interest, but may find it hard to do so if investors seek investments with more potential for capital gains.

8.2

In essence financial claims fall into two types: *equity* and *debt*. As will be explored in some detail in Chapter 11, each one has its attractions from the firm's (i.e. as represented by its existing shareholders) point of view. One of the reasons for having some claims which are, in essence, equity and some which are basically debt, is that it enables the firm to strike the appropriate balance. This does not really explain the wide diversity of equity and debt 'instruments' used by firms.

The major reason for firms going beyond simple equity and debt is generally to try to meet the precise investment requirements of a variety of potential investors. This is much the same as a shoe shop stocking a range of different styles and sizes of footwear. By doing this it can appeal to the needs and tastes of a wide variety of customers. Firms which limit their financial instruments to two, will find it much more difficult to raise finance than those firms who can offer investors something which caters more precisely to their needs and tastes.

8.4   Memphis plc

Pre-contract announcement value of the firm	20m × £1.20	£24m
NPV of the contract		4
Pre-rights value of the firm		28
Rights issue (number of shares = £10m/£0.80)	12.5	10
Post rights value of the firm	32.5	38
Ex-rights price per share	£38m/32.5m =	£1.1692

The right to buy one of the new shares would theoretically cost £0.3692 each, because a buyer could pay this amount for the right to pay the firm a further £0.80 and obtain a share worth £1.1692.

CHAPTER 9

9.1 XYZ plc

The statement implies that the person making it has superior knowledge than do those who by their actions, i.e. buying and selling, in the stock market influence share prices. Evidence on the efficiency of the capital market, cited in Chapter 9, suggests that this is only likely to be true if the person making the statement has 'inside' information. Otherwise the evidence shows that the market knows best on average.

9.2

CME does not imply that all investors know all that there is to know about all securities traded in the market. It does not even imply that any individual investor knows all that there is to know about any particular security. CME simply implies that the current market price of a security at any given moment reflects a consensus view of the security and therefore reflects all information which is known by investors.

9.3

If the market is efficient in the semi-strong form, then all published information is impounded in the price of securities. The statement refers to unpublished information and for it to be true that this is impounded in the share price would require that the market is strong-form efficient. Evidence shows the ISE to be semi-strong, but not strong-form efficient. Thus the statement is incorrect.

CHAPTER 10

10.1 Gregoris plc

$$104 = \frac{8}{(1+k_L)^1} + \frac{8}{(1+k_L)^2} + \frac{8}{(1+k_L)^3} + \frac{108}{(1+k_L)^4}$$

This looks like a return of a little below 8% because the stock with an 8% 'coupon' is worth more than £100. Try 7%:

$$104 = \frac{8}{(1+0.07)^1} + \frac{8}{(1+0.07)^2} + \frac{8}{(1+0.07)^3} + \frac{108}{(1+0.07)^4}$$

$$= 7.48 + 6.99 + 6.53 + 82.39 = 103.39$$

i.e. k_L is very close to 7%.

10.3 **Fortunate plc**

Summarised prospective profit and loss account for each future year

	£ million
Profit before interest and tax	9.0
Less: Debenture interest	1.2
	7.8
Less: Taxation (50%)	3.9
Profit after interest and tax	3.9
Less: Preference dividend	0.5
Profit attributable to Ordinary shareholders	3.4

Cost of debentures = 12% before tax

$$\text{Cost of preference shares} = \frac{£0.5\text{m}}{(5\text{m} \times £0.65)} \times 100\% = 15.4\%$$

$$\text{Cost of ordinary shares} = \frac{£3.4\text{m}}{(8\text{m} \times 2 \times £0.80)} \times 100\% = 26.6\%$$

Weighted average cost of capital

$$= \frac{(£12\% \,(1 - 0.50) \times £10\text{m}) + (15.4\% \times 5\text{m} \times £0.65) + (26.6\% \times 8\text{m} \times 2 \times £0.80)}{£10\text{m} + (5\text{m} \times £0.65) + (8\text{m} \times 2 \times £0.80)}$$

$$= \frac{£0.6\text{m} + £500\,500 + £3\,404\,800}{£10\text{m} + £3.25\text{m} + £12.8\text{m}}$$

$$= \frac{£4\,505\,300}{£26\,050\,000}$$

$$= \underline{\underline{17.3\%}}$$

10.5 **Da Silva plc**

19X1	$(0.0900 - 0.0800)/0.0800 = 0.125$
19X2	$(0.1050 - 0.0900)/0.0900 = 0.167$
19X3	$(0.1125 - 0.1050)/0.1050 = 0.071$
19X4	$(0.1250 - 0.1125)/0.1125 = 0.111$
19X5	$(0.1350 - 0.1250)/0.1250 = 0.080$
19X6	$(0.1450 - 0.1350)/0.1350 = 0.074$
19X7	$(0.1550 - 0.1450)/0.1450 = 0.069$
Sum	0.697
Arithmetic mean	10%

(The mean could be calculated from the more recent data and/or a weighting used)

$$k_e = [d_0(1 + g)/V_0] + g$$

$$k_e = [£0.1550\,(1 + 0.1)/2.75] + 0.10$$

$$k_e = 16.2\%$$

$$\text{WACC} = \frac{(£5.5\text{m} \times 16.2\%) + (£1.5\text{m} \times 10\% \times (1 - 0.33))}{£5.5\text{m} + £1.5\text{m}} = 14.2\%9$$

The main assumption being made in the estimation of the WACC figure is that past experience is a good guide to the future. More specifically:

- That the risk of the proposed investment is similar to the average risk of the firm's recent past activities.
- That past dividend growth is similar to future prospects. This seems a dubious assumption in this particular case since the dividend growth rate has been very erratic from one year to the next.
- That future interest and tax rates are likely to be similar to current ones.

CHAPTER 11

11.1   Shiraz plc

According to MM:

$$E(r_{EG}) = E(r_{EE}) + (E(r_{EE}) - r_L) L_G)/S_G$$

Where $E(r_{EG})$ = the cost of equity in the geared firm
$E(r_{EE})$ = the cost of equity in the all equity firm
r_L = the cost of loan finance
L_G = the value of loan stock in the geared firm
S_G = the value of equity in the geared firm

Thus in the case of Shiraz plc:

$$20\% = E(r_{EE}) + (E(r_{EE}) - 10\%) \pounds14m/(10m \times \pounds2.40)$$
$$1.583 \, E(r_{EE}) = 20\% + 5.833\%$$
$$E(r_{EE}) = 16.3\%$$

The share price would be identical (£2.40) because the lower risk attaching to the returns in the all-equity firm would be exactly compensated by lower returns as a result of the absence of the cheap loan finance.

11.3   Particulate plc

According to Modigliani and Miller (MM) the value of a geared firm (V_G) is equal to the value of the equivalent all equity financed (V_U) firm *plus* the value of the, so called, tax shield provided by the tax relief on loan interest (*TD*).

i.e. $V_G = V_U + TD$

Thus for Particulate plc:

$$V_G = \pounds35m + (\pounds8m \times 0.33) = \underline{\pounds37.64m}$$

This is made up of £8m loan finance and £29.64m equity.
Expected equity earnings are expected to be constant as follows:

	£m
Annual earnings after tax £35m × 20%	7.00
Add: Tax £7.00m × 33/67	3.45
Annual earnings before tax	10.45
Less: Interest (£8m × 10%)	0.80
	9.65
Less: Tax at 33%	3.18
Available for shareholders	£6.47m

$k_e = 6.47/29.64 \times 100\% = \underline{21.8\%}$

The weighted average cost of capital (WACC)

$$= \frac{(21.8 \times 29.64 + [10 \times (1 - 0.33) \times 8]}{29.64 + 8} = \underline{\underline{18.6\%}}$$

Thus WACC has decreased from 20 per cent to 18.6 per cent as a result of introducing the debt finance. At the same time the cost of equity has increased from 20 per cent to 21.8 per cent as a result of the increased risk which shareholders will have to bear.

11.5   Ali plc

Return on equity earned by the firm = $(12.80/(10 \times 4 \times 1.60) \times 100\% = 20\%$.

Assuming that the same level of return is earned on the additional finance, after the rights issue, Lee's investment in the firm would be:

Original investment	10 000 × £1.60	£16 000
Rights issue	(10 000/4) × £1.20	3 000
		19 000

After the expansion, by either means, the pre-interest profit of the firm would be $20\% \times [(10\text{m} \times 4 \times £1.60) + (2.5\text{m} \times 4 \times 1.20)] = £15.2\text{m}$. Therefore the dividend per share = 15.2/50 = £0.304.

(a) Personal borrowing

Lee's dividend after the issue = 12 500 × £0.304 –		£3800
Less: Interest = 10% × £3000		300
		£3500

(b) The firm borrowing

Firm profit (pre-interest)		£15.2m
Less: Interest = 10% × £12.0m =		1.2
		£14.0m
Earnings and dividend per share = £14.0m/50m =	£0.28	
Lee's income = 12 500 × £0.28 =		£3500

Thus Lee's income is identical for identical risk. Since 'homemade' gearing is a perfect substitute for corporate gearing, logically investors will not pay a premium to invest in geared equities. Thus the cost of capital will be independent of the level of gearing, subject to the MM assumptions.

CHAPTER 12

12.1   Distributors plc

The dividend will need to be such that its present value, discounted at the shareholders' opportunity cost of capital, is £25 million.
    That is:

$$£25\text{m} \times (1 + 0.20)^3 = £43.20\text{m}$$

    Together with the normal dividend of £25 million makes a total of £68.20 million.
    If the payoff were to be more than £43.20 million the shareholders would, in theory, prefer the investment to be made. If the payoff were to be less than this amount the shareholders would prefer the immediate dividend of £25 million.

12.3   HLM plc

The equity cost of capital is $1.5/10 \times 100\% = 15\%$ p.a.

In effect, the investment amounts to two outlays of £1.0 million after one year and two years respectively, and an annual inflow of £0.4 million in perpetuity starting after three years.

The NPV (in £m) of this investment is:

$$-\frac{1.0}{(1+0.15)} - \frac{1.0}{(1+0.15)^2} + \frac{0.4/0.15}{(1+0.15)^2} = -0.870 - 0.756 + 2.016$$

= £0.39 million increase in the value of the firm or a 3.9 pence increase in the value of each share.

12.5   Images plc

NPVs of projects

I	$-2.00 + (0.75 \times 2.283)$	$= -0.288$
II	$-2.00 + (0.65 \times 3.352)$	$= +0.179$
III	$-3.00 + (0.80 \times 3.352)$	$= -0.318$
IV	$-1.00 + (0.50 \times 2.283)$	$= +0.142$

Thus logically the cash generated from profits should be invested in projects II and IV, a total investment of £3m. This would leave £2m to be distributed as a dividend, since the shareholders can employ the cash more effectively than can the firm. This assumes that shareholders are indifferent between receiving dividends and the firm investing available cash at the relevant cost of capital.

Other factors
MM said that since the profits belong to the shareholders they will be indifferent as to whether they receive a dividend or whether the firm retains the assets concerned, all other things being equal. Thus provided that the firm can invest the funds at a rate above that which is available to the shareholders, the shareholders will prefer the firm to invest these funds rather than to pay dividends. If the firm can only achieve an investment return equal to the rate available to shareholders on investments made outside the firm, shareholders will be indifferent as to whether they receive a dividend or whether the firm invests the available funds. Only where the firm cannot achieve investment returns as high as the shareholders can achieve by investing outside the firm, will the shareholders have a positive preference for dividends. This means that, in theory, the firm's management should make all investments which yield a positive NPV when discounted at the opportunity cost of capital, up to a maximum of the funds available. Any funds which the firm cannot invest at the opportunity cost of capital should be returned to the shareholders as dividends, enabling shareholders to make their own investments. Thus the level of dividends is a residual, i.e. what is left after the firm has made all of the beneficial investments available. In the case of Images the dividend should be what is left after making the two advantageous investments (II and IV).

This assumes that the shareholders will always wish to invest all of their wealth. In fact they may wish to consume some of it, and may find the level of dividends paid by the firm insufficient for their consumption requirements. MM argued that any shareholder who wished to consume could sell as many shares as necessary to provide the cash required for consumption. It can easily be shown that such shareholders will be better off by the firm investing in projects II and IV because the price of the shares will be enhanced by making these investments, meaning that shareholders will need to sell a lesser number of shares to produce the amount of cash which they wish to consume.

The following points also need to be raised:

- *Availability of cash.* Profit does not equal cash. Given the firm's steady level of profit, however, net cash inflows should exceed profit, unless there has been new investment in fixed or current assets or a net repayment of finance.

- *Clientele effect.* It is claimed by some people that investors are attracted to buy the shares in one firm or another because of its dividend policy. Thus many of the shareholders of Images plc may be attracted by the generous dividend policy. If this is now altered these shareholders may feel disadvantaged. As MM pointed out, it is open to these shareholders to create 'dividends' by selling some of their shares. However dealing charges are not trivial in amount and a disposal of some shares could trigger a Capital Gains Tax charge, which would otherwise be delayed or even avoided.

   This means that a change in the dividend policy of Images plc could be disadvantageous to its shareholders. This might outweigh the advantage to the shareholders of the firm investing in projects II and IV. The shareholders' best interests may lie with Images paying the usual level of dividend and investing the balance of available funds.

- *Taxation.* Dividends are subject to Income Tax, whereas retained profit, leading to higher share prices, attracts Capital Gains Tax. Though the legislation has sought recently to equalise the effect of these two taxes in the UK, there are still significant differences between them. Perhaps the most important of these is the fact that Capital Gains only come within the scope of taxation when the shares are disposed of, whereas the tax on dividends bites when the dividend is paid.

- *Informational effect of dividends.* It is argued by some people that directors of companies use dividend payment levels as a device to signal information to the outside world. It is claimed that high dividend payments signal confidence in the future of the firm while small payments signal a lack of confidence. If it is true that small dividends will be interpreted by the market as a sign of an uncertain future, then the fact that Images plc is paying a smaller than usual dividend could have an adverse effect on the wealth of its shareholders.

CHAPTER 13

13.1   **Dixon plc**

(a)

$$E = \sqrt{\frac{2AC}{H}}$$

Where E is the economic order quality
             A is the annual usage
             C is the cost of placing each order
     and H is the annual holding cost of one unit

$$\text{i.e. } E = \sqrt{\frac{2 \times 23\,000 \times £50}{£1.50}}$$

$$= \sqrt{1\,533\,333} = 1\,238.3 \text{ units}$$

so orders should be placed of 1238 or 1239 units, but since the round figure of 1250 is not too far away, orders of that size would probably be placed.

(b) During the three week lead time $1/52 \times 23\,000 = 442$ units would be used, so the order must be placed when the stock is no lower than 442 units if 'stock outs' are to be avoided.

13.3   Arcadia Ltd

Cash budget for six months to June

		January £	February £	March £	April £	May £	June £
Receipts from debtors		2 800	3 200	3 200	4 000	4 800	5 200
Receipts from cash sales		4 800	6 000	7 200	7 800	8 400	9 600
	(A)	7 600	9 200	10 400	11 800	13 200	14 800
Outflows							
Payments to creditors		4 000	4 800	4 800	5 600	6 000	6 000
Wages etc.		3 000	3 600	3 600	4 200	4 500	4 500
Advertising		1 000	—	—	1 500	—	—
Salaries etc. 80%		1 280	1 280	1 280	1 280	1 600	1 600
20%		280	320	320	320	320	400
Fixed assets acquired		—	—	2 000	2 000	2 000	—
Dividend		—	—	—	600	—	—
	(B)	9 560	10 000	12 000	15 500	14 420	12 500
Surplus/deficit for the month (A–B)		(1 960)	(800)	(1 600)	(3 700)	(1 220)	2 300
(Cumulative surplus/deficit)		5 540	4 740	3 140	(560)	(1 780)	520

13.5   North Anglia Engineering Ltd

Optimum level of stock holding

Firms hold stocks to the extent that the financial benefits of holding stock are outweighed by those of not holding stock to the maximum extent.

The costs of holding stock include:

- *The cost of financing the stock.* Finance is tied up in stock.
- *Storage costs.* Storing stock costs money. If the stock is valuable or fragile these costs could be considerable.
- *Insurance costs.* Stock would normally be insured against losses and damage.
- *Obsolescence costs.* Items of stock may become obsolescent during the stockholding period. This may seriously reduce their value.

The costs of holding insufficient stock include:

- *Loss of customer goodwill.* If a customer cannot be supplied from stock that customer may go elsewhere, never to return.
- *Production dislocation.* Running out of a stock line may mean that production has to cease which can be very expensive in terms of lost production time and other production costs.
- *Loss of flexibility.* Holding very low stocks makes it difficult for the firm to respond rapidly to an opportunity to increase output to meet an unexpected demand or to engage in large production runs which could yield economies of scale.

Reasons for large stock levels

The points which should be investigated in an attempt to identify the reason for large stock levels include the following:

- *Optimum order quantities.* Does the firm use any technique for deducing the optimum size of order or manufacturing batch?
- *Stock re-order levels.* Are there established stock re-order levels for each stock line such that a new order is triggered when the re-order level is reached?
- *Budgets.* Are stock requirements carefully planned and budgeted?
- *Reliable stock records.* Is there reliable information available on a day-to-day basis which provides a basis for decisions relating to stock management?
- *Ratios.* Are ratios such as stock turnover systematically used to monitor stock levels, both generally and in respect of particular stock lines?
- *Security and authorisation.* Are there clear rules established surrounding the authority to order and issue stock?

CHAPTER 14

14.1   ABB plc and CDD Ltd

Pre-merger value of ABB plc = £12m/20% = £60m
Post-merger value of ABB plc = £60m + £27.5m = £87.5m
Estimated rate of return = £14m/£87.5m × 100% = 16%

14.3   Thruster plc and Relaxation plc

Pre-takeover price per share of Thruster plc	
EPS = 48/(170 × 2) =	£0.1412
Price per share = £0.1412 × 18	£2.5412
Pre-takeover price per share of Relaxation plc	
EPS = 11/(90 × 2) =	£0.0611
Price per share = £0.0611 × 14	£0.8556
Price for three shares 3 × £0.8556 =	£2.5668

Combined after tax earnings of the post-takeover firm:	*£m*
Pre-takeover earnings of Thruster plc	48
Pre-takeover earnings of Relaxation plc	11
Cost savings	8
Total earnings	67

Number of shares	*shares (m)*
Pre-takeover shares of Thruster plc (170 × 2)	340
Shares issued to Relaxation plc shareholders ((90 × 2)/3)	60
Total shares	400

Earnings per share = £67m/400 =	£0.1675
At new PE ratio each share is worth £0.1675 × 16	£2.68

Thus, on the assumption that share price was the only criterion, both sets of shareholders would welcome the takeover since both will be better off.

CHAPTER 15

15.1   Tiny Tim Ltd and Mega plc

$$\text{Price earnings ratio} = \frac{\text{market price of a firm (or single share)}}{\text{after-tax earnings of the firm (or a single share)}}$$

OR

Market price of a firm = price earnings ratio × after-tax earnings of the firm

Market price of Tiny Tim Ltd = 16 × £350 000 = £5.6 million.

This needs to be adjusted to take account of the fact that Tiny Tim Ltd is relatively un-marketable, compared to Mega plc. A discount of, say, 25 per cent should be applied giving an estimated value of about £4 million relative to £4.5 million for Tiny Tim Ltd.

15.3 PR Industries and Howard Pope Ltd

On the basis of the information provided, the following approaches can be taken to valuing the shares of Howard Pope Ltd:

(i) *Price earnings basis*

$$\text{Price earnings ratio} = \frac{\text{market price of a share}}{\text{after-tax earnings per share}}$$

Market price of a share = price earnings ratio × after-tax earnings per share

$$\text{Market price of a share of HP Ltd} = 15 \times \frac{£15.3m}{(2m \times 20)} = \underline{\underline{£5.74}}$$

(ii) *Dividend growth model basis*
According to Gordon:

$$\text{Cost of equity} = \frac{\text{next year's dividend per share}}{\text{current share price}} + \text{growth rate of dividends}$$

OR

$$\text{Current share price} = \frac{\text{next year's dividend per share}}{\text{cost of equity} - \text{growth rate of dividends}}$$

$$\text{Current price of an HP Ltd share} = \frac{[£5m/(2 \times 20)] \times 1.10}{0.13 - 0.10} = \underline{\underline{£4.58}}$$

(iii) *Net (balance sheet) assets basis*

$$\text{Price per share} = \frac{\text{Net assets (from the balance sheet)}}{\text{number of shares}}$$

$$\text{Price of an HP Ltd share} = \frac{(143.42 - 30.00)}{2 \times 20} = \underline{\underline{£2.84}}$$

The figures resulting from the use of the first two methods would need to be fairly heavily discounted (say by 25 or 30 per cent) to take account of the fact that the HP Ltd are very unlikely to be easy to sell, HP Ltd being a private company.

There are many problems with these valuations, for example:

(1) The first two methods rely on finding a suitable firm, or firms, whose shares are traded in an 'efficient' market, to use as a basis for comparison. The principle of these two approaches is that the PE ratio and cost of equity of listed firms can be applied directly to the unlisted firm. This makes all sorts of assumptions about the comparability of such factors as:

- activities;
- dividend policy;
- operating risk; and
- financial risk (gearing).

The use of the Gordon growth model also assumes constant dividend growth of HP Ltd into the future.

(2) The net assets basis assumes that the balance sheet represents a fair value of assets and claims, on a going concern basis. It also assumes that all assets and claims are included on the balance sheet. These assumptions are unlikely to be valid. The balance sheet is (and is intended to be) a historical record of the assets, still in existence, acquired by the firm as a result of transactions and the sources of funds used to finance them. Thus the balance sheet has little to do with current values of assets and claims, and still less to do with assets like goodwill which were not acquired as a result of a particular transaction but through a gradual process.

The PE and net assets bases of valuation tend to be applied where the buyer is interested in acquiring the whole or, at least a controlling interest, in the firm, i.e. a *majority stake.*

Dividend valuation methods tend to be used where a minority stake is involved. The logic of this is that for the minority shareholders, their only economic interest in the firm is related to dividends.

Other approaches which could have been used include:

- *Dividend yield*. Here, the valuation is obtained by taking the view that two similar firms, one listed and the other not listed, will have a similar dividend yield. Normally a 25 to 30 per cent discount will be applied to the valuation obtained to allow for the lack of marketability of the unlisted firm's shares.

- *Economic value*. This is, without doubt, the most theoretically correct approach. It is based on estimations of the amount and timing of the net cash flows which are likely to be generated by the shares and an appropriate discount rate. Estimating cash flows and discount rates is difficult, which may well explain the popularity of 'market' and balance sheet based methods. Nevertheless, an approach which has a sound base in logic has a head start on other approaches.

Index